05 July 19

THE WORLD'S MOST TRAVELLED MAN

MIKE SPENCER BOWN

A Twenty-Three-Year Odyssey

THE WORLD'S MOST

to and through

TRAVELLED MAN

Every Country on the Planet

Douglas & McIntyre

DOUGLAS AND MCINTYRE (2013) LTD.
P.O. Box 219, Madeira Park, BC, V0N 2H0
www.douglas-mcintyre.com

Edited by Derek Fairbridge
Dust jacket design by Anna Comfort O'Keeffe
Text design by Shed Simas / Onça Design
Printed and bound in Canada
Printed on paper made from 100% post-consumer waste

Douglas and McIntyre (2013) Ltd. acknowledges the support of the Canada Council for the Arts, which last year invested $153 million to bring the arts to Canadians throughout the country. We also gratefully acknowledge financial support from the Government of Canada and from the Province of British Columbia through the BC Arts Council and the Book Publishing Tax Credit.

LIBRARY AND ARCHIVES CANADA CATALOGUING IN PUBLICATION

Bown, Mike Spencer, author
  The world's most travelled man : a twenty-three-year odyssey to and through every country on the planet / Mike Spencer Bown.

Issued in print and electronic formats.
ISBN 978-1-77162-142-7 (hardcover).--ISBN 978-1-77162-143-4 (HTML)

  1. Bown, Mike Spencer--Travel. 2. Voyages around the world.
I. Title.

G465.B69 2017   910.4'1   C2017-903932-6
                                                 C2017-903933-4

CONTENTS

AUTHOR'S NOTE

W HAT FOLLOWS IS THE ACCOUNT OF TWENTY-THREE of my past twenty-five years spent wandering through wilderness, voyaging across oceans, and trekking overland to survey the earth, with no home or possessions other than what fit in my trusty backpack. There was no specific destination in mind except to visit countries—not the airports and luxury hotels, but the country itself—to experience local culture and ways of life. My travel journals from every country stack up to a height twice that of the notoriously lengthy *Moby Dick*, so selectivity was prudent if this volume were to be more readable than Melville's classic. I wanted a variety of regions, characters, and moods. My riskiest countries tended to be solo trips, and many of my friskiest trips were with friends. The best mix for this book was some of each, half and half, with a range of perspectives from continent-spanning to human-scale adventures. This life has been lived on the move: sleeping in tribesmen's huts and cheap hostels, using local transportation whenever possible: traversing jungle roads in Gabon, packed in the bed of a Hilux pickup truck with thirteen souls and four enormous bunches of plantains; boating the length of the Amazon, snacking on roasted piranha; and hitchhiking across Iraq during the fighting following the officially three-week-long Second Gulf War. I've floated on dilapidated ferries across surging estuaries, ridden horseback or in military trucks across deserts and plains, followed the course of rivers, crossed wastelands, bussed and trekked through deep jungle, traversed mountain ranges, and lounged on the remotest beaches. I adopted local customs and ate local food: roasted goat's eye as the guest of honour at a Mongolian tribal feast, alligator nuggets, mystery kebabs, "bush meat" ubiquitous in certain regions of Africa ... but drew the line at wheelbarrows brimming over with smoked monkey corpses. A man's got to know his limitations.

The author aboard local transportation in Mongolia after a fifty hour, nearly non-stop, journey in 2009.

"Well, in our country," said Alice, still panting a little, "you'd generally get to somewhere else—if you run very fast for a long time, as we've been doing."

"A slow sort of country!" said the Queen. "Now, here, you see, it takes all the running you can do, to keep in the same place. If you want to get somewhere else, you must run at least twice as fast as that!"

— "The Red Queen's Race" in *Through the Looking-Glass*,
   by Lewis Carroll

THE PALACE OF THE WINDS

I N THE DEPARTURE LOUNGE OF THE ASMARA INTERNATIONAL Airport during the rainy season in 2013, waiting on a flight out of Asmara, Eritrea, an elderly woman approached me for a chat. Presumably she chose me because I was the only other non-Eritrean in sight. As she, likewise, was the first other traveller I'd met in Eritrea, I was curious to hear her impressions of this dictatorship, where it's a struggle to get official permission to see much of anything.

"Have you been to the magic fertility baobab?" I asked.

"No."

"The Red Sea coast?"

"No."

"The last forest on the Horn of Africa?"

"No. No to everything—I stuck close to my hotel."

Turns out she was a country-counter, whose lifelong list totalled 170 countries to date. I should have guessed by her choice of reading material: a list of the location identifier codes for the world's major airports. She was proud that she could name all the busiest, from ABC (Albacete, Spain) to ZRH (Zurich, Switzerland). Now, short trips are fine, if that's how it works out, and different people have different tolerances for new experiences, but for me, unlike my new acquaintance, transportation, per se, holds no special interest. Planes can sometimes fit as part of the adventure, or boats, or buses, depending on the circumstances, but much of the time transportation is, to my mind, merely a technicality. The real prize is exploring the earth and its bewildering variety of people and environments.

When she heard me say that I'd been to almost all the countries, and those that remained would only last me a few more months, she assumed that she'd met a kindred spirit and smiled. So I said, "At least you got to taste some interesting Eritrean food."

"Luckily I did not have to," she said. "On my flight over from Minsk, where I deplaned to check off Belarus, I saved all the extra food the airline gave me, in plastic bags. Then, in Eritrea, I reheated these." I must have looked askance at this, since she added, "They were clean plastic bags."

"Do you ever eat local food?" I asked.

"Hmm, once in North Africa a Bedouin offered tea. When I refused, he muttered a curse: 'Death to those who refuse an offer of tea.' So I drank, even though the glass was probably dirty. Police here demand you ask permission to travel outside of the city, so that means I didn't have to go anywhere, but can still add Eritrea."

IN THE BLUE CITY OF JAIPUR IN DUSTY RAJASTHAN, INDIA, IS A sweeping edifice of carved pink stone. There is no depth to this building, which is little more than a soaring façade of screened viewing perches. It was built by the Maharaja Singh so that upper-caste women could observe a bustling market without danger or exposure to dirt and un-pleasant smells—to see the life of others unfold but not experience it, or be sullied by it, themselves.

"The Palace of the Winds," as this great façade is called, has its modern counterpart, awesomely amplified, in the conference centres, world-class hotels, fine restaurants, and tourist developments of the "small world" that globalization promotes and that country-counters positively fetishize. Taxis, limousines, and high-speed trains take VIPs to and from airports, with their business lounges, security procedures, and duty-free luxury shopping—making today's upper castes feel as snug as a Jaipuri princess in the corridors of a standardized palace of culture. With a few changes of plane and maybe an online hotel booking, one can travel from anywhere to anywhere else in perfect comfort and safety. Formerly exotic and wondrously remote places are now firmly on the circuit of package tours. Lhasa, Tibet, once one of the most inaccessible places on the planet, can be visited on an "Eight Most Spiritual Sites in the World in Eight Days" tour. Machu Picchu, the last refuge of the Inca, high in the Andes Mountains, can be reached by train and an air-conditioned bus.

This is the latter-day Palace of the Winds, globalized, and this is where, inevitably, you will bump into the guy you met on the beach in the Cayman Islands, or that marketing director lady from Frankfurt. For the platinum-card-holding business traveller, delegate, package tourist, and aid worker, who spend an inordinate amount of time in airports and lobbies of hotels, it is indeed "a small world."

There is nothing wrong with this global palace of culture, but what about the "fly-over" states and other seldom-visited places of the world—what is found there? Level desert stretching as far as the eye can see? Jungles teeming with monkeys and feral men? Sprawling cities of suburb and slum? The reality is that most of the world's population lives in these regions, and it is not all bad. Only venture out from the Palace of the Winds and backpack through our planet's nations, regions, and ecosystems, and plenty of weird and wonderful things will educate your mind and delight your senses.

Cultural anthropologists are notoriously rancorous, but present a united front when taking issue with broad statements about humankind, save, perhaps, the claim that cultures most invested in the ideal of progress are often w.e.i.r.d. (Western, Educated, Industrial, Rich, Democratic). This certainly describes Canada, my country of birth, which furnished me with a powerful passport allowing visa-free access to over 140 countries; all the more reason to leave the rhetoric to the academics and go out to see for myself. That I did. Now forty-eight years old, I've lived out of my backpack for nearly my entire adult life. Our planet is full of surprises, so my urge to explore never dwindled as it drove me far and wide; the landscape is demarcated into a patchwork of countries, and after some time wandering in one patch, the grass starts to look greener on the other side of the border fence. New countries become familiar, one by one by one.

Four years ago, as a weird side effect of so much travel, reporters celebrated in print and on television, on radio and in video, my achievement of having been to every country. This same quixotic metric is the cherished goal of the epic passengers who ride for passport stamps. However, travellers and passengers can be easily told apart: travellers have stories. These last four years I've continued travelling in ten countries on three continents, thinking and writing, to try to answer the question: If not to collect stamps, and when you are certainly not the fastest or the first, what is the point of travel? Is it merely a fun way to get older? Because travellers have nothing material to show for their time, no more than passengers. Some might say, spying another record up for grabs, the point is to do the most. This book tries to illustrate my answer: I travel for the stories that mean the world to me.

Most people don't want to find themselves on their deathbed, rueing that they never got out and saw the world. If there was such a dreadful thing as a bucket list of regrets, it's safe to say this would not be among mine: many reporters and other travellers consider me the world's most travelled man, the most extensively travelled man, the patron saint of backpackers, or some other such honorarium. Is this justified? I think it depends very much on what travel means for you.

In the few hundred years of the Golden Age of Sail, the way to see the world was by crewing on tall ships, and the genuine sea dogs had a yellowish complexion they could only get from tar and salt spray, the wind and the searing sun. It could not be faked. To them, travel meant sailing, and it was a matter of pride what ports you'd called at, particularly as continental interiors were places of disease and impassable patchworks of savage tribes. For these hearty souls, transportation by sail was enough of an adventure that if they had called at Peking and Batavia, they could boldly say they had seen the Orient. Just so. They could tell outlandish or blood-curdling tales of simply doing their jobs. With the opening of the age of the steamship, and the early days of air and rail, there was still enough adventure to rightly feel no need to separate the concept of travel from this heroic transportation.

Those days are gone. If you fly to Micronesia, you are no Amelia Earhart; you are a United Airways customer, who was doubly sure to check that they added all those points on a frequent flyer card. And if your cruise ship stops in Singapore, you have not really seen the Orient, not really, no matter if you indulge in Singapore slings at Raffles Hotel till the floor heaves like the choppy Straits of Malacca. We can now safely ignore the warning of woe to anyone who found himself in Far Tatarstan without correct documents, sage advice during the nineteenth century's "Great Game" of spy versus spy striving to sway Central Asia's irascible rulers. If there is an irregularity with your documents today, you are inconvenienced, not tossed to perish in the bug hole of Bukhara.

I mean no particular disrespect to country-counters; in fact, scores of those who have crossed paths with me have counted past their sacred (because it is three digits?) number of "one hundred." Often their conversation is stimulating; necessarily, the theme can't stray far from the transport schedules and visa applications that are their bread and butter. All these country-counters, after hearing what else travel is for me, beyond the mechanics of it, say something to the effect of, *You are doing something completely different than me.*

So be it.

Lately there has been a slew of such persons, usually young men, who have recently done every country on earth in four years, or without using planes, or have done it in record time, as the youngest, or youngest American, or first to do it by pogo-stick, or what have you. They tell me of their arrival in, say, Bhutan—The Land of the Thunder Dragon, with its ancient culture, Tiger's Nest monastery perched on a misty cliff, and painted fortresses from whose roofs dangle gigantic hives of honeybees—where, perversely, their wanderlust is quenched with a poke of their foot over the border and a passport stamp, after which they turn tail and scurry to the next country on their official list. I'm reminded of the words of Seneca, written over two thousand years ago:

For suppose you should think that a man had had a long voyage who had been caught in a raging storm as he left harbour, and carried hither and thither and driven round and round in a circle by the rage of opposing winds? He did not have a long voyage, just a long tossing about.

Literally hundreds of people have contrived to be tossed up on the shores of every country on earth, the vast bulk of this horde of "tossers" padding their worldly experience with countries done as a gimmick. Of course the minimalist ideal is to "Leave only footprints, take only memories," but it is an extreme of minimalism to reduce this to leaving often a single footstep, and taking out no life-enhancing memories whatsoever. If you've just collected your last visa stamp from a four-year trip that took in every country on earth, it is obvious to me and every other experienced traveller that your entire journey consisted of arranging transport, riding on said transport, applying for visas, picking up visas, and navigating the formalities of border crossings. There is time, in 193-plus countries over four years, for nought else.

Even seeing every country in Asia long enough to get a feel for them takes well over four years, and that assumes that you are blazingly fast and super organized; eight years is more reasonable. Local radio stations and national news programs that want to interview a traveller back from a four- or eight-year trip would do better to interview someone returning from a trip to a sensible number of countries; they'd have far more interesting stories than someone who wasted their energy on the ruse of finishing the whole world over the same time period. Stories, not stamps, should be our mantra. These "done the whole world" guys know that other travellers know they are gaming the system and deluding themselves, rather than entering into the spirit of travel. They know that when people say, "I hope I'll find a way and the time to see the world one day," they are not yearning to play footsie with geopolitical borders and collect stamps. Besides, what if you were such a person, and tragically, a car crash sheared off that very foot: who, then, had been to every country? You or your foot?

A Brazilian guy sat beside me once in a beach bar in China, chatting over a few beers. We quickly determined that we both travelled full-time.

"London, Paris, Berlin, Rio, Hong Kong, which do you prefer?" he asked.

"London, because of my friends there," I said, "but these megacities are only one facet of travel, and not the be-all and end-all. A better time is had taking a jeep across Tibet, or a boat to the Togian Islands, or following the Nile to the Horn of Africa."

"What about the girls, and the dance clubs, and shopping, and, don't forget, the girls?"

His mention of shopping established him as a fellow of what was once called the "jet set."

"I prefer to live as the locals do, mud or grass huts, faded colonial hotels, local transport, even if it's walking or hitchhiking."

"How awful," he said, laughing. "Don't you feel you wasted your life? It should have been one long party, man."

How difficult it is to bandy about a concept of travel that doesn't touch on the philosophy of how and why you travel in the first place. People ask me often, and often very earnestly, if I have a special technique that makes travel cheap and easy, and conjures up a readymade "purpose," anticipating some answer that is the modern equivalent of how being an English-as-a-second-language teacher expedited Asian travel in the early '90s, and presuming I may well be the guru of a sort of ESL-teacher-on-steroids advice. I am not, and I find that if someone has clarity of purpose and abundant finances—enough to see the world and then some—he'll only find that it's a curse like Midas's touch. No one with the means to see the world in style can ever see the real world; the temptation to fall in with whatever now passes for the jet set, and to avoid the unpleasant, dusty, or tedious, is too high. Every stay in a mud hut or rainforest lean-to is at risk of being transformed into a four-star hotel or rainforest spa.

And often I hear: where are the best girls? Ha ha ha—best how? I suppose I could point you to primitive villages in road-less reaches of Madagascar, where you could gather more girls than you could shake a stick at. And if, in the morning, you handed one such lovely a piece of paper with your email address on it, she'd likely try to eat it.

Also, apparently, there's this notion that my having seen so much of the world ought to have tendered me a trove of solid common sense. If only it were true.

In 2008 I was trying to cross on foot from Herat, Afghanistan, to Turkmenistan, and had made my way to an old bridge, past which was the Turkmen customs. As it happened, the officer in charge was a strikingly beautiful Turkmen woman (never called a Turkwoman, sadly; I couldn't resist inquiring) who had a crew of eight dedicated border official fellows working under her. They had all my worldly possessions out on the table and ran their thumbs along every seam of my backpack, interrogating me about scraps of paper and old receipts—such papers are few; I discard them to avoid hassles in situations like this—so she had to focus on grilling me about my lifestyle, with a deepening frown on her face the more of my answers she heard.

"Stop all your travel," she yelled. "Find a wife, get married, and make children!"

"Yes, ma'am," I said, saluting her smartly. "I'll get right on that."

Bam, she stamped my passport and let me through. Honestly, what could I possibly have to say on the subject of common sense? Would someone with an iota of common sense to spare be crossing the Afghan/Turkmen border on foot? No. He'd have a house somewhere nice and safe, with a wife he'd met through friends at some party, and sufficient kids to placate a border guard if he should ever find himself in far Turkmenistan.

So what, then? I do have an abundance of un-common sense from dealing with random and ever-changing conditions, unusual cultures, impossible officials, puzzled locals, wild animals, wild tribesmen, and even wilder police, all gained from roaming our big planet.

CHAPTER ONE

ROUGHING IT IN THE BUSH

Canada

ONCE, MORE THAN NINE YEARS AGO, NEAR THE HEAD-waters of the Amazon, where it levels out after rushing down from the Andes, I was staying with some Yuacho tribesmen who were accustomed to visitors boating in to view the area's pink dolphins. The tribesmen lived on a platform made of hewn timber, erected above the floodplain that is a mosquito marsh much of the year. One muggy afternoon, all the adults were napping in hammocks, and the one baby among them (the only one they had left?) was suspended by straps into one of those baby walkers with plastic wheels that allows the little one to move, before he can take his first steps, by bracing his dangling legs against the ground. This baby would roll closer and closer to the edge of the platform, and then, just as I was gathering myself to rush over, he would swerve, only to approach another edge. Bad enough that it was a 2-metre drop to mud and roots on the south-facing edges, or a similar drop to murky river on the northern edges, but there were also schools of piranha in the river, and, worse, a huge black caiman, with a grinning zipper of interlocking teeth, lurking in the mud. Can you imagine what social services would say on a home inspection in a Western country if they found you had an ungated reptile pit and moat of carnivorous fish in your baby's romper room?

Modern Western countries are at the other extreme. Recently, when I was visiting nieces and nephews in Canada, I asked one of my brothers why the kids didn't just disappear into the woods and peaks around his home in the Rocky Mountains, and only show their faces at mealtimes and to attend school. He told me that's not how it works anymore: everything is done to a schedule and under adult supervision. If the kids go mountain biking, it will be from such a time to such a time, with an age- and skill-sorted cohort, under the guidance of a trained adult, with everything coordinated by these mini-supercomputers that are modern phones.

"But," I said, "can't they also choose to run off and play with the neighbourhood pack of kids?"

"There is no neighbourhood pack of kids, for better or worse—mostly worse."

It was my privilege to grow up in those slack decades, the '70s into the '80s, after kids had been freed from work in factory and on farm, but before parents began to fret about how much idle time this allowed them, and put them to work on activities that were structured, seemingly, with an eye to pleasing a university admission board or rounding out a resume when applying for an internship. This happy but now lost middle ground was the one I knew, and it gave me the confidence to explore.

For my sixth birthday, my mom gave me a hatchet, a saw, and a little orange knife that went with me everywhere, even to school. A couple of my uncles were teenagers, and they had built a dune buggy out of parts from the dump, where they'd go to shoot rats. They offered rides to my brothers and me, sometimes playing practical jokes like taking out the floor panel on our side of the vehicle and then driving over gravel so it would shoot up and sting us, or discharging firearms as we roared along, angling the gun so the hot bullet casings would fall in our laps.

One fine morning on Groundhog Day, when I had just turned seven years old, a Class 2 hurricane was barrelling toward Nova Scotia and our home in the Annapolis Valley. Our mom told my brothers and me that we would have to stay inside all day. Usually when we had to pass such a daunting stretch of time indoors, we took the precaution of catching bullfrogs from the pond in front of the house; the previous time was on a rainy day in the autumn, when boredom drove us into the kitchen where our mom was stirring beans in a pot on the stove. We entertained ourselves by letting our frogs leap; one almost fell into the beans, landing smack on the lip of the pot, but tipping out rather than in. We had fled from Mom's wooden spoon to take our chances with driving rain.

This being February and far too icy, a day's confinement was even harder to tolerate, and we managed to make ourselves a nuisance even without the customary amphibians. Soon the hurricane was howling, tearing limbs off towering elms—one crashed through an upstairs dormer—and even uprooting a few tall maples on the premises. Then sunlight poured in through the windows.

Our mom, seeing that it was now sunny and ominously calm, chased us out of the kitchen with the wooden spoon, saying, "Out, out, out."

We scooted into the forest, and so into the full blast of the hurricane. It had not subsided. Rather, the eye of the storm had been passing directly over the house.

On the run back home, I was nearly blown off a footbridge over a creek, holding on to the railing, flapping in the air like a flag, above the haunted swamp that was the site of the Moccasin Hollow Massacre. Fun times.

Later, having moved out west to Alberta in the winter of 1977, I learned basic canoeing, fishing, and hunting skills, vital then and especially when I became an adult. My home was on the ridge of Fish Creek Park, which was the edge of the city of Calgary at the time, with only farmers' fields and prairie to the south, and the foothills and Rocky Mountains a jaunt away to the west. This bushcraft was built on a foundation of rock-throwing talent. We did a lot of rock throwing, perhaps four hours a day, not counting the hours we were battling each other with sticks and thrown clubs, or against packs of kids from more distant communities. A few of us got so good at throwing that we used these skills to hunt. An illustration: just as you release a rock, after having put your whole body into the throw, you usually snap your wrists to impart whatever kind of spin is called for. Well, I and one of my friends could pick up a rock, hold it out at arm's length in front of our chests, and snap our wrists: the rock would jump and appear to defy gravity, emitting a weird hum as it spun, which would cease the instant we reached out and plucked it from the air. When we could afford our first shotguns, rock throwing fell by the wayside, and the new focus was the wilderness, abundant in western Canada.

While still teenagers in the late '80s, I, along with Chad, a tall and gregarious friend of Cree descent, got out into the wilderness whenever possible, exploring the Pacific coast and rain forests, and climbing mountains without equipment or really any planning. Anyone looking over Chad's bookshelf before meeting him might expect to find someone cerebral, perhaps a wandering scholar. In person he's very athletic: rock climbing, backcountry skiing, surfing, biking; he owns little beyond what he needs for these activities, and his free time is filled with sport, travel, and charity.

One winter morning during our late teens we went "up-Island" to clamber through rainforested slopes and reach the Carmanah Giant, a newly identified example of Canada's tallest tree, which was situated on Vancouver Island in what is now Carmanah Walbran Provincial Park. Chad's shambolic 1961 F-100 unibody truck carried us there with its straight-6 engine, three-on-the-tree transmission, and manual choke. This beast was banana-coloured, with a yellow steel interior, including yellow steel dash (perfect as a forehead maul in case of an accident), no seatbelts, and, because of bubbles in the brake lines, frequently no brakes. We didn't discover until we were at what can generously be called the trailhead that neither of us had any food—also, no matches or sleeping bags. We had a tent, however, so couldn't complain, as it was to be only a three-day excursion.

Off we went, climbing over, up and up and over gigantic deadfall spruce, slathered in bright green moss and snow. We slept the first night, back to back, in a mess of freezing mud, and then waded down Carmanah Creek, busting through a thin glaze of ice clinging to its banks, until we reached the giant Sitka spruce, 112 metres tall; a lightning bolt has struck some off since that time. The effort had drained our energy, especially now that we were into the second day of highly technical hiking without food, so we decided to bushwhack our way up a clear-cut and try for the logging road that must be in there somewhere. Also, and this is important, we were enjoying ourselves the whole time.

Hiking up clear-cut slopes is challenging on the West Coast, since the stumps are huge, and rainfall has eroded much of the soil. At any moment your entire leg might be swallowed up to the hip between the sprawling root buttresses. Night fell and we kept climbing, by feel, as there was nowhere to put up a tent on such terrain, and it would be too cold to sleep anyhow. Finally we came across a logging road and had to make a call: left or right? Right it was, and after some ways, there was the trusty old yellow Ford, our deliverance to pizza and jugs of beer at the nearest mill town.

On other days a favourite way to plan a trip was to throw a dart at an aviation map of Vancouver Island and go where it landed, with the proviso that it be sufficiently remote and wild—not typically a problem out there; we had wolves in the campsite once, and bears were common, or bald eagles glowering from every suitable snag of deadwood.

It was around this time that I purchased a new backpack for the first time, rather than just using old canvas hand-me-downs. This was a bright purple, teal, and black Serratus, from Mountain Equipment Co-op. Remarkably, it has carried my every possession from then on. I've lived out of it practically everywhere over the whole planet for twenty-five years and counting, with no sign of settling down.

ONE SUMMER IN THE EARLY '90S, I WENT WITH MY OLDER BROTHER Steve on a car-camping trip into the Rockies. At Ya Ha Tinda Ranch, where horses were trained for Parks Canada rangers, we'd used loose stones to make a beer corral in the shallows of the Red Deer River. Now most of us were relaxing after getting the tents set up, including Leon, a farm boy from northern Alberta. He'd found me crouching in the mud on my haunches, listening to birdcalls in the forest beyond the gurgle of the river.

"I can tell you don't have much experience camping," he remarked to me.

"How do you figure?" I said.

"First off, if you'd just flip over that round of wood over there, you'd have a comfy seat. And better yet, you should own a folding chair like this one with armrest drink holders."

"I don't sit in chairs anymore. I find them uncomfortable," I admitted.

As a matter of fact, I'd been disappearing more and more into the wilderness, such that, besides falling out of the habit of sitting in chairs, being around townsfolk made me uneasy. The people I liked best were what could be termed colourful characters: aging American draft dodgers, outlaws, growers, anarchists, cultists, raver girls, sawyers, prospectors, bank robbers, lumberjacks, hip-hop-ers, hippies, and hip-hoppies. I knew a junkie drifter for whom bulrushes were a dietary staple, who showed me how to make a stove out of old tins and to eat rat root to boost endurance. I was spending a lot of time in the Selkirk Mountains of British Columbia, between the Salmo–Creston Pass and Anarchist Summit.

Ken, a close friend, lived in these mountains, and would join me on some Asian and Russian travel a decade later. His family were not only Doukhobor anarchists, but also members of the "Sons of Freedom" sect, notorious for protests, usually conducted in the nude, arson, and bombings. This heritage also accounts for his looks—a mix of central Asian and white Russian features—and attributes: middling stature, brown as a nut in summer, pale in winter, and nimble when crossing streams and climbing forested slopes. He was a peaceful young man, but his dad, while charismatic, was adamant that Communists would soon rule the world, and he had done some jail time for destroying a 100-metre-tall hydroelectric-transmission tower and plunging thousands into darkness as part of an anarchist bombing spree back in 1962. This was frowned upon as terrorism, even back then.

The Selkirks seem to attract misfits and dreamers, often to the annoyance of the sensible folk. Even so, necessarily, it was an unusually tolerant place at that time. And this suited me fine, as I had become the sort of person who wanted nothing to do with regulations, forms, licences, and other trappings of civilization. Extended wilderness stays were more normal for me than stints in settled areas; my sessions of sub-arctic tree planting north of Prince George were positively social in comparison. While I had enjoyed many full and half summers on mountains or in swamps and meadows, my longest without human contact was eighty-six days in the Valhalla Range of the Selkirk Mountains, hundreds of kilometres from civilization, without speech, and without bathing.

If you bathe, you smell worse, and you attract mosquitoes and black-flies. Also, any animal can detect you from over the next rise if you wash, whereas somehow you blend in when you don't. On three occasions squirrels chased each other in a spiral up my body, presuming me to be a tree trunk, until they squared off with each other on either side of my face, saw my lips curve into a smile, and dashed down in alarm; and not a peep out of them for a half hour after that, which is quite a sign of a shocked squirrel during mating season. This will never happen, even once, if your skin reeks of soap.

I'd learned to barge bears, throwing up my arms and running at them, then pissing on their marker trees and scoring the bark with a hatchet higher than the reach of their own claw marks. Bears are actually kind of fun to mess with, once you get to know them. One August in Little Slocan Valley, asleep atop my sleeping bag as it was a hot, sweaty night, I gently awoke as a bear snuffled closer to my tarp. I sat up slowly, listening to nostrils sniffing at the flap of plastic that served as my door. Chuckling softly to myself, I decided to give it a scare and gingerly stood up, then swung my fist so that the flap of plastic loudly crumpled aside. Angling my feet so that my toes would catch in the clay of the hillside, I leapt out, buck naked, into the darkness, emitting a traditional bear-barging growl. The bear went *zing*, straight up the hill. What's more, a second bear went *zing*, crashing through boxwood shrubs, up the hill after it. Laughing, I rearranged the plastic flap and fell back to sleep.

I'd save broken E-strings from guitars to snare rabbits and grouse, and thrived on wild salmon, hazelnuts, and berries. For a time I made a pet of a huge and vicious-looking wasp, coloured black and that day-glow chartreuse yellow, the same hue as the rubbery lichen that dangles from fir trees. As I lay in a hammock writing a novel for my own amusement (*Living Off the Land* I titled it, before tucking it away in a box) or plucking wild strawberries, the wasp would cruise in a holding pattern over my body. When a biting fly dared enter my airspace, the wasp would seize it, methodically barber its limbs and head, then fly to parts unknown with this prize torso, reappearing later to continue the hunt for which it had selected me as live bait. If the wasp wasn't truly a pet, at least it was a win-win relationship.

What did I learn from nature? The aptitude and impulses that first beckoned and then compelled me to see the world. That same year, while admiring the Little Slocan Valley's lakes, connected like a string of pearls, and listening to the lizards scurrying under the orange puzzle-piece bark of the trees, I considered how strange this place, so familiar to me, would seem to people of a frozen tundra or tropical jungle or shifting sand dunes. It made me wonder, Had anyone ever set out to see the whole world? So in a way, it was love of nature that lent purpose to my adult life.

The wilderness taught me other useful things, one of them being: nature is fair to a fault—this is why a man's got to know his limitations. The other is hard to put into words. Civilized people are clueless. Hunter-gatherers get it, but they are scarce nowadays. There is a human nature attuned to living with the band back at camp—social life in the band with family, friends, and rivals is something we have evolved a social and conceptual mindset to cope with. But this amounts to precisely half of what it is to be human—there is a flip side, an entire second half to human nature, which is the human nature sculpted for use when alone in wilderness. Few people ever experience it. This second human nature fascinated me.

To experience this second human nature, you must go alone to deep wilderness, without seeing people, speaking, or seeing human structures.

Human structures and altered landscapes are like manifested thoughts. You can feel the concepts and the human striving behind them—to look at them is to be reminded of others. If you are alone but around artifice made by the hand and mind of man, you don't get the second human nature, bush-mode; instead you get its miserable cousin, cabin fever. Same goes if you are with or near another person, unless you can salvage some fractional bush-mode by being exquisitely in tune with that person and so communicate without speech.

But get away from all artifice and everyone else, and the changes are profound. After ten days you'll feel a simple distortion of your unexamined obsession with time—time will stretch like rubber, and you'll no longer know or care if it has been eight or twelve days, as the sun and the moon phase come to mean more than the date. This is not an especially mind-bending result, but it is the first sign of your conscious and unconscious reversing polarity. After a few weeks your world starts to become interesting; you begin to lose a habit that you don't even know you have: the habit of compressing your thoughts so that they are succinct enough to put words to them, an absolutely essential precondition for speaking.

When you never speak, those parts of your mind get repurposed. Something over a month without speech or human contact and the transformation is complete—dismissal of concepts from one's mind, and a weakening of the self, such that you have no longing or habit for either. In two more weeks your waking and sleeping are similar. If you sleep on the forest floor like I did, open to the elements save for a bit of an overhead shelter to keep rain away, your mind can experience reality as you sleep, and if you dream, as I once did one drizzling night, that a deer tiptoes across the mountainside, eating tiger lilies, in the morning your eyes behold, as mine did, the missing line of lilies. What you dream is real. Similarly, during the day, instead of thoughts, daydreams will float in your head, and by following your dreams, all necessary things will be done, in the times and order that is best, all without thought ... rather, you are in the same flow as reality, and you don't ever feel the need to flap or fuss.

If you are making a mistake or blundering into a dangerous wilderness situation, you will experience a vision that will correct your path as long as you heed its deep meaning. Hereafter your bushcraft is like something out of this world, or maybe deeply of this world, an altered state of consciousness, the other way to experience what it is to be human.

I could intuit the identities and intentions of any animal moving in the forests around me or on the slopes above by the reactions of squirrels and chipmunks and birds. Wolves and deer and moose gave away their species by how "thick" their legs sounded stepping through shrubbery in the next meadow over. When, during my mind-bending personal record of eighty-six days of solitude, a black bear tried to spy on me, off to one side, through 40 metres of dense brush, while hiding behind a black stump and poking out only a black ear and one eye, I turned my head, gazed into its eye for a fraction of a second as a sign of mutual awareness, and walked on without breaking stride. It was as if my mind could recognize anything amiss in the patterns of wilderness around me, and the disturbance in the background pattern would emerge and come to my attention as if by intuition.

At times I would play a game with deer, where the goal was to approach them, undetected, by moving inside the gaps in their consciousness. If you are fully in tune with nature, you'll note that deer cycle through various states of consciousness, and in the gaps you can draw closer, as long as you are downwind. Attend especially to their browsing state, and also one of the other states, a faux browsing state, as these are the most important. In the faux state they appear to browse, but they are secretly doing a scan with all their senses. When a deer is in this state, move not a muscle, not even your eyeballs; then, when the deer thinks itself safe and sinks into full browsing, with its sensing dimmed to save brain power, slink ever so silently forward. When again it attends—in fact, a split second before it forms the intent to shift states, which will be at irregular intervals—freeze without forming the notion to freeze, but freeze.

The game was to approach a deer like this until it was within arm's reach, but rather than touch the deer, I would wait till it went into the most alert form of consciousness, where it lifts its neck and does a full eye and ear swivel and scan, and then flick my eyeballs to one side, nothing more, to expose the whites for a split second. Frantically, the deer would bounce away through the bush, probably astonished that a huge animal such as me had appeared beside it: magic.

I'm sure that these experiences are common to humanity, as other people I've talked to who have spent long stints in the wilderness tell me similar tales. And I've yet to meet anyone who has done more than sixty-five days alone in this way and maintained an ego. That is to say, we all enter a mode where our days and nights of dreams and aspirations are no longer filtered through any kind of self or "me." There is no such entity as "me or I" after this point. And when you go back to civilization, it's a long slog back into the mindset needed to deal with chattering people and their world of battling, thrusting, concepts, and artifice. Usually it's one for one: if you had minimal human contact for five months, it will be five months of strenuous effort, equivalent to learning a foreign language, to flip back to normal, during which time you'll appear to others to be "bush-crazy."

Some of the effects of bush-craziness are minor and easily dealt with. Your expressions will be exaggerated; you'll have to tone them down. And you'll find you will have to be careful in shops not to knock over shelves, especially if you fell into the habit of careening off tree trunks for controlled descents down forested slopes. But this is nothing compared to the most mind-bending effect that comes with being around other people again. The part of your mind tasked to deal with others, closely twinned if not co-mingled with the deactivated self, wakes up with such fury that you attend with a laser focus to every expression, every word spoken or not spoken, in order to determine what was implied and when, who might have mimicked earlier wordings or reflected earlier facial expressions, and what subtle clues to group dynamics were thereby revealed.

Furthermore, civilized humans come across as all bluster and crassness, trampling one another's feelings, working angles on the psyches of their friends and lovers with all the subtlety of demolition crews with crowbars and dynamite clearing slums for an expressway. If you don't cultivate compassion, and see how civilization is so demanding of time and attention that it is necessarily quick and dirty, you might end up with a dim view of civilized humanity, which is especially troubling as you know that you'll fall into the same habits once your "self" is up to strength and wrestles you back to the city mindset.

What does this have to do with travel? For me, everything. This insight into our second human nature was a cherished gem of un-common sense, an honest treasure for someone who aspires to be a student of the will-o'-the-wisp that is reality, down wherever paths that may lead. This, the vital edge for surviving "failed states" and dangerous travel situations, comes to me from dream-time. Because while it's too mentally taxing to keep this ultra-expanded "theory of mind" working in real time beyond a few weeks or months, I've found that I could retain some as a precious treasure, an intuition worthy of my trust, especially a heightened intuition when someone in my company is not who he claims, a false persona, who may want to do harm.

Not everyone who has spent too much time alone in the wilderness gets to keep something of value. A case in point: up in the hills of southern British Columbia near the town of Fruitvale in the early 1990s there lived a one-eyed mountain-man who imagined he was a wizard, and who liked to take potshots at people with a .303 rifle from his homesteaded back acres. I empathize with the path he probably took to be who he became, but I also feel sorry that he forgot about the umbilical you need to be able to return from the dream-time of bush-mode to the mode suited for human companionship—that is, a firm grounding in reality, and a healthy measure of compassion. If you are not grounded in reality, extensive time alone in the wilderness will leave you as the most insufferable kind of new-age hippie, and if you don't have a healthy measure of compassion, you'll end up as a vicious hillbilly. Or, like our one-eyed friend there, you may be lacking in both, with a result that combines the worst of both worlds.

What I took away from the wilderness became the tool I'd use to know good from bad intentions amid that mess of strangers daily met in strange lands, and each encounter was a learning experience to sharpen my intuition. How exactly did that guy's voice inflect as he tried to sell me a dodgy bus ticket? What precisely was that odd vibe coming from the one who turned out to be secret police? Was there any expression askew on the face of the hawker who tried to rip me off with overpriced salak (snake fruit) in the market? These are all learning opportunities to school yourself in flint-hard reality, and they are vital for doing business too; you can't get this stuff from university, no matter if the tuition is sky-high.

Striving to flip back from bush-mode into people-mode encouraged me to school my intuition, actively using the world available around me, the way a mountain lion hones its claws on rocks. These predators of the North and South American wilderness are superb testers and teachers of survival skills to human interlopers.

Just once, a mountain lion tried to kill me. I'd been practising my lamp-less night-hiking skills, climbing high in the hope these dark ridges might funnel me to Mount Gimli in the Kootenays. In the middle of the night, up in steep alpine zone where the terrain was a mix of sheer precipices and meadows dotted with stunted trees, a large animal startled as I crossed a gully in the rock. My ears detected it quietly swerve in behind to follow me, uncharacteristic behaviour for wapiti or deer. Stopping in my tracks was a test; it took one step, then two, and it also froze. No more wondering if it were bear or mountain lion—only a mountain lion will stalk humans that way.

That same animal had worried me the week before. I'd dropped a sweaty little daypack and stepped into a streambed to guzzle water; the air was 37 degrees Celsius, and the pine forests were burning, with one fire atop this mountain, another across the valley. The mountain lion had darted in and taken a swipe at the bag. Then it was gone. The result was that the thick foam shoulder strap, with two rows of double stitching and a heavy nylon outer fabric, was shredded as if it had been cut half through by a razor. I could bend the strap open like a puppet's mouth. And this was the work of the central claw alone; the others dug in to either side.

Weapon-less, I adjusted my walking in this black of night, affecting a confident stride down the mountain. The instant this animal sensed my blindness it would pounce on my back and go for the kill. So at the whisper of a paw's swish through bunchgrass, I'd crane my neck to glare behind me into darkness, feigning vision, and I'd growl. How to avoid walking straight off one of the many cliffs? Let's just say I've never "minded my step" more than I did in the hour that big cat followed me down the mountain. Even the flat meadows up here were like ski slopes. I descended several kilometres with the animal shadowing me, only to overshoot my camp a little way to the left. It was still stalking me, and closely, perhaps 10 metres back. But here I was lucky to recognize a peculiar J-shaped branch against a sliver of moon, and I veered to where I'd set up camp: a sheet of plastic and my precious stockpile of a couple of weeks' emergency rations of rice and canned goods.

Then and there, in the glow just before dawn, it decided to have a go at me—striding directly in, not making any snarling noise that they are known for, but ears back and ghostly silent. I was the one snarling. Having grabbed a staff of hawthorn wood—used to hold up my plastic tarp—I swung to club the top of its skull, careful not to overcommit. Striving to get inside my swings, it would dodge and dart back, then circle and come at me again from another angle. I drove it off but passed a sleepless night. In the morning my first task was to write a note: "If you don't find me here, get away fast, as I've been killed by a mountain lion: likely still prowling the area." Nails fixed the paper to the bright orange puzzle-piece bark on the side of a huge ponderosa pine. This rather alarming note could be torn down a couple of days later as the mountain lion only came back briefly the afternoon of the following day. Then it was gone for good.

CHAPTER TWO

THE TRIP OF MANY FIRSTS

Costa Rica · Nicaragua · Guatemala ·
Honduras · El Salvador · Belize · Mexico

T HAT NOTE WAS MEANT FOR THE WOMAN WHO WOULD hike up to join me in a few days. Brenda was my first proper girlfriend, and it was she who would convince me that while backpacking through North American wilderness is all well and good, there is also such a thing as travel on a shoestring budget in foreign lands, the tropics being especially tantalizing compared with Canadian winters. I'd done some travel in the UK and Western Europe, and Hawaii, and had driven coast to coast across North America many times, in both the United States and Canada, but I felt it was time for a change. Just before I first encountered Brenda's charming ways, an exquisite flavour of loneliness compelled me to adopt a lifestyle that included people, the kind of loneliness that gets into your spine and pulses down each vertebra in turn, before clawing its way back up to your brain. Although I was not done with the bush and had many more cherished experiences, intercontinental travel started to edge out American wilderness as a focus of my life.

Brenda had naturally curly dark hair, the poise of a dancer, and an easygoing disposition with a tendency to empathize with the plight of others and also to look on the bright side during troubles. This sunny disposition would prove useful as we explored farther south than either of us had ventured before, past the claw-shaped Sonoran Desert to where the Isthmus of Panama, segmented like a scorpion's tail into small countries, jabs into South America. From her earlier experience in Mexico, Brenda knew her Spanish pronunciation of the stock-phrases she had memorized was perfect, eliciting a torrent of words in reply from Latinos who assumed her fluency, when really she understood little and slowly. Handier was her experience dealing with hustlers and tourist-touts, gained on a solo road trip around Jamaica.

As for skills at my disposal to ensure a thrilling Latin American trip together that skirted disaster? It is hard to imagine a greater dunce regarding practical travel skills, since I had none whatsoever. My assumptions, picked up on travels in Europe, the United States, and Canada, that other people would drive safely, that men loitering at bus stations would provide honest information, and that I would find hot running water and toilet paper in public restrooms weren't worth jackshit. I lacked any foreign language ability, had no talent for bargaining with sleazy taxi drivers or sleazy bus conductors or sleazy people who approached us on the street. As a gringo in Central and South America you are a buzzing electromagnet for every sleazebag from Punta Arenas to Belize City.

And what of my intuition, so carefully honed? This only took me so far and no more. My intuition would be that this local guy is trying to rip us off; actually so are the rest of his low-life associates crowding around us—so now what? This is when your travel skill ought to kick in, if you have any, which I didn't.

Another thing, how do you get from here to there in undeveloped places? Do they have buses? Do you rent a car, like in Hawaii? Drive an ox-cart? Does a peasant pull you in a rickshaw, and you hurry him along with judiciously placed smacks of a riding crop? How should I know? I hadn't a clue what to expect or where to go or what was a fair price, and it had never occurred to me that there might be such a thing as a guidebook. Later, I would overhear other backpackers (it hadn't even occurred to me that there would be other backpackers) sprinkling their dialogues with extraordinary statements like "of course, it's best to catch the bus from the plaza in front of the church of Santo Tomás if you want to get to Antigua from Chichicastenango," leaving me in awe of this apparent geographical prowess. Perhaps hard-core backpackers obsess over maps and encyclopedias for months before setting out travelling. Given that a fair few of them were willing to spend untold months living in remote villages, trying to learn the local language, who's to say they weren't equally keen on geography? It never crossed my mind that someone would have written it all down for them, and that they'd arrive with such an unlikely thing as a guidebook they bought back in their home country. A couple of weeks passed before we realized everyone but us had them. Lonely Planet and Rough Guide were new ideas back then, like Tesla Motors or Oculus Rift are now, but the word was starting to spread mouth to mouth about this newfangled travel aide.

We had bought a package holiday return flight from Vancouver, where Brenda was living, to Costa Rica, as it was much cheaper than a one-way ticket. We just tossed the return and came back overland. Costa Rica was expensive, with twenty-dollar-a-night hotel rooms, even in the early '90s. Before this trip I'd thought it was the Europeans who suffered a poor standard of living in stuffy, old, sagging, stained hotel rooms that cost a king's ransom, in filthy cities with wondrous paintings and sculpture but scowling people, and sidewalks strewn with dog shit. But once we got out of Costa Rica, it was a revelation that there are degrees of poverty much worse than that in Europe. Of course, if this was the third world, then I was accustomed to the fourth world, the wilderness, where you are grateful just to have shelter from rain under a tree, and dinner is whatever you can find. So it was not filth and want that amazed me, but the fact that so many people were living like this, not because they preferred to be in a state of nature, but because this was the highest level of living offered up to them as the fruits of their civilization.

Compensating for my lack of any travel skills, I discovered I had an innate toughness. Some of this was physical, carried over from the wilderness and evidenced by such experiences as the time when, resting up after a couple of months of Selkirk mountaineering in early 1993, I figured my toes were past due for a medical inspection. Sprawled in the mud by the campfire, I heaved my feet out of both sopping-wet Zamberlans, known affectionately by me as my bear boots on account of all the fang punctures those animals made in the leather of the "upper" and scree collar. My toes were perfect, every nail pink and shiny, like new—suspiciously so: it had snowed or rained every day, so my boots hadn't come off the whole time, not even in the sleeping bag. Tapping the boots on a rock caused five entire loose toenails to tumble out of each. They'd all been ripped out during ascents and then regenerated.

And sure, my shoulders didn't tire carrying my pack, and sometimes Brenda's too, even when we were walking all day with them. As well, I seem to have a cast-iron stomach and a good immune system, never having any contact with doctors or checkups for anything beyond a few minutes of paperwork, but that's not what I'm getting at. Humans generally are much stronger than we give ourselves credit for. If we really had to, most of us can pull off the most astounding feats, living for weeks without food, scrambling through 100 kilometres of scab-land and gulch: humans are big, tough animals, and they die hard.

The thing is, if you are challenging yourself and having adventures in this life you're living, a fair stretch of it is going to be spent suffering, and some people see that as carte blanche to become insufferable. I can only hope it's not my misfortune to find myself next to them. For me, the epitome of tough is not only mind over matter; it's being able to joke and have a laugh about situations that aren't going to kill you, and even many that might.

So there was that one advantage, and also a burning curiosity about new peoples and ecosystems. Something as basic as a novel species of palm tree was thrilling to me, and a jungle or a volcano was positively mesmerizing. New things and new lifeways filled me with an ambition to experience them. If you tire of seeing too many Spanish forts on your trip, and skip the next one, you might say, slangily, that you are castled-out. Same goes for museums or jungles or ruins; non-surfers can find themselves beached-out. What of the larger sense: Can a person sock away too many experiences that are new and shiny? To feel those pangs is simply to be homesick; this did not describe me: my traveller's boots were never coming off. For Brenda this last tendency might have seemed more an oddity than an advantage; she might have wondered what was so compelling out a dusty bus window.

If anything was going to keep me up at night, it wouldn't be village firework festivals or sweltering heat and bugs as much as it would be trying to corral my excitement that tomorrow was going to be as new and fascinating as today. I was like a kid before Christmas, save that as a little kid I'd tell my folks all I wanted was socks and underwear, and to sleep in Christmas morning. Here in travel I found a spirit I could believe in.

In Costa Rica we did the usual things: sunburn on our first day splashing in the Pacific Ocean; soak in Tabacon's magma-fuelled hot springs; gawk at the tropical paradises surrounding golden slivers of beach in Manuel Antonia Park; and stare into greener than green jungle alive with ring-tailed coatis slinking through the undergrowth. Apart from all the natural beauty, it's obvious that there is real poverty and lack of development here. Nowadays, there is some economic activity in Central America, but a couple of decades ago it was practically medieval.

This is a morbidly fascinating thing to see—cultural stagnation. And it was a while before I understood that for thousands of years it was the rule rather than the exception around the globe. Most civilizations are not founded on the pillars that support progress, but are based on different values, often religious or social, that are fervently upheld. In much of Central America the plantation-owning "hacendados" have optimized the system to conserve social norms and stick to time-honoured and time-tested means, not generate progress. If the locals weren't there—if, say, a land similar in every respect but uninhabited just appeared out of the mist—you could sell every flattish hectare of it for a million dollars each, and the lots would be gone in a snap, bought up by Westerners. In the early 1990s, many of these Latin American countries were the nation-state equivalent of what, in the language of modern Western real estate, would be termed a "teardown," and the value of the country was greatly reduced when you threw in the centuries' worth of accumulated accomplishments of their civilization and their human resources, which amounted to a subjugated peasantry rather than a workforce.

Impressions of this trip are still sharp in my mind. It was another ten years before any real travel skill accrued to me, as it takes that long to mature as an observer, so much of what I experienced didn't immediately make much sense—instead raising a multitude of questions without ready answers. Costa Rica was truly rich, a nation that put social progress over military prowess, and I suppose it reflects well on their neighbours that they have gotten away with this. On the Pacific coast, on sickle-shaped Jaco Beach, I let myself be battered by the waves and sizzled in the sun. It was my first time seeing boys with assault rifles, here guarding against bank robbers, and an older woman, also a tourist, said to me, "It's not guns that make me nervous; it is that these boys with guns have no life experience."

After revelling in leaf-shrouded waterfalls with bathing pools and windy lakes and rivulets of glowing red lava, we skipped across the border to Nicaragua, just barely opening to a trickle of backpackers, with the treaty ending the horrendous Contra War only four years old.

This was a trip of many firsts for me. First encounter with travel snobbery: near the southern frontier, in San Juan del Sur, a dilapidated fishing village and former base for steamships servicing the California gold rush, we met some people with the polar bear licence plate of the Northwest Territories, who were disappointed that they'd driven from the Arctic only to find such relatively inexperienced travellers as us, spoiling the coolness of this destination with our naivety.

We also met a young Swedish woman, Zara, who had recently suffered a life-altering burn: part of her face and shoulder had melted. We had such fun hanging out and chatting that we ended up travelling together for a while, which was my first experience of how groups of backpackers can coalesce and dissolve as fun and circumstances dictate.

The night we met her, Brenda and I discreetly discussed the obvious question: Should we ask her how it happened? We decided to, casually, NOT bring up the question of her burn, as she had almost certainly come on this trip to get her mind off such matters and to count her blessings ... she had only mentioned that the sun helps with the problem of tightness in her scar tissue. We never spoke of it in the time we travelled together. When we eventually split, she thanked us for this and told us her insurance company had warned her to be extremely wary of anyone she met while travelling who wanted to talk about the accident. Apparently it was not unheard of for insurance companies to hire private investigators to trail claimants on holiday, the stakes are that high. Zara was deft at turning away crowds of beggars who accosted us for change—she'd simply thrust out her own hand, and they would shy away.

Getting to know dreadfully shabby hotels filled a crucial gap in our backpacker skill set. We needed to pass the night in a Nicaraguan market town, whose name was best forgotten come morning, and asked the woman at reception for the price of a suite with enough beds for the three of us, and a private bathroom. She named her price—ten cents. Rather than bargain her down, as is the custom, we couldn't help but laugh. Suspicious now, she insisted that we pay upfront for the room; we were obviously intending to do a runner, or else why had we not haggled for a lower price? We paid up our three cents each and took possession of our suite. Of course, to some extent you get what you pay for. In this case, mattresses that were burlap sacks stuffed with straw, and a hot, mosquito-filled room; what's more, our Swedish friend tended to snore, and locals celebrated one of their festivals, which seem to fall every other day, resulting in drunken shouting and fireworks late into the night.

An upgrade was in order. From then on we looked for mid-price hotels, in the one- to three-dollar range. Such a hotel we found only a few days later; moreover, it had prime access to one of Nicaragua's lovely beaches, golden and lined with a distant palisade of volcanic cones. The hotel was old, weathered, and wooden, such as you'd see in a Wild West film, with saloon doors, and, if anything, the beach was too accessible: waves had eaten away at the seaward foundation posts, so the building slumped and the floors were as steeply slanted toward the crashing waves as the sand around it. The proprietor led us through the saloon and up a wide spiral staircase to show us our rooms. He made a point of explaining carefully that we were to make sure we opened only our own doors and not the doors to either side or the one farther up the corridor. This warning didn't make immediate sense to us, as guests usually enter only their own rooms, and our Spanish was too poor to understand the word that would have explained all.

We went out and watched a family dig for tiny ghost crabs along the shore, the children running back to their mother to hand off what they'd caught, so she could hold them in a fold of her skirt, and we enjoyed a few beers at the bar. Only later, when we were in bed, did we hear the squeaking, smell the distinctive odour, and notice the dark shapes wheeling outside the window—the Spanish we could not understand was the word for bats. Brenda and I snuggled in our bed and congratulated ourselves on not coming up tipsy from the saloon, stumbling to open one of those wrong doors, and having the bats emerge in flapping, reeking gusts, probably contriving to snag in the curls of Brenda's hair.

MANAGUA BECKONED: THE BIG CITY OF A MILLION PEOPLE ON THE shores of disgustingly polluted Lake Managua, and just north of Lake Nicaragua, home to freshwater bull sharks. It was a sprawling slum, dotted with high-rise apartments that had been wrecked in an earthquake in 1972, condemned, and never repaired, as President Somoza and his ministers absconded with much of the money raised for earthquake relief, sparking a revolt that became a revolution and devastating civil war. The apartments were dark, and only the lower floors were inhabited, by vagrants. The sole signs of life were the glow from an occasional black-and-white, cathode-ray-tube television.

An election was scheduled and, presumably to show their civic spirit, the army had decorated the cityscape with lofty black cut-outs, like billboards but cut in the shape of titanic soldiers, rifles at the ready, seemingly, against the citizenry below, so that everywhere you looked you saw the black silhouette of a soldier looming over you. We feasted on mangos and found a very fine hotel, five bucks a night. Our room was daub and hewn timber, with a nice whitewash on the walls. The single manufactured item in sight was a cheap plastic shower curtain, such as you could buy in the markets that were just beginning to fill up with stuff from China—to the amazement of locals, who could hardly believe that such exotic things could be theirs, and all the way from the Orient. The only decoration was a framed picture on one wall, and the colour picture in the frame was none other than the printed sheet that must have come in the package with the shower curtain, showing a woman enjoying a shower behind exactly that plastic curtain.

Brenda, Zara, and I wandered out into the darkness to explore, finding many destitute children scampering here and there, and more tasty tropical fruit for sale, as well as an amusement ride down by the stinking lake. I declined to go on it, but Brenda and Zara did, to their regret; a clanking diesel engine whirled them about like an egg beater in a miasma of choking black fumes. Brenda said she would have puked if her esophagus could have managed to counter the centrifugal force.

Back at our hotel, we couldn't help overhearing a heated argument from the lobby between young and idealistic aid workers, with the leader of the group perhaps proving the most idealistic. He was browbeating the rest of them for going out and spending ten dollars at a bar, explaining how many days' wages that was for a labourer. One of the volunteers was not having it and countered that he was not a Nicaraguan labourer, the money was given to him by his mother, and it didn't have any bearing on his work. The intrepid leader was struggling to explain the rarefied concept of solidarity with the poor they were helping, and under the primordial rules of morality, he had a point. Of course, it was hard to see how, in the greater scheme of things, the poor would have been made richer overall by any visitor deliberately spending less money while in the country.

I got talking to one of this group, and he admitted that their project had gone wrong for an odd and unanticipated reason. They had chosen one of the poorest towns in the area to help by setting up a sewer system, but over the years since the project began, the town they were helping emptied out as everyone left to look for better opportunities in a more prosperous town in the next valley. Too late the aid group realized that the town was poor for a solid reason: the soil was thin and rocky, and the microclimate such that vital crops were no sure thing. So when the possibility of jobs opened up elsewhere, the townspeople piled out of this hopeless place of bare subsistence and left those gleaming new toilets behind. Ironically, the aid group should have elected instead to set up the sewer system in the wealthiest town in the area, because that's where the poor people ended up. I was scratching my head when I heard this, thinking that there is more to doing charity well than meets the eye.

The next couple of days we spent seeing the sights of this interesting city, the capital of Nicaragua since 1852. Managua boasted a cathedral as ornate and magnificent as anything you'd find in Europe, except that the roof was torn off and it was haunted by a gang of cocaine dealers armed with automatic rifles. We'd heard that if they took a dislike to you, they would not let you see inside, but we must have seemed pleasant enough people, since we looked around without incident. The interior was covered in graffiti, especially the smashed altar, which was carved from wonderful coloured slabs of imported stone, now scarred and chipped. Particularly offensive and sexual anti-Catholic doggerel was chipped into the altar stones, deciphered by Zara. We didn't explore too far, as many of the rooms and apses now doubled as impromptu fecal minefields.

It was a great relief to get out of there and back into the sunny streets. Brenda had mentioned once in conversation to another woman that her father could be strict, especially on account of his profession. The woman said, "Let me guess, is he a policeman, a priest maybe?"

"Ha," Brenda replied. "Both: a chaplain for the police."

Her father had spoken to me on the telephone, man to man, before I took his daughter on this extensive backpacking trip through all of Central America, famed for dust, donkeys, and dictators, and we established that my duty was to keep her perfectly safe, no matter what.

In the area around the cathedral, some government buildings were in somewhat better repair, but still pockmarked from the war, and political graffiti marked nearly every surface. It would have made a fine parliament for a nation of skate-punks.

TRANSPORT ON MOST CENTRAL AMERICAN ROADS WAS VIA DECREPIT school buses, Cardinal or Bluebird models, usually ones that started service in the United States, migrated to Mexico in old age, and came to Central America to die. The starter was often burned out, and everyone would have to push the bus to get it going again after each stop. Some bus conductors tried to get separated groups of gringos to pay twice by telling each group in turn that the other had said they would pay for all. This ploy was often exposed, but they were shameless. At each stop a crowd of vendors would flank the bus and raise bread, sacks of nuts and cubed papaya for snacking, and plastic bags of fruit juice on poles, level with the window. Toss some money and you could be well fed.

On the way to Antigua, Guatemala, a thief was standing right next to my pack. I had to watch him like a hawk the whole way, as whenever I began to nod off, his hands would creep toward our bags. It was an exhausting grind of a journey, and when we finally arrived after midnight, Brenda burst into tears. We were in what appeared to be an alarmingly insalubrious dark, filthy slum, with rats in the street.

We wandered, hoping not to get mugged, until we saw an ornate door along a dark alley. Thinking to get off the street, I banged with a brass knocker and the door opened, revealing a well-dressed boy who ushered us into a lovely hotel, built around a courtyard orange tree garden. There was clean white linen on the beds, and antique hardwood furniture.

Antigua by day was wonderful, and a celebratory excursion was in order: we would climb the volcanic cone of Mount Fuego looming over the city. This was at first a vigorous slog through jungle-slathered slopes, our happy group in the company of a couple of guides. When we started the climb in earnest, in more open grassy slopes over black rock, I found myself up front with one of the guides. He asked me to take several pictures showing the whole string of climbing tourists, while making sure to get each tourist's face. He stood smiling where he might also fit into the frame, and he thanked me.

"For advertising?" I asked.

"No," he said. "Banditos, heavily armed, sometimes operate at the foot of this volcano. Not long ago they got one of our tour groups. The photos are if we have to show police who was out here, and I'm going to head back now with this camera. The other guide will go with you to the top. Don't worry, they didn't kill anyone—they just robbed and beat the shit out of the men, and gang-raped all the women."

The volcano top at night was a marvellous show of glowing orange lava blobs, spurting up in a fountain that threatened to engulf us and scorch us to the bone, but always fell short with a shower of molten sparks. Intense heat coming up from the ground threatened to melt the soles of our boots, but before that could happen we were told to run down the slope of the volcanic cone, which was directly in front of us. Formed out of the black sand of crumbled old lava, this slope was invisible in the pitch blackness. After a last look at the orange eruption against the black sky, we sprinted down the cone and emerged at the base, boots full of sand, after a thrilling night.

TRAVEL-SAVVY READERS MIGHT BE WONDERING, HOW DID YOU GET all those visas if you didn't know anything about travel and had no guidebook to tell you they were necessary?

Simple, we bribed our way across every border. These borders were laughably, ridiculously corrupt: in some dank, sweaty, tobacco-stained room with an ominously squeaky ceiling fan, among stereotypically mustachioed men packing pistols and assault rifles, the same conversation played out again and again, and twenty dollars was handed over. Thank goodness for rampant border corruption or this backpacking trip would have been a logistical nightmare.

We also changed money at these borders. One or two of my thin stack of American hundred-dollar bills were transformed into gargantuan bricks of ripped filthy rags: bank notes, allegedly, that were embossed with murky messes of filth and ink. Sometimes only the curly moustaches lingered, like the grins of Cheshire cats, to hint that it was some father of the nation being depicted. Locals had the notion that the physical condition of the note should have a bearing on its desirability, as if it were perishable avocados on offer at a roadside stall. Clean notes were preferentially given to those of high social status.

In Honduras we traced sinuous roads through dry, pine-studded mountains, exploring Mayan ruins and the city of Tegucigalpa. Nowadays it is infamous for having one of the highest murder rates in the world, but back then it was merely an unheralded, violent slum consisting largely of rusty, corrugated metal sheets tacked together to make shacks. Locals warned us that some of the buses were run by pirates, who grabbed anyone foolish enough to come aboard, so gangs of thieves could strip them at their leisure before tossing them out the back door. Also, half a dozen people warned Brenda not to wear earrings, using the universal hand signal for an earring being ripped from an ear. Here was a city with steady work for armed guards. A little corner store would have a man with a pistol outside; a better-stocked shop would have a man bearing a rifle; a fancy restaurant with nicely dressed waiters, such as Pizza Hut, had a pair of soldiers with assault rifles, controlling who might approach.

Brenda and I once entered a Chinese restaurant, rifleman outside, and found it to be thick with dust, furnished with white plastic chairs and tables that were cracked and wobbly and duct-taped in several places. Overhead a noisy fan vibrated, also filthy and poxied with mummified dead flies. We were hungry enough to risk it; after all, what could go wrong with a simple noodle-and-chicken plate? When our food arrived, though, we were skeptical: the noodles were burned on top and mush beneath. The chicken was alarmingly fresh, having been hacked apart and tossed into the wok in such a way that you could deduce how it might slide back together, feathers, beak, and claw intact. Gravy with the look of grey mould smothered this whole mess. As a final touch, the proprietor now threw wide the door and allowed a swarm of astonishingly filthy beggar kids into the premises; they commenced to moan and clutch at our clothes with grubby fingers. This might seem another demerit from the original ambience of filth and flies but really was a stroke of luck: plates slid over to grateful kids, a dollar passed to the cook, problem solved and we were out of there.

I HAD PROMISED BRENDA THAT IF SHE REALLY DIDN'T FEEL SAFE IN any country, she should just tell me and we'd leave. She was very brave and only exercised this prerogative once, when we were touring El Salvador. I'd met a few Salvadorans back in Canada, especially during my one summer working in northern tree-planting camps, and each had shared this odd tendency: in the first conversation after they met me and gave me their name, Salvadorans would add, "In El Salvador you can hire a hit man for 300 bucks."

Eroded hilltops were crawling with peasants, who had climbed up to slip a few maize kernels into cracks in the rocks that still held a healthy vein of soil: a medieval Malthusian nightmare. Whenever we walked around on the street, a gang of young men would coalesce from shady alleys and doorways in a most suspicious and furtive way. Our only respite was to duck into restaurants or take taxis to throw them off our trail. We were not the only foreigners with an interest in El Salvador, knowledgeable locals informed me, but it was small comfort to hear that an American-trained and -funded group was active in the hills around our area, especially since the locals asserted that group was the Atlatl Death Brigade, with a penchant for making fleshy dioramas of murdered peasants, featuring ingenious use of disjointed baby parts and bowls of blood.

Brenda had discovered the limit of her comfort zone, and our Salvadoran side trip was cut short. El Salvador wasn't yet ready for backpackers, let alone tourists. I question whether much of it was fit habitat for humanity either: if they had a motto in the early '90s it would have been *A place that makes you not want to bring children into the world*. While we were there, we met mostly kind and hardy people who had to endure this dysfunction through no fault of their own. I later learned that this is a characteristic of bad situations globally—and also learned to be suspicious of simplistic remedies touted by those without the stomach for a dog's breakfast of unpalatable truths concerning development.

A visit to the Mayan ruins at Tikal enticed us, but they were all the way back over in Guatemala, and to get there we had to endure more long bus rides. We had started to get the hang of this Central American bussing and knew what to expect, though we were a bit worried when soldiers blocked the road near Lake Petén Itzá, ordered everyone out, and had us line up along the road. After noticing that we were foreign, they dismissed us. They wanted to search indigenous locals as suspected leftists, since the civil war, with its infamous "disappearances," wasn't to end until 1996. Other undesirables were known to travel these roads, including bandits who lived in the wilderness hereabouts. We stayed in the drowning lake town of Flores, now an island with half its houses submerged, and connected to the mainland by a causeway that was built ever higher as the lake waters rose.

Tikal was famously used as a filming location for the rebel Massassi base in the original *Star Wars* film. At the time Brenda and I were there, people were allowed to climb the many steep temples—at some personal risk, as a fall would cause you to bounce painfully all the way down, likely resulting in broken bones or neck. Temple IV was the highest, rising 70 metres above the ruined plaza below. After climbing to the top and noticing the beginning of a ledge, as narrow as a scaffold plank, I decided to trust the ancient masonry and take in the view from around the back side, edging out carefully, shuffling my feet along the ledge. At last my shoulders were flat against the cracked blocks of the shrine of the celestial serpent, with a catastrophic drop just beneath my toes. It was like flying over green jungle, mostly overgrown orchards of breadfruit trees, mottled with hidden ruins, stretching to the horizon. I'd assumed that I would have the experience to myself, but no: beside me were two giggling American teenage girls who'd had the same notion.

Next was Belize, every inch of which is claimed by its neighbour. The country was hard to find on our locally bought map, as it was coloured the same as Guatemala, and neither a border nor the name Belize was displayed. Asking locals didn't help, as they said, "No Belize, all is Guatemala." Belize City was a scuzzy place, full of bedbugs and worse, according to everyone's guidebooks, which also counselled to avoid it outright. Two rival Afro-Caribbean hustlers, named Chocolate and Stud, offered to help us do just that and take us by motorboat out to the islands or cayes near the reef. One of them prevailed, but as there was not much to distinguish between them in terms of personality, I can't remember whom we came to hire in the end, except that he was a good skipper and wound through the mazes of cresting waves with a minimum of bouncing and crashing. Caye Caulker was a small paradise, with children selling lobster and coconut pies on the beach, including one boy who was very little and very shy and had to be encouraged to wait for us to put the money in his bag.

A minor miracle happened on the cayes: Brenda often wore a particular elastic top, with no bra needed. As we discovered, the ultraviolet radiation had been slowly degrading the clear plastic hasp that held the whole kit and caboodle. It could have failed any place: in a crowded restaurant, in the street, in front of an official at a border crossing, on a bus. But when it did fail, spronging skyward like a long rubber band and releasing her boobs for display, it was during the two-minute interval that we were traipsing through, for the only time on our entire trip, a clothing-optional beach.

From here we were back to tamer travel, north into Mexico, eating chicken feet in the plaza, tasting chocolate sauce as a savoury flavour on meat, marvelling at all the Volkswagen beetles swarming Mexico City, climbing pyramids, and finding that, for us, Cancún was too touristy, even before it had been built up, and the atmospheric old Mexican city of Mérida was more our style. This whole trip felt over once we'd crossed to San Diego, with its odd culture of high-rise prisons in the downtown, super-friendly and well-meaning local people warning us in a frenzy of fear not to venture out of certain safe zones, strange and gleaming modern glass buildings, and the impressive navy in the harbour.

Back in Canada, Brenda and I eventually parted ways, on friendly terms and staying in touch over the years. She wanted to settle and have children immediately, whereas my thoughts were on the next adventure. There is a truism that travelling either brings a couple together or breaks a relationship. Our trips together did both, bringing us together to show that it was not to be. These first months were just a taste of third-world backpacking, but they had shown me more things than my mind could possibly assimilate, dispelling my school-days notion that famous, and thus justly popular, places like Cancún, with five million tourists a year, will be the memorable highlights of travel, and that images of a family digging for ghost crabs in the moonlight by some unknown village on the shore will be forgotten. Though it would be some time before I knew what to make of it, my eyes were now opened to human geography as they had been to the natural world. There was no going back.

CHAPTER THREE

TROPICS AND THE BUSINESS OF TRAVEL

Indonesia · Thailand · Burma · Cambodia · Singapore

T HE FIVE YEARS THAT FOLLOWED WERE A TIME OF CHAOTIC travel, including some in Africa, Europe, the Middle East, the Caribbean, and former British colonies, but dominated by Asian destinations, especially Southeast Asia, my logistical base for visas, flights, and schemes to earn travel funds. These travels laid the foundations for my acquisition of backpacker habits and skills. They were not yet intuitive, but at least they could be called upon when needed.

It took until the later years of the '90s for me to feel comfortable being stared at as the centre of attention in whatever village I'd crop up in. In Asia I would tower above most of the locals, a sea of heads with black hair, rather than being anonymous in a crowd as is the norm in the big multi-ethnic cities of the Anglo-sphere. And even after all that time living out of my trusty backpack, intense dreams would tantalize me the night after I arrived in a new country. These visions, akin to my experiences alone in the wilderness, were summoned by seeing somewhere marvellous for the first time.

My new pastime of swapping travel tales with other backpackers had an added bonus of helping me remember details that would have faded if I'd kept my experiences to myself or relied entirely on my notes. Keeping a journal was one of my long-standing quirks: I recorded my experiences, daily thoughts, and interesting conversations in a pocket notebook as they happened, or, failing that, remembered those details when everything was transcribed into a larger journal in the evening before I went to sleep. Looking at the notes I wrote in these years, from the mid to late '90s, there were three recurring questions from other backpackers: Don't you get homesick? What about money? How do you communicate—or are you content to be lost to the world? I'd answer each of these with a story. Any substantial block of my time that failed to generate adventures fit to relate as an interesting story seemed such a waste to me now, and made me redouble my efforts to live so as to have something to tell for it.

Stay-at-home types or casual visitors often mused that I must have the motherlode of photographs of me mugging in front of every tourist trap. They were shocked to hear me say that I had nothing against photography, but I've never owned a camera. Cue the bemoaning of lost opportunity, all traces of irony gone from their voices. To each their own: many photographers have accompanied or crossed paths with me, and they often send photos, now stowed in a hefty box at my mom's house, but I have no special desire to capture a place or an instant. In fact, I suspect that indulging in such photos might cheat me out of seeing something for the first time for real. My passion is for the long now, and the best way for me to capture that sort of moment is in a story.

Often, over these five years, new acquaintances would say something to the effect of "You want to do years of backpacking? How will you not be bored out of your mind?" If they didn't say it, they were likely thinking it. But backpacking is nothing like a beach holiday or charter bus tour. Package tours get just as boring, just as fast, for me as for the next guy. If that was the only or main thing that travel was, then you'd likely find me home-bound on a front porch, reading books about long-dead explorers. Sometimes it's a matter of many or most people not understanding the difference between, say, a package tour and backpacking. To explain the allure of travel to these doubters, telling one of my growing collection of travel tales would often do nicely, such as a version of this account of the curious events of a week in Indonesia, from the beginning of 1996.

Flores is an island in the Indonesian province of Nusa Tenggara (sometimes called the Sunda Isles), which is a long, fascinating chain of islands arching south and east from Java. Flores is rather jungle-y compared to more frequently visited islands, such as Lombok. In the '90s the way to reach it was by boat or Fokker airplane, and getting around on the island meant old buses with bald tires on awful roads. A ten-hour drive would expand to eighteen when you factor in the four or five tire changes, ditch-side tire repair with little rubber patches, and much inspection, hemming, and hawing. The main draw for visitors is Kelimutu, a forested volcanic mountain with a crater atop it that holds three lakes, each a different intense colour like oil paints. The lakes were turquoise, emerald, and burgundy for me, but these colours are prone to shift over the years as concentrations of dissolved minerals wax and wane. After a coloured lake viewing, a 30-kilometre hike down the mountain at night, and a character-building bus trip out of there, I ended up in a little town called Bajawa, known for the colourful pom-poms that dangle from the men's hefty agricultural knives. I was sharing a room, separate beds, with my new friend, a young Canadian woman from Guelph named Joanna.

"Do you think that there is malaria here?" she asked, noticing me putting up a spanking-new mosquito net.

"Yes," I said. "Probably vivax, the kind that settles in your blood forever."

"Is it okay if I sleep under your net too?" she asked.

"It'll be a tight squeeze, but sure."

She was an adventurous blonde with a sharp mind for business, who preferred to roam the tropics, buying silver jewellery and gemstones and selling them in Canada at outdoor music festivals and universities.

These characteristics I'd learned from chats during "jam-karet" (rubber-time), when we were waiting for bus conductors to patch burst inner tubes, and a few nights at the backpackers' hotel in the settlement of Moni, near the base of Kelimutu, where the youthful guests would refer to each other by their country of origin rather than bother with names— my first encounter with this convention. But we would have time to get to know more about each other later. What we needed now was a box of condoms. None were at hand, so I offered to go out on a mission.

"I'll be bored here alone. I'll come along too," she said. And so we wandered all about a maze of mud roads and shabby wooden shacks, lit by the occasional bare bulb.

The streets were deserted except for a pack of kids, thirty or more of them, who, having nothing better to do, followed us around shouting the usual "What is your name?" and "Where are you going?" then laughing hysterically. To each other they said, speaking Bahasa language, "Moon people, moon people, where are the moon people going?" Moon people on account of our white skin, naturally. One of the slightly older kids must have figured we were out searching in the dark of night for dodgy hooch, since the madding crowd nudged us to a purveyor of Chinese whisky with special herbs, produced from a trapdoor (this whisky came in useful afterward, though I'm pretty sure the special herbs were some sort of narcotic).

The dealer pointed us and our horde of shouting children to a make-shift pharmacy. I ducked inside, and rather than standing outside, look-ing foolish, so did Joanna.

The pharmacists were asleep, but they had left their pubescent son in charge of the shop. Of course, he was the peer and school chum of the street kids, who now all poured in to see what the moon people were up to. Lacking the necessary Bahasa language skills, I was having trouble communicating and resorted to pantomiming my needs with gestures toward my amorous companion. The pharmacist's son blushed more than I thought possible for an Indonesian boy, but he did produce a pack of "Long Love" condoms. The swarm of kids shrieked with laughter, pointing at unfortunate Joanna, who had turned beet red.

There wasn't much to see in Bajawa—in fact, we had been the main entertainment—so we took what was left of our whisky and hopped on the bus to Labuan Bajo, a beachside town and port. Many burst tires later, we arrived and settled in. A fun town for backpackers, but even more intriguing was a wooden boat, built in a top-heavy manner like a junk; the skipper was asking if any foreigners were interested in a voyage of some days, ending up in Lombok. To sweeten the deal, he was calling on Rinca Island to view komodo dragons, and we would sleep the first night near Komodo Island, sheltered in the bay near the main town. After that it was a long voyage across the sea of Sumbawa.

The voyage began splendidly: gentle waves; the little hidden green and silver tussles of flying fish and needlefish sporadically bursting out of the water; stops for a bit of snorkelling on some likely reefs. On Rinca we went ashore to look for dragons. There were eight passengers who had an interest in dragons, all foreigners, all backpackers; we decided to roam as a group with a local guy we hired to show us the wildlife. He spoke some English too, enough to inform me that when dragons see the colour red, they lunge and kill. Fairly warned, since I was wearing a "loud" red shirt; on such a bright tropical day, though, it would have been more useful if he'd told me this when we came ashore, and not after a long hike through low hills of rubble with tufts of dried grass. Weighing venomous dragon bites against possible sunburn, I doffed my shirt.

The first dragon we saw was chubby, just lying on the ground. Word was these creatures can gather wolfishly in packs and run down horses and deer, or lurk in ambush and take down these or even more hulking animals, like water buffalo. It was hard to credit these stories looking at this lounging lizard. Shortly after, we heard a screaming noise from a nearby forest of giant cactus-like euphorbia plants and rushed over to investigate. It was a deer in a battle for survival with a large dragon. The deer had lost but didn't know it yet. Both hind legs had been snapped off and the hide on her belly torn completely away, but her guts were still intact; she stood on her bone stumps and remaining set of legs, screaming, and came wobbling over to me, since I stood in front of the group. The dragon hung back, waiting. Our group talked over the situation as we backed away, and concluded that it was best if we departed so the dragon would finish killing.

Back on the boat, it was a short motor over to Komodo Island for a visit to the park headquarters. Joanna had been there a couple of years earlier, when the rangers would feed a goat to the dragons for the amusement of tourists. A team of visiting biologists had put a stop to that, saying the dragons were all getting fat and arthritic, waiting around to get the goat instead of hunting up-island. Joanna said the park headquarters had also been heaving with rats; they were all over the kitchen and running over the blankets of any tourists sleeping in the hotel. We didn't find out if the rats had gone the way of the goats, as we slept anchored out in the bay.

That night was calm and lovely, and after some rice and squid we heard the call to prayer from the mosque on shore. We settled down to watch the stars and, later, to be gently rocked to sleep, all lying out on the wooden planks of the deck. Next morning we could scarcely feel we were afloat; it was dead calm, water smooth as glass, as far as the eye could see. The crew fired up the engine. Soon we were chugging out into a surreal seascape, eerily lacking so much as a ripple. A couple of the tourists decided it would be fun to ride on the roof, not possible the day before as it tended to sway a lot.

As the afternoon wore on, a wind picked up and waves appeared. The wind and waves built and built until all passengers, tourists and locals alike, were huddled down where we could clutch the gunwales and try to avoid being seasick.

Come nightfall, the waves were huge and menacing us from directions that took expertise to predict. The crew were keeping our bow facing these monstrous swells, assisted by the beautiful disco-blue glow all along their crests: diatoms in the sea were being disturbed and glowing in the turbulence. We had been caught in a raging typhoon. I found enough peace of mind to marvel that I was out in such a beautiful and deadly show, admiring the glowing blue topology of furious wave crests. Little did we know that a 555-ton steel-hulled car ferry from Java, the *Gurita*, was sent to the bottom by the storm, and other boats were wrecked in the seas off Sumbawa around us. Up to 340 lives were lost, and a few dozen survivors told of sharks indiscriminately feasting on the flesh of the living and the dead.

The typhoon and its casualties made the news in places as far away as Europe, but at the time we knew only that we had to hold on for dear life. Then a tourist started yelling and beckoning to an Indonesian crewman. This man was with the rest of the crew, clustered around the engine, striving to ensure it didn't cut out. The waves were so violent that they kept wrenching our stern clean out of the water; at that point the propeller would be running without resistance, and we could hear the engine over-rev. If the engine quit, we would be in dire straits. We were all cognizant of the thin line of blue glow in the black of night, where the sea thrashed upon the base of a cliff. The propeller alone was keeping us from being dashed to our doom on the rocks, not to mention keeping us from going broadside to a wave.

Despite this, the crewman made an effort to attend to the squawking tourist. He ran and grabbed hold, waited for that momentary lull between titanic impacts, ran and grabbed hold again; his timing was marvellous to behold. Then he was bending an ear to the passenger. I cupped my hand to shield the shrieking wind and listened in, worried what this emergency was, so serious that he would call a crewman off all-important engine duty.

"Three meals a day is what the captain promised on this voyage," the tourist said. "So where is my chicken and rice?"

A flicker of perplexity, incredulity, showed on the crewman's face, quickly shifting to a model example of Indonesian composure. He pointed to the galley. "Eat," he said, his mind already judging the timing of the surges to rush and wrestle his way back to the engine.

If you'd gone into the galley and put a pot on the stove, a couple of seconds would pass and then *bang*, the pot would be clanging off the ceiling. Then *bang*, off the floor ... Go at a chicken with a knife, and I'd give better odds to the chicken. Envision putting yourself, a knife, and a chicken into one of those glass globes that churn to pop up numbered balls for a lottery—and gamble that pieces of chicken would pop out before chunks of your own self. We battled the storm all night, and, come morning, in a feat of expert seamanship, we managed to slip into the entrance to a narrow passage in the cliffs of Sumbawa, a place called Bima, that proved to be such good shelter the winds buffeting us were no fiercer than a gale.

The crew started cheering wildly once they had timed the swells and waves and got into this passage without crashing up against the veritable Scylla and Charybdis to either side. Joanna and I could tell from their stupefied, relieved faces what a near thing it had been.

The skipper assembled us for a speech, once we were at the dock. "Is it better to continue by sea?" he asked, rhetorically. "Or is everyone better on land?"

When a couple of German motorcycle tourists started to debate the merits of each, he stated the obvious.

"Better you stay on land."

Shouldering my pack and stepping onto the gangplank, I heard a clucking from a wicker-work box in the bow: yesterday's twice-lucky chicken, in double peril from a typhoon and hungry humans. These jeopardies had miraculously cancelled one another out, leaving him crowing at a new dawn.

SOUTHEAST ASIA IN THE '90S WAS THE IDEAL PLACE TO LEARN backpacking skills. It was like Africa is today, a place where, with a little luck, crazy, dangerous, and fun stuff could happen at any moment. I had an opportunity to explore all this with Joanna. She possessed all the backpacker virtues. Her stomach could tolerate even the nastiest street food, her fit legs carried her over the roughest terrain at a steady pace, even with a pack geared for camping, and she could bargain hard in the markets while keeping it friendly. I found her, and her laissez-faire lifestyle, fascinating, and we became inseparable for several years. We explored Southeast Asia, always with an eye for jewellery-buying opportunities and, later, opportunities to manufacture unique items for our "Earthly Delights" line of home, garden, and patio products. We were seldom alone, as we tackled life as a team.

When exploring a region, it's convenient to have bases of operation—places you know fairly well—that you can fly into and out of, or from which you can arrange forward travel. For Joanna and me, our base for visas and most international flights was Bangkok; for business it was Kuta, on Bali; and for occasional magic mushrooms and frisky midnight strolls on lonely beaches of coral fragments that rubbed musically under our toes, we would go to nearby deserted islands. Thailand was the beating heart of the backpacking scene, where the now-legendary full-moon parties on Koh Phangan, an island east of the Isthmus of Kra, were enough of a draw, even back then, that they caused a lunar monthly pulsation in the movements of backpackers through Southeast Asia. Most would organize their trip so that they could be on that beach just before the full moon, with a place to stay sorted.

Joanna had been to some of the first moon parties, which then amounted to little more than a bunch of hippie backpackers gathering to smoke weed—often with the town's chief of police—play their guitars, and trip on magic mushrooms. The locals were bemused but not involved. By the time I'd attended my first one in the mid-'90s, local Thai-style houses with their saddle-shaped, double-peaked thatch roof, carved ornamentation, and attendant orange-and-blue hut-master gecko were getting harder to find; concrete structures were encroaching, and the Thais began to show an interest in these goings-on. Some small bars along the beach, most centrally the Cactus Club, were blasting out discordant pop music. The scene was solidly backpacker; if you had a hankering for hookers, you had landed on the wrong island. For that, Koh Samui was your place, the first to be touristed, now morphed into a package-hotel island with drunks, aggression, hookers, bar stars, and transvestites adding a yeasty component to the original mix of friendly Thais, casual visitors, and expats.

But always we found ourselves returning to Indonesia—for business and pleasure. Arriving in Bali brought a frisson of instant joy, from the first aromas of curbside incense offerings—ylang ylang, frangipani, *sedap malam*—and gentle gamelan music to my first taste of fish ball soup from little carts, buzzing with wasps. This joy was often magnified if the sneaky pleasure of escaping the grip of a northern hemisphere winter was thrown in. While its near neighbour Thailand is a kingdom of excellent food and military coups, Indonesia is an empire conquered and consolidated by the Dutch, which, in a stroke of luck, the Javanese inherited.

Similar to the Roman Empire, with its Mediterranean Sea as a Roman lake, Indonesia was a Javanese Empire, home to many cultures tied together through sea lanes and shipping. Now, and as of 1999, it is a democracy, but back in the day, dictatorship held sway, with the usual shenanigans: you might read that a new law had been passed saying that people riding motorbikes must wear helmets, and then hear the buzz in the streets that the monopoly allowed to sell motorcycle helmets was owned by the son of the dictator, President Suharto. Or a new law said you must have insurance to drive a car; how modern, you might think, until you heard the taxi drivers grumbling that the insurance never paid out for any reason, so it was essentially just a burdensome tax, and the only company that issued policies was owned by cronies of Suharto. Despite these quibbles, and largely because of the intelligence and skill of the people, Indonesia was growing economically at a ferocious rate. It makes you wonder what rate of growth is possible if somehow corruption could be stamped out. But we as a species will never know, as it'll never happen.

Joanna and I were busy working smart, and sometimes hard, to fund our trips, happily immersed in making a success of "Earthly Delights," then in full swing. It took just days to have a sample of a new product made, and for these short waits we could hang out on the nearby Gili Islands or Sulawesi. When it came time to make thousands of items to fill orders, though, months would pass, and further months as the containers crossed the ocean. At various times we shipped things like coffee tables made of coffee wood (My sales pitch was "It's not just a coffee table, it's a coffee-coffee table"), replicas of a thousand-year-old Scottish box decorated with stylized designs of the leaves and berries of heather, and wrought-iron tripod planters. These substantial runs of wood and metal products were all sold at once in big flower and garden and home furnishing shows, usually in the early spring. While villages of Indonesian artisans worked on our orders for months, we would explore farther afield, places like the outermost islands of Indonesia, Malaysia, Indochina, and beyond, all over Asia.

Once we got on the second of two identical buses in Nepal—a lucky thing, too, since the first bus plunged off a cliff, destroying a footbridge on the way down, and leaving few survivors. After weeks of trekking around the Annapurnas, we were caught in a blizzard at 5,000 metres. This was followed by days huddled in a Tibetan yak herder's mud and rock shelter, squatting by the smouldering dung-fire, unable to communicate with him except through smiles and laughter, until one of the yaks bestirred itself and ploughed through the snow, opening a path to the village of Manang (where we were able to skedaddle in a dual-rotor Russian helicopter). On another occasion, in Sri Lanka, we found ourselves between the front lines of opposing armies, within earshot of the bursting artillery shells, as we explored a lost ancient city in the jungle.

When we ventured away from Southeast Asia on a side trip to the southern part of Africa, I learned that the world was not divided into developed and developing countries as the television news is apt to assume. There is a third category not much talked about: non-developing countries, like Zimbabwe, where human potential is bottled up by a governance that can only be described as an unholy blend of feudalism and socialism. The society seemed lethargic and stunted, while villagers focused their considerable talent and energy on raising huge numbers of children, their sole security. Only a fool would do business there, and since we needed local business opportunities to finance our adventures, we returned to vibrant Asia: to the wild west of the Philippines; to Palawan, with its underground river, mud, soldiers riding "shotgun" atop the buses, and bandits. To India, which served up a heap of crazy in the year it took to get a glimpse of its bewildering variety and teeming cities. People forget that Asia used to be a chaotic place where life was cheap.

The cultures of Asia were so strange and mystifying to me, it got me seriously thinking about diverse and divergent lifeways. A Sanskrit scholar smuggled me into the holiest area of Vishnu's greatest temple, where I saw cross-dressing Brahmans loving Vishnu as a wife loves her husband. An auditor for an international umbrella of charities, staggered by the fraudulent books, muttered "never again," disabused of his idealism. Barefoot Indian workers swarmed like ants over the hulks of ships, cutting through asbestos and steel with oxyacetylene torches, winching the fallen slabs up the beach. In the Gir forest, five male lions approached, taking turns to roar. And, looking behind me, I laughed to see that the Indians who had set out wildlife viewing with me had cleverly arranged themselves in a column so that, to a lion's eye, there was only me: they shuffled to stay in sync with my motions, hidden, with my body as the only prey in view, so I had a tail of Indians, as it were, to swish behind me as I pleased.

Following the maxim that a change is as good as a rest, in between long stretches of travel in Asia, Africa, and the Caribbean, and these business trips to Bali, we would criss-cross North America in an old green truck, following music festivals when it was the season for them. I had a knack for sales, once I learned to handle the till, and discovered myself to be simultaneously talented and hopeless as a businessman. I enjoyed huge profits from mere weeks of work importing innovative products, but then I let the exporting and importing lapse to max-out on more travel to destinations just opening to tourism.

Burma (Myanmar) was such a place, just opened, according to the traveller's grapevine in those years when most information about unpopular destinations was rumour, and phoning ahead was usually more trouble than it was worth. According to the oft-quoted opening sentence of L.P. Hartley's novel *The Go-Between*, "The past is a foreign country: they do things differently there." Burma, meanwhile made you wonder: Can a foreign country be the past? Travel in Burma is more like *time* travel, a concept not especially popular in anthropology, just as the special existence of a moment called "now" is not popular in physics. But when you are travelling by horse and buggy, and this is not just for tourists but the usual way people get around, you are as close as you will get to time travel. I had slipped the Yangon customs official a dollar bill as a bribe, so we were in without having to change too much hard currency into dicey foreign exchange certificates.

East of the former royal capital of Mandalay there is a lake called Inle that could be accessed by a new Korean-built bus—bought, according to the locals, with heroin money from the Golden Triangle (the mountainous region famed for renegade opium cultivation). Some locals and sensitive backpackers wouldn't ride the new bus for moral reasons, objecting to the fact that it had been bought with heroin money, but Joanna and I made the trip. The drive to the lake was along a rudimentary road, more of a modestly widened goat track. Rice is grown along the shore of this lake, and people live in stilt houses out in the depths, tending floating tomato gardens. Several islands were scattered about the shallow waters too, but these had been entirely occupied by Buddhist stupas, bell-shaped buildings that house shrines. These shrines held golden blobs, purportedly statues of Buddha; tradition held it to be meritorious to buy sheets of gold and drape these onto the statue, which had become so gilded that it was like the gum of a gobstopper candy, secreted deep inside a blob of gold.

A market at one end of the lake allowed the tomato- and vegetable-growing lake dwellers to trade with the shore people. At one stall we saw a woman sitting at a table piled with goat heads, her face fixed in a frown that mirrored the slack look of a disembodied goat. Many women sold cheap Chinese goods while puffing on big green cheroots (cigars). The stilt-house dwellers travelled to the market—indeed, they got about their whole life—in little canoes, and so developed the most extraordinary sense of balance. They would not sit while paddling, but stood, and they would do this not in the canoe, but, rather, on a narrow tail of wood that projected out the stern. They would stand on one foot, as the other leg was busy manipulating a paddle and propelling them along, thereby leaving both arms free to cast a net or tend vines.

At that time, tickets for air travel were made of paper, and they sometimes had to be reconfirmed a few days before use or they would be cancelled. This was the case with our flight from Burma on Biman Bangladesh Airlines. We looked over the ticket and realized we needed a phone so we could call the nearest airline office in Yangon. No problem, we'd simply take a boat back to the town on the shore.

Once ashore, the locals tending the rice paddies pondered our request for directions to a phone. After talking at length among themselves, they indicated a tuk-tuk, a small three-wheeled vehicle with a motorcycle engine, and pointed north. North it was, and at each town we reached, enquiries led to much discussion, scratching of heads, and fingers pointing yet farther north. When we passed out of the range that one tuk-tuk driver was comfortable with, we'd swap for another. The longer this went on, the more nervous we became about how far north we had got, especially after finding our little tuk-tuk sandwiched between two army trucks carting loads of 500-pound bombs to the front lines. But we'd come this far, we decided, so we might as well see it through, and ended up in what the locals joked(?) was no man's land between the Burmese army and the rebels of the Shan State Army in a small dingy town of decaying lumber and dirt alleys. What now? It wasn't obvious that there should be any telephones here, and there were no transmission towers or poles or any sign of technology.

After a while wandering the streets, we noticed a Chinese man standing on the corner of an intersection. Every so often a few locals would approach and show him something in the palm of their hands; he would take a look and then either shoo them away or, occasionally, pass them American dollars and pocket whatever it was they held. Having found no sign of a phone, and with nothing better to do, we wandered over to introduce ourselves.

Turned out he could speak a bit of English, and he explained he was a buyer of conflict rubies, blood rubies, sold by people mining in the homeland of the Karen, who used the money to finance their war. The ruby buyer's name didn't make it into my notes, but he had much whiter skin than the Karens or Shan, and his face was remarkably round, like a porcelain plate, so I'll call him China.

He showed us two rubies from his pocket, one worth 300 dollars, the other barely fifteen dollars. Could we spot the difference? We looked, and even though we had some experience buying semi-precious stones, they appeared remarkably similar to our eyes. He explained that you needed years of practice to price a ruby. I told him about a ruby buyer we'd talked to in our hotel when we first passed through Yangon: he was trying to have money wired in from his brother in Singapore, but someone in the bank had skimmed the transfer, and he was trying to confirm with his brother and find out which bank employee had made off with it.

China laughed, and lamented that if only he had $200,000 in cash, he could get a licence to buy directly from the government mines. Or, for the same fee, he could lease a square kilometre in the Golden Triangle. There he could do as he pleased for a number of years—heroin lab, methamphetamine factory, marijuana or opium plantation, counterfeit Thai baht operation—until the junta gave a warning to wrap up operations and then sent in armed forces, with cameras, to document how they were busting this illegal operation and were oh-so-tough on crime. Then he'd fork over another two-hundred grand and set up on a new square kilometre nearby. We wished him luck amassing this cash, and explained over lunch that we had come here looking for a phone.

"Ah, I can help you," he said.

He led us down an alley to where a hatch opened on a vertical shaft, with a ladder; we descended into near darkness, finding a humid dirt tunnel with bare bulbs illuminating it at intervals. A long queue of locals filled this tunnel, but China must have been a man of importance since he led on, squeezing past everyone to the front of the line, which terminated at a wooden wall. There a square hatch opened in the wall at chest height, revealing an antiquated bulky black rotary-dial telephone. A woman stood behind this shelf, the keeper of the phone. We understood that this was our chance to make a call, so we took out our scrap of paper with the airline's number in Yangon, and tried to remember how to use one of those rotary-dial phones. Our call got through, and despite the strong Bengali accent of the woman who answered, we were fairly certain our flights were reconfirmed.

After we had climbed back out into the daylight, we had to ask: Why were there no phones except this museum piece in the middle of nowhere, up near the front lines? China explained that when the

British were fighting the Japanese in the jungle during World War II, they needed to be able to take orders from headquarters back in Yangon. The phone had been there since the war, which is why it was down in that tunnel. People kept it working all those decades, repairing whenever there was a break in the line.

To this day, that was my most troublesome phone call.

CHAPTER FOUR

COLONIZED AND BALKANIZED: LUMPERS AND SPLITTERS

Australia · New Zealand · Albania · Croatia ·
Bosnia-Herzegovina · Albania · Macedonia

ETTLING DOWN WITH JOANNA WOULD HAVE BEEN THE sensible thing to do. Conventionally, a life is supposed to go only one way and entails a job, then marriage and kids. A guard on the borders of Far Turkistan and a Westerner can agree on this subject, though for the former it is normal, and the latter will call it "perfect," with a little sarcasm intended. Perhaps there exists some truly perfect Xanadu in the back of beyond, where a dream life doesn't have to be one way or the other.

In Alberta, we parted ways. She moved to Bali, eventually marrying, starting a family, and fulfilling her dream of becoming a silver jewellery "tycoon." After we folded our business, I stayed in Vancouver for a month but soon had itchy feet. It was December 1999, so it was possible to score a ridiculously cheap flight across the Pacific on New Year's Eve

1999 because the dreaded Y2K bug had deterred customers from flying in case the airplane's computer failed at the stroke of midnight, causing it to plummet from the sky. The 747 was empty except for me, stretched out over a middle row of seats, sleeping through the change of the millennium, newly single and heading for a solo tour of Asia.

Such a relaxing flight allowed me to get over the hectic experience of running around Vancouver trying to arrange those crisp new US hundred-dollar bills needed for travelling. Twice I'd had to bus downtown for banking, since the first time everything had been shut—for Christmas Eve. It was often thus for me, only figuring out that it was some major holiday after I had tried to do some banking or go to a museum and found the doors locked during normal business hours. Weekends are nothing special to me either, as they mean only hardship finding a hostel bed, and closed embassies forcing longer waits in national capitals than would be my preference. About a third of the time during my years of travel I'd neglect my own birthday, and only realize a few weeks later that I was indeed a year older.

At any rate, I had managed to get the banking done between Christmas and New Year's Eve, and the money was in the sturdy SunDog-brand bag that was always on my person, even when I was taking a shower inside a locked hotel room. Occasionally other backpackers would tease me about carrying a "man-purse." Little did they know it held dog-choking wads of cash, organized into envelopes, each filled with US$10,000. This fact didn't make me wealthy, which is a concept implying generations of financial security. Nor did I feel rich. Many, if not most, thirty-year-old Westerners had more assets, whether they were invested in a house or took the form of a college degree or valuable job training. My cash was vulnerable to total loss from force or trickery at any moment. A sharp blade rode along in the front pocket of my bag, and I was well-trained and mentally prepared to risk my life and peace of mind for the rest of the contents. If my intuition told me muggers were casing my bag, I would let my gaze flick to their watch or their wallet pocket, and when my hand drifted toward the hilt of my blade, they would take me for a fellow predator and go after easier prey.

Why take such a terrible risk? A degree for teaching English or practising medicine, worth the equivalent to what was on me, had the advantage of being intrinsically safe, and would allow me to work for half
the year to fund the other half year's travel. Not good enough, I thought.
And hindsight has proved me right: travelling and working half and half
would have meant a forty-six-year trip to see the world to my satisfaction.
What I needed was a way to fund my travels with a couple of weeks' work
spread over the year, leaving the other fifty weeks free.

This bag of money permitted me to exploit a peculiar, now vanished,
economic niche that was a continuation of what I'd practised doing
business in Asia with Joanna. For about ten years after 2000 there were
many regions with poor or nonexistent banking, and someone keeping
an eye out for trading opportunities could manage, at great personal risk,
to make about what a worker in a fast-food outlet would take home in
Canada. Opportunities might arise to, say, buy lapis lazuli from Afghan
merchants in Laos and ship it to Mexico to sell, or buy wrought iron
in China and ship it to Malaysia. This was more than enough to fund
budget travel and to grow my stash a bit in good years. The situational
awareness needed to stay alive also proved handy for spotting trading
opportunities. This time it would be semi-precious stones and jewellery;
next time, whatever caught my eye.

Apart from the temptation of a cheap flight, my goal was to explore
new Asian countries or make return visits to ones that held, for me, parts
unknown. Already people regarded me as well travelled; some of them
were competitive, so after hearing travel tales on a porch or in a common
room, they would ask me how many countries were under my belt. These
conversations didn't interest me, as in my experience they always ended
quickly, mired in ethical disagreement. Twice I had visited Seoul, thus
having been to Seoul, not South Korea. One day in my life had been
spent rafting in Zambia, below Victoria Falls. A fun fact but no excuse
for me to claim I had "done" Zambia.

Friends and socializing were also on my agenda. As usual, bouncing between countries meant stops in Bangkok to forage for fresh visas,

sometimes in the company of Ken, my Sons of Freedom anarchist friend from Canada. Nearby in Ko Tao, Thailand, we met two people from the UK: Tim, a big, tall, blond chap, quick to make friends and organize parties; and Molly, a pierced and dreadlocked photographer, trying to live a life true to deep ethical convictions. Tim doesn't consider himself a traveller, but he has been to as many countries and continents as many who so fancy themselves, and he returns with stories that most people would consider the rightful subject of action films. He certainly manages to experience an amazing amount of the fringe culture of Europe, often hidden in plain sight. Molly fills her spare time with travel and otherwise documents rave culture, where bands of DJs with truck-borne sound systems squat abandoned buildings or out-of-the-way places until the police shut them down, making for a life most interesting and hectic. Both became close friends and later introduced me to the underground party scene then in full swing in Europe.

My friend Chad, from the days of hapless camping trips on Vancouver Island, had come with me to Borneo. He also went through Cambodia before me, one of the few countries I had missed in Southeast Asia. He told me of armed robberies, rocket-propelled-grenade battles in the streets of the capital, and a close encounter with death, when every man, woman, and child at the hotel he was supposed to be staying in was massacred by machine-gun-wielding gangsters. Fortunately he had been delayed by a truculent taxi driver, arriving too late for the grim reaper. So when I set out for Cambodia myself, chaos and danger were on my mind. Instead I found women fishing in the swamps using baskets, rickety ferry boats, and peasants chipping away at the concrete of old bunkers to scavenge the rebar—but no explosions or murder. Still, one guy in my hotel was shot (only a flesh wound), the mango-mongering kids on the beaches of Sihanoukville threatened to stab visitors who refused to buy, and the Khmer Rouge demanded twenty bucks to allow me to see the northern part of the temple complex of Angkor Wat. All in all a good trip, and it proved the small blessing of starting with rock-bottom expectations.

SINGAPORE HAD BEEN MORE EXCITING THAN EXPECTED, FEATURING a Swiss woman, Barbara, who I met in the lounge of the Perak Guesthouse. We went out to a disco and then snuck into her hotel, past the perhaps disapproving elderly man at the reception desk. This could have been a one-off—we didn't even have a common language—but little did I know I'd end up seeing her on and off for years afterward. A tall woman with wavy black hair and a swimmer's build, Barbara was certainly pretty and, as my intuition told me, a woman of many talents and eclectic interests, but we had to solve the language problem. She made me understand that her native German dialect was not practical, so we would speak in English, which she would learn with my help. She was a physiotherapist and master of shiatsu massage, and a practitioner of Zen, as I'd confirm later when I could have a proper conversation with her.

Some of my first efforts at teaching Barbara English involved convincing her we should head east to check out East Timor, a new country that had popped up. This former Portuguese colony on the Indonesian island of Timor fought successfully for independence from what it saw as new colonial masters, Indonesia's government in Java. Timor means "east" in Bahasa, so the country's name meant East East. It was a place infamous for war and human rights abuse, but newly under a United Nations transitional authority with some foreign armed forces stationed on the frontier.

Off we went. The final leg of the journey involved thumping over the waves to West Timor on a catamaran and beginning a long process of taking vans from one village to the next as we slowly approached the militarized new frontier. The more traditional villages were divided among a patchwork of clans, with special tartan cloth designs to match, as in the historical Scottish Highlands.

Other backpackers were few and mostly fakes. They were dressed as we were, but when we sat down to talk to them, the conversation was stilted and, on two occasions, dull as dishwater. It became even more awkward when they realized that we were bona fide backpackers and that I had guessed they were missionaries in disguise. Otherwise my travelling skills were not serving me well: we were always the only guests in the guesthouses, when they weren't shut entirely and overgrown with weeds. The hotel restaurants were always shut too, so it took a lot of wandering to get food, which was often what they called Padang style, where meat and rice had been precooked and then kept in the open air, behind a net to ward off flies. Once I had to drag Barbara around a town for almost an hour, asking here, there, and everywhere for directions to the nearest restaurant. There were none, and this was a big town. In desperation I dropped the Bahasa and changed to the universal sign for eating, a mimicry of hand to mouth and a rubbing of my belly: success. I'd been too formal in my questions, asking for a restaurant when those didn't exist; only many eateries, any one of which they were happy to show us.

At the eatery we chose, I saw a man with a suspicious face. Nothing out of the ordinary in terms of features, but I could swear his face kept popping up again and again, which was impossible because we kept changing towns as we made for the border. After ordering a Bintang beer and sending it to his table, I said, "Cheers," raising my own beer. He nodded and smiled and took up the bottle, then started to drink, as quickly as a kid might chug fruit juice. Clearly he was parched, so I sent him another beer, and he came to sit with us. Already he was tipsy. "I'm a secret agent," he said, "pretending to be a West Timorese Christian." He lifted his shirt to show the grip of a 9mm pistol.

"Interesting. What is your mission?"

"To spy," he said.

"Cheers to that," and we clinked bottles. "Who are you spying on?"

"You."

"I'll make it easy; what do you want to know?" I explained that we were backpackers travelling the world.

As he had finished his second beer, I shouted a third. Now he was wasted and admitted that he'd never tasted alcohol before, but he had to drink it so people would think he was a Christian, as everyone knows Christians drink beer. He said he came from a little town in east Java and had been posted for a couple of years in Dili as secret police. And now he was a spy. I thought: Spy, yes, but not exactly James Bond material.

He started to complain that he didn't like it in West Timor and wished he could be sent back to his parents' village. None of the girls here would talk to him because they had discovered he is Muslim and they were Christian. He was almost certainly involved in the terrible atrocities that had taken place in East Timor during the 1990s, given the time he was active and his position, but at the same time he was just a young man. I wished him luck getting transferred somewhere he could feel more at home.

On the frontier we had to wait in a long barbed-wire-flanked queue at the border, and with everyone but us carrying chickens and goats, we felt a little out of place. I'd worn a silk shirt by mistake, so I was sweltering in the jungle humidity. The Australian 2nd Battalion was manning the border post, and we got stamped in: UN Transitional Authority in East Timor. But not before an interview with the commander. He wanted to know if it was true that the refugee camps were emptying out. I told him that they were nearly empty, and he was happy to hear my independent voice confirming there wasn't any military buildup on the other side. Obviously not many backpackers were coming in overland.

The military, Australians and Brazilians, were doing a top-notch job checking for weapons and minding the borders, camping in difficult jungle environments. I wish I could say the same for the United Nations. It was not their finest hour. They had decided that none of the local hotels or restaurants were good enough for UN bigwigs, so they brought a couple of large ships over and anchored them just off the docks in Dili. One was a luxury cruise liner. We checked the prices: $350 a night for a room and $50 just for breakfast. I'm sure the price hardly mattered, since it was all charged to the UN accounts. The other ship had shops and a disco. A man at the gangplank ensured only UN clerks and the local girls on their arms could pass. Barbara and I found we could pass too, on account of our first-world status, but computer geeks macking on village girls was not our scene.

Convoys of white UN trucks would head down to the beaches for volleyball and parties. I'm sure it was a blast, and they had to get to the beaches somehow, and I don't doubt that these guys knew their stuff when it comes to providing economic and political advice. But there was a deeper problem with all this. They were supposed to help the bureaucrats and politicians of the world's newest democracy act the part. They apprehend not only what you say, but also how you act. You might make an excellent speech, and your PowerPoint slides show unequivocally that you should be exceedingly careful with the public's money, especially as you are a public servant and your country is underdeveloped and so on. But your message is undermined if the newly minted bureaucrats see you showboating with 500 bucks a day charged to your expense account.

For our part, Barbara and I found the local hotels suited us fine, and there was nothing wrong with rice and fish with a Timorese Portuguese twist. And the UN presence wasn't all bad. Someone had set up a café to entice UN types with an amazing blueberry cheesecake. And a man we'd met on the last van into Dili, a guy exuding a slimy vibe with eyes like a lizard, departed in disappointment. He'd come to scout if this was the place for another in his chain of whorehouses, but he just wasn't feeling it.

IN BETWEEN TRIPS TO CLUSTERS OF NEW COUNTRIES, I MADE SHORT jaunts to Canada, helped by my ability to find ridiculously cheap return flights from Asian hubs such as Bangkok to Vancouver. My first return was in the summer of 2000 and included hiking the famous West Coast Trail, through the ancient rain forest and beaches of Vancouver Island, with various family members. The next summer, joining my brother Steve and his wife, Nicky, I went on a long canoe and hiking expedition over the glaciated spine of the Rocky Mountains to retrace the lost trail of intrepid fur-trader David Thompson. This was the last of my North American wilderness pursuits, although I didn't know it at the time. I seldom came home in the summers after that, aside from a final visit one year later when both of my brothers became fathers in 2002.

My brothers were not only starting in on kids, but were also gainfully employed—Stephen writes popular history books and biographies of explorers, and Dave has his web-design company. And then there was me, in January 2003, jetting off across the Pacific for a quick stop in

China and then on to Koh Phangan for a full-moon party to get me in the proper mindset for some strange lands. The choices they had made were right for them, and certainly reduced any potential parental pressure on me to settle down and have kids. Just as well, since, even as I entered my early thirties, I felt the same rush as the roaming teenagers on their gap year when new geography was made real to me.

After spending days getting into Haad Rin and setting up for the party, and a couple of days drinking to put me in fine form, I had second thoughts. Maybe it was better to skip the party and get an early start on travel. The days before the party are the most fun anyhow, and the party itself can be a letdown. Too many people don't pace themselves; they stagger into a third night without sleep, as long-tails (watercraft with an automobile engine and a prop mounted on a long shaft) motor over from Koh Samui, unloading boatload after boatload of package-tour bar stars. And the party always ends the same way: at dawn, with a plump heap of shirtless youngsters passed out on Sunrise Beach, so sticky with toxic sweat that a coat of sand clings to them as if they were sugar-sprinkled donuts.

Anyhow, Barbara and I were supposed to meet in Indonesia. Problem was, my Yahoo account had stopped working, the problem didn't resolve itself until three weeks later, I couldn't remember her email address without access to where I'd typed it, in my glitch-paralyzed Yahoo account, and all this time Barbara was wondering what had happened to me. What followed was a surprise solo back-roads tour of Australia and New Zealand. I'd woken with a hangover, clasping some airline tickets, with vague memories of having bought them but not where they led, and sleepiness overcame me on the flights so that I failed to check the destination on the final ticket. These countries are cushy, yet memorable, especially the spectacular landscape and animals.

New Zealand is a place of fascinating natural and social experimentation. The race of penguin evolved here, as did giant flightless birds called moa, 3 metres tall, and the prodigious pouakai, an eagle that preyed on them, something like the Roc in the Sinbad-the-sailor myth. Polynesians arrived in a few boats, settled around the late thirteenth century, and proceeded to eat all the moa. If you can imagine those drumsticks, you can't blame them. These islands are prone to apocalyptic volcanism, and one such eruption had the population reduced to eating ferns but generally the land and sea provided.

After the seventeenth century another maritime people rowed ashore, Europeans. The locals were almost all Maori, and by then also fierce warriors, save for the Moriori, peace-loving social reformers living on the Chatham Islands off the coast, who had experimented with banning weapons and living a life of tranquillity. When the Maori encountered the British, one chief was astonished that the British king, George, had soldiers who would kill on command, regardless of whether the war was morally justifiable. Likewise, when British sailors spoke of the island of the Moriori, some Maori set out in a war party and attacked, clubbing all the men and old folks to death, and keeping all the fertile females. It would appear that the Maori idea of right and wrong was different from our modern take on the issue, and also that the Moriori social experiment in radical government war-club control was an idea a century or so ahead of its time. Unsurprisingly, the maritime warrior Maori and maritime warrior British had enough culture in common to get along adequately and co-found a modern nation.

Hostels were another social experiment. Worldwide, the hostel as a business concept was lame and unpopular, so hostels kept their doors open only with government subsidies from taxpayers. Backpackers didn't like them; with their curfews and drinking bans it felt like you were in an institution—which you were, since the government wielded the subsidy. In an important way, the government was the true customer, not the backpacker. The hostels in New Zealand and Australia were the first to change this. A few must have decided to ditch the government subsidy and instead provide what the backpackers actually wanted: no curfew, mixed dorms, a travel agent in the building, and a bar downstairs. This revolutionary model, of the guest being the customer, worked like a charm, and older government-subsidized hostels couldn't compete. It turns out that, all along, hostels had only "needed" a subsidy because they had been subsidized. The end result was that travel was "too easy."

I plundered the Franz Josef Glacier; cruised Milford Sound; hiked Abel Tasman Park, with its golden crescent beaches and shady fern trees; viewed the volcanoes, lakes, traditional longhouses, and mighty Kia trees of the North Island; and watched the America's Cup yacht race, then skipped over to Sydney.

Partway through this trip, my Yahoo account started working again, as if a digital curse was lifted. A succession of increasingly angry emails from Barbara filled my inbox, the last few describing her decision to devote weeks to intensive martial arts training with fists and offensive weapons. Discretion being the better part of valour, I decided to carry on from Sydney to visit Australia and make it up to Barbara later by flying to Central Europe, where I hoped the brisk Alpine climate would have soothed her anger.

Australia was the ends of the earth to ancient humankind, filled with a host of bizarre hopping creatures that had taken over from even stranger egg-laying mammals. The duck-billed platypus and echidna were the only ones to survive the marsupial onslaught: turns out they both used to be swamp dwellers, and marsupials have trouble competing in that niche, as the babies are tucked in a pouch and liable to drown. According to some scientists, particularly ones trying to focus on a thrilling narrative for documentaries, humans arrived in an epic migration perhaps fifty or sixty thousand years ago. According to aboriginals there was no migration; their ancestors have always been there. Who is correct? The aboriginals, without a doubt.

A long time ago, or dream-time, the ancestors moved about on an earth that would be familiar to fans of high fantasy. There were towering terror birds, slavering giant beasts, oversized lizards like dragons, and a menagerie of demi-humans—stocky Neanderthals, mysterious Denisovans, Hobbits, and undoubtedly other strange and wondrous races. These groups of humans lived in a world where the odds favoured a person burning out long before he might fade away, though I'm sure people might have packed two hundred years of adventure into their average thirty or forty whirls around the sun. As far as they were concerned, they were born into the world and died in the world; there was no concept of Australia, any more than when they left Africa they would consider celebrating that they were leaving Africa for Asia, or imagine they were going to Australia. It was one creation, and yes, they were always here. What was not always here was the notion to divide creation, conceptually speaking. From the moment the concept of Australia was invented, the aboriginals were already smack dab in the middle of it, and had been for fifty thousand years.

In contrast, the British are in Australia because the colonies of New England were expensive failures, and the ruling imperialists needed another dumping ground for surplus people—such as one of my ancestors in Scotland, who was sentenced to be transported for stealing a wheel of cheese. In the midst of nineteenth-century social upheaval, where the death penalty was in effect for nearly every crime, the magistrates decided that rather than riling up the already revolting lower classes by carrying out too many capital sentences, it was better to deposit them in Australia against their will. The idea was that the Empire would dip into the supply when cannon fodder was needed, the traditional use for these human surpluses. England availed itself generously of these people on the occasion of the Great War, and took another helping a generation later.

In Australia I headed up the coast from Sydney until I reached the Daintree Rainforest in the far north, then backtracked to the small city of Cairns to swim among some specks of the Great Barrier Reef, before swinging inland through the heat, fascinating rock formations, and, sometimes, plagues of flies that are the Outback to modern Australians, who look seaward and cluster in ocean-side cities. A flight took me from the extreme centre of the continent to the far west, from Alice Springs to Perth, and I hitchhiked back to Sydney along the coast while combing long stretches of beach, with side trips to explore places like Kangaroo Island, Tasmania, the Blue Mountains, and any cities I found myself in.

Travelling thus for a few smooth months, all around the continent, was relaxing and perfect for meeting neighbourly Australians, with their practical and philosophically sound "mate-ship" culture of friendly co-operation. Also, Australians with ancient ties to this land were happy to talk with me about the merits of walkabout. It matched my own experience of the wilderness.

Midway through my trip, a well-meaning ethnic European guide, at the base of the iconic Uluru rock in the centre of the continent, told an aboriginal story about the creation of the world and finished with "We have our own story about how the earth was formed and life evolved. Who can say one belief is right and another wrong? We need to respect the beliefs of other cultures."

I felt his comment was so silly that I told him, "How European of you. Questioning our own model is the central ancestral trait in the telling of our European origin story of science."

By speaking this way, he'd revealed his deep allegiance to Western thought. Other cultures don't value or praise doubting their own myths. People can be respected, not beliefs, which have no rights or expectations. And our focus on conceptualizing over walkabout comes at a price. When you live also among the other side of human nature, you don't need to believe illusions to fill a void that is half your soul and half your world: you have dream-time, and dream-time simply is. Dream-time is not an aboriginal belief, akin to concepts like Heaven or Hades or Valhalla. Dream-time is real, like gravity, kangaroos, and red dust, and is always there for anyone who wants to explore what it is to be human and alive on the landscape and dwelling in the myths we spring from.

NEARLY EVERYWHERE MY TRAVELS HAD TAKEN ME, THE LOCAL history involved conquest and cultural dominance by Westerners. In Australia, particularly, backpackers had been glued to the television news for months, the channel set to CNN and the Iraq War. Just why did Europe loom so disproportionately large over world history? North and Central America, the Anglo-sphere, and Asia were familiar to me now. Apart from a few stopovers and a family trip when I was sixteen, I knew nothing of Europe. It was time to visit the source of Western civilization.

My plan was for a three-month trip to the Balkans and Central Europe—a region of the world I knew nothing about—starting in July, after a month in the UK couch surfing and attending a party among the monuments of Stonehenge with Tim, Molly, and some French friends. Before starting on the Balkans, I had a stop in Central Europe. My Swiss Miss, Barbara, was running a physiotherapy and shiatsu business in Winterthur, a small city near Zurich, so I dropped in to do a road trip with her. This included some very long tunnels, as the Swiss like to go through mountains as much as around them, some hiking through the Alps, and guesthouses in villages. The Swiss have a waterfall, called the Rheinfall, which is meant to be impressive, though I have seen similar falls in Canada that haven't yet been ennobled with so much as a name. Apparently the Rheinfall is the largest in Europe.

Switzerland is a mosaic of languages, ethnicities, and Christian sects: the Protestant churches are austere and cerebral, while some of the Catholic churches in these little villages really go all out on the vibrantly painted idols depicting torture. In Val Calanca, a southern valley known for stone quarrying, I experienced what has become one of my favourite activities: buying a loaf of bread, butter, sliced meat, cheese, and wine, and picnicking in the Alps. When Southeast Asians tell me they don't like bread, I tell them they should try it first, since that white sliced stuff they munch on is not bread.

Barbara and I made plans to meet again in Croatia in a few weeks' time—she would fly there while I set out by train. Little did I know that gypsies had been using their Czech passports to fly to Canada and engage in the most brazen forms of professional shoplifting. Canadian officials became angered and required that Czechs get a visa to visit. This led to some bitter words and hard feelings, including reciprocal visa trouble for Canadians. In the middle of the night, Czech police came onto the train, identified me as Canadian, and kicked me off. The train pulled away, leaving me on a lonely stretch of tracks in a dark forest in an unknown country. My only choice was to shoulder my pack and walk back along the tracks from whence the train had come.

After a long moonlit trek, there was a small concrete platform with a backpacker standing on it. A short conversation revealed he was an American frat-boy from the Deep South, and he said, "You must also be trying to reach that super-hard-to-find mountain hostel."

"Sure," I said. "You're in luck. I have all the information here." We were in Austria, and I made the best of it.

After that things went more according to my plan to visit unusual countries in the Balkans, and especially to see some of the remnants of feudal Europe. The UN was still in place, keeping order. Everything was ridiculously cheap, as the region was recovering economically from the Yugoslav civil war of the early '90s and the campaign to bomb them into peace.

In Croatia I hooked up again with Barbara for a holiday. We swam the azure waters, tiptoed over hot limestone, and avoided black sea urchins. After we got past the urchins on our first swim, I remarked how it was like a minefield; she hadn't noticed them and was lucky not to have had her foot lanced with painful spines. The island of Hvar was spectacular, with audacious yachts and purple fields of lavender, outgassing enough fragrant xenoestrogens to sprout tits on a boar. The fortress of Diocletian was remarkable, preserved from a time when the Illyrians were the backbone of the Roman Empire. Nearby, we enjoyed octopus salad on a gleaming white marble terrace above a cerulean sea, while squadrons of fat day-tripping orange moths batted about in the sun beams.

In Split we split, Barbara heading back to Switzerland to take care of business, while Bosnia-Herzegovina was a bus ride away for me. Sarajevo bore scars of the war, including ruined buildings and Sarajevo roses (shell bursts on the pavement). On one occasion I watched tattooed, red-necked, shirtless locals fill dirty plastic bags with minnows and tiny crayfish, presumably dinner. I'd done my share of noodling, a fine hillbilly sport in which you feel under riverbanks, often for eels or catfish. It's usually the big sons of a gun that you are after, so these friendly folks had me thoroughly out-rednecked: the animals they were after were minuscule and dwelt in old tires in a stream that was little more than a sewer clogged with trash; to catch them you had to wade crotch-deep and grope through the sludge in the bellies of these tires.

The breakup of the former Yugoslavia caused a terrible conflict, and the region fractured along lines of religion, ethnicity, and tradition. We may shake our heads at this foolishness, but when we examine our own societies, we will likely find that we applaud the very forces that drive the conflict. It's as if we praise plate tectonics but claim to despise earthquakes as unnatural. Should the Balkans praise holding onto beliefs and the resulting Balkanization? I'd like to occasionally see historical plaques proudly displayed that honour the various people of different creeds who ditched aspects of their culture in order to contribute to a new reality. Few people stop to think that all the deep-seated and cherished aspects of each and every culture were at some time radical and new, displacing some earlier notion.

My travels took me through Republika Srpska to Serbia proper. While in Belgrade, I decided to spend some time foraging for visas. My guidebook and other writings insisted Canadians needed a visa for Albania, but could pass visa-free to Kosovo. I waved for a taxi and tried my best to pronounce the address for the Albanian embassy that was listed in my guidebook. After a drive past the Chinese embassy, left in ruins from an American bombing in 1999, four years before my visit, I was dropped at what proved to be the memorial for General Tito. Hmm. Another taxi, which took some walking to find, dropped me again at the memorial, this time the back side or I would have realized the mistake. Another effort, this time writing out and showing the address, had me back again, now on the eastern side. Rather than see if I could be the first to be dropped by taxi at all four sides of General Tito's memorial, like some *omphalos* (navel of the world) approached in ritual from the homes of the four sacred winds, I sat in contemplation, munching on plums from a tree that had sprung from the distinguished leader's grave.

Thus fortified, and inspired by the images of the late leader's Balkan triumphs dancing in my head, I set out on foot, wandering around and checking large houses in the neighbourhood that looked most likely to house embassies. After a hot and sweaty search, I found it. Knocking at the door produced no result, but the door was unlocked. I went in and called out to see if there was a guard or secretary. Silence and nobody so, floor by floor, I explored and finally discovered a man hunched alone at a desk in a small room on the third floor. He was the ambassador and friendly, lucky for me. He took the time to explain that, despite all the ink expended on printing documents to the contrary, Westerners didn't need a visa to enter Albania.

This tidbit of information had taken me an entire exhausting day to discover. However, it did give me confidence that, since the visa restriction had been lifted for Albania, I could trust the advice that I didn't need a Kosovo visa. After all, the Albania information was an omen visa restrictions were being relaxed. Yet when my hitchhiking finally brought me to the Kosovo border, following some pretty impressive canyons and a fjord in Montenegro, and after many military checks, I was refused entry. A visa was needed, and it was a 10-kilometre trek back over Serbian roads before I could get a ride to Belgrade to find the embassy and start in on fresh bureaucracy.

Later that week I checked in to a three-dollar-a-night hotel in a Kosovo town whose historic sites were central to the ethnic conflict between Serbs and Muslims. On the pavement of one of the streets outside the hotel, I met a hawker of pressed corn-juice who showed me a ruined Turkish bath and the Serbian Orthodox Church buildings around town. He also pointed out the decals on UN armoured vehicles; always some acronym followed by "FOR," meaning force. A joke about town, he told me, was that they should all be tagged "what-FOR."

You might charitably allow that I had "inspected" the historical sites of this town, for a total cost amounting to pocket change. As luck would have it, the American delegation arrived for an official inspection the next day. They also concluded the sites were in tip-top shape. By "they" I mean a man and a woman, habitual bureaucrats slumped from too much screen-time at desks, guarded by security dudes with microphones in their ears and automatic weapons, plus troops and armoured personnel carriers. Must have cost the US taxpayer a tidy sum.

But to understand the logic of the disparity between my costs and theirs, one must abandon conventional measures of productivity. Their presence was not only a ritual, but a ritual show of force. World news should report on royal weddings shamelessly, by all means, since most of what passes for news is ceremony anyhow. In Kosovo, all of that inspection was ceremony. I didn't fully understand this until I was visiting Haiti years later, after the earthquake. World news is largely reporting on nobility, ceremony, and symbols, with symbolic displays of emotion that speak to people's identity—a lumping of kindred concepts that in feudal times used to be known as Heraldry.

From Kosovo I managed to find a bus going to Albania. There was only one other foreign traveller aboard, and even he admitted he was a UN worker.

Albania was possibly the bleakest country in the region, rivalling some of the places in Central America I'd seen a decade earlier. Instead of highways, it had a network of ruts filled with dust, but it was possible to hitch around if you didn't mind waiting for hours at crossroads. The nation is dotted with concrete bunkers that look like mushrooms armoured for war; literally thousands of these things popped up in the most unlikely places in the landscape. In the north, crowds of peasants attacked cars with sticks and stones. But things were more civilized in the south, and the trucks passed the occasional shack looking like a saloon from an Arizona ghost town. My favourite had two old men on rocking chairs out front, and a fly-blown rag of a wolf skin nailed to the door.

I had trouble making myself understood. For Albanians, nodding is no and shaking the head is yes, but pointing is universal: the house goulash was tops. Finding any variety of food outside the capital, Tirana, was not easy, and even there it was mostly pizza on offer. There was no shortage of colossal statues of sword-wielding warriors or bleak Stalinist architecture, and the citizens were in a testy mood, many of them having just destroyed their life savings on a Ponzi scheme of national scope.

A side trip to a place called "The country formerly known as Macedonia" was irresistible. I wanted to see how a nation whose culture is that of seventh-century Slavic invaders got itself into the odd position of claiming to be the heirs of Alexander the Great and his Macedonian culture, more naturally associated with northern Greece. And this despite Macedonia's Lake Ohrid being the dwelling place of Saint Cyril of Cyrillic alphabet fame, and Greece already having a province of the same name. Simply, the Macedonians were restoring a castle and had big plans for attracting tourists. The local thinking was, essentially, if an orthodox Christian nation of Greece can make such good tourism cash out of exploiting the ruins of a long-dead pagan culture that worshipped gym-buffed fitness, beauty of the human form, wine-fuelled symposiums, philosophy, and art, then perhaps the pickings are rich enough that another orthodox Christian nation of gym shunning, non-philosophizing citizens can arrogate some of that juicy history to itself. Bring on the faux classical architecture, if that's what it takes.

Back in Albania I spent long dusty days hitchhiking to sites of ancient ruins. One particularly desolate site was famous for a school of philosophy a couple of thousand years ago; another was a former Greek colony, but much of what was left standing were fortifications, including the Lion Gate, with stone steps that were deliberately uneven in order to confound attackers by forcing them to mind their feet rather than blocking spears with their shields.

In a nearby southern port city I rented a cot in a nondescript concrete room from an old man, one of countless similar flats with identical concrete steps and doors. Key safely pocketed, I wandered about town and down to the corniche to promenade with the assembled townsfolk along the seaside at sunset. I ended up drinking beer and chatting with a student of ethics by the sea when, abruptly, all the lights went out. I had to retrace my steps without a torch through a labyrinth of dark alleys, looking for a concrete stair by moonlight with no number or any other characteristic to distinguish it, and no idea what street it was on. Somehow, trusting my instinct in the dark led me to the right door.

The morning was lucky too, as a freighter was leaving port and could drop me off on the island of Corfu in Greece. The whole ship vibrated from the engine, enough to rattle my teeth as I sprawled on the rusty red deck in the sun. In Corfu I discovered I'd made a mistake not changing the last of my Albanian money to something generally more useful. Attempts to change it in banks in Corfu failed. So I checked in to the biggest hostel I could find, the pink palace, which had a massive common room serving hundreds of backpackers. Just before dinner, when everyone was getting seated, I called out that I had forty bucks' worth of Albanian money to change, at an excellent rate, to anyone who was heading north. No takers. And none the next few days either. Not one of these hundreds of so-called backpackers would even consider going to Albania, logically the next destination.

The Balkans were my first experience travelling solo in regions with few other tourists or travellers: I bookended the trip with jaunts in London, home to numerous traveller friends, and a city that grew in my esteem as quirky details became known to me: the unsanctioned raves under Festival Pier, an Egyptian obelisk damaged by Zeppelin bombing, the "Red Star" bar—an establishment so insalubrious that it's a wonder they kept their liquor licence long enough for the ink to dry. I visited people met through travel and also made new friends. A return trip to Canada lasted for barely a month, just long enough to attend a family gathering to celebrate my grandmother's eightieth birthday and visit my brothers and their one-year-old children, before I was back in London, poring over maps.

CHAPTER FIVE

IRAN, IRAQ—WHAT'S THE DIFFERENCE?

*England · Qatar · Iran · Bahrain · Oman ·
Jordan · Iraq · Turkey · Egypt*

HUNDRED-DOLLAR RETURN FLIGHTS TO CANADA COULD be found in the first few years after the new millennium. It was while I was across the Atlantic in Ottawa in the autumn of 2003 that an email arrived from Molly in London. She wanted to do a photo shoot of the underground party scene in Iran as a final project for her university degree and asked me to accompany her; if I pretended to be her husband, she would be free to move about in this Islamic, decidedly Shi'ite, country. The first task was photocopying one of my brothers' marriage certificates and changing the names, just in case hotel managers got nosey. Then I wrote an essay about my interest in Islamic architecture, to facilitate the tricky visa process. There was little risk to this, since the certificate was not for officials but only for hotel managers who might object to us occasionally sharing a two-bed suite, and my interest in Islamic architecture is real. However, a thousand-dollar risk remained. It was necessary to commit to the trip and buy the airline tickets before I could be sure of my visa, but the gamble paid off.

I also stuffed a bag with stacks of American hundred-dollar bills, as ATMs couldn't be relied on in the Middle East, and there was no way to guess how long we'd be in areas poorly served by banks. My habit was to walk around with heaps of cash anyhow, as this was 2003, still years before the bank card transitioned from practically useless to an essential part of any travel kit. Besides, stacks of bills were my float for small-scale international trade and business opportunities.

Molly had a guidebook, keenly studied and highlighted in yellow marker, so she was good to go, with ample camera equipment and a list of possible contacts to sniff out underground parties. She had a hijab at the ready to cover her dreads, and a supply of drab and shapeless clothes, but was worried about her piercings. Initially, her idea was to replace them with flesh-coloured plastic bars, but she later discovered the bars attracted more attention than the piercing itself, which had the advantage of at least being obviously jewellery.

We made a stop in Qatar, in the Persian Gulf. Molly had lived there after her parents fled the revolution in Iran and before they had ended up in the UK as a compromise between her Scottish architect father's commonwealth New Zealand connections and her mother's Jewish New York academic background. Molly wanted to see some of the places she remembered from when she was a schoolgirl, and I wanted to get to a bank and establish a base of operations for travelling in the region.

We stepped out of the air-conditioned airport into a degree of heat that makes a place like this unsuitable for humans. Even the local Arabs are nocturnal and have arranged an economy where any sweaty daylight work is done by migrant underlings who brave the sun and furnace-like heat for some drips and drizzles of oil money. A man with a mobile kiosk had set up in a prime location, selling little bottles of chilled water. I sipped some water and was accosted by a policeman.

"It is the fast of Ramadan," he bellowed, so now it was off to jail for me.

I apologized and said I didn't know, having just stepped off a flight, adding that the Asian Muslim countries more familiar to me didn't take their fasting so seriously, and certainly didn't expect foreigners to join in.

"In every country, ignorance of the law is no excuse," he said.

It seemed my arrest was imminent, but he let me off with a warning instead. From then on we slunk behind palm trees and pillars to drink.

Molly enjoyed her stroll down memory lane and prepped for Iran, but success eluded me: no bank would let me open an account or rent a safety deposit box, either here or in Bahrain. Iran would be receiving me with my full travel fund and international business float carried as cash on my person.

One day we went to check out a fancy hotel on Doha's Corniche, a waterfront promenade along Doha Bay. I approached the concierge at his desk.

"This is an Islamic country, so no one has alcohol," I said. "And also Ramadan, so most definitively no alcohol, but is there any way for me to get a drink?"

"Certainly not, sir," he said. "Alcohol is never allowed."

As he spoke, he slid a piece of paper across the counter into my hand; best to look at it after stepping away from the desk. There was jotted the number of a room in the hotel. Hmm. Molly and I got into the elevator and rose to the fourth floor. The door to the room looked like any other. We knocked and the door opened to a full bar staffed with Eastern European girls, beckoning us in for cocktails.

WE TOOK A SHORT FLIGHT ROUTING THROUGH BAHRAIN TO IRAN'S capital. Tehran is a big friendly megacity, prone to horrific traffic snarls and crust-busting nine-on-the-Richter-scale earthquakes. It hasn't had a temblor in a while, so shoddily built high-rises have risen like scabs over the lower urban sprawl. Tensions with the West were the same then as they are now. Americans couldn't travel without a government "minder"; Canadians were less controversial as visitors, and Molly had entered on her New Zealand passport, to dodge any hard feelings about those former imperialists, the UK. At first we roamed the city. Molly also asked about, and gently persuaded her way into, some underground parties. She was noticeably foreign, with her spiky piercings and blonde dreads peeking out from her hijab. Iranian men sometimes literally walked into lampposts trying to pass us on the sidewalks; ironically, she complained of feeling invisible—if we talked to someone, she was completely ignored, and all questions were directed to me.

The streets were a like a honking mechanical Serengeti, but rather than wildebeest stretching to the horizon there were white Paykans, which are replicas of a vanished British auto, the Hillman Hunter. Safety in numbers was the best method for crossing a street. Molly and I would tuck ourselves into groups of old ladies and plunge across the road all together.

Iranian food was a pleasure to explore: we had pistachio-flavoured ice cream in carrot juice, dill soup from vendors in fog-shrouded parks, sour yogurt drinks, huge flatbreads hot from the oven, and rice dripping in butter. Molly was trying to be vegetarian at the time, and it was no easy matter. A restaurant was selling chipped potatoes out of a bin by the window; heaped to either side were bins of brains on the right, and to the left, tongues. One set of tongs served all. Another time I was keeping an eye out for plausible fast food and peered through a filthy window: two men sat at a white plastic table with the severed head of a camel lying between them like a centrepiece. Precious gems were easier to find than vegetarian-suitable dining.

We perused museums that displayed what seemed to be the highest calling of the Persians: paving everyday items with as many gemstones as can be shoehorned onto the surface, functionality be damned. I half expected to see bejewelled toilet paper and knickers. And we talked with locals, especially students at the university. Persians are a sophisticated and proud people, and have a sense of themselves as one of our planet's great and ancient civilizations, greater than those upstart Arabs and Turks.

The students we spoke with casually informed us of certain ugly facts. We'd often see a peculiar kind of beggar: women lying at the sides of streets, completely covered by a wrinkly blanket so they resembled black poppy blossoms, with a gnarled hand protruding like a stamen questing for bees or, in this case, loose change and Iranian dinars. We were told they were addicted to heroin. They hide themselves completely so that you can't see the signs, especially the tracks on their arms. Winter was setting in, so this crop would perish and a fresh crop of women would be splayed out in these mean meadows of paved paradise come spring.

Also, Laleh Park, where we often went for strolls near our hotel in central Tehran, was notorious for prostitutes. We laughed, at first incredulous, as everyone looked so cloaked and demure. Not so, the students told us; they can see signs, missed by our eyes, but brazen to them. I asked how they communicate their intent. The trick was for a customer to pull up in a share taxi and ask the woman who signalled to the car the usual question, "How far are you going?" She might then reply, "As far as you want."

Iranians are generally a practical people; one example of this is the clerics, who are not confined to giving mere relationship advice, but aspire to double duty, working as something like a powerful official "wingman." Under certain circumstances, men and women can contract for a marriage of a month, a week, an hour, or a lifetime, as they like, and a fee goes to the Shi'ite cleric who marries them. Congress between men and women who are not of the same family is otherwise strictly proscribed; there can be no willy-nilly mixed gender bunching of citizens in the street or in private, and sex that is unsanctified by society is punishable by flogging or even death in some cases. Foreigners are not exempt; a German businessman, Mr. Hofer, was on death row for the crime of sex outside of wedlock. He spent years in prison, but his death sentence was then commuted, for political reasons. Postbox-like receptacles, shaped like praying hands, litter the sidewalks: the open slit is for dropping off notes to rat out a friend or neighbour to the morality police.

How did this ultra-conservative revolution take hold? Educated older locals told me that it was a case of the Iranian intellectuals and elites being too civilized and progressive for their own good. In the 1960s and '70s the Shah was allied with the West and modernizing his nation at a frantic clip. This was the time of Vietnam War protests in London and

America, and flower power generally, a movement that had at its heart a desire to return to a purer form of spirituality. Iranians studying in the West caught the spirit of the times, and, noticing that corruption and injustice were far worse in Iran than in Europe or America, they had ample cause to demonstrate. When it came to the crucial moment for the Shah to crack down and spill blood, he proved too soft for the task and unleashed only half-hearted torture and suppression, enough to delegitimize his government but not enough to quell the demonstrations.

The opposition to the Shah's rule was funded by bazaar merchants, who were afraid of losing out to shopping centres—the same sentiment that makes some modern Westerners try to block Walmart. Stepping up were certain clerics, the Ayatollahs, and just as the hippies were enamoured of early Christian and Hindu spirituality, the Iranian youth were besotted with dreams of a return to Islamic ethics. The Shah was overthrown, leaving a power vacuum. The Ayatollahs were not squeamish like the Shah, and initially they were trusted by the population; they seized power and directed the war against Saddam Hussein's Iraqi army, which had tried to take over the oil fields in Iran's moment of weakness. The result was trench warfare, and then the conservative theocracy that shapes today's Iran.

Molly had secured an invite to our first party, and when we got there, it was full on. Mainly wealthy Iranians were involved; the girls would arrive in long-sleeved coats (*roo-poosh*) and head scarfs, only to toss them off once past the door. Underneath, they were dressed in halter tops and miniskirts, and they made free with the makeup and cleavage, presumably compensating for pent-up frustrations. Dealers, usually Azerbaijani, had different kinds of booze for sale from refrigerated trucks. There used to be more Iraqis dealing booze, but with the war raging, the Azerbaijanis had the market to themselves for the time being. Alcohol was the main vice, though one Afghan girl had some of her homegrown weed, and some guys were racking up lines of cocaine. The DJ favoured Western music, and music that included a female voice, as this had an extra frisson of illegality. Of course, partying in Iran is risky, and partiers are often caught in police raids: loud music and dancing, enflamed by illegal booze, is anything but quiet. But partying was a form of protest against the rigid moral laws of the regime; most of these free spirits really knew what it meant to fight, and suffer, for their right to party.

Molly had her camera out and was careful to never take any shots that might identify anyone. I asked if there were still any bars secretly open, like the speakeasies in Prohibition-era America. A guy told me that they were systematically hunted and shut down until none remained. People still have raves and big outdoor parties near the Caspian Sea in summer, but Tehran house parties, like the one we were attending, were the best to be found this late in the season. Party-goers have to be more careful, and a policeman has to be bribed to give a last-minute warning if they were coming for a bust.

We were curious what would happen to us if the party was raided and were told that as we were foreigners, things wouldn't go as badly for us as for them. The Iranian party-goers get captured quite a lot, and the boys get whipped with twenty lashes, or just beaten up. (One guy said to Molly, "It's great fun, you should try it.") The girls are supposed to be beaten too, but a recent verdict in Islamic court was that it is un-Islamic for a male judge to witness a woman's exposed skin being whipped, getting perverse pleasure, I suppose, while witnessing this mortification of female flesh. The girls were laughing about how they could usually wiggle out of any whipping now, as they simply slip some cash to the woman police officer or prison guard sent to do the evil deed. As these women would just as soon not do the whipping, they take the money and crack the whip, and the girl can scream like she's suffering. After she slips on her *roo-poosh*, the judge is none the wiser.

Recently, the police were particularly cruel to this group of partiers, and kept both sexes of captured youngsters in outside pens overnight while they waited to come before a judge: the temperature was freezing, and many were dressed in skimpy party clothes. Some of the girls needed sanitary supplies, which the police relished not providing.

One stylish young woman had a lapdog. I was surprised to see it, as they are considered unclean. She admitted as much, saying, "The official stance is that if someone is seen with a dog, the police are meant to shoot it dead on sight, and then bill the owner for the cost of the bullet."

"When I walk my dog," she added, "I carry a can of mace." She explained that if she timed her walk wrong and encountered a policeman in a killing mood, she would mace him in order to escape, though it was important to remember to go down to the police station afterward and give a bribe to the officer in charge so the incident could be swept under the rug.

There was no raid that night, and the next morning we looked into means of getting around the country. Buses promised to be slow and boring, as the place is mostly flat desert, but due to a budget-crippling subsidy of kerosene (jet fuel), the airline seats were only ten or twenty dollars, even for very long internal flights. I bought a thick stack of tickets, and we made a plan to zip around by air, then branch out from each place we landed in to get a good feel for the country.

Later that night we stopped in at Sufi shrines and Shi'ite mosques. They were segregated by gender, and my experience of the sombre and contemplative men's side contrasted with Molly's experience of the feverish excitement and fervour of the women's, as female worshippers wept and wailed and clutched at the gate that protected the saintly treasures.

We hired a car and driver to have a look at the Zagros Mountains that shield Iran's western frontier, clad in the degraded remnant of a once idyllic oak forest. We would be stopping at the ruined castles of the original Assassins, who were once feared but now extinct fanatical specialists in blackmail, poison, and backstabbing. The way was long and spooky, with narrow, muddy switchbacks, cliffs, and clinging mist. Before we got to our first castle, Molly insisted that I promise we wouldn't go anywhere steep and that I would not run ahead and leave her on some precipice in the ruins. "Sure thing" were my exact words, but it was obvious to me that the site of the castle wasn't particularly steep and held no danger. I promptly ran off to explore the ruins, as Molly seemed to be dawdling, and there were lots of old towers and crumbling walls to take a look at. When we got back in the car, I suspected she was angry about something, but had no idea what. It turned out she reckoned the assassin's castle was a terrifying place of cliffs and slippery slopes, and she didn't enjoy the cliffside drive either.

"Six-hour drive," she wrote in her journal. "Constantly winding back and forth on narrow switchback 'roads' in solid thick fog was altogether the most terrifying day of my life, without a doubt. Nothing at all could be seen through the windscreen. The driver could only navigate from memory. What an awful day."

WE STARTED FLYING AROUND THE COUNTRY ON ARCHAIC RUSSIAN Tupolev jets, with ratty interiors, and fuselages stained black with kerosene soot from poorly combusting engines. The flights were convivial, even jolly, and felt much like getting on an aerial version of an Asian "chicken (local) bus," with the pleasure of knowing that we would be deplaning within an hour, not after some all-day, all-night marathon.

Yazd, a city at an oasis beneath Mount Shirkuh where two deserts meet in the centre of Iran, is the birthplace of Mohammad Khatami, former president of Iran, and also Moshe Katsav, former president of Israel. It is one of the more religiously diverse cities in Iran, as it holds the largest sacred fire remaining from pre-Islamic worship. Ancient Persia is where the metaphysics of "the people of the book" (Jews, Christians, and Muslims) first evolved, the western mythical universe with its idea of the struggle of light and darkness, good and evil, demons/Satan and angels with halos—an ancient solar disk symbol. Christian mythology that grips one's imagination is usually based on the ancient Persian beliefs and not later teachings in the Abrahamic tradition. Followers of the old faith could be recognized by the flower patterns on the dresses of the women, and they were especially common near the fire temple sacred to Ahura Mazda.

The streets were a warren of mud walls, with two knockers on each door—a hefty manly sounding knocker if you are a man, and a petite knocker to ply should you be a visiting woman. These traditional buildings are disappearing, as modern Iranians don't consider them safe during earthquakes. A passenger sitting beside me on the flight in told me he worked for UNESCO and was trying to convince the locals to preserve their tradition of living in thick-walled mud-brick abodes, but many such homes had already been demolished, replaced with reinforced concrete. While Molly and I were in Yazd, we stayed in an old caravanserai that looked like something out of the *Thousand and One Nights*. We smoked nargilas (hookahs), while supping on stewed eggplants in walnut sauce.

There were ancient ruins to be explored in Persepolis, including the palace of Xerxes, decorated with hulking blue statues of stylized bull heads, magnificent pillars, and frescoes of winged angels with golden halos, from the time of the magi. And we visited ancient cities like Esfahan, with wondrous gardens, wind towers, blue domes for scholars and philosophers, and reflecting pools.

Hopping over to Kerman, we saw the only place in Iran where people keep bowls of opium on their tables, as a sign of hospitality. On road trips we climbed up to spy into old crumbling towers of silence. Molly noticed a rare example of anti-Zoroastrian-fire-worshipper graffiti—"All is Vanity except the One!"—on the wall of a pit atop an abandoned Tower of Silence. This was where predatory and carrion birds used to strip the flesh off human corpses to afford them a sky-burial; a priest would watch the vultures pluck out the eyes, since the soul's destination, heaven or hell, was indicated by which one, right or left, was gobbled first. With the march of Islam, the place is truly silent save for this plea to embrace the one god. When we climbed down from the tower, we chatted with teenage Afghan refugee boys on dirt bikes, and carried on by car.

In Bam we explored the great Arg-e (mud fort) and tasted the famous dates, as well as candies made with pistachios, dates, yogurt, and honey. Even our first night in Bam proved favourable for sweets: we arrived late, and all restaurants and shops were closed. A glum night was improved when, digging laundry soap out of my backpack, I realized the detergent was not what it appeared but, rather, Turkish delights bought long ago in Albania, disguised by copious icing sugar and relegated to the washing-up bag.

Friendly Mr. Akbar had the best beds in town. There, at the aptly named Akbar's Guesthouse, we met a Japanese guy who had just travelled across Iraq. I asked how he got the visa. It ought to have been nigh impossible. He explained that he bribed his way through the border, then scooted across the country in three days and two nights, travelling only at night and confining himself to hotels during the day so that as few Iraqis as possible could note his presence. He was overjoyed to have made it out alive. Another Japanese backpacker guest and I were all ears. And suddenly I started forming my own plan to backpack Iraq. I wanted to do it by hitchhiking all around, thoroughly and at sensible hours so I could meet Iraqis. The seed was planted. My first decade of travel had taught me that "no-go" countries and war zones were accessible to solo travellers willing to go in cheaply, under the radar, provided they were also willing to put their traveller's bag of tricks to the ultimate test, including, most importantly, ability in making rapid and accurate first impressions of newly met locals, skill at taking calculated risks, and situational awareness. It was time to up my game.

Molly had to go back to Tehran to continue documenting the underground party scene, while I chose to fly to Shiraz. She agreed to ask if anyone among the Iranians she met at the parties was planning to drive to Baghdad, as I figured I might as well do Iraq now, while I was in the neighbourhood.

It turned out that Molly and I were among the last people for some time to wander along the curvy, sun-dappled walls and towers of the Arg-e Bam, or to walk the streets in good spirits. On Boxing Day 2003, a terrible earthquake struck Bam—and that was the end of the place. Since it was built of UNESCO-approved traditional mud architecture, it collapsed in the middle of the night, killing a huge swathe of the townsfolk; the talk was of fifty thousand dead, though it may have been lower, a few tens of thousands.

Amplifying the ordeal of the surviving townsfolk, most of the houses were uninhabitable ruins, so the people settled into tents on the outskirts of the city. (Many months later I learned that Akbar's Guesthouse, where we'd been staying, collapsed, killing the guests, though friendly Mr. Akbar survived.) The government wanted to fix Bam and get the people housed again, but they didn't really want to pay much money to do this; after all, money was in short supply, with the

Western sanctions and sluggish economy. They thought it best to ask the construction companies in Tehran to supply workers for what should be a patriotic project. Here's where things get even darker, because what kind of worker is a company likely to supply for patriotic duty? Why, the underperforming ones, of course. And why might a construction worker in Tehran underperform and be found dispensable? In short, heroin. Thousands of city-slicker smack-heads were sent to live in the tent cities of the stunned and grieving survivors of the earthquake. Since they were bedded down in the same tents while the workers were shooting heroin, the survivors had a go, to numb their pain. Thousands of them ended up addicted to smack, and seeing as they were sharing dirty needles, an HIV outbreak was piled on top of their other complaints.

NEAR SHIRAZ, I WENT TO MUSALLA GARDEN TO VISIT THE SHRINE OF Hafez, where I read some government-sponsored signage praising him as a national hero. He was and is famous as one of the greatest of the Persian poets—and the Persians are renowned for poetry. Looking high and low, I couldn't find much of his poetry. Proud locals told me the problem was that Hafez wrote about partying, drinking wine, and beautiful youths. His poetry was frowned on as subversive, but the fact that he was a poet of supreme talent meant that the government couldn't forgo trumpeting his success. They only asked that you praise this poet while refraining from reading his poetry. In one poem he says:

What good in being a solitary, secret drinker?

We're all drunkards together—let's leave it at that.

Eventually I was back in the capital, to find that Molly was successful in finding more parties and couldn't wait to develop her stash of film, including some she hoped would represent the spirit of Iranian partiers, carrying on like Hafez in difficult times. One party had been raided by the police. Someone had paid off a patrolman to give them a warning phone call ten minutes before the other police were on their way, so everyone wiggled into their conservative clothes and scrammed. They were lucky that time. A couple assumed responsibility for Molly and made sure she was not left behind in the rush to escape.

Iranian youth, like youth everywhere, are awash in disruptive hormones, just awakening to what it's like to be fully man or woman, but any mixed-gender non-family gatherings are serious crimes, so the bravest young Iranians figure they might as well grab the bull by the horns, dancing and drinking at illegal parties. If the police are catching these young people and mingling these formative memories with episodes of handcuffs, brutality, and whippings in police dungeons, mightn't the experiences become inseparable in those impressionable young minds? The Ayatollahs are almost certain to achieve the opposite effect to what they intend, and Iran may end up as one of the biggest S&M markets. Perhaps Iran in the future will have more than the "normal" number of shops peddling whips and ball gags and fuzzy pink handcuffs.

MOLLY HAD MET A LOCAL GUY FROM TEHRAN WHO WAS DRIVING TO Iraq, and introduced us so I might catch a ride. His father was in the business of selling walk-in meat freezers and was sending his son to Baghdad to see if business was good now that Saddam had been overthrown. Then, at the last minute, this careful father decided he couldn't risk his son.

I flew back to the Gulf with Molly, and she left for London with her undeveloped film. This left me to circulate through other countries in the area, including Bahrain, Oman, Qatar, and Jordan, enjoying Arab hospitality and trying to find a viable way into Iraq.

At one point it was looking promising for me to simply board a flight to Baghdad; I had a ticket in hand and was waiting in the lounge with a large group of what turned out to be American military personnel. Several young men were talking about the procedures they must follow with respect to securing the secret battlefield codes they were carrying; they noticed me and included me in their conversation, only afterward sussing that I was not US military. After exchanging conspiratorial glances, they launched into an earnest new conversation discussing how, as a matter of course, they were actually not entrusted with any devices that contain codes and would never openly discuss those codes even if they were.

As we prepared to board, a man called out that there would be one last check as we got on the plane. "Everyone have your navy ID card in hand to show at the gate."

"Showing a US navy card might be a problem for me," I said when I got up to the gate. "I'm not American and not in the navy."

They wouldn't let me board, so back at the ticket kiosk I said, "Swap my ticket for something I can use. Your man there didn't let me on the flight."

They stuck me on the next plane to Oman instead, landing in Muscat, a city of bright green grass and charming little mosques, nestled in a bumpy landscape of crumbling black rock, with hills capped by old towers. The country was ruled by Sultan Qaboos, an elderly confirmed bachelor who was widely hailed as an enlightened ruler. He lived by the sea, in a palace that looked like a gargantuan mushroom; his lawn was polka-dotted with howitzers, the protruding barrels flagrantly candy-striped in what had to be a fancy custom paint job. It seemed he was still busy with the business of governance. His motorcade, consisting of open-topped jeeps with machine guns manned by soldiers in gas masks, ominous and standing stiff as statuary, raced along the corniche, carrying him to the airport and back, the vehicles so close together they seemed like segments of a zany centipede on roller skates.

Oman has much to see. This ancient land is the home of the stunted desert tree that yields dried sap known as frankincense, long the darling of Arab rent-collecting before being dumped for a sexy new rent-boy: oil. Frankincense is no gift for kings these days, and Oman is short on oil, so the Sultan is trying to get his people used to the idea of working for a living. He is gradually sending guest workers back to the subcontinent, while mandating that Omanis must hold all jobs as waiters, cooks, and even taxi drivers. The country is built for car travel, not public transport, so I got around by hitchhiking or often just hiking, as cars were sometimes few and far between. The red dunes of the Wahiba Sands were especially fun to explore on foot as long as I managed to find shade during the heat of day.

The expression "going around the bend" is said to be inspired by the bend in the Strait of Hormuz, in Oman's north, where the British Empire used to have a relay centre for its London-to-Karachi telegraph cable until the mid-1870s. The operator at the post was liable to be driven mad, with nothing to occupy his time but endless dots and dashes, oppressive heat, and seabirds. Nowadays there is air conditioning throughout the land, and people much prefer to stick to their cars, driving extremely fast. The government is trying to lessen the carnage on the road, so the law says that all cars must have a device that pings if the speed climbs above the maximum speed limit on the open road; as a result, whenever I was in a taxi, my ears were irritated by an incessant pinging as the pavement flashed past at 160 kilometres per hour.

My travels after leaving Iran were frantic; I was breezing through countries dawn to dusk as my main objective wasn't seeing these lands, which I would return to, but gaining access to Iraq in what my intuition told me would be a narrow window before the insurgency against the us-led invasion picked up momentum. I flew back to Bahrain to plan onward travels, but with no better luck than before, and there didn't seem to be any way to cross Saudi Arabia.

I kept circling around Iraq, flying to Jordan to try again, this time overland. The country proved pleasantly distracting, with so many amazing wadis (valleys or gorges) and castles and ancient ruins. It was a joy meeting shepherds on eroded hillsides and watching the sheep and goats make their way through the landscape—one always opting for the low road and one the high—or bantering with the city hustlers as I munched on honeyed pastry. Visiting Petra, the ancient remains of the mysterious Nabatean civilization, was well worth the effort of hiking all the way to the nearby modern town, then out into the ruins and back by nightfall. I was tired, but my mind was steeped in the experience of tombs and amphitheatres cut out of the pink rock, and the shimmering abysses of reds and oranges and shadows down *siqs* (canyons) cut deep and narrow from eons of flash floods. Ruins like the famous treasury have lost all plaster and painted decoration, but a guide at one archeological site nearby, called Little Petra, showed me an intricate fresco dedicated to Dionysius (the god of wine, theatre, and things beyond human reason but also epiphany, "who comes as a foreigner") and explained the Nabatean culture of sitting together at leisure, chatting, socializing through the "grapevine," playing musical instruments, and enjoying cups of wine. It struck me that even though two thousand years had passed, the scene was alike in everything important to the one in the common room of the hostel where I stayed, a remarkable preservation of human culture over the millennia.

At last, back at the cliff hostel near the old centre of Amman, I met a guy who knew a guy who was going to Iraq. I'll call him Mo. Mo was an Iraqi refugee living in Sweden, but he thought it was just now, in December 2003, possible to cross into Iraq and see if all was well with those family members he'd left behind. We learned that there was a roadside out of town where Iraqi drivers loitered between transits; they regularly did the drive from Amman to Baghdad in convoys, since insurgents are more likely to attack lone vehicles. We agreed on a price with a shady-looking Iraqi hustler—sixty bucks us, so thirty dollars each.

At the border, a bribe saw us through, one dinar each. Mo could speak a bit of English, and he complained that this was sad for him to see: his first experience of a new Iraqi regime is corruption.

Our driver waited until we had a sizable convoy, and then we all sped off across the desert at 180 kilometres per hour or more. It was good that we had not tried to drive ourselves, as it was important to know where bombs had cratered the highway, making it necessary to slow down and detour around the resulting rubble. Sometimes we'd pass scenes of carnage, where a Bedouin's flock of sheep had been converted to appalling mutton by a speeding night-convoy—stopping was out of the question at those speeds. Regularly the driver and Mo would dispute in Arabic, and Mo would translate for me, always something like: He says that the road is rougher than usual and orders us to pay twenty more dollars to cover wear to his tires. I would say, Tell him we already shook on a price and paid it. The car owner is responsible for his own tires. But my intuition told me he would be trouble later. This situation kept me hyper-alert, and I didn't nap over the course of the 900-kilometre drive. A calmness spread through me instead. Using my skill set, I would adapt to whatever situation was in store for me. That or be destroyed. Any potential stress could be discounted for now, and would, typically, arrive like an echo weeks later, as joy or creeping anxiety, or both.

We reached the outskirts of Baghdad in the darkest part of night, just before dawn. The city didn't look exactly salubrious, with helicopters whirling overhead, searchlights probing the curfewed neighbourhoods, and sporadic rifle fire, and I felt uneasy. We swung around to let Mo off.

"Are you going to be all right?" he asked me.

"Sure," I said. "I'll just find a hotel somewhere, using this guidebook I bought." I wished him luck and waved as he hauled his suitcase down a dark alley.

Now I was alone with this driver who'd been angling for more money, and he was speaking to me in Arabic; obviously he must be asking me where I'd like to be dropped. Out came my trusty new Lonely Planet guide to the Middle East, which had Iraq as one of the featured countries. I indicated for the driver to pull up under a working street light so I could take a gander. I must say that Lonely Planet really let me down here: when I got the guide opened to Iraq, instead of the usual map of the city and numbered list of hotels, there was merely a disclaimer explaining that their researchers were afraid to research, so they couldn't convey much information other than a block segment on history, chronicling how the ancient Mesopotamians were the first to invent beer and build hanging gardens. The guidebook had a rough sketch of the country and some roads, but otherwise practically nothing of use to me.

Resorting to universal pointing and gestures, I indicated he should show me around to a few hotels so I could pick one. He conveyed with his fingers that he wanted, naturally, twenty dollars for this service. It was a scam, of course. Later conversations with locals proved that five dollars was more the fair price for that sort of thing, as I suspected, but my situation was delicate. There wasn't another car in sight, just empty streets ringing with the occasional gunshot, so it would not be wise to get out and walk with my backpack. Furthermore, there was only a twenty-dollar bill handy in my pocket, while my smaller change was somewhere at the bottom of my little SunDog travel bag. If I opened it in front of him, he might see that it also was chockablock with more than fifty grand in US hundred-dollar bills. It was more sensible to show the twenty in my hand. Off we sped.

First he carried me to the Sheraton, in a neighbourhood without much gunfire. I waved him on to the next without even checking; it was a four-star hotel and probably cost a hundred dollars or more a night. Just as well, as my later reading revealed that a rocket-propelled grenade had been fired at the Sheraton not long before my visit, perhaps the week just past. Though few travellers know exactly how they award these hotel stars, mightn't it be enough to knock off a star for each grenade attack— and perhaps two stars if there were any guests pulped by shrapnel?

Budget hotels were scarce; eventually I checked in to a place that used to cater to Turkish businessmen. Exhausted, I crashed on my bed, and the first day found me so disoriented from that night on the road to Baghdad that the highlights of this legendary city eluded me. Instead it served as my "training day" for this new kind of travel and for tactical planning. The day included a walk around the neighbourhood, marvelling at the lovely buildings and palm-tree-lined boulevards.

Happily, I managed to concoct a strategy for doing Iraq, which involved dressing myself in the manner of a local and being particularly mindful of mimicking the facial expression of the Iraqi dudes passing me on the street. This worked like a charm. My hair had been blond in my childhood, but had darkened enough over time for me to try to pass as an Arab. Sometimes there would be the flicker of a funny look, as if someone was entertaining the notion of my not being Iraqi, but they must have thought, *Maybe he's Azerbaijani or Syrian.* Back in Iran, people had often said I looked Azerbaijani. Years later when I was in Azerbaijan, the locals said, No, not a chance, and they were right. But as long as I looked how people thought an Azerbaijani ought to look, it was enough to get by. A local guy who ended up chatting with me said he had simply dismissed as crazy the notion that I might be a Westerner strolling around unarmed and unguarded. My blending-in strategy only failed occasionally, sometimes in bazaars, where the children would run over saying, "Americani, Americani." I hastened to correct them: "*Canadian.*"

If there was something that interested me, say a building where a cruise missile had struck, it wasn't safe to stand there gawking; wiser to go around the block to take another look. I was used to seeing in various war zones how 500-pound bombs take a chunk out of reinforced concrete—almost like a bite out of a crispy apple—and Baghdad had more of this, but the damage from the thousand-pound cruise missile warheads were different and caught my eye: they were powerful enough to put a little twist into the building's frame, so you could see the whole structure might have to be demolished.

TURNING DOLLARS INTO DINARS, THE IRAQI CURRENCY, WAS FUN. Both times low funds compelled this, the money changer was a scruffy-looking chap standing in the street holding an assault rifle and a stack of dinars. I'd come up to him, grinning, with some American cash, and when he discovered that I could only speak English, he'd double over with laughter. My take on this was that it was a sign that, despite what the camera angles try to convey on the news, there were not many Westerners wandering around in Iraq. Later I'd see how it was usually done: news crews in the Green Zone (the international zone in central Baghdad that had been secured by the US-led coalition and was surrounded by blast walls and barbed wire) looked for camera angles to suggest that they were out and about in the city, and soldiers bristling with equipment would go down the same streets as me, but GI Joe style, with one covering the other from a corner, and then being covered in turn as he caught up to the squad. All their guns were at the ready, pointed at nearby locals—as is only sensible given that these were Americans in uniform and obvious targets.

A hotel janitor agreed to drive me around Baghdad in his gas-guzzling brown '70s sedan that looked something like a Lincoln Continental and was really beat-up and cobbled together out of spare parts. He showed me some more of the sites, including a plethora of Saddam's palaces and the Assassins' Gate—before a suicide bombing at the gate increased the security measures. The National Museum was closed, and it turned out that many former tourist sites and war monuments had been used to base troops. This makes sense, as they would have had both public toilets and parking spaces already installed. Sadr City, a suburb of Baghdad, had an unwholesome look to it, the streets strewn with rubble and the denizens suspicious of passers-through, making me decide to forgo exploring it on foot.

One of the managers at my hotel was chuffed that he had a Canadian tourist as a guest, and he took it upon himself to try to keep me alive. On a couple of occasions he ran over to me when I was about to go out the front door for a stroll and wouldn't let me leave. Both his hands would be pushing against my chest. Under the circumstances, I had gone to sit in a plush red velvet chair in the reception area, and waited to see what the matter was. And both times, not ten minutes later, gunfire, and once an explosion, reverberated in the street outside. The manager, and probably the whole neighbourhood, must have known that it was about to kick off. I had no way to tell if it was the 1st Armoured Division clearing the streets in a continuation of Operation Iron Grip or some spat between rival insurgent groups. The Iraqis in the lobby, accustomed to decades of stop-and-go war, and finding comic relief in the situation, would laugh and gesticulate as they deliberated when it was safe to let their Canadian tourist out the door. Their mood was contagious, and I had to remind myself to mimic a dour Iraqi wartime face when out on the street.

There was a fancy restaurant within walking distance, where for less than four bucks I could get a ridiculous amount of food; they'd bring a whole roast chicken to the table, stack of bread, heaping platters of rice. Usually I took my evening meal in the Baghdad Tower Hotel's rooftop restaurant. A fat, jolly, expat Egyptian waiter at the restaurant was so insistent about suggesting bottles of wine to accompany my food that I felt sure he must be getting a cut. He lamented the damage the wars had done to beautiful Baghdad, the Paris on the Euphrates, but he was also a helicopter watcher the way some people are bird watchers, and would throw open the windows to afford a better view, calling out, happily, "Apache" or "Blackhawk" or "Iraqi police helicopter." For three nights in a row there was skulduggery afoot below the window, with figures skulking out of alleys and attacking the building next to us, which had soldiers defending behind sandbags. I would sit and sip my wine, and watch the firefight in the darkness below.

I DECIDED A TOUR OF HILLAH, A CITY SPLIT BY A BRANCH OF THE Euphrates River that was the archeological site of ancient Babylon, and parts south would suit me. My initial arrangements were to go with the janitor again, a road trip in his beater of a car. For a third time the hotel manager intervened and bid me travel instead with a capped and smartly uniformed driver carrying a sidearm. He had been right to intervene twice already, so I acquiesced. The driver pulled up in an old but snazzy dark Mercedes, with a powerful engine, and we cruised away to the south.

Hillah was disappointing—ordinary save for the pretty date palms lining the riverbanks and a whole mess of slaughtered sheep bleeding out into the drains. When we got closer to Babylon, the traffic around us became more and more military. We'd be stuck between convoys consisting of Hummers, equipped with chassis-mounted machine guns front and back, that drove at the beginning and end, and occasionally in the middle, of what otherwise was a procession of tanker truck after tanker truck, heavy with refined petroleum. Often there was an attack helicopter flying above the convoys, whereas elsewhere in Iraq I would see two for a single convoy, weaving back and forth in the sky above the trucks. Despite this effort, or perhaps only because of reckless driving, the highways were littered with blackened burnt-out tankers.

We got to Babylon. My guidebook had furnished a scrap of information describing this site as empty fields with a couple of forlorn statues of lions. The main danger might be bandits, so I had brought a bit of cash in order to have something to hand over quickly if we ran into trouble, leaving my passport back with my "business float" in the hotel safe in Baghdad.

Conditions had changed. Babylon was a sprawling helicopter base, buzzing like an angry hornet's nest. My driver took me up to the gate, where there was a US soldier named Neil in charge. I asked him about coming in for a visit, describing myself as a curious traveller. He seemed surprised, then bemused, and asked if I was some rich guy who jetted around the world.

"Minus the part about being rich," I said. "So think hitchhiking in place of the jet setting, but sure, that's me."

"What do you intend to do if I allowed you in?"

"Chat with some of the guys here if they have the time, see how they're doing."

"I suppose I can let it happen if you can get permission from the civilian authority," he said, directing a local translator to give directions to my driver. Then he walked away, shaking his head.

We found the place we needed to go not so far away down near-by roads. Here was another barbed wire and gated situation, this time with a very sturdy British soldier in charge, whose bearing and walk suggested Special Forces. It was mostly scruffy-looking locals trying to get onto the base, for whatever reason, and he was striding around the gate, keeping good order. He refused me entry.

"Thanks anyway," I said. "Bye." And I left.

"Come back," he said, reversing his position. "I'll let you in, just show your passport first."

Alas, no passport, no permission. My driver was annoyed by these developments, whereas for me, misadventures are often better than adventures. I tried to explain to him that it was okay; I think he had it in his mind that my task was somehow important and now a failure. While it would have been interesting to get in to talk with the guys at the Babylon base, as I'd met only Iraqis thus far in Iraq and had yet to speak with any Americans, the view from the other side of the barbed wire made for an interesting day on its own. We cruised around some more but not much farther south, then headed back to the capital.

After a while, with local buses and hitching, I saw more small cities or large towns, including Mahmudiyah and Ishaqi, not far from Baghdad. Lacking an adequate map, I was never exactly sure of my position, so I just drifted around, meeting Iraqis, who were mostly friendly once they discovered, to their joy, that I was a tourist; maybe they thought that more tourists would follow, and this was a sign Iraq was on its way to being a normal prosperous country again. Usually one who could speak some English would help find me a hotel and show me the best restaurants, sometimes staying for a meal and translating questions from curious locals.

ONE MORNING, SOMETHING IN MY POCKET CAUGHT MY ATTENTION: the nifty-looking brass key of the last hotel I'd checked out of when leaving Baghdad. I thought it would be a shame if they had to make another one. I was in the city of Samarra, where my turning up in restaurants for plates of chicken, bread, and pickles always caused a neighbourhood sensation, and where the traffic was snarled by a long line of US military vehicles trying to inch their way through a horrible self-inflicted traffic jam on narrow roads never designed to handle a mechanized invasion. Some guys embodied boots on the ground, and everyone was training their rifles at passersby on the streets, as was established practice.

A search of the town revealed a post office. Time to find out if Iraq's postal service was up and working again. There was a room convenient to box up the key and copy the address from the business card I'd fortunately retained. By this time, word must have spread that a Western man was trying to post something. Suddenly it was as if I was a secret agent, and my little package was a matter of national security. A phalanx of a half-dozen AK-toting Iraqi troops arrived, a couple of them communicating through earpieces as they shepherded me through my mission of queuing at the post office. Afterward the commanding officer shook my hand, and they escorted me safely away, parting with a smart salute.

It was January 2004 and time to go north. Winter was setting in, and it would be wise to get through the mountains of eastern Anatolia before too much snow fell. Hitched rides carried me back to a bus station outside Samarra, there to wait. My bus arrived, looking like the usual dented crate on wheels. Just then a friendly local guy managed to convey that a nearby fellow was about to motor north and was open to my hitching a ride.

This guy who didn't mind a foreign hitchhiker was also able to speak some English. He tried to get me to understand that Iraqis used to be an important, cultured people and would be again. He was also, it became clear, a big fan of Saddam Hussein and could point to nearly finished mosques as proof that the former dictator was a good Muslim. We were passing the occasional city and town; in between there were loads of those petroleum convoys with helicopter support, or sometimes Hummers and American soldiers. A whole mess of destroyed Iraqi tanks and other armour lined stretches of the road. I didn't stop to peer into them, as some of this armour was likely pierced by depleted uranium shells. Though the residue is meant to be safe, there was no sense in taking a chance just to sneak a peek inside busted T-series tanks, which are as common as discarded beer cans on the world's battlefields.

Finally, as we passed through yet another city, my driver called out, "Tikrit, Saddam's home town; we stop for lunch."

My thoughts were: Tikrit? That's probably the one place to steer clear of if it were up to me. Saddam had been captured by American soldiers in Operation Red Dawn while hiding in a hole at a farm near here on December 13, just a few weeks earlier, and his people must be seething with rage toward invading Westerners.

We parked near a big open-air chicken restaurant and sat down for a meal. My driver was talking to me in English, compelling me to carry on publicly in English too.

"Are all these Saddam's tribesmen?" I asked.

"Yes, look at the head scarf."

There were scores of Saddam's kin all around, and many had stopped eating; others sat muttering and giving me the evil eye. It occurred to me that someone might stride over and slice off my head. If this were going to happen, though, logic dictated that it should have happened right away, so I soon relaxed and enjoyed my meal before leaving unscathed.

Late in the day I was dropped off in Mosul, in the far north of Iraq. Once again my driver was kind enough to help me find a good hotel. Mosul had a few towers and a museum (closed due to looting, I was told, and no one answered the door). There was also a squad of Americans, possibly 10th Mountain Division or 101st Airborne Division, as these were now the earliest days of 2004. The soldiers would set up behind walls of sandbags on a floor of the same building downtown every morning, weapons at the ready, and scan the road below. The thought crossed my mind that they ought to set someone to watch at night, because an insurgent might tuck a bomb and timer up there, to devastating effect. They were in a fairly central location, so they must have seen me passing below them often while I was wandering around the city. Once I waved, but no one waved back.

Seeing as the sites here in town had been looted, I hired a Kurdish guy to drive me out to some of the ancient Assyrian ruins nearby. I could spot an ethnic Kurdish man a mile away, as they have a distinctive look in the frontier region: often big faces with thick features and prodigious mustaches. Also, they exceeded any other group or nation in exuberance for President Bush and Americans. The Kurds imagined a bright future, and perhaps they were right. And I met my first Westerners—a North American couple who had popped over the border to research a book on the Kurds. The woman, especially, seemed on edge, and she appreciated my words of encouragement. I told them that as long as they stayed in this northern part of the country, it was way calmer than the rest in terms of gunfire at night and tension in the crowds.

The site now called Nimrud, ancient Kalhu, was occupied with Peshmerga fighters, the military arm of the Kurds. One of them showed me around the whole place for a dollar. Half the original monuments have been carted away; the other half matches the stuff on display in the British Museum. But it's interesting to see these giant carvings and statues of weird and wonderful beasts in situ, stuck in mounds of dirt and at the bottom of shafts.

King Shalmaneser ruled the city over three thousand years ago, and another king, Ashurnasirpal II, made the place his capital. He had a palace built of costly woods such as tamarisk, pistachio, and cedar, erecting monumental limestone and alabaster friezes, black obelisks, a great ziggurat, and statues of colossal winged lions and bulls, up to thirty tons in weight, known as lamassu. The British made off with some of these lamassu, and much else besides, in the mid-nineteenth century, and put them on display in London. And a good thing they did, too; it has preserved much that would have been lost to looters stealing pieces to order for wealthy collectors, chiselling and smashing to get what they want. The destruction has been tremendous since 2015, when barbaric ISIS armies conquered the region. It gives me no pleasure to realize that I visited all the major ancient sites here and elsewhere before they were bulldozed and dynamited, a world heritage that is denied to future generations.

Inscriptions on limestone slabs have yielded to deciphering scholars; they boast of the ancient king's war crimes: "Many of the captives I have taken and burned in a fire. Many I took alive. From some I cut off their hands to the wrists, from others I cut off their noses, ears and fingers; I put out the eyes of many of the soldiers. I burned their young men, women and children to death."

The descendants of the Assyrians still live in the area, but society's notion of what is acceptable has evolved over the millennia since Ashurnasirpal's rule. Committing, and boasting of, war crimes, including burning captives alive, beheading, torture, and slavery, is as popular as ever, with ISIS the most enthusiastic modern participant. But no VIPs are going to pay good money for sculptors to carve new lamassu for their mansions. Their neighbours would laugh at them. Nowadays it is hoarding antiques like looted lamassu and stele that indicate a refined character.

BACK IN MOSUL, FOR THE FIRST TIME SINCE MY ARRIVAL IN IRAQ I had a slow day, somewhat boring. I told myself that this feeling was impossible; hitchhiking around Iraq just after the December 2003 Operation Iron Grip phase of the war should be relentlessly stimulating, producing a fine collection of stories to cherish. Indeed, every day until this one had been interesting and new—and yet ... a glum mood of inexplicable boredom came over me, leaving me wishing for some further excitement.

That night my wish was granted. I was in a building that had a restaurant, just finishing my meal, watching Arabic music videos on the dining room TV, when, suddenly, the lights went out, leaving me to sit in the dark, eating olives.

There was soon a commotion at the door—the US army burst into the building. A squad of soldiers with Petzl lights on their helmets began interrogating and searching the Iraqis. There was a noticeable difference in the squad's behaviour when they were around their commanding officer: when he was in the room, they were polite; whenever he stepped out, the boys got more rowdy. One Iraqi who could speak a little English said, "I'm only the assistant manager." The young soldier holding him at gunpoint prodded him in the belly with a rifle barrel and said, "Shut up or I'll shoot you." The soldiers were annoyed because two AK-47s had been found already.

Then I said hello to them. They swarmed over, pointing their assault rifles at first, interrogating me from every direction. Because of my perfect English they might have wondered if they had captured a spy or special agent or something. Had a Canadian tourist just fallen into the clutches of the latest Iron-monikered Operation? I knew even then that it's best to keep your sense of humour in cases like this; if you can't and it gets serious, and they get angry for real, heaven help you.

"What are you doing in Iraq?"

"The usual, I'm on vacation; what—are you guys working?"

"Where's your gun?"

"No gun. I'm a tourist."

They couldn't believe it at first, especially when they learned of my inability to speak a word of Arabic, and I told them I was just wandering the country unarmed, looking at archeological ruins and buying bread and dates in the bazaars. Contrast this with the experience of these soldiers. For good reason, the Americans didn't typically leave their bases except in a Hummer or tank or armoured personnel carrier, and even then only with a rifle and body armour and grenades and laser-guided gizmos, goggles, and helmets so that you can't even see there's a human under all that materiel.

When they tried to impress on me that Iraq was a dangerous country and a war zone, I said, "Yeah, I'd rate it a medium to severe on the danger scale, depending where you are." And I listed other dangerous countries familiar to me, war zones or places where nasty bandits proliferate—

Khmer Rouge–controlled northern Cambodia, Palawan's jungle roads, the rusty sheet-metal slums of Tegucigalpa with its murderous gangs. Actually Iraq was dangerous, but it suited me to downplay this, obviously, as it was not in my interests that they overreact and restrict my movement.

One soldier asked me if I was the person they had seen walking past a few times—so I knew these were the same guys who manned that post every day. That was me, I said, and another said he had thought I didn't look like an Iraqi. Then they were asking where I'd gone in the country, and I listed some places visited until I mentioned Babylon.

"You've visited Babylon?!"

"Yeah, but I only got to the perimeter. It was full of American military—some sort of an attack helicopter base."

Maybe it was supposed to be a secret attack helicopter base, I thought.

Now the commander was trying to do a proper interrogation, but his guys were just chatting with me in between his questions—one asked me about watching television in the hotels I'd stayed in, and if I'd seen the latest NFL game. My descriptions of partying in Iran entertained them. They seemed to find it interesting that someone could be hitchhiking around without any gun or knowledge of Arabic, despite my telling them how the people had been helpful and kind.

"You've got balls, man," one soldier said. "Vacationing in Iraq."

The commander wanted to see my passport. He took down information, then asked after any other ID. I showed him my Alberta driver's licence, whose details he also jotted down. "One last question," he said. "What bombs or RPGs [rocket-propelled grenades] have you seen in the building?"

None, as it turned out.

"If you value your life ... get out of Iraq as fast as you can."

"I'm going to try to hitch farther north tomorrow," I said.

They departed with the two AK-47s they'd seized, and that was that. Of course those Iraqis from the restaurant would now have to buy some more on the street tomorrow, and it seemed likely to me they would be angry at the Americans for taking the rifles that they needed to defend their homes and family.

Indeed, with "nation building" accomplished and the Americans out of earshot, the Iraqis showed their anger. A couple had been in the restaurant celebrating their wedding, and they felt it had been disrupted. One large gentleman was yelling, to me, "Pentagon is worse *qaeda*"— *qaeda* meaning "base" in Arabic. The Iraqis had my sympathy, but I also sympathized with the American troops, who were merely following orders. There were cultural misunderstandings all around. I tried to explain to one Iraqi that in America the police and army, in the course of their duty, are expected to act with unquestioned authority. They routinely hold citizens at gunpoint, even for trivial things like traffic stops, and sometimes issue commands in a manner that may seem strikingly direct and rude. This is simply a peculiarity of American culture.

Later that year, in Egypt, I learned I was lucky to be Canadian: a Lithuanian told me the story of another traveller who had tried to come into Iraq across the border from Turkey, and hadn't got far before being confronted by American troops. They asked him his nationality. When he said Lithuanian, they weren't familiar with the place, reckoned it might be one of those troublesome little places like Dagestan or Ingushetia, and arrested him. After the arresting process starts, it takes on a life of its own, and it was a month before he was released.

Next morning found me packed and hitching a ride with an Iraqi, passing by windswept grass and stony plains. He spoke English, but just a little. We got to talking about our home cities, and it was hard for me to explain that I once lived in a village. It wasn't sinking in; he thought any Westerner must hail from somewhere at least as big as Baghdad. We were passing towns every fifteen minutes or so, and as we approached one that was about the size of Glade, my home for a while in British Columbia, I saw my chance.

"My town same this town," I said.

"This town Yazidi town, people who worship Satan," he spat.

IN JANUARY 2004, NORTHERNMOST IRAQ AND EASTERN TURKEY were a plain of snow and stones, a staging area for the convoys of tanker trucks I'd seen in Iraq. The border was a mess of mud and red tape. My exit stamp was on a slip of paper and indicated not Iraq but Kurdistan. Passing over to the Turkish side involved a lot of paperwork to get what is typically an easy visa. It made sense to pay a scrounger ten bucks to help me navigate the procedure more efficiently, and once I got to the other side, I found a car picking up passengers on a windy and chill winter's day.

It had been a memorable couple of weeks in Iraq before the American soldiers recommended my departure. Every day was a whirlwind of adventure, but a feeling of relief swept over me when I made it safely to the hinterland of Turkey, where it was possible to contact friends and family to tell them of my health, throat yet un-slashed. I'd learned something about my tolerance for personal risk, but was glad of my decision not to drop any hints to my family about my plans for hitchhiking Iraq. Although, if your parents aren't worried, are you even travelling?

The risk was real. Later in 2004, a younger, less experienced, and even less lucky Japanese traveller, Shosei Koda, entered Baghdad using the same route that I'd taken. He was almost immediately kidnapped by terrorists and murdered in a videotaped beheading four days later.

As a young man in the second month of my eighty-six days alone in the wilderness, I found it necessary to obtain an accurate description of fear for my novel. Like a painter looking for a picturesque meadow in which to set up an easel, I trudged off in search of fear, with notebook in hand, and found just the thing: a bear—in this case a cinnamon bear, not gigantic but above average size. He would do. The bear rose up on its hind legs to have a look-see, close enough for each of us to recognize a threat from the other. Instead of barging the beast, I glanced down several times while jotting notes. What fear I could muster expressed itself as an unstable emotion, like a pine cone balanced on its tip, poised frozen between a smidgeon less than a full commitment to either flight or fight.

What surprised me was that my time in Iraq was not like that—at least, not much. What I experienced was more the fear you feel when asking a girl out, poised in the instant before she might say no. The relief of passing unscathed through places like Tikrit was like the transformation of fear into elation in the moment after you see her lips shape themselves to say yes.

But the alertness induced by this intense apprehension, when I asked the world to let me take the liberty of another day's or moment's helping of life, wore on me and left me mentally tired and searching for a place to recharge.

It was always thus for me, in that mere fear of a violent death from an attack by a human is more an animal thing, so it doesn't disturb me. I've made friends with this fear over my years in the wilderness. My maximum anxiety as a young man came not from danger of attack by the few predators in an otherwise familiar landscape, but from, for instance, arriving in a huge city, new to me, with no map and no ability to speak the language, perhaps even at an odd hour, where people are leery of strangers on the street, and having to somehow communicate with them to find out where to go. (As an older man, I find this same challenge counts as fun.) For this mild species of anxiety, it did my nerves good to admire the tall Nakhla date palms in Baghdad or, better yet, some bushes scrambling forth from cracks in the masonry where a bird had deposited the seed.

For nerves frayed by weeks of intrusive alertness, it was best for me to return to the source. Snow, mud, dead residue of crop stalks, and freezing rain as I passed through cities like Diyarbakir, didn't do it for me. Neither did Istanbul, though some places leave mental traces, as if trains of thought and moods can be geo-tagged. Istanbul is one such place; over the years I've returned a dozen times to this city and picked up strands of thought, often right where I left off years earlier.

I collected a Syrian visa and set off on the road to Damascus, proceeding slowly along Turkey's Mediterranean coast. I only felt completely relaxed and comfortable again in my own skin after a stay on the idyllic beach at Olympos, breathing sea air, snacking on oranges from the grove around my A-frame shack, and wandering to explore the ruins, then largely unexcavated and overgrown by forest. I stepped over cylindrical sections of toppled pillars and discovered ancient sarcophagi incised with funerary inscriptions in ancient Greek, all the while listening to the waves toss a shoreline of colourful pebbles.

For some years afterward, I'd surprise fellow backpackers by naming Syria as the top destination in the Mediterranean area ... cheap and excellent hotels, the castles of Aleppo and Krak des Chevaliers, ancient sites like the city of Zenobia in Palmyra, good street-food cafés. The sites are largely ruined now, sadly, as are many of the people.

Damascus was a fine place for sipping coffee and people watching, now in the company of a wandering Turkish professor, who confessed to a penchant for letting his female students sleep their way to better grades. He found it amusing that he, secretly an atheist, could visit all the mosques normally closed to non-Muslims, just by showing a Turkish passport. As we sipped coffee and watched the girls pass on the streets, he expounded on the virtues of Turkish coffee, the best in the world, he asserted. He got me to agree that it was pretty good, once you learned not to disturb the sludge at the bottom of the minuscule cups.

Not all mosques were so restrictive, and some of the most fascinating had been converted from temples to Roman gods such as Jupiter. I especially enjoyed the shrine to a leader who rose to great fame, despite the southern, foreign origins of his patriarch's harem, and his espousing a religious sect different from that of the local gentry—something like Mitt Romney, I suppose, only in this case, he didn't go down to defeat but rather rose to be King Saladin, a Sunni Kurd from Tikrit, and victor over Richard the Lionheart of England. For hundreds of years, local Muslim rulers were not particularly interested in converting the population of these formerly Byzantine lands, because they could tax them higher as infidels, and Saladin even encouraged the Jews to return to Jerusalem. But the continuing intrusion of crusaders—who built magnificent castles, such as Krak des Chevaliers—made them see the advantage of subjects who were co-religionist and thus more loyal, and the peoples of Syria were gradually converted.

Blanketed in thick snow, the trans-Lebanon Mountains held the likeliest pass to the coast, which our bus's engine strained to climb. A young Englishman had joined the Turk and me, and he became concerned that I didn't have a visa to cross into Lebanon. He had spent weeks preparing, while I was merely intending to try my luck on the spot.

However, my border guard spent a few minutes chatting with me about his relatives in Ottawa and where to buy the best shawarma on Elgin Street, then stamped me in despite my lack of a visa or other supporting documents, while the English guy was aggressively vetted for over half an hour even with his visa and sheaves of documents, all in order.

In Beirut we passed a Starbucks, and I explained to the curious professor that this was American-style coffee. After a few sips he changed his tune; from then on it was "Starbucks, the best coffee in the world." The city was mostly peaceful and still rather beautiful, notwithstanding the odd building wrecked by street fighting, or chunks blasted out of high-rise apartments by artillery fire from the surrounding hillsides. We sampled the nightlife, famous cedar forests, and valley with ruined temples, and also took this rare opportunity to check email.

Barbara, messaging me from Winterthur, wanted to take some time off and meet me in Egypt. Lebanon was the end of the road anyhow, there being no way to cross to Israel or back to Syria, so I said goodbye to my travelling companions and flew to Cairo. The idea was to find a good hotel and get an idea of the lay of the land before Barbara arrived, as she favoured Swiss standards over my indifference born of frequenting slums.

I felt sure the old British officers' club would be the perfect hotel for us, possessed of retro-shabby colonial styling, and an elevator attendant in a starched uniform to work the screen and buttons. A thought that was comforting to me, though far less so to the local youth, was that Cairo remains always the same—a polluted honking, stressed-out, Arabic megacity. The civilization predates that of the Arabs by thousands of years, but the locals are thoroughly Arabicized, so I never see any displays of science or engineering books or magazines but, rather, a preponderance of religious tracts and salacious nonsense for sale in the shops.

With nothing to read, I had more time for hanging out with locals while waiting for Barbara. One businessman managed a Radio Shack and told me his main problem was that his containers were being plundered as they passed through Italian ports on the way to Egypt. The Italian longshoremen must have figured that he'd blame Egyptian corruption, but he'd used tracking technology and determined the thefts were happening in Italy. Another Egyptian businessman said it was a safe bet to expect Egyptian corruption; one of his relatives had just had to sign over, or else, a chunk of his company to the son of President Mubarak. I mentioned that doing business in Egypt sounded a lot like doing business in Syria. I'd talked to a guy in the carpet business in Homs who told me he'd had a knack for management and was growing his company so well four years earlier that government thugs knocked on the door and extorted $40,000 out of him, on pain of death. It nearly ruined his extended family, and in order to prevent a repeat of the demand, which would end with him dead or maimed, he'd abandoned his dreams and sacked his employees, resigning himself to running a family operation that he could keep so small it would be beneath notice, *inshallah*.

Whilst sipping tea late one night in a souk, I joined the table of an American from Detroit. He also had French citizenship, and he began to complain that he didn't want to see any more North Africans immigrating to France. They were a disgrace to Islam, he stated, chasing women and drinking alcohol, losing Muslim identity to French culture. "Are you a Christian American?" he asked.

"No," I replied.

He asked where home was for me, and I told him of living out of a backpack, constantly on the move, having recently passed through Turkey, Syria, Lebanon, and before that, Iraq.

"Did you have any trouble in Iraq?" he asked.

"Not so much. A close call with explosives in Baghdad, and I was surrounded by the American troops in Mosul, but managed to avoid arrest."

"I've just come from Iraq too, brother. I was setting up safe houses and stocking them with weapons to strike back at the invading Americans."

He'd mistaken me for a fellow terrorist. I neglected to set him straight in order to hear him orate on the evil of Christian Americans. The conversation switched to global jihad, and I let him do most of the talking. He asked if I wanted to hear how we had won the great victory over the Christians in Chechnya. I nodded. His story was essentially this: Russian soldiers are predictable. They long for victories like they had during World War II. So the Chechen commanders set up a ring of defences around Grozny, just enough to be plausible. Then they stacked crates of vodka in the city hall and hid most of the fighters atop the high-rise apartments, with rocket-propelled grenades. Russians yearned to burst through the city defences and drive armoured columns to the city centre, where they would be sure to film themselves raising the Russian flag for the evening news. This happened exactly to plan, and naturally the Russians got into the vodka to celebrate the victory. After they were good and drunk, the signal was given and the fighters on the roofs fired their RPGs down on the tanks below. "The thing about a T-72 tank," he said, "is that with one RPG hit to the hatch on top, it buckles. A second hit will punch right through and kill the crew. We won a great victory. Of course, afterward, the Russians surrounded the city with artillery and shelled Grozny until it was a ruin ... " his voice trailed off. But he soon was back in good spirits, and we chatted about the Shi'ite–Sunni rift. When the hour was late, he gave me his email address on a scrap of paper, and we parted ways.

Next morning I met a Lithuanian, Erlandas, who was just finishing his Egypt trip. I asked him if he'd got out to the pyramids, since I was planning to do that first thing when Barbara arrived the next day. He hadn't, instead spending all his time photographing frogs on the banks of the Nile, hoping to spin it into a magazine article. We talked for a while over breakfast, and when I mentioned my surreal conversation in the souk the night before, he asked if he could contact the Western terrorist to try to get an interview. I couldn't find the scrap of paper, and I told Erlandas I had a vague recollection of tossing it away, for obvious reasons. I already had a huge problem with profiling on western frontiers, with long detentions and border guards going through every scrap of paper in my backpack and pockets. My strange lifestyle may have produced a knee-jerk prison-and-torture response, for both me and the young American guy, if I decided to go to the Egyptian police, even if he had been exaggerating his Iraq activities. My impression was that he was not a major player; rather, I would bet he just hung out with Iraqi insurgents, bigging himself up, like he must do with his buddies at home in Detroit.

BARBARA FLEW IN FROM SWITZERLAND, AND WE LOOKED AT pyramids, where Barbara was shocked that all these titanic stone blocks were shifted just to make a tomb. I'd seen more than my fair share of pyramids over the years, so I already knew this; what I didn't know, and learned just then from a touristic handout, was that an ancient Pharaoh, not Punks or Goths, was the originator of the notion of crafting women's clothing from fishnets.

According to a tourist information pamphlet, Pharaoh Sneferu, being bored, said to Djadjaemankh, his priest and magician: "I have gone through all the rooms of my palace in search of relaxation and found none." Djadjaemankh said to him: "May your majesty proceed to the lake of the palace. Fill a boat with all the beautiful girls of your palace. Your majesty's heart will be refreshed by seeing them row." Said his majesty: "Indeed, I shall go boating! Let there be brought to me twenty oars of ebony plated with gold, their handles of sandalwood plated with electrum. Let there be brought to me twenty women with the shapeliest bodies, breasts, and braids, who have not yet given birth. Also let there be brought to me twenty nets and give these nets to these women in place of their clothes!" All was done as his majesty commanded ... he pronounced himself well pleased.

We toured the temple of Karnak and sailed the Nile by felucca, ending up in St. Catherine's Monastery in the Sinai. Here we met a Serbian icon researcher with intriguing stories of years spent fruitlessly trying to negotiate a viewing of the secret icons stored therein. The monks would lure her to Egypt with promises of a viewing of exceedingly rare and never-before-seen icons; then at the last minute they would demur and send her home. They'd baited and teased her four times already, but this time she felt it must be for real. She looked so wound-up she seemed ready to burst.

"I don't know why I'm so fascinated by icons," she admitted, and Barbara and I exchanged glances.

The fact was, she looked like an icon: a handsome, vaguely andro-gynous woman, with a face not completely symmetrical, just as icons are portrayed with one half perfect and divine, the other half mortal and flawed.

We were not the only ones exchanging glances. "Why is everyone at the table glaring at us and muttering curses?" I asked her.

"It's not you. It's directed at me. Excuse me a minute." She walked over to another table at the cafeteria and spoke to the hostile group in Serbian. When she finished, everyone was laughing and smiling.

She came back to sit with us and explained: "They are all Serbians, like me, but earlier today I greeted one of them, and he must have no-ticed that I have a slight Croatian accent. I just now explained to them that I'm entirely Serbian; it's only that my family lived for many years in Croatia. It's all good now."

St. Catherine's Monastery harbours a copy of the "Ashtiname of Muhammad," likely a bona fide cartoon of the Prophet Muhammad, which has a fascinating origin story. It is a cartoon of the prophet's hand, drawn perhaps by the holy prophet himself, for a reason that few would guess: to declare that all Muslims have a duty to show respect and mercy to his friends, the Christians living in the monastery. Other cartoons of Muhammad fail to be cartoons of him according to this simple test: say a cartoonist wanted to poke fun at President George W. Bush and draws a cartoon that bears a remarkable resemblance to President Barack Obama. If it succeeds as a cartoon, it is not a cartoon of Bush but of Obama. To be a bona fide cartoon of someone, it must resemble some part of the intended subject's body or visage at least well enough to be recognizable. There are no contemporaneous paintings or drawings of the entire form or most body parts of Prophet Muhammad. So only a cartoon such as this hand has any probability of satisfying this sensible test.

The Holy Prophet intended for this tracing of his hand to remain on the wall of the monastery, but in this his will was thwarted somewhat by people who decided they knew better: it was removed to Topkapi Palace (now a museum), and replaced by a copy in the monastery. Otherwise, the spirit of his command, sealed with a cartoon, has been obeyed for fourteen centuries.

A fierce sandstorm limited our visibility and movement for over a week in Sinai until, fed up with grit in our clothes and stinging wind on our faces, we retreated west by bus to Cairo. Besides, Barbara needed to attend to her business in Switzerland, and I had to leave Egypt for London by the end of March, then home to Canada for a quick visit.

CHAPTER SIX

HUB AND SPOKES

Central, Eastern, Southern Europe · Scandinavia

I**N APRIL BOTH OF MY BROTHERS BECAME FATHERS FOR THE**
second time while I wandered, adapting not to home and hearth
but to backpacking challenges. These babies would be great fun
to visit as they grew—and as I grew into my new role of "Uncle Mike."
Collectively they satisfied any potential need on the part of my parents
for grandchildren, leaving me free to travel to my heart's desire, and also
ensuring there would be ears eager for stories on my returns to Canada
to change out over-filled passports.

It's a commonly held belief that after ten years doing something,
you become an expert. Apparently this is not so for me: with backpacking, each continent requires unique ways and means. European travel is
very strange compared to that in the Middle East—people with luggage
on wheels, eclectic architecture with sprinklings of castles, a fair share

of pretty girls out in the open, all viewed, ideally, while licking an ice cream cone. It took me a while to figure out how to make the best of the continent, which to my eye, and especially after seeing many other places, seemed like a vast outdoor museum: interesting, but exclusive and well ordered. Many young people backpacking here scarcely have a travel tale worth telling that doesn't begin "First we got appallingly drunk ..." Since I was now in my early thirties, this had lost some, but not all, of its lustre.

From London I branched out, couch surfing or living in hostels or sometimes in squats, in what was a blur of urban decay and iconic modern cities. Molly and Tim introduced me to the wonderfully filthy free party scene, then thriving in Europe. Parties in abandoned warehouses would go on for days or weeks before the police shut them down. I didn't have quite that much time to devote to partying, but it was fascinating to find a tribal sub-culture evolving in the decay and liminal spaces of these intensively urbanized and ostensibly sophisticated nations.

Germany beckoned. I had considered Bavaria first, but had been swayed to make for Berlin, the most interesting city in that land I was told. For the traveller, the city's history is its most obvious asset, once cleft right down the middle by east-west tension, but now plumped together. Modern-day Berlin, aged yet beautiful, displays this history front and centre, so to speak, more aware of its charms than any Bavarian barmaid. Making reservations is not my way, so it was luck that brought me to Circus Hostel, where I could enjoy prog-rock music over breakfast and get to know the city in the company of a chatty Jewish-American girl, Bonnie, and a Dane, whose short stature would have easily gone unremarked had he been born on southern shores; however, he was blond, a son of the North Sea, and so comported himself with an impeccable spine like a drill-sergeant.

Berlin's museums, public buildings, and slabs of Comrade Khrushchev's wall, often freckled with bomb damage on exposed surfaces, or tattooed with colourful graffiti, were fascinating. Both experimental and practical architecture was abundant and, likewise, citizens who were business-minded and those who were experimenting with their lifestyles seemed to mix well in the leafy parks and energetic neighbourhoods. Beers and conversations at streetside tables kept me occupied on warm evenings.

A winding path took me through Central Europe, dipping south to see Barbara at her home in Winterthur, Switzerland, and then to a rowdy CzechTek rave in Czech Republic that was attacked and tear-gassed by the police because of a failure to agree on the size of a bribe to let the party go on. Slovakia's capital, Bratislava, had me marching around for three hours in darkness and rain, trying to find a bed for the night. Part of the delay was due to my decision to take a gander at a castle while I was passing so near. Then I bushwhacked down the forested slope below its walls in rain so hard I could scarcely see my boots. Once a cheap bed was secured, I wrung out my clothes and unfolded a soggy map to dry.

The next morning I went into a Ukrainian embassy I'd chanced upon the night before in my wanderings, and presented various documents that were the usual fetishes for demanding a visa. I met with the administrator and he scrutinized everything, finding fault here and there. "You won't be able to make your application today," he said, smiling, "and we will be closed until Monday." He folded his arms.

"Perfect, thank you," I said. He seemed taken aback, so I added, "This was only a trial run. My intention was always to make my application out of Warsaw, and now I know exactly what I am up against. So next, I enjoy Slovakia and hike in the High Tatras Mountains."

These mountains were pretty, and the hiking sublime; I saw on the map an asterisk marking "the highest peak," and struck out for it. Soon after a short stop at a petrol station for supplies, I'd reached the base and started up. Much of the route was scree; some of the rocks large enough that it felt like bouldering. Due to my late start, it was only near the top that I began to pass other climbers, mostly Germans. To me they seemed geared to the max in Gore-Tex and gloves, packs, hydration bottle strap-ons, mountaineering boots, ski poles, and some with goggles. In turn, perhaps they saw me as woefully under-prepared, in black nylon fast-dry trousers and a T-shirt; dangling from one of my hands was a plastic bag holding a sandwich and a fruit drink. We stood atop the peak as they took photos in drizzle that had turned to light snow with gusting wind. When it would have been my turn to stand on the highest prominence, one German offered to take a photo of me with my camera. I told them I didn't own a camera. We chatted a few minutes, but I began to feel the chill so skipped back down. The weather broke when I was halfway off the slope to reveal green valleys and awesome god-clouds pierced by golden sunbeams.

In Krakow my dorm mate was an Irishman, Connor, who made a living off horse racing and professional golf. He'd go to events and phone in to bookies with immediate updates. This gave them a few seconds' or minutes' advantage over people watching on television, and this edge could be golden. He met lots of wealthy Arabs at the races, and told of a tantalizing buffet spread, fit for a sultan, that all went into the trash. A royal aide saw one of the caterers pluck an olive out of a dish on his way past the dining chamber, so he bellowed, "Nobody eats before the Sultan! Throw this out, and replace everything." Connor met a Polish girl that night in a smoky cellar-turned-bar under the streets. She had the most wonderful accent when speaking English, a mix of Polish and Italian. I distracted the hostel clerk at the desk so Connor could sneak her into the dorm. She warned us against entering a nearby bar, as there were too many stabbings, but then later she got slashed herself—having not taken her own advice, I suppose. Her main worry was about the blade leaving a scar, as she worked in the fashion industry.

Warsaw coughed up a Ukrainian visa for me, but I had a while to use it, so I decided to swirl around, enjoying the summer in Eastern Europe, including Slovenia and Hungary, and boating the Danube from Budapest. Come September, I had an email from Erlandas, photographer of frogs on the banks of the Nile, he invited me to visit Lithuania, so I hitched a ride on a tractor-trailer driving north to the Baltic Sea. When I arrived he told me, among other things, about Lithuania's prowess at basketball, and the country's origins in Cold War opposition to foreign domination. Oddly, for a people so dead set against being dominated, their Statehood Day is a celebration of the time a king allied himself with invading German knights, massacred the locals, and shoved Christianity down the throats of the survivors. (Meanwhile, in Belarus, a nation seemingly content to be dominated by a foreign government in Moscow, they celebrate Victory Day, which commemorates locals massacring invading Germans and afterward trying to dislodge Christianity.)

It was refreshing to wander the Curonian Spit on the Baltic, with its sandy dunes, wooden statuary, and whispering pines, and to read up on history on rainy days. One fact stuck in my mind: there was a court case from a time contemporaneous with slavery in the United States involving a runaway serf in the Grand Duchy of Lithuania. His master found him in a town and cut this insolent serf down with a sword blow. The master was flabbergasted when the town militia arrested him and put him on trial; this serf had been on the loose for some time and had made many friends in the neighbourhood. At trial, the master called for outright dismissal of the case, confident of the facts of the matter: the man had been his, so he could do with him as he damn well pleased. In a surprising turn of events, the master was hung for this murder of his own serf, a first.

These little Baltic states held me only a couple of weeks, as I had to get over to Ukraine before I started cutting into the limited dates on my visa, but I did enjoy the time I had there. The roadside toilets used for the public buses were the direst I'd ever encountered anywhere outside of Asia, but this was more than compensated for by charming cities, especially the dark Teutonic castle town of Tallinn in Estonia. I had visited just a little too late to be welcomed with open arms as a foreigner. Ryanair had already started offering cheap flights to loutish tourists from the British Isles, all of them over for stag-night weekends of drinking, fighting, and vomiting. Still, the people at bars and hostels were friendly enough once they sussed that I was not one of those.

A flight dropped me in a Ukrainian city. I have no record or recollection of which one, though I can picture many of the streets, parks, and shops in my mind's eye. At one time there was a fair handful of these ghost destinations in my memory, but usually over the years the names would reassert themselves (one was the city of Dahab—not the resort, but the city—with blue shadows, narrow alleys, sand, drifting plastic trash—an orphan in my memory for years until, out of nowhere, my mind placed it). A train carried me to Kiev, with its leafy riverbank parks, golden onion-domed churches, and couples kissing on escalators that run so deep no atomic blast could touch the speedy clattering metro.

On the Crimean Peninsula I tried but failed to visit Sevastopol. Instead I marched until my legs were sore, past rows of military housing blocks and formidable Russian warships at anchor. A bed for the night could not be found, so, accepting defeat, I bussed on to Yalta and checked into the Bristol Hotel. In Yalta, a promenade by the Black Sea is lined with people who make a living by taking pictures of tourists with a curiosity like a lizard or a hawk, or dressed in archaic costumes, or seated on a motorbike. A couple of Africans were standing there too, and for a fee you could have your picture taken with a *neger* guy—to wow your friends in small-town Ukraine. *Neger* just means "black" around here, but if politeness wasn't important to you, and you thought someone's skin was too dark and wanted to tease him about it, rather than calling him *neger*, you'd call him a Caucasian—people from the Caucasus Mountains are notoriously swarthy.

Often when I'm exploring the same continent for many months or years, I find that my tempo speeds up noticeably about two and a half to three months in; around here I found my groove and breezed along effortlessly, feeling healthy, fit, and happy, through hundreds of cities, towns, and interesting places between the Black Sea and the Atlantic coast of Iberia. The journey left impressions of the shifting landscape that only extensive overland travel can furnish: in the south, this little continent is a series of mountainous peninsulas jutting into temperate seas. The peninsulas have long been civilized, farmed, and fought over by peoples unified by their appreciation for long evening conversations over wine and good food.

Before Christmas I found myself in Calais in northern France, eager to take a ferry to England. I obtained a ticket and set off on the long journey to the dock on foot. I got there in time, but for one problem. Everything had been set up for vehicular traffic, and it was hard to see how walk-on passengers who arrived by foot instead of bus entered the terminal. There was certainly no gate for people who tramped in like vagabonds from the city along the highway, and the on-ramps were designed to thwart any access by pedestrians. I scouted the perimeter, probing the primary defence: an enormous, unscalable, chain-link wall. With minutes to spare I prised open a door that led to a passage with further doors, unlocked; racing along this passage took me so deep into the facility that I met the line of passengers having their identities verified before boarding. A stunned official noticed me standing among the facility staff on the wrong side of the security barrier.

"Oh my god. Please don't tell me you are going to claim status," he gasped, his eyes darting to take in my scruffy appearance and the backpack I'd lived out of for more than a decade.

"Do you possess any documentation?" asked another nervous official.

I produced my passport and ferry ticket, and the first officer's relief was plain on his face. "How ever did you get in here?" he asked.

"By way of a series of doors in the exterior fencing," I said. "I hope I'm not in trouble."

"It is us who might have been in trouble. Someone might have lost his job over this ... If you had been an undocumented immigrant, you could have claimed status by having got as far as you have."

I laughed and said, "I'm just a regular Canadian trying to get onto the ferry. You guys don't make it easy for passengers arriving on foot."

"No, we most certainly don't. That's the whole point of this facility. Clearly there is a flaw in our security," he added and started making phone calls.

I shuffled in with the other passengers and off we sailed for the white cliffs of Dover.

From England it was easy to catch a cheap return flight to Canada. These runs home were not a break in my journey, but, rather, spurts of particularly hectic travel. My family and friends are spread across the entire continent, from sea to shining sea, quite literally: my dad has a house on the North Atlantic shore, my mom on the North Pacific, and there are plenty of kinfolk in between. If necessary, my passport could be renewed in Ottawa.

Soon I was resting in an airplane seat, jetting back to London. Transoceanic flights are not, for me, tedious. They give me time to think. In the old days airlines used to have one or more movies for a planeload of eyeballs, but by 2005 the impetus was for individual entertainment systems; made no difference to me, as I seldom used either option. You don't so much enjoy a movie as wreck a movie if you see it on a plane; I read magazines or books, or sometimes studied the map of the world at the back of the in-flight magazine. Funny, my travel style was much like an airline, I realized. Despite travelling overland if at all possible, with only the vaguest of itineraries, I used the same hub-and-spoke logistics. Here was London, my new hub.

I had visited so many countries in Europe over the past year that my old friend Chad started calling me a "European" traveller. Europe cannot be rushed, though, if you want a feel for modern history, which until recently danced to a European tune. But now my gaze flickered over to Asia, following the thick dotted flight paths connecting the intercontinental hubs. There was Hong Kong, Singapore, Denpasar, Bangkok, Delhi. Bangkok, especially, was an old hub, ideally situated to gather visas and access South and Southeast Asia. It had been a while since my last trip over the Pacific, and this had me wondering, Would the staff in the traveller haunts still recognize me? Or the people on Khao San Road? Joanna lived thereabouts now, just over in Indonesia; she'd married a Balinese guy, had some kids, and they owned a bunch of silver shops. I looked at the diverse colours of the countries sketched out in an arc many thousand kilometres wide around Bangkok, and felt the flood of fond memories; my travels don't take me back there anymore, of course. I'm on to fresh pastures.

That's the beauty of hub and-spoke travel—you flit in and out of a hub, maybe with a girlfriend nearby. As your choice hub is a major city in an area that is a magnet for travellers, all your traveller friends come and go from there anyhow, joining you on trips. In the meantime, or while you wait for them, you discover your region, a rich pasture of unexplored lands and experiences. I was comfortable with this type of travel, this lifestyle. I could go on forever like this.

My new but increasingly close friends were in London. We'd catch up on each other's lives and crack a beer after lengthy UK customs and that familiar tube ride into town. Barbara was nearby in Switzerland, so it was easy to pop over for a good time; she was taking some days off from running her business for a road trip, and the plan was she'd join me for the fjords of Norway. Chad had written to tell me he'd asked for a leave of absence from his career to travel Asia, perhaps to join me in Kathmandu or Lhasa. Molly was up for Tibet too, and maybe some coastal China or Nepal. It would be autumn by the time they were ready, so naturally I'd spend the summer exploring the near abroad. My gaze flicked back to Europe, that motherlode of countries—not mere names on a map but, for me, bursting with memories. And here was northern Europe, terra incognita to me. Sweden, especially, is a big country.

An experienced traveller can look at a region and have a pretty good idea of how long it will take to backpack it. Scandinavia is good for a summer. Norway with Barbara will be fun. After which I will join my friends on our way to the Tibetan Plateau. I pored over the map of Europe and felt some unease, quickly suppressed: the plane would be landing soon, and I had some inkling of a strategy for a whole year. What more could I expect, or want?

A short central-European road trip got me warmed up, and some more Spain. There were oodles of time: Molly didn't want to consider Tibet until after the festival season in Europe, which she had been photographing for years in what was her life's work. And the best trekking in Nepal was October or later anyway, when the air is crisper and the chill drives away the blood-sucking leeches.

Instead I was off to Denmark, Sweden, the Faroe Islands, and Iceland. Barbara would meet me for Norway. Then I would cross Sweden again to take a ferry to Finland, and head back to the UK to check if my friends were stoked yet for Tibet.

The public transport system, buses and tube, were bombed by terrorists on July 7, 2005, just hours after I used them to leave from Heathrow. The Stockholm newspaper covered the attack. Fifty-two people were murdered. Measured responses to these sorts of outrages are easier said than done, but certainly must include greater scrutiny of suspicious characters stepping off planes. This would include me. Heightened security procedures in the UK, especially Heathrow, meant long interrogations became the norm for me, one lasting seven hours. The police there knew me well enough to joke around when they saw me being brought in and thought, Not you again. If I'd got to know them any better, we'd have been obliged to send each other Christmas cards.

SCANDINAVIA, INCLUDING ICELAND AND THE FAROE ISLANDS, GREEN, sunny, and blonde, occupied my summer of 2005. Barbara and I took the ferry up the coast of Norway, sleeping on the deck (kindly crewmembers let us occupy the carpeted audio-visual room, as long as we were out by six in the morning). We took turns rowing around Gieranger Fjord, spin-casting for fish, and then returned south overland, spotting reindeer and gangly-legged moose on the barrens. Barbara returned to Switzerland, and as the shadows grew longer my path led to the forests and swamps of Finland. My flight back to the UK was out of Arlanda Airport in Sweden. I rushed back and found a hostel in Stockholm, waking early for the trip to the airport and check-in, only to discover that my boots had been stolen. They were old and cracked and well worn, but also broken in. And, most of all, they were my boots. Who does that? Can you even imagine stealing a man's boots as he sleeps? Stuffed with the feet of some particularly unscrupulous backpacker, they continued, no doubt, to plod around Sweden. Plastic flip-flops saved the day. My new leather boots, bought in Kingston upon Thames while staying with Tim, would carry me to Tibet.

CHAPTER SEVEN

ROOF OF THE WORLD

China · Tibet · Nepal · India

MOLLY WAS PACKED AND READY, HER EMAIL informed me, but rather than applying for a Chinese visa in London, we decided it was smarter to fly to Hong Kong, where potent Chinese visas are granted the same day you apply for them. Molly met me at Heathrow Airport in late September 2005, and we did just that. The trip was freestyle but, as it turned out, a chart of this trip would show a great circling of the Roof of the World, anticlockwise, through China, India, and Indochina, with dashed and solid lines showing flights and overland journeys. Years later I would wheel around the Tibetan Plateau again, wider that time and clockwise, a solid circle of overland transport, taking in entirely different landscapes.

Chinese officials often seem puzzled by the concept of independent travel: they can't shake the notion that solo travellers are somehow trying to save money by figuring out their own tour, and the officials wonder why the travellers aren't more forthcoming with their itinerary. Anyhow, we picked up a visa each, to supplement our short-stay visas on arrival, and now we had choices to make: did we credit the rumour that at Dragon Guesthouse, operating out of a converted traditional court-yard manse in Szechuan's Chengdu, a city of ten million, it was possible to find a package-tour operator who could arrange a (fake) tour of Tibet, thus providing us with the paperwork that was mandatory if we were to be let into Tibet so we could see it properly as backpackers? That we could find giant pandas in Chengdu decided the matter for us.

Hong Kong is always good for a few days' look-see: it has interesting buildings and museums, and a shallow pool in a park I always visit when passing through, where people play with their remote-controlled model boats. The skyscrapers make a nightly show of lights, in our case aug-mented by the fireworks display over the harbour on China's National Day (October 1). A last check of email told me that Bali had fireworks of its own that same night: Joanna wrote that she and her family were unharmed when the island was terror-bombed a second time in three years. Restaurants had been the targets, and twenty people were killed, with a hundred injured by shrapnel. The first bombing, in 2002, had destroyed places Joanna and I used to frequent: the Sari club, Aromas restaurant, and Yusuf's silver. But she didn't write what the exact targets were in this latest Islamo-fascism outrage.

After five days, Molly and I reached Szechuan, a region of moun-tains, hills, rice paddies, rivers, lakes, dams, and earthquakes. Near the great cities, and anywhere else worth the investment of time and aching backs, the landscape has been transformed by human hands: terraced for paddies, and the water sluiced, dammed, and channelled to serve up rice and other foodstuffs. Ducks wade, chickens scratch, and pigs watch the world go by and grow fat for the slaughter. This is Chinese traditional agriculture—if not quite as old as the hills, certainly as old as the terraces. The Szechuan hinterlands, beyond the sculpting of the rice farmer's callused palms, can be as misty, thought-provoking, and peaceful as a subtle Chinese watercolour. There are spooky canyons, rushing streams, bamboo stands clacking musically in the breeze, and mirror lakes.

Legend tells how earthquakes are normally rigid rock shaken by the motions of dragons deep underground. Dragon Guesthouse was a building that had survived something worse than an earthquake, the destructive Cultural Revolution, with ornate wood carvings and a traditional courtyard intact. As enough travellers coalesced to make up a plausible "fake" tour, we wandered through red and gold temples full of great urns bristling with joss sticks, and gawked at impossibly cute pandas, including one mother with a squeaking baby.

Sure enough, normally rigid rules yielded to our hundred-dollar payment, and papers were drawn up showing Molly and me as part of a tour. This sort of thing is frowned upon, but only mildly, since what is important to Szechuan officials is that travellers keep up appearances. Our group got on a flight together, collectively passed through customs at Gonggar Airport, just 60 kilometres from Lhasa, and then scattered to the winds.

WHEN, IN THE LATE '90S, WESTERN ART EXPERTS FUNDED BY THE American Himalayan Foundation were assisting a group of monks in the restoration of sacred paintings at Thubchen Gompa, they agonized over how to duplicate the fading, mellowing, and subdued colours. The monks protested that they didn't want that; they wanted bright paint fresh from the tube, new and better.

Just as some Tibetan monks don't understand what Westerners see in those old murals, some Chinese officials don't understand what tourists see in Tibet, so cold and smelly and backward.

The Tibetan Plateau is an unpromising place to colonize, but Chinese generals saw it as important to hold the high ground in any future Great Game versus India. Usually, if enough colonizers move into a country, eventually enough will have been born there for the country to become theirs. This certainly worked with Cambodia for the Khmer, who replaced the native Negritos, or Rakshas (ogres), as they were referred to in ancient Sanskrit. There is a problem with Tibet, however:

just as cows cannot thrive on the Roof of the World, since they fail to calve, so Han Chinese and other lowlanders have trouble getting pregnant and bringing a baby to term. The Roof of the World is the abode of yaks and Tibetans. It's hard to feel you are living in your homeland if you cannot bring children into the world. There is something alien and alienating about having to return to the lowlands to spawn, like a frog to the swamp. The genes that allow the Tibetans to thrive on the plateau include some that have pride of place, like Bon relics: one is possibly a match to a gene from the Denisovan genome, Denisovans being ice-age-adapted humanoids from the primordial past.

Otherwise, genetically, the Tibetans are akin to Han Chinese, just with those few biochemical tricks up their sleeves, and when they were strong and the lowlanders were weak, they poured down from the plateau, raiding, conquering, raping, and pillaging their way to a Tibetan Empire around the year AD 800. This fact is the key to the Chinese take on who is Chinese and who is not Chinese. Over long millennia, a rogues' gallery of jostling barbarians have bided their time and then conquered the Han when they saw their chance. The Han scholars take the long view of history and patiently add another dynasty to the scroll. The flip side of this for the triumphant barbarian is that now his heirs and ethnicity figure into Chinese history. The Han absorb their enemies and become one with them, so if you will strive and wrestle and rape and kill, violently insisting that your people and the Han live under one law, you might master them, but in consequence, you and your barbarian kin are Chinese for good.

On the first day in Lhasa, where the slab-sided white and ochre Potala Palace dominates the Kyi-chu Valley, any strenuous exertion would have me seeing stars. I'm usually fine at elevation, with just a little loss of appetite at 3,300 metres that passes after a single sleep, which previously allowed me to enjoy Thorong La and Annapurna Sanctuary in Nepal, and the top of Borneo's Mount Kinabalu. But here we had flown in, stepped out of our "tour group," and started breathing thin air. We explored markets selling candy dishes of silver-chased human skull, animal pelts, and painstakingly detailed pictograms with gold-leaf symbols that displayed the universe as it is, without the illusion of desire; we climbed inside those gigantic, sprawling, monastic fortresses stuffed with golden Buddhas and precious gems; and we circled the Jokhang with the ear-muffed mumbling mendicants come in from afar, for this is a place of pilgrimage.

For us it was also a starting point: we needed two more travellers to efficiently rent a Land Cruiser and driver; foreigners have to use the driver provided, and public buses are off-limits. We found our companions in Al and Sarah; he was British army, and both of them were from York and good company.

When we toured cliffside monasteries, the monks made a rare exception to their vows and let the girls blow on their prodigious horns; both Molly and Sarah were skilled with sax and trumpet, respectively, and surprised the monks by sustaining a note on such ungainly instruments. We picnicked on shining sacred lakes, some of the highest in the world at over 4,000 metres of elevation, living on instant noodles and porridge and big bottles of cider. Scorchingly chilied wind-dried yak meat tested my jaw. The girls learned not to give candy if bunches of nomad children crowded around at windswept outposts; the biggest beat the others bloody and made off with all the treats. And we learned to stoop for rocks to reach an understanding with the hulking Tibetan mastiffs that tried us on for size.

On chilly evenings Molly would chuckle over passages in a novel she was reading, *Shantaram*, or read choice paragraphs aloud. The author was an Australian, Gregory David Roberts, writing fiction reportedly based on his own life as a gangster in India.

"Mike, finally here's someone who could give even you a run for your money in terms of suffering in the line of duty for adventure," she said.

"By what you've described," I said, "the worst of that is from stints in horrifying Maharashtra State prisons, so in effect he's had government assistance, while I've had to manage solo."

"You can read it after me," she said, smiling.

THE DALAI LAMA IS WELL PRACTISED AT CONTROLLING HIS URGES and desires, yet he yearns to return from exile one day to settle near

Reting Monastery and live as a hermit among the juniper forest and dzo (cow-yak hybrids). So no shame, then, that we less-enlightened souls also felt compelled to take bumpy dirt roads to see for ourselves. A gilded image of the goddess Green Tārā rendered us contemplative in spooky chambers; beyond the double doorways, creaking ajar on ornate hinges, dzo contemplated only the vibrant green of the meadow grass, their tongues and damp snouts glistening, hooves stamping the dirt to furnish dancing dust motes for the sunbeams spilling past the door. Juniper and grass owed their luxuriant growth to a spring that was said to be home to the demons Dzin-pa-lag-mang and Klu Dung-skyong.

Darkness fell. What a perfect place for a mini-rave. Molly had a portable music player with EDM tracks of "old skool" and "raga" beats. In the darkness of a meadow in the forest, halfway up the mountain, we perched the player on an interesting-looking rock surrounded by yak skulls. Foraging Tibetans had, by day, scoured the slopes clear of dead-fall; little chance, then, to find wood by night. Nevertheless, I showed them how we do things in the backwoods and started a campfire in no time. Our fire was not a finicky one; it consumed yak dung and an old boot, bone, and horn when brambles did not suffice. Beer and cider accompanied the music. A family of Tibetans appeared out of the darkness—an old man, a couple of women, and a kid. We offered them cider, which they declined, but they began to circle the large rock in our midst, chanting and making offerings. Was it their holy rock? We noticed a symbol splashed on the side. But they were relaxed and friendly, completed their ceremony, and departed, leaving us with all the stars in the ultra-black night sky, and lonesome yaks shambling by in the darkness.

Back from this gravel side road and onto a main road, also gravel, I caught sight of an odd muddy message on the wall of a mud-brick outbuilding among the plops of yak dung drying in the wind. It read *Pete from Kamloops was here*. I remembered meeting the guy in the mid-'90s on a bus in Himachal Pradesh in India. He had been travelling for four years at the time, and had picked up a peculiar habit: when conversing with a group, he would occasionally stop mid-syllable, wander off to buy a drink, then return and continue on the next syllable as if he had never left. He had announced that if anyone was ever in Tibet, they should look out for this wall of mud and dung where his finger had traced letters to immortalize himself.

A road that dwindled to a four-wheel-drive track wound its way south to a famous peak, and here we were, with a Land Cruiser, plenty of cider to ease lips parched by dry winds and thin air, and a driver. "Everest," he heard us say, and veered south. Squeaking marmots kept us entertained at picnic stops, as the track hugged precipitous terrain; triangular ridges slapped with yellow pastures softened into blunt, rolling hills that had opened onto stony barrens when at last the shining white mountain assumed its rightful station above the horizon, growing improbably large as we drew near, our way marked only by scuffs in the rocky debris fields that skirted its base.

At Mount Everest we sheltered behind a wall constructed entirely of stacked beer bottles, which took the bite out of the minus-twenty wind. Base camp was free to explore, but it would cost a bundle to climb any farther. Molly took a picture, since lost, of me positioning my fingers so that Mount Everest was being squeezed between them. It was good for a laugh, as was a nearby Buddhist shrine or monastery, lonely and deserted apart from the cat that made its home here in the ruins and was content to be Molly's playmate while we warmed our ears and fingers. The walls of the monastery were painted with murals. Art is a window on the soul, and the monks took this opportunity to express themselves: demons eating and dismembering men and women, demons shagging other demons, demons shagging men and women as they eat them. Hmmm. Come to think of it, is it entirely healthy to dedicate one's life to repressing all human desires?

Those weeks we made our way through an unforgettable rush of experiences, sweeping vistas, sun-dappled colours, black crows, black yaks, golden grasslands, and dazzling snow. Somewhere along the way, Molly lost her novel just before she could finish, and I felt the same sadness when, deep into October, we had to leave.

Tibet held one last thrill: the longest sustained downward road in the world, to the border town of Zhangmu. This cleft in our world was so deep it could be from Mars or a moon of Jupiter. In our 4x4 we passed many a gear-grinding Dong truck stuck in the snow, and our driver became so accustomed to ramming his way through snowpacks to avoid the trucks that he took to off-roading straight down between the upper switchbacks; at times we felt like we were skiing, and the wheels scarcely turned, we had so much slide to our roll. After many hours it became too steep for this, but the road kept on, always down, down, down into this abyss, this fissure in the roof the world. We stopped once in a cliffside city built into the switchbacks, clogged with honking trucks, and every square metre of it furnished the most astounding view. To live there is to know what it is like to be a fledgling in an eagle's aerie. At last the mountains soared steeper, yet now trees found purchase, and mist clung.

We visa-ed-up in Kodari, a community of sheet-metal-roofed shacks lining the Araniko Highway, and crossed the Friendship Bridge on foot into Nepal. A new Jeep-like Kijang with a broken leaf spring hastily welded, and we were back in the Nepalese Himalayas: young, humid, crumbly rock faces; wet earth; everywhere green and, after fresh rain, shot through with burbling streams and brown rivers.

AL AND SARAH WOULD BE AROUND FOR A FEW DAYS MORE, DEPARTING from Kathmandu, where we would soon be meeting Chad. For now, the four of us sat at a crude table made of hewn rhododendron wood, in a roadside restaurant perched on a garbage-strewn ridge. Third-world bussing was the topic of conversation: Molly can't stand them on account of a dodgy back. I'm only a little over six feet tall and don't have a problem, but I mentioned that Chad was too tall to fit, and every bump was torture.

"When Chad was in Tibet a couple of years ago, he was riding the local buses. You're not supposed to, so he would have to duck at every army checkpoint. The Tibetans would help hide him. If the checkpoint was too serious, he'd get out and hike around it, then try to pick up another bus on the far side. The worst part was sometimes the Tibetans would be carting around homemade dynamite they use to blast rocks out of their barley fields. Once, the Tibetan seated next to him had a crate full of it in his lap, badly made, because Chad saw it sweat nitroglycerin, falling, *drip, drip, drip*, at his feet, while the bus bounced over potholes and ruts ... Exploding buses are a big problem in Tibet."

"Happily, we rented a jeep," Molly said, adding, "Are you guys being bitten by mosquitoes?"

"There are no mosquitoes," I said, looking over my arms.

But Molly, way more covered up, had whirling mosquitoes above any exposed skin, and little welts were rising.

"Except around you, it would appear," I said, pointing them out.

"I knew it," she said, "they always go for me." We laughed.

"Chad is Cree," I said, "and his tribe live in the muskeg, which is swamp with permafrost just under it. The mosquitoes are thick as thieves. You can kill ten with every slap," and I mimicked slapping my arm three times with a two-second interval between. "They have an ancient Cree method to keep them away."

"Go on, what is it?"

"They used to rub themselves with rancid bear grease."

"Do either of you have any Deet handy?" Molly asked.

AL AND SARAH HAD LEFT. NEPAL WOULD HAVE BEEN FUN WITH US three—me, Molly, and Chad—but Molly got an email in Kathmandu. Her flatmates said they were moving out, which left her in a frenzy of worry; no way could she afford the rent on a three-bedroom flat on her own. She had to rush back to the UK to find a new place to live. She booked a flight the next day. Upon stepping in the door in Green Lanes, her flatmates told her, "Actually, all is decided: we are not moving out. Why are you upset? Everything is fine."

Up in her room, she checked her email and opened a note from me, telling her that on the day she had left for the airport there was a massive street party in Kathmandu—DJs Mukul, Ankit, Sickfreak, Djital, D-rex, and B.man from London had come to help the Nepalese have a good time. The streets were thronged, and several stages for rigs were set up, one at the intersection near our hotel beside an outdoor shop selling knives and swords. The air was sweet with the smell of burning hashish, and the people danced without a concern in the world, not even the encroaching army of rebels marching on the city.

Chad and I quickly procured FIT (free individual trekker) permits for Langtang National Park. Neither of us had trekked it before. Besides, I'd just been to Everest, and Chad had heard there was lots of Maoist rebel activity in the Annapurna region at the moment, more than usual. Rumour was they had taken over the Annapurna trailhead and were taxing foreigners on top of the usual permit fees. I had already done that trail twice, so Langtang it was, and the lower passes—only 4,000 metres, not 5,000—suited our late start to the season. It was already late October, and we would not be finished until well past mid-November.

Many people, especially car-commuting urbanites, don't understand why someone would deliberately go trekking, putting one foot in front of another for the better part of each day. The problem is, they never learned how to walk: which is ironic because humans are specialized bipedal endurance hunters. That's our "thing," the way giraffes have long necks, and flipper-y penguins fly through the seas. So you don't put one foot in front of another: that's what you might do if you conceived of humans, to quote poet Russell Edson, as "teetering bulbs of dread and dream."

When trekking properly, you inhabit your body as much as your head, so you are not a bulb, nor are you teetering, so there is nothing to dread. Since you are also living in the moment, you feel alive and awake in the day, while there is plenty of time to dream while you sleep—in villages with such spectacular views and intact sense of community that it warms your heart to know that such places still grace the earth.

I had trekked through Nepal previously, with Joanna. With Chad I settled into a faster pace. A squad of young Israeli guys just out of the army couldn't keep up—except one, who was motivated to make an effort. "If I'd wanted to talk to Israelis, I would have stayed home," he explained.

When Joanna had first done the Annapurna in '95, farther west, it was also the first time she saw a mountain. She was starting with the highest in the world, and had agreed to do the trek with a crew of avid mountain climbers. Her biggest concern was that she would hold everyone back. She needn't have worried; she was the only one to finish on time. The men had been training by climbing Alaskan mountains when they should have been training by eating out of garbage bins. It was their stomachs that failed them. Joanna was accustomed to living on Asian street food.

She had been impressed by the way I could point to some of the fastest, fittest trekkers and say, "That guy, and that guy." And sure enough, a couple of days later we'd pass them with wrappings on their knees, limping, and a newly hired porter carrying their packs. I knew they would be in trouble because they were putting one foot in front of another, and taking the impact of walking with their nice bouncy tendons, instead of absorbing it with the meat on their bones, no matter how sore. Muscle regenerates at night, tendons and ligaments do not.

A Warner Brothers cartoon illustrates it best. A couple of hillbillies are being fooled by Bugs Bunny, who has them acting out the ill-advised instructions of a square dance. When I saw it, I thought, The cartoonist knew mountain men. They're bent at the knee, centre of gravity low, almost like they're crouching, with legs splayed to the side, and these legs find their own purchase. Your body feels the terrain that way, while your eyes look ahead, soaking up knowledge of the route, and your feet run patterns that feed from the memory, as if it were sheet music you see, that your body sublimates directly into a sort of dance. This way of trekking frees you from the mud, rocks, and slippery fears so you can enjoy the butterflies, conversations, and views.

Chad and I crossed gleaming snowfields, and passed frozen lakes and villages so picturesque we felt envy for the crones peering out from their cottages, since they had seized a lifetime in such a place. We saw, where warmth allowed, shrubs and trees and busy little animals, also making their way while the sun was shining. After dark and jokes and beers by the guesthouse's fireplace, I enjoyed invigorating sleeps, with dreams in vibrant colour, once sleeping through a minute-long earthquake that woke Chad. For me, it was only my dreamscape that shook.

You could welcome many lifetimes' worth of views in Langtang, watching the seasons shift and the play of the light, the moods of the weather. The mountains are so big that they leave no place for personas to plump up, as in cities, where faces loom and shade one another: one-upping, ego-buffeted, shouting out, Oh, the humanity. Instead, mountains extend down, to their ridge's roots, and also reach high, above patient canyon-cutting rivers; they show men legging it and resting, each true to size: minuscule. Life-sized. You sit with your friend and joke and talk about this and that, but inside you are also laughing because we are so small on the face of the earth that it's impossible to take your own self seriously. People are fairly ridiculous, and that's an extra something to smile about.

We had to take a bus back to Kathmandu, and Chad was folded up like a pretzel in his seat. He used to sedate himself with alcohol for such buses, but none was at hand. As we passed into the urban encrustation, glimpsing from the window crunchy layer upon layer of stacked concrete, where each tenant family's life between two slabs was demarcated with curtains of red brick, a young woman tried to fling herself under the bus. She was so violent in her effort to cast herself into oblivion that she overshot, and the wheels passed on either side of her prone body. The look on her face stuck with me, and I thought, Perhaps she can't endure another day in this slum. But then I realized that she was not like me; she saw no slum. She was born to this. Perhaps this sad matter was something to do with love and loss.

IN KATHMANDU, AFTER OUR TRADITIONAL STOP FOR WATER BUFFALO at the Everest Steak House, Chad told me he was off to India, to the western state of Goa.

"That's a long way," I said.

"Not by plane. Why don't you join me? I'll email you with my hotel details once I get there."

Some shopping detained me. I needed to get something to send to Tim in London for his birthday. (He eventually opened the package in front of a huge crowd in a bar. One problem: who would have thought massive Gurkha knives, with blood-dripper just above the tang, are illegal in the UK?) Anyhow, I thought about it while I shopped, and decided to go to Goa.

Since those Maoist guerrillas had surrounded Kathmandu and demanded the overthrow of the government, there was an unusual rush of people at the embassies applying for visas so they could flee. Chad had his Indian visa from Vancouver, so off he went. I was still waiting on mine, and waiting. His taunting email arrived, alluding to an imminent beach party on Anjuna, and tasty fish curry. So I slipped the guy in the Indian high commission an extra hundred bucks, walked out with the visa, and booked a flight to Goa for the following morning.

I awoke to cold smog from mist and burnt coal, and a series of annoyances: my belly was bad, unusual for me, and the taxi driver tried to cheat me. Then when the plane made a stopover in Delhi, the Indian authorities kept me in a holding room over a four-hour wait for the connector. What to do for four hours? There were two magazine-vending machines side by side in the centre of the room. The contents were probably all Bollywood trash magazines written in Hindi, but it was worth a look, and my eyes spotted an English-language magazine, *Scientific American*, inexplicably in stock. Checking my change, I found I had just enough, but not the necessary denominations. I asked the men at three kiosks serving the room if they might help me make change, but all refused. Hmph. I crouched with my back against the wall and waited.

Then a slender, somewhat prim man arrived, set up a small table, and unfolded a chair. Before plunking himself down, he balanced a sign on the tabletop: *Make change here to use the vending machine*. I strode over and pulled out my money, and he took out a tray of coins, about to make the conversion, until he noticed the direction of my gaze.

"Oh, no, mister. I see you are looking to buy a magazine from the vending machine on the right, while I am only here to provide change for people who want to use the vending machine on the left."

"But those are all written in Hindi," I said.

He was unmoved, and no rhetoric on my part could shift him from his principled position. I returned to my section of wall and crouched there for another three and a half hours, until my flight started boarding.

Another short security check turned up the lighter in my pocket. Though a non-smoker, I'd carried this same Colt lighter practically forever, taking it out whenever a campfire was needed or if someone asked me for a light. Normally it's not possible to keep a lighter any length of time, since every other person who asks to borrow it will pocket it and walk off. I would always tell them, Don't walk off with my lighter. I've had it a year, or two years, or three. The last guy who asked to use it heard me say, "This same lighter has been with me for thirteen years, so you get that back to me."

"New rule," said the security guy as he tossed it into the trash. "No lighters allowed on planes."

IN GOA AT LAST, I CHECKED EMAIL TO SEE WHERE CHAD WAS STAYING: hmm, no reply to my last email asking for hotel details. He had read my message telling him I was flying in that day, so I figured he must be having a good time and had forgotten to send me a note on his whereabouts.

Goa is not a big state, but it is still a big place, and I'd only spent one week there more than a decade earlier. My best guess was that Chad would be in a beach town, Arambol, and the cheapest way to get there was on a jam-packed standing-room-only local bus. My idea was to check email again once I was there. If his hotel was at another nearby beach, there might be time to shift. In Arambol, a search revealed an internet café among the shops and markets: again, no reply.

It was now dark, and my only wish was for a bed and for this string of annoyances to end. A boy asked me if I wanted to have a room in the Ganesh hotel on the cliffs; the price was good, and so was the location—as promised, on the cliffs, and with a blue Ganesh painted on the wall. I flopped down and slept, waking early to the sound of a guitar on the balcony of the room next to mine. They were familiar tunes, the songs Chad typically played.

I popped my head out the window, saying to him, "Good morning, neighbour."

On the Goan beaches I struggled with a series of debilitating illnesses—a cold, then a terrible stomach, then another cold that caused me to lose my voice. I made the best of it, as anyone would do under the circumstances, by roaming the tidal muck, examining dead sea snakes (striped yellow and black, like wasps) and the sun-dried fishes. Luckily my health returned for the one party that was thrown on Anjuna beach. I had fun despite taking it easy, and Chad went skinny-dipping in the ocean while the party was in full swing on the beach around him. Otherwise he kept busy swimming back and forth along the shore each morning. After a few days he left to motorbike around Sri Lanka, looking for surf breaks, and I stayed behind with Bryn and Vicky, a couple from Manchester we had been hanging out with. Soon they'd also had their fun in Goa and hopped on a train north to Mumbai. I accompanied them. I had remembered that Barbara was about to arrive in that very city, on December 9. I'd be rolling in on the 8th. She was surprised to see me, and I explained that I just happened to be in the neighbourhood, so I could travel with her for a few days if she'd like.

While waiting to hop on another train back south on my last night in Mumbai, I was in Leopold Café. A trendy expat hangout, it was established in 1871, but the interior is art deco, so it must have had a major reno at some point. It's also noisy and crowded. I saw a guy signing a book for someone at the table just behind me. He was blond and grinning, with long hair and gold chains hung over an unbuttoned white shirt and tanned chest. Seemed like an interesting character, so I made my way through the crowd to see what book he was signing. *Shantaram*. So this must be Greg. We had a chat, and I mentioned how my friend Molly had been enjoying his book but then lost it in Tibet before she could finish the last few chapters. He had some extra for sale, so I bought one, and he signed it with a kind note to Molly. I sent it off to London before taking the train to Kerala.

This was not my first trip to the south of India, and at first I didn't think I'd learn much that was new. In recent history the area had been a battleground for conflicting French and English imperialism. Now, a point of national pride, it was a centre of India's world-class software industry. By mid-December I'd made my way to an old favourite, Mamallapuram, in the southeast. This is where they work in hard stone to make statuary for Hindu temples, among other things. I found that the damage from the 2004 Indian Ocean tsunami wasn't as bad as it could have been—only two deaths—as the wave struck in the early morning before anyone was on the beach.

Soon I had taken a train over to Trivandrum, relaxing for a few days while wondering where to spend Christmas. I noticed a tower along a main road in the centre of town—a round tower like you might see on a castle. My first thought was that it could be a restaurant, but then a whole bunch of nuns came out of the opening at the base that served as the entrance. I went in anyway. The entire inside of the tower is a smooth spiral passage winding up and around and around, lined with red- and black-granite benches that were built into the ramp-like floor, each of them abutting the inside of the tower's round outer wall—a wall pierced with geometric holes that served as windows for light and breezes.

There was no kitchen anywhere in sight, but mustachioed waiters with matching turbans swirled up and down that singular passage with trays of curries and fruit juices. This was a cool place to sit and think. I couldn't spend Christmas here because—at the risk of sounding nauseatingly over-travelled—I'd done Christmas in Trivandrum before, back in '96. I took a tuk-tuk to a travel agent and booked a flight to the Maldives, passing through Colombo, Sri Lanka, on my way out.

Security in Colombo was still ultra-tight because of the threat from Tamil Tiger suicide squads, and the airport was a shock to me—it was big, brand new, and sparkling clean. The last time I had been in Sri Lanka, the airport was a giant dusty warehouse, like something you might scout for a squat party. It was surrounded by barbed wire and soldiers behind sandbag walls. There were gaping holes in the corrugated iron roof, and birds were flapping around inside the terminal. Now it was transformed, from being worse than Kathmandu airport to nicer than an English terminal. One of the original employees must have kept his job; he followed me around, watching for signs of a detour to use the urinal so he could crowd in and help with water and tissue towels, angling for a tip. I spent a comical half hour evading him before using the loo just in time for my flight.

Maldives customs were a bit of a pain. The sight of a single male backpacker getting off the plane was so unusual that they questioned me, and when they found that I intended to stay in the city rather than on a resort, they searched my backpack for drugs. They had a sniffer-dog but decided to do it by hand.

Maldives was laughably unsuitable for me. I found it had become one of those Islamic republics where alcohol is banned—you can't even bring it in from the duty-free. The country consists of a central island city of 80,000 people, where there's no drinking or bars or nightlife or, indeed, anything contrary to religion. The other islands are exclusive resorts—one to each island—with leases from the government. These are all ultra-expensive, $300 or more a night. Drinks are served at the resorts, but aside from the off-putting cost, they all cater to couples and honeymoons and such. So here I was in a nation whose economy is devoted to providing romantic seclusion for married people and lovers.

The main island is flat, sandy, and barely above sea level, entirely occupied by the city of Malé, with low buildings laid out in a grid. It's obvious from even an hour of wandering that no tourists alight here. I discovered later that they go straight from the airport to speedboats that whisk them away to whichever private atoll their five-star resort has claimed. It took me an hour to find a hotel, and there was nothing to do and no time to eat, so I slept instead. The following morning, crowds were drawn by the call to prayer. The city was mine to quietly explore.

Boatloads of sleek silvery tuna were being unloaded at a dock; huge blue-and-green parrotfish surfed in the breakers where the buildings met the sea, magnified to comical sizes by the bellying lenses of wave water; girls in black hijabs played volleyball on a sweltering beach. There were no restaurants open anywhere, reminding me that this was Friday in a city that, despite being the capital and the only city of a country that relies on tourism, never gets any tourists. After a few hours, still before noon, I returned to watch the tuna boats. Inside a building on a concrete floor they were sized and displayed for market. While I admired them, a local guy struck up a conversation with me. When I mentioned the complete lack of anywhere to eat, he led me to the only place open on Friday: upstairs above the market they sell Friday fish soup.

We found seats and sat around talking for some hours. He was trying to open a resort hotel and was very open about the process. He had completed stage one: his consortium had raised $10 million, packed it in a briefcase, and sent him in.

"Is this to make the hotel or buy the atoll to put it on?" I asked.

"Neither. Anyway, the atoll is free to anyone willing to invest in a resort. You schedule a meeting with the official in charge, then you slide the cash over to him and he counts it. Then, if he sees it is all there, he tells you that you are in consideration for being gifted the use of an atoll. Then you wait while they decide which one. That's what I'm doing now, waiting."

I laughed and said, "I wondered how the president of this tiny country could afford one of the most expensive yachts in the world. I suppose the $10 million is divided among the president and his cronies?"

"Exactly, but there is lots of money to be made here, as you can recover your investment in four years of operation if all goes well, and after that it's all profit. The economy here is all about these resorts. The tuna fishing is really small business."

"They weren't too happy when I told them I wasn't going to a resort. They had everything out of my pack for a search."

"Did you notice the dog in a cage?"

"Yes."

"That's our nation's new drug-sniffing dog. It cost about 40,000 dollars to train it. There were drugs being smuggled in, and the police suspected it was the tourists going to the resorts who were bringing them. But when they set the dog to work at the airport on the tourists' bags, clean. Then a private jet full of government ministers happened to land. The dog 'indicated' as the ministers walked by with their special passports that allow them to avoid searches. The ministers weren't searched or questioned—the dog was declared by them to be 'crazy,' and it's been locked up in a tiny cage at the airport ever since."

I asked him about all the Islamic dress I'd seen around. What did these people think of tourists in bikinis at the resorts?

Everyone becoming so pious is a new trend, he said. It wasn't like that when he was young. He thought it might be Saudi influence, but he wasn't sure. He added it was lucky they didn't see all that went on at the atolls, though the workers there must have plenty to gossip about.

Still, there are no guarantees that you will make money out of a resort. I don't begrudge resort owners in Maldives making a handsome profit if they can. It's a risky business in a way an investment elsewhere is not. The problem is what could be called your social licence to operate. This is something that's hard to quantify, but a Gurkha who opens a guesthouse in his home village in the Himalayas when he retires from the British army has it. A bunch of foreigners who were forced to slip $10 million under the table to a dictator do not.

This is apart from the extra risk of trying to run an operation catering to the super-rich in a foreign land. In Churchill, Manitoba, they have armoured buggies with giant wheels that go out roaming in search of a polar bear experience. Imagine if you were a tour company in the UK and decided to run similar vehicles, but for clientele who were Arab sheiks at a rave or the Glastonbury music festival, while someone with a megaphone gave a lecture on the cultural significance of this or that. You have to be careful how and what you market in all circumstances. This is why Nepalese tourism is more resilient than the Maldives version. No matter if Maoists take the capital; the tourists will keep coming, and everything will run as normal. In Maldives, after a change of government, you could find yourself unpopular with the locals whose former dictator you were forced to fund, and you have no convincing papers to show you paid for the privilege of taking over one of the nation's atolls.

There wasn't much to keep me here, so I booked a seat on the Christmas Eve red-eye out of Maldives, and arrived in Bangkok on Christmas morning. Without bothering to sleep or even shave, I went out drinking on Khao San Road. Boxing Day morning I was still drinking—onto the second night of missed sleep—and got kicked out of the bar for snogging a pretty English girl from Brighton. We went back to my room to fool around, and she couldn't believe what a grimy backpacker dive I was staying in. I explained that I'd always stayed here, it wasn't so bad.

"But there are places now with a pool and new furniture and a TV," she said.

The receptionist, a Karen refugee known only half-jokingly as "servant to boss" who had been there when I used to frequent the hotel in the '90s, recognized me when I checked in. He looked much older now on account of grey bags under his eyes. Asian megacities will do that to you, with the greasy air, din of noise, and unrelenting stress.

It seemed like it had been ages since my last trip to Haad Rin, so I went over for the New Year's party in 2006, for old time's sake more than anything. As the party began, everyone was gathering on the beach, in the darkness. The waves were lapping against the sinuous little dunes and ripples of sand. Funny, that dune was just a little too sinuous—what could it be?

Most people are so unobservant. Here, midway along the beach, I could have asked my fellow party-goers, "Guess how many gigantic 12-foot-long pythons slithered past while you were standing here?" And they would have said "None" and been wrong. I touched the python; it had such soft skin, and I did then point it out to a few tourists, but not to any locals out of fear they'd kill it.

The next morning I checked email and saw that Chad had finished surfing Sri Lanka and was now also in Thailand, stopping in for the wedding of one of his friends, a mathematics professor from UBC who was marrying a Thai woman, also a professor. He'd dressed in traditional Thai style for the wedding and was now on the islands in Koh Lanta. I joined him there; not so exciting a place, but fine for a rest. We went out on a speedboat with twin 200 hp engines for some snorkelling at a national marine park: Chad was trying to improve his free diving by going down to the bottom to look for turtles. Thai food is superb, of course, and I took the time to branch out and try more than the soups, curries, and green papaya salad, though plenty of these were had as well. At the beach bar we gave our livers a workout with the local whisky, though the service was glum. Our waiter had worked serving drinks for ten years, his life on hold so he could save all his money to start his own beach bar. The week after his grand opening, the 2004 tsunami had washed away the whole shebang, and he was back to serving drinks for tips.

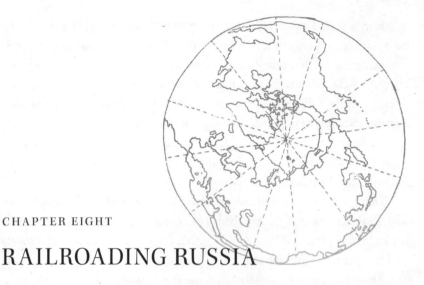

CHAPTER EIGHT

RAILROADING RUSSIA

Russia · Siberia

ROM THAILAND, CHAD AND I BOTH RETURNED TO CANADA in the opening weeks of 2006. He went to Vancouver, and my destination was the Kootenays. I went there, in the dead of winter, to reconnect with my Doukhobor friend Ken, who wanted to talk to me about a Russian trip he was planning. He was going to take the Trans-Siberian from Moscow to Vladivostok, boarding the train in the Baltic for the extra Saint Petersburg leg, and stopping along the way to see the highlights in between. I wanted in on this trip, of course, and after sixty hours of non-stop travel—starting under a beach umbrella in Koh Lanta and enlisting two tuk-tuks, three boats of increasing size, and two long bus rides sandwiching an even longer flight—I called him from a freezing payphone in the bus depot in Castlegar, jet-lagged and exhausted.

Ken was also planning a surprise party for me. A surprise party can be an anxious thing for a host, because he can't be certain how it will go: either the party is indeed a surprise, or the guest of honour finds out and you make do. But the host usually doesn't anticipate a party being a *double* surprise. I'll explain: about twenty people showed for it, despite a snow warning being issued, and I was duly surprised when they all yelled "Surprise!" Later I said, "This is great, my first surprise party, but what's the occasion?" And they said, "It's your birthday." And so it was, for my second surprise of the evening.

There were a couple of feet of snow outside, and all the trees were white with their boughs laden down. It looked fantastic. Perfect for walks in the snow and binge-reading all the dozens of new books Ken had bought since my last visit.

After that, I bussed east through the Rockies to Alberta and stopped in to see nieces and nephews. It's important to visit as much as practical, or I would find I had seen the world only to return and have them say, "Who is this Uncle Mike stranger?" In Canmore, my three-year-old nephew Andrew had a ski lesson: they start them early out there.

I got an email from Molly: she had a room to let in her flat. Did I want it for a while? Sure, I wrote back. It was getting to be spring in England while it was still winter here in Canada. Better to wait over there for Russia to warm up, and for Ken to make preparations. He would surely be ready soon, or so I thought. I had no idea I'd spend half the summer in Europe again, waiting. It was fun, but Europe was getting familiar to me, and it felt like I was killing time—which I suppose was true.

I couldn't shake the feeling that times had changed. I had never had to wait so long for someone to agree to or suggest some travels. It was as if everyone favoured careers now, or was starting families: they talked about travel as if it were a species of guilty pleasure. Even Molly. Although she asked me to tell her the dates for our trans-Siberia journey once Ken was ready, since she might want to drop in for the Moscow-to-Vladivostok leg, just one month of it, she sounded as guilty as the rest, as if she had more important things to do.

ONE OF THE HIGHLIGHTS OF THE WORLD IS RIDING THE RAILS FROM Saint Petersburg on the Baltic Sea to Vladivostok on the Pacific Ocean. I started in Saint Petersburg with Ken, who was eager to explore his Doukhobor heritage. Molly showed up in time for the actual Trans-Siberian train trip, meeting us in Moscow. She had fond memories of Russia from a school trip her parents had carefully budgeted to send her on as a sixteen-year-old. She dabbled in secret smoking back then, like all the London girls, so she stepped out from the home of her host family to have a puff. A passing soldier grabbed one of her arms and started hauling her away; the host family's babushka (granny) rushed out and grabbed her other arm, so that she was pulled back and forth in a tug-o-war between the two. In Russia back then, girls who smoked in the street were invariably prostitutes. Her parents were wise to sacrifice so they could afford to send her on that trip, and it goes to show the value of cultural exchanges to youth: these are experiences you just can't get in a London middle school.

We did our trip in stages, frequently getting off the train to explore the countryside and cities, riding with the Buryat horse tribe of Lake Baikal, the deepest and oldest lake in the world, with a fifth of the globe's fresh water; indulging in the ubiquitous vodka swilling on the train; and visiting the Yakuts, nomadic herders near the Arctic Circle, where a Yakut man taught me how to drive a reindeer sleigh out for some ice fishing. This 9,000-kilometre train ride is best experienced over many months, three in my case. A spare month at the end was spent largely in Russian bars.

My next stop was in London, to couch surf at Molly's newly rented flat, and a good thing too. I felt so ill that my legs could scarcely pry me up from her sofa. I wasn't sick so much as aching everywhere, and I admitted to a bit too much drinking.

"A bit too much drinking? You think?" Molly said.

Russia had been the exception that proves the rule: my usual suspects weren't travelling anymore, having aged out of it. And I had some thinking to do, thinking while on the move. After so long accustomed to travel, moving was now my default state. Remaining in one place required precious willpower, which I couldn't seem to muster.

All I knew for sure was that my hub-and-spoke, friend-centric travel style was starting to show its limitations. Its advantage is that the hub becomes like a little home, and a place to recover. Also, when the hub is in Europe or Indochina, I am sitting in the midst of choice adjacent destinations for my friends, and I need only dally some days or a week: one or more of them will head out for a trip; we'll meet up, wander, and enjoy adventures; then, typically, I return to the hub city to visa-up and do some banking and communication. Also, I had travelling girlfriends whose biological clocks had not yet started ringing, eager to squeeze in experiences before looking to settle down and start families. The hub-and-spoke style worked best when there were vast regions to explore, a seamless Earth spread out in front of me. It relied on my carrying cash, in a balance of major currencies, and choosing a likely megacity in which to forage for visas.

It worked like a charm for over a decade and then some. But as I learned in 2006, there is a typical age for travelling. Even devoted travellers tend to do most of their exploring early in their lives. They drop out of it, or only dabble, through the primes of their lives, which are devoted to marriage and kids and career. Then I would see examples of how they picked it up again after retirement or when the kids left school. The patterns in Australia had been particularly stark—kids backpacking and older retired folks with rented vehicles on road trips.

Once they were pushing forty, my usual travel mates switched priorities: no more six-month "trips of a lifetime." They could get only a few weeks off work, and this meant returning to familiar areas so they could make the most of their short time by hitting the ground running—and avoiding the risk of disappointment on such a short stay by forgoing visits to unfamiliar places. Their trips had to serve double duty as vacations from stressful careers.

Settling down in the manner of my friends was impossible for me: my minimum standard of living was having one adventure after another, a World Heritage Site or other magnificent place around every corner, and a life without tedium. This lifestyle was a dream come true, and well worth the calculated risks that came with defending my bag of cash, traversing war zones, doing small-scale business in items like semi-precious stones or carved wooden statuettes of chickens, and accepting local, or lower, rather than Western, standards of comfort.

And yet even my pace was slowing, though not because of age. My hub-and-spoke travel style was becoming not fit for its purpose, especially as my coverage approached half the globe, and it was increasingly harder to find "blue sky" zones: clusters of unfamiliar and thus excitingly new countries to experience near my hubs in Europe and Indochina. In hindsight, for example, there was no advantage to going to Europe in preparation for my trip to Russia with Ken: Vladivostok was as easy to access from Vancouver as Saint Petersburg was from London, so what had been the point in spending time in London waiting for him?

There was one indispensable hub, Canada, to keep me supplied with fresh passports. Even those passports with forty-eight pages don't suffice for heavy travel; I could blow through one of them in a couple of years. This was the case in 2007, when I found a cheap flight to take me across the Atlantic from Europe. First thing back in Canada, I sailed with my dad to Brimstone Head in Newfoundland, one of the four corners of the earth according to the Flat Earth Society of Canada. Then a flight carried me west to Alberta, and I stopped in to see both brothers and get family news. While hiking and having a good chat in the snow behind my older brother's backyard, I met a mighty bighorn sheep ram, with spiral curved horns, and his harem; they were scraping snow away with their hooves to get at the dried grass beneath.

Thereafter, my spare time, and much of my time that couldn't be spared, was spent struggling with an unusual problem, a first for Canada. My passport was nearly full, but President Bush the Second had decided that now Canadians would need to show a passport to visit the United States. There was a 300,000-passport backlog at the office, as casual Canadian travellers suddenly realized they'd better get a passport for the first time. This had me skittering between Alberta and British Columbia, trying to figure out a way to get to the front of the passport queue. The arms of this federal bureaucracy were particularly alien and divergent. I had better luck with a Pacific octopus I found stranded on the sands of

Boundary Bay, bedevilled by gulls, which turned red and then purple while I carried it to a deeper tidal pool, its suckers gripping my arms.

By mid-March, drastic action was in order. I reasoned that the many diplomats and government officials in Ottawa must have a workaround for this problem. And they did: I could take my documents in to the passport office near the Parliament Buildings, and they would have it ready for me in a few days, neatly avoiding the massive backlog. My picture in it looked as alien as a Pacific octopus, all red and purple and blotchy. The machines must have been running hot from round-the-clock use. Anyhow, a fresh passport meant a spell of interrogation-free travel until it began to fill up again with exotic stamps.

This virgin passport needed to be broken in, so I flew from Montreal over to London, where Ken had returned after a full-on extended experience in Russia. He had just fallen for a lovely English girl named Sally, Tim's sister as a matter of fact—they make a great couple, as she's pretty and smart with a personality that complements Ken's. We were happy for Ken; he had met the woman he was to marry.

Molly, meanwhile, was struggling to make progress on publishing a photography book, *Out of Order*, with a selection of the shots she had taken of the underground party scene. These parties meant so much to her, and she had thousands of photos to sift through so she could choose, prepare, and develop the ones for the book, as well as all sorts of work I can't even begin to describe. She spent some days telling me how the party scene used to be something new for the misfits and the more artistic people. It sounds corny, but Molly believed that if all people were like the party people, societies would have limited need for police. She had to take leave of mere travel-for-the-sake-of-travel until she completed this project.

Molly and I furnished one another with the best advice we could. Molly had been agonizing over whether to move to Bristol for the next year. She wouldn't see a whole whack of her friends nearly as much, but she had a younger group of friends in that city who were still deeply involved in the party scene. If she was going to document this moment in social history, she had to be there. I told her to move, even though it meant I'd seldom see her anymore, as I would only be making very short stops in London from then on. Europe was finished in terms of major trips.

As for me, it wasn't clear where I should go next. Having seen a little more than half the world in sixteen years, I struggled to envision travelling like this for that many years again without going barking mad. At that point, a lot of my friends and my brothers would be seeing their kids off to university, and while they were paying off their mortgages as they prepared to retire, I'd be checking out of my last hostel, with no marketable skills and no employment record, and probably laced with dozens of tropical diseases, some of which were yet to be named.

Molly's advice to me: "Go travelling, and the answer will come to you" and "You won't be satisfied unless you finish what you started."

THIS WAS TIME TO TAKE STOCK OF MY PROGRESS. WHEN FACEBOOK first started out, software developers came up with some apps that tried to take advantage of the "wall," where they would jostle for space and try to keep front and centre. The big idea was that these apps would use the wall as a means to muscle their way to dominance, turning Facebook into a dumb pipe and leaving the app triumphant. Facebook administrators eventually clued in to what they were doing and shut them out, but back then, one of these programs, amateur and buggy, allowed travellers to fill in a map of the countries they'd visited. I duly filled in my countries and had a look.

My coverage was impressive: I would likely be the most travelled guy in any small city I entered—well travelled, but not to the point of being a freak of nature. On my map, the east-west axis of Eurasia was well represented, and also North and Central America down to Panama, and Australia, but I hadn't touched on Antarctica or South America, and I'd done enough of Africa to know that, because of the size, poor infrastructure, and problem countries, I'd need at least three or four more years of gruelling travel, lethal disease, and exhaustion—hard core years—to finish it. South America and Africa are north-south axis, so climate comes into the picture in a big way, necessitating extra communication that would make Facebook a handy tool.

The idea that any of my usual travel friends would be up for this was laughable, and the notion that it was possible to base this effort out of London or India or one of my Indo-Chinese megacity hubs was equally absurd. I needed to invent a new way to travel and take it up a notch to have any hope of seeing the world. Banking would be a problem; many of the destinations that interested me now had shockingly high rates of robbery with pistols, more than a match for my knife. And without a hub to store my bag of cash at, I'd have to run off bank cards and credit cards. This made me uncomfortable. I'd seen some Europeans and Americans get away with it, but they were doing the usual countries. There was no way to test beforehand whether cards might work in the kind of countries ahead of me. With my own eyes I had seen card-based travel attempts result in some epic fails, particularly for Canadians, whose cards often failed to work for no obvious reason.

PARTIES WITH MY EUROPEAN FRIENDS DELAYED ME UNTIL THE weather got colder, and then a flight dropped me in Vancouver by mid-November 2007. Hours after arrival, walking on the Boundary Bay beach near my mom's house, I saw something like Stonehenge and drew close to have a look at what appeared to be the bombed-out ruins of a fortress overgrown with ivy, giant beams of twisted iron thrusting up from a collapsed roof, and scores of soldiers and robots trudging around in the vicinity. Weird: I'd been away longer than planned, but hadn't expected civilization to collapse in my absence. Then I noticed all the cameras, and row upon row of tractor-trailers, and got out of there. *Battlestar Galactica* was being filmed. Security had the paths blocked but hadn't anticipated anyone coming from the beach.

While I walked the beach, I had ample time to think about what to do next. To see the world in one lifetime to my satisfaction (a much longer task than merely visiting all the countries), I'd need to leave my comfort zone of hubs and travel mates. It was pretty clear I needed to travel for seven more years non-stop. And all solo. Also, I'd have to do it all freestyle: not just the countries, but the entire series of trips.

Then came an amazing surprise that decided the matter: Jim and Sharon, my stepdad and mom, bought me a ticket for the adventure tour that was the best way to do Antarctica. They told me they'd used the money that would have gone toward my house and wedding and helping with my kids, as they had done with my brothers. Any wistful thoughts of salvaging a normal life were dismissed. My assets, already liquid, were adjusted to be even more liquid, to accommodate spending at a rate much higher than any investment income—a burn rate that, toward the end, finished off the business float that had allowed me to take advantage of opportunities to pay my way. This burn rate would leave me with empty pockets at the end, but rich in experiences.

The trip to reconnect with Canadian family and friends had been exhausting but rewarding, because I knew I wouldn't be seeing nearly as much of them in the years to come. This was a big change for me. I'd become attached to the idea of shared experiences with close friends in foreign lands, as it provided structure for my helter-skelter existence. But subconsciously, as I've mentioned, it was clear to me that it was late summer for this kind of travel rooted in hubs and spokes with friends, and the Eurasian patchwork of destinations was losing its freshness. If there was to be any hope of seeing the world in a single lifetime, I would need to float free as dandelion fluff.

There is an expression in the Bahasa language that Joanna used to use, *Io chaboot*. When she said it once in Kuala Lumpur, these sophisticated Malays laughed.

"Where did you learn that?" they asked.

"From my villager friends," she said.

"You sound like a hillbilly. It means 'let's go' but, literally, 'pull up roots.'"

I was ready to *Io chaboot*. But first I stopped in at Mountain Equipment Co-op to buy clothes for Antarctica. Then I flew to Calgary to visit an old friend, Bruce, whom I hadn't seen in years but had found through Facebook. His brother Stewart and I had been inseparable in high school and earlier, and I'd been the best man at Stewart's wedding to his wife Jennifer, but I'd lost touch in the days before email and Facebook, and Stewart had died, with me missing the funeral.

Bruce was successful in business, founding a stock photo company called iStock. An assistant picked me up at the airport and conveyed me in style to one of his five houses spread from here to Berlin. This one was full of funky Chinese antiques and cool artwork, and was on a ridge with a panoramic view of the skyscrapers—where Calgary would have situated its castle if it had been a European city. Bruce said he only used it for parties a few times a year. He looked just as I remembered him, except he had a wide black armband tattooed onto one arm in tribute to his brother Stewart, and a mermaid tattooed up a forearm.

When he heard that I'd left my Nokia in London, he gave me a phone to use for the weekend, encrusted in black jewels with a crystal skull and crossbones on the back. Then we went to the iStock Christmas party, which was set up like a casino but with a buffet. Later, in the carpark, the crystal skull phone beeped once, with what I thought was a text for him. When I showed it to him, he cracked a smile. He had set it to beep when a stock he had bought at $70 had reached $200. I asked him how much he owned, and he said he'd bought $3 million of it.

"I guess you're buying the beers tonight," I said.

We drank a dozen beers each and chatted about old times. We'd gone to school in a neighbourhood that was on the outskirts of the city at the time. Of course, neither of us had any idea what we wanted to do when we grew up, nor do I remember either of us voicing a desire to become richer than a comic-book super-villain. He showed me a website he'd made that had been voted very cool; he used it to showcase new bands. He had an interesting lifestyle, partying with A-list celebrities in Los Angeles and hanging out with smart tech-sector entrepreneurs—a very different path in life to my own.

I was turning south to start my seven-year non-stop trip, beginning in Antarctica, but with Bruce's business trips to megacities and houses everywhere—and maybe a secret volcano lair too, I suspected—and me criss-crossing the globe, I was certain I had not seen the last of him.

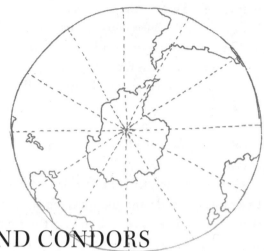

CHAPTER NINE

PENGUINS AND CONDORS

Uruguay · Paraguay · Peru · Chile ·
Bolivia · Argentina · Antarctica

THIS JOURNEY TO THE POLAR SOUTH WAS THE FIRST LEG OF a burst of sustained travel that my younger self would not have credited. In my early years I would feel loose around the joints of my mind and need to cool my heels after just six to eight months. But now, every instinct told me Go. I'd pored over maps of the world; two of these maps, of Africa and South America, would absorb many years' worth of scrutiny, outright frustration, and sometimes little triumphs when impossible routes and borders yielded to persistence or luck or improvised tactics. I was sorry to see those maps go after they crumbled beyond repair.

I had been doing things ass-backward. Typically, people start to travel with travel buddies; then they gradually move over to more travel with girlfriends. Then they stop and settle down, often with the girl they travelled with—the travel was a test to see how they were together. For me it was travel as couples first, then I began travelling more with buddies and far less with girlfriends. But maybe asses are supposed to be backward, because finally, instead of settling down, I was embarking on a stint of travel that would draw on all my previous experience, and needed my full package of skills to contemplate and, if fortune smiled on me, complete. This journey to Antarctica would give my new freestyling, Facebooking, and bank-card-based minimalist travel a hectic summer of chasing the sun.

People call it a trip of a lifetime when you do a six-monther. Well, I went beast-mode and did fourteen trips of a lifetime back to back, scratching a seven-year itch to give the remaining half of our planet the once-over.

The South American continent was my destination. It would all be new to me, and the trip to Antarctica was set to go in late January. I opened with a trip to Cuba, hanging out at a resort with family members for a couple of weeks, and then touring the island with a happy-go-lucky Brit named Antony. He joined me again a couple of weeks later in Panama for a bit more fun, after which I boarded a flight to Ushuaia, a small city in Argentina, at the southernmost tip of Cape Horn, where the ships leave for Antarctica, less than 700 kilometres farther south. Ushuaia is also one of the southernmost inhabited places on earth, some other contenders being Cape Town near the Cape of Good Hope in Africa; Tasmania; and South Island, New Zealand. Now I'd been to them all, and in less than a week I was to board a ship to cruise the Southern Ocean. Snow began to fall in what was locally high summer, and the sky remained bright until ten o'clock at night.

By January 8 I was just finishing a run of bad luck. First, a couple of days earlier, the other three people in the bunks in my dorm room at the hostel had cranked the heat, leaving me sweating and barely able to sleep. They were from Brazil and were trying to replicate the Amazon rainforest conditions they were used to at home. I was glad when they left, until discovering that my new dorm mates were three Dutchmen, who were just back from sailing around Antarctica for a month in ferocious cold and storms; they kept the heat off and the window open, freezing my ass for two nights. As compensation, I chatted up a pretty backpacker girl I'd met in a restaurant and took her out to the bar. Afterward we kissed, and she said she wanted to see me the next evening at eight o'clock at the Dublin, an Irish pub. I was there, but she was not.

I had to hang around Ushuaia, as my ship didn't leave till the 14th. I found a squad of Israelis with whom to pass the time when not hiking or visiting Mount Darwin or doing any of the many fun things there are to do in the south. They all deferred to one of their group, who worked for Mossad, the secret service. He'd been in Iraq too; he didn't bribe his way in like me, as his unit was even less fussed about border formalities. He told an amusing story of setting out electronic surveillance of an Iraqi base. While installing their devices, they discovered the place was already being surveilled. The equipment was the latest American stuff, technology that the Americans hadn't shared with them. They scooped it all and carried it back to Israel for reverse engineering.

There's not much variety of restaurants in Ushuaia, but most days I'd go to a place on the main drag called the Banana Bar. Its logo was an anthropomorphized banana that somehow managed to look degenerate—a smoke in one hand, a whisky in the other, and a sallow face with the red-rimmed eyes of an opium addict, brooding under the brim of a black hat.

I'D LONG BEEN FOND OF TALES OF THE GOLDEN AGE OF SAIL, AN AGE of wooden ships and explorers. And an age not long passed. Ships such as these carried my Scottish ancestors to New Brunswick and supported my British grandfather, captain of a Banks schooner from his seventeenth year, off Labrador trapping cod. My father remembers caulking those 120-foot hulls and spreading the fish on the sapling-wrought flakes to dry. This family tradition ended with me, alas: the exacting model of a dory, made for me by my grandfather to begin my education in naval carpentry, sits dusty on a garage shelf near Boundary Bay, south of Vancouver.

But it was a heroic age, when the Scottish people scattered to distant shores, borne like thistle fluff in the wind. And of all the fantastic reaches conquered by these fearless Scots, with their characteristic monomaniacal will, what could be more fraught than the Scotia Sea, whose waves lap the shores and glacial cliffs of Antarctica? The sea is not, as some assume, named after famous polar explorer Robert Scott, but after the *Scotia*, a ship used on the Scottish National Antarctic Expedition, from 1902 to 1904, by explorer William Bruce, who navigated and mapped those waters. What adventure, then, to sail the Scotia Sea, where one of my distant relatives sailed with the Scott expedition of 1910–1913. After braving the Scotia Sea, the pounding waves and storms off Cape Horn, and the Roaring Forties—a circumpolar wind that locks Antarctica in an eternal deep freeze, I would bask in the romantic vistas of glistening blue icebergs, coldly malevolent ... On second thought, that last of my family connections (on my grandmother's side) to venture there didn't fare as well as might be hoped: toes eaten away by frostbite, and realizing that he was dangerously slowing the retreat of his (doomed) shipmates, who had reached the South Pole only to find a fresh Norwegian flag planted there, he wandered off to perish alone in the blizzard.

But I was not the sort to be daunted by negativity. Along with dozens more big-spending tourists, I would explore the Scotia Sea by ship. In a slight nod to modernity, this ship would be a converted steel-hulled Russian icebreaker, equipped with sonar. But do not imagine that technology has banished all hardship and heroism; we were warned that in the heaviest weather, no soup would accompany dinner.

We set off from Ushuaia, the city at world's end, into the Beagle Channel, and then across the roughest ocean on the planet: first destination, the Falkland Islands. More British than Britain, the local papers are full of pictures of the dukes in full military regalia, quoted praising the determination and British pluck of the Falklanders. Besides fighting spirit, the place is given over to sheep farming. Their flag is an image of a particularly plump sheep with big, dreamy, come-hither eyes. The motto beneath reads "Desire the Right."

Being the youngest of the passengers, I gained valuable practice making formal dinner conversation with elderly English, Dutch, German, and American travellers. They were remarkably spry and lively for their age, which I guess stands to reason, as they had to be healthy enough for a strenuous adventure cruise, but retired to have the time for it and old enough to have saved the money to afford it. My bunk mate, Keith, was in his sixties and the quintessential Brit: worked in insurance in London's Square Mile; a keen rugby player when he was a schoolboy; involved with his alma mater, where he is a member of a historical preservation club; invariably polite, apologizing even for matters outside his control.

We skirted a seamount, partly emerged from the water, called Shag Rock. If you were the skipper of an Antarctic Zeppelin service, this would not be the place to land—three knife-edge mounts thrust out of a thrashing sea, smothered in nesting birds.

This was also where we encountered our first icebergs—some of them melted into fantastic shapes but still towering above the ship, with colours of white and deep blue and green. A few were tabular icebergs with ice faces hundreds of feet high, and an area as big as some European countries. A Southern right whale was also there, feeding on krill. These whales are incredibly rare; they were called right whales because they were the right ones to harpoon, since their thick blubber meant they floated when dead. The whale cavorted around the ship, then rolled on its belly and squeezed out a long poo, like pink ice cream, to show us what it thought of humans.

We sailed away, destination South Georgia Island. This island holds an immense heap of wildlife, and visiting is like stepping inside a BBC documentary; in fact, this is where they obtained penguin and seal footage for *Planet Earth*. Mostly we kept in the lee of the main island, and still we had to thump through heavy seas. The waters swarmed with fur seals, elephant seals, wandering albatross, and a good mix of penguin species. I couldn't begin to describe all, but here are a couple impressions.

Once I was standing on the bow, alone, as the sky became obscured by a hovering mist layer. Then a sun-sized hole opened directly astern, in just the place to let in select beams of sunshine. These scintillated beneath the mist layer, transforming the slate-coloured waters to a tropical lagoon–like turquoise wherever they reflected. The sea was frothing with thousands of seals and penguins. Imagine if a huge trawler was just pulling in its net, and the fish were churning about at the surface in the mesh—it was like that everywhere, and the animals were porpoising in all directions, or rolling on their sides to look at me, or just skipping around in sheer abundance. The wind was catching the ripples made by their liveliness and whipping it into whitecaps. Then the beams of sunshine made a day-glow circular rainbow, and through this our ship sailed.

The remains of the old whaling stations at Grytviken and Leith Harbour, built in 1904 and 1909, respectively, were surreal. At Leith Harbour I hiked down from the mountains onto beaches of glacial till, where I found these huge factories for slaughtering mammals on an industrial scale and rendering their blubber down in enormous vats, now rusting and derelict and rotting away. There were giant tanks riveted together from plates of iron, caving in and stained with whale sludge. There were tremendous saws for dicing the largest animals the world has ever known—and the bones were strewn about: the ground was practically made up of these bones. I stood on fragments of skulls as big as lorry cabs; there were ribs too heavy to lift, and everywhere also cool debris like grenade-harpoon heads, blubber ovens, and hulks of R-2 whale-catcher boats—the ones that almost wiped out the blue whale, which once numbered in the hundreds of thousands.

These ruins of factories for killing marine mammals were now frolicking with, and colonized by, some of the very marine mammals that used to be fed to the machines. Elephant seals in blubbery piles totalling thirty tons or more, with individuals in the one- to three-ton range, lounged together making rude noises and flapping their flippery bums. They live nearly all their lives in the deepest abysses of the ocean, using their huge black eyes to see in the dark and hunt bioluminescent squid, and needing their blubber to keep warm. Super-cute crèches of fur seal pups played among the huge propellers of whaling ships, probably British, and other maritime debris abandoned to rust away on the beach. There were also thousands of 200-kilogram adult fur seals, which gallop over with a look like a dog that's about to bite you and think that's pretty funny, and it is—and they will. I boxed a few away, and a guy had to kick one to get it to back off. I marvelled at herds of (introduced) reindeer sweeping through meadows beneath glaciers, dividing to cross wallows of elephant seals.

Next it was on to the South Orkney Islands, and then to Antarctica itself. By Zodiac we visited a place where a volcano had exploded under the ice, which had since been colonized by chinstrap penguins. And we went to the places where the Swedish/Norwegian Antarctic expedition had overwintered back in 1902. It's funny how national characteristics, well known to us in the present century, show even at that early stage. The Swedes brought a pre-fab house and pre-fab furniture and assembled it out of a kit that they loaded off the ship. The Norwegians overwintered in a heap of stone slabs glued together with penguin shit. Guess which of the two nations produced the founder of IKEA? On the other hand, the Norwegians long ago named Greenland, in the north, to encourage settlers. I can only suppose that it was the more matter-of-fact Swedes who took over the naming on that 1902 expedition, as we sailed through Terror Gulf past Danger Island.

By a strange coincidence, one of the days we spent on mainland Antarctica, January 29, was also my birthday. The crew provided a cake, while the dozens of passengers helped me celebrate. This was the largest cake and best-attended birthday party I had ever had, and easily the most remote, as it was celebrated on a continent nearly empty save for some scientists and us.

All journeys must come to an end, and eventually it was time to cross the infamous Drake Passage back to Cape Horn. The winds nearly thrashed me out of bed, and when I dared to stand outside, I learned that not only can cheeks vibrate in gale-force winds, but so can one's nostrils.

When I was at sea, it was as if I had fallen off the face of the earth: the only form of communication was a kind of ship-to-shore radio. It would have cost me 250 bucks to call up someone's Facebook profile using this system, and another ten bucks to send some short text—for instance, "a fool and his money are soon parted." Under the circumstances, I lived by the motto *No news is good news.* It was good to check up on family and friends after these three weeks of cruising, and an email from my mom informed me that the whole family would be gathering in Hawaii.

For the first few nights on dry land, it felt like my bed was swirling beneath me, and as if the earth moved under my feet. As soon as my land legs were back under me, I headed north to Patagonia, finding a whole new ecosystem. I'd forgotten that it was high summer, shorts and T-shirt weather, find-some-chocolate-ice-cream-and-eat-it-before-it-melts weather. There were rolling hills covered in sagebrush all around me, and a bright blue river snaked out of a mountain range in the middle distance. The next day I visited one of the largest and most spectacular glaciers in the world, Perito Moreno, with chunks of ice crashing down into a moraine lake beneath it. Then I was off again, west to the bustling and beautiful city of Santiago. Set in the temperate strip of land between the Andes and the upwelling cold Pacific, it is a good place to explore on foot, with many plazas and cathedrals and fancy restaurants. Combing the Chilean coast would have to wait, though: from here it was possible to fly to Easter Island, with its stone heads, and French Polynesia, and then on to Hawaii.

FUN HAWAII FAMILY REUNION ACCOMPLISHED, I BOOMERANGED back to Buenos Aires, visiting Uruguay and the Iguazu waterfall, where the Iguazu River drops from a plateau to create nearly 3 kilometres of cascades, then stayed in the shabby-chic Hotel Embajador in Paraguay, in what my guidebook called the no-go zone by the malarial swamp. South America north of the Horn is riddled with long-established backpacker routes, and it was simple to connect the dots for a taste of everything of great cultural or geographical significance: Inca ruins, Andean ski towns, Amazon nature retreats, even salt flats and surf beaches. The hostels were bustling and very social, and more and more I'd run into backpackers who, on introduction, would say they had heard of me, or new friends would tell me later on Facebook that they had met someone who had heard of someone who had met me. On a dozen or more occasions I'd join the conversation of a group of travellers, only to discover they were discussing various tales about me and my travel exploits. They'd be surprised when I said, "That's me you're talking about."

Normally this sort of backpacker-scene notoriety would start to happen only after someone had been travelling in an area for at least two years, but I'd not yet finished a full year in South America. And, oddly, some of the stories I was hearing were of experiences in Asia, Europe, and elsewhere, and were tales I hadn't told in ages. This was evidence I was becoming a minor celebrity of backpacking; even before stories about me went viral on the internet, there was a sort of global grapevine among backpackers, sustained not by any particular backpacker, since the members of this group come and go, and the planet is so big, but by backpackers' need to exchange information to facilitate travel. There is obviously opportunity around that grapevine to indulge in a little gossip as well. In hindsight, my notoriety was to be expected. If anyone devotes his life to one unusual activity—not just travel but, say, surfing, base-jumping, growing giant pumpkins, anything—he ought to be well known after keeping at it for a while. Either famous for it, if he had any knack, or at least a respected elder.

Wending my way through the Andes allowed me to make the first of many trips to Peru, a country ideal for backpackers. Cuzco, the former Inca royal seat, is one of those rare small cities where you can spend weeks doing daytrips and wandering around town with no risk of boredom. Some of the hostels, including the one I stayed at, are built on the remains of amazing Inca stonework, interlocked boulders that resist earthquakes while pleasing the eye.

After dropping down to the Chilean coast, climbing by jeep through the salt flats of the Atacama Desert, then continuing by bus to Bolivia, I ascended over 4,000 metres to the silver-mine works at Potosí (one of the highest cities in the world, and at one time the richest) and then descended into the mines, coming face to face with some problems of developing-world poverty tied to productivity. The horrifying child labour (kids start work at age ten and often die by age thirty according to my former child-miner turned guide) is managed by co-operatives. The Bolivian state stopped mining here in the mid-'80s, and no corporation wanted to take over, so families of workers kept on mining those last veins of silver, zinc, and tin. The members of the co-ops are willing to inflict on themselves conditions that would be considered inhuman if imposed by a global corporation. This illustrates something I knew well from doing business in Indonesia: for many of these impoverished downtrodden masses, often the only thing worse than being exploited by global capitalism is not being exploited by global capitalism.

That was enough of dry thin air and rattling buses along switchback roads over cactus-strewn mountainsides; after enjoying some weeks around sparkling Lake Titicaca, an enormous, deep Andean lake, and the islands of the sun, I headed off to the Bolivian Amazon for a refreshing swim with the pink dolphins and a paddle through submerged jungle trees, fishing for piranha and marvelling at swarms of spider monkeys in the drooping branches and black caimans basking on the muddy riverbanks.

When I bid farewell to Paul and Sandra, a cheerful British/Irish/Australian couple who had been my travel companions for the last two weeks in Bolivia, Paul gave me some Advil for a toothache I'd developed. Popping one allowed me to eat again, but also spoiled my lifelong claim to never having taken a painkiller, leaving only the lesser claim of never having seen a doctor for a checkup or experienced a medical complaint serious enough for me to consider booking an appointment. Pain-free, I dashed back to Peru and met my Uncle Ross and cousins in Cuzco to tour the sacred valley and do my first hike of the Inca trail to Machu Picchu.

A message from Paul and Sandra reached me before the start of my hike: they had been robbed at knifepoint in an Andean town just after our paths had diverged. I had a bit of a scare myself: after bussing in to the trailhead for the week-long hike, I was at first unable to find my backpack. But it was located, and apologetic locals explained that when the porters had unloaded the baggage from atop the bus, they had put my backpack to rest amid the bags and sacks belonging to Quechua villagers, where, I suppose, it looked like it belonged.

The Inca trail is fantastic, a highlight of the world, and everyone should do it, if they have the time and money, before it becomes too popular and the odds of getting a permit too long. Something of a full-time porter myself (of my own goods), I walked with the porters most of the time, or ahead of them, stopping when I got to the place we were meant to have lunch or sleep. This feat would not have been so easy if this had been the Himalayas and the porters Sherpa. Much of North and South America's Indigenous population burgeoned from a tiny base, just a few families, and they didn't have the genetic variety to work with the way East Asians did when settling the Himalayas. Lacking the variation in biochemical pathways to get a foothold, as it were, the only recourse was a physically expensive alteration—that is, large lungs and hearts, and the heavy ribs and chest to carry them—and even then they were not much better at coping at altitude than me.

Machu Picchu was wondrous in May, so much so that I hoped to be able to return and see "the hitching post of the sun" again one day. Magically, on this day, the morning rain subsided and sunbeams pierced the mist to spotlight green cliffs and intricate ancient stonework with gold, a place of delightful vistas, proportioned and balanced with well-placed stairways, walls, temples, and houses betwixt mountains and thrilling heights, encouraging wonderful thoughts: such beauty and serenity was uplifting. To be here is to be somehow more alive.

Places such as Machu Picchu are worth seeing as many times as you can manage. These are still the glory years of backpacking, for a decade or maybe two yet. In the near future, travellers will be amazed to hear that anyone but the ultra-rich could visit world highlights like this. Twenty or thirty years hence, the Andean peoples will likely be aware of the importance of personally experiencing their own heritage. If there are thirty million Quechua speakers, and each would like to visit Machu Picchu just once in their lifetime, that would fill the entire daily quota every day of every year, with no space left for foreign tourists. More and more premier sites will become inaccessible due to high demand. Even today, if you want to raft the Grand Canyon, you have to spend a small fortune and wait for many years. If there were no queue to limit visitors, it would cost a jaw-dropping fortune instead. In aggregate, my own travel experiences, those that have not become priceless, will soon be valued in the multi-millions of dollars, even adjusted for inflation—and I'd experienced them for an average travel budget of about twenty-five dollars a day. Backpackers should get in while the getting is good, because this opportunity to carpetbag travel experiences cannot last.

To the Inca, this sacred valley was the fertile core of a powerful empire. To someone born here, it must seem a valley blessed by the gods. To the tourists beside me on the buses and trains, it was enchanting because they saw how people lived, invoking dreams of a golden age when people were steeped in tradition, honouring the ways of their ancestors. World travellers see a different valley, and think different thoughts, because they have a global perspective. The sacred valley is fertile, especially compared to nearby valleys, but there are many such places on earth. The locals are not uniquely blessed by the gods. This does not make the valley less sacred, but, rather, the earth more sacred and precious. And where tourists see changeless tradition, I see valleys lush with African grass, and groves of Australian eucalyptus, Indochinese chickens, European pigs, and Mexican avocados. Similarly, the locally bred potatoes are now rooted in every compatible soil on the planet.

Office workers are very chatty and well connected, so when globalization affected them, it was a big new thing, and much talk ensued, while articles on this phenomenon were written and widely circulated. What few realize is that subsistence farmers were among the first to have their lives disrupted and remade by globalization. Lives that were deeply integrated with the cycles and rhythms of ancestral crops were disrupted. Now, if you want to understand the lifeways of subsistence farmers, it is better to ask about the local microclimate and soil rather than historical crops, because efficiency is king. These farmers of the sacred valley got the globalization before, and without, the industrialization, for want of capital and capitalism.

Looking over this retreat for Inca royalty, I reflected on how assured I was feeling now compared to the doubts that had plagued me a year earlier. Benefiting from a second wind, and with a little bit more attention to maps, I was often getting a pretty good experience of a country after only one or two visits. This not only reduced my airfare costs, but also reduced time wasted on visa procedures and gave me some hope that I'd see the world before my hair was grey or dwindling funds rendered me destitute.

My switch of travel style from hub-and-spoke to freestyle had been wildly successful, and I'd hit the sweet spot, with little need for guidebooks or plans—after all, no travel plan survives contact with friendly forces, and friendly people can be found at every turn. Anyone travelling with an open mind will be constantly meeting locals who provide all manner of excellent suggestions and opportunities. Having no plan gave me flexibility for maximum fun and the ability to see things the guidebooks and package tours miss. But it was still necessary to know the basics about a country or region and its culture. For best results as a freestyle traveller, believe in going plan-less, not clueless.

CHAPTER TEN

RED SANDS, BLACK SEA

Kazakhstan · Kyrgyzstan · Uzbekistan · Tajikistan ·
Afghanistan · Turkmenistan · Azerbaijan · Armenia · Georgia

T HAT YEAR IN SOUTH AMERICA HAD LEFT ME WITH MANY fond memories and energized from much socializing in hostels brimming with backpackers. South America is an easy training ground for travellers, with just a couple of languages to dabble in, and so many backpackers dilly-dallying around that advice and guidance are always available and up to date. It's possible to do the continent drunk, and some people do, feeding wallets and cameras to muggers every month or so in a kind of intemperance toll. So it was especially easy for me, with my relative moderation born of maturity; another year here would have been pleasant, with much new territory to visit, especially toward the north. But for a change of scene, my sights were set on a Silk Road less travelled.

Following a brief stop in Vancouver, and another in England (to visit the northern city of York and then south again to party on London's Tube system—Mayor Boris Johnson had decreed "no more drinking on the London Underground trains," so citizens occupied them for a last piss-up), I was all set for a spring 2008 tour of the "Stans" of Central Asia—Kazakhstan, Kyrgyzstan, Uzbekistan, Tajikistan, Afghanistan, Turkmenistan—as well as Azerbaijan, Armenia, and Georgia, before heading farther west.

On my flight from London to Kazakhstan, there was time for a stop-over in Malta where my old friend Bruce was doing an event for iStock. He'd arranged a get-together for stock photographers, hired models to pose in castles and beaches, and otherwise made it interesting.and fun for photographers to get together, talk shop, and practise their art. My stay was not long, just enough for a visit and to see the island.

I needed to get going on Central Asia and confront the notoriously horrendous visa difficulties. The entire region is something of a backwater now, but it used to be the crucible of ancient empires, so there is no shortage of imposing monuments and strange legends. Kazakhstan presented the least visa trouble for its size, so any visitor is wise to start there. I touched down in Almaty, a pleasant city (named after apples) of parks and stately buildings, many built by Japanese POWs, within easy reach of the Tian Shan (Heavenly Mountains). Almaty nestles in the foothills of this range, which also shelter diverse wild apple trees, the ancestors of the popular modern fruit.

Kazakhstan is a huge nation, reminding me strongly of Alberta in Canada: it has the same high, dry prairie, oil and ranching mentality, and mountains, though these peaks loom to the east instead of the west. The people are a mix of ethnic Russians and majority Kazakhs: a pale Asian race traditionally skilled on horseback and living off nomadic herding.

A tall Kazakh woman, Karlygash, who had rented me her flat, wanted me to sign up for an organized tour.

"I'm not so sure if tours are my thing," I said. "Can you describe this tour?"

"My van with ten passengers, mostly Kazakhs," she said, "will drive high into the mountains, after stockpiling watermelons and crates of vodka. We'll picnic and see the mountains until dark, by which time we'll have reached an abandoned Soviet observatory, which is optical, not electric, so it still works. After that, a party, watch stars, and sleep in the former astronomers' dorm building. Cost is twenty dollars."

She made a sale.

In the van was a Kazakh woman named Dana, smiley, dark haired, golden tanned, and petite compared to me—we later discovered her running shoes could fit entirely inside my boots. Viewing the moon and stars and galaxies provided a magical atmosphere; with this prompting, not to mention drunken Ping-Pong playing, romance was in the air. She worked for the United Nations, running a program for preventing child labour. With help and advice from Dana and the UN office, needful visas accumulated more quickly than expected—merely excruciatingly slowly, but not as excruciatingly slowly as for a guy I later met in Tashkent who was staying in a hostel with a nice persimmon tree, watching the fruit ripen as he filled out documents for six weeks.

While working on my Uzbek and other visas, I spent my free time with Dana and a succession of American diplomats, a couple of them very senior, important enough that their kidnapping or killing would make the news and possibly spark congressional hearings. Only one of them was embarrassing to walk with at first, as he was on the prowl for local women and kept using the word "prostitutes," even though I hastened to inform him that the Russian word is nearly the same, so everyone passing in the street knew what he was on about.

Another distinguished gentleman was in charge of security for the United Nations building. When he gave me his card, I had it laminated and tucked it away for safekeeping. The UN logo was on it, and my intuition told me this was just the thing to aid travel in certain African countries. For some years now I'd pondered the difficulty of travel in countries like Democratic Republic of Congo. Other backpackers had warned me that as soon as they had encountered militants, army, or police in the wild east, usually their first day in the country, they had been robbed and left nearly naked, and had to limp back to the border in an epic backpacking fail. Many old Africa hands declared certain countries to be no-go zones. I thought this white-and-blue card might do the trick for me.

One diplomat had an especially hard go of it: he was the economic advisor to Afghanistan on behalf of the United States, and his experience of Afghanistan had been eighteen months living in one or another metal shipping container, which was full of computers and guarded by hundreds of American troops. He would tap away on his computer, and every so often a helicopter would arrive and carry him to the palace to talk with President Karzai. While he and I were talking about economics, the subject of fair trade, that modern economic thalidomide, came up. He admitted with a laugh that he was involved in the decisions that led to the collapse in coffee prices, leading to poverty that set off that whole misguided fair-trade attempt to "help."

I was fascinated. I knew the coffee collapse was triggered by a massive attempt at development aid but had never heard the details.

"Someone had figured that there should be more effort to alleviate poverty in the mountains of Vietnam," this diplomat explained. "A decision was taken to scale up an effort to introduce coffee production, to the tune of millions and millions of dollars."

"Didn't anyone point out, pre-implementation, that agricultural products are relatively inelastic?" I asked. "If coffee beans are cheaper, it doesn't mean that the guy who has a cup of coffee in the morning now drinks an extra cup."

"That fact came up in committee," he said. "We had some farmers and businessmen who told us that even a 10-percent oversupply in an agricultural good like coffee can cause a glut. They told us to proceed only very slowly and carefully, and put as much effort into finding a market for the new coffee as growing it."

"Then what the hell happened?"

"They got kicked off the committee for not being team players, and we proceeded to massively scale up our project," he said, adding something to the effect that "Slow careful projects are useless to huge development entities: we need massive bling projects to justify our massive funding. The media was happy to blame the Western coffee buyers instead of us, so everyone covered their asses and moved on. My involvement was only peripheral, as a consultant, so I wouldn't have taken any flack for it anyhow."

IN ALMATY I HAD A FAVOURITE PARK, WHERE KIDS WOULD ROLLER-blade in an area near an orthodox church and a war memorial sculptural that showed the determination of impossibly square-jawed bronze Kazakh soldiers. These soldiers watched over wedding ceremonies now, with Kazakh brides in their traditional Disney princess dresses and conical hats streaming with ribbons, posing for photos with tuxedoed grooms by the eternal flame.

"We had some problems the year before," Dana said, "of trouble-makers attacking Kazakhs seen going into church. Extremists say it is a violation of our Kazakh religious traditions."

"What are Kazakh religious traditions?" I asked. "Because to me the Kazakhs seem highly tolerant."

Dana was nominally Muslim, but she drank alcohol, tried not to eat pork if it wasn't too much trouble, and had never been to mosque. Pagan traditions like holy lakes and visiting shrines and shamans were more important to her, and even these she didn't take seriously.

"Kazakh tradition is to be very open and tolerant about religion," she said. "That's why the attacks were so weird. Central Asian governments found the problem started from mosques funded by Gulf States, especially Saudi Arabia. At first, when Arabs said they wanted to fund mosques, the governments all said, good, thank you. But now we don't want this funding because they are Wahhabi school of Islam. It is not a good fit for us. Uzbekistan has now a rule that all sermons must pass censorship before they are allowed to be preached."

After foraging successfully for a few visas, I said goodbye to Dana, arranging to meet her later in the consonant-enriched nation of Kyrgyzstan, east of Kazakhstan, when she had time off work. Eventually, like every other passerby, I was drawn to deep, wondrous Issyk-Kul, a lake whose shore is lined with trees and old Soviet holiday resorts. In

Karakol, a former Imperial Russian fort now a small city on the eastern lakeshore, I was sharing a dorm with a German physics student, Simon, and a Dane, Jacob, who did business in Shanghai. We decided that the three of us would hire a guide and climb in the Tian Shan Mountains, but when it came time to hire the guide, Jacob was hungover.

"You two guys go and decide for me," he said blearily.

"Okay," I said, "but tell us, are you physically strong, or weak, or something average? We have to decide how ambitious a climb to attempt."

"I was on the Danish national water polo team—so very strong."

Good to know, because we were directed to a monoglot ethnic Russian guide, and he offered to show us something easy, or something difficult. The next morning, after a long trip by van to the base of the mountains, we started our difficult climb. The level of exertion was fine for Simon and me, but Jacob lagged. He didn't want us to slow down to wait for him, but then he got lost. After we found him, we pretended to go at our usual speed, but really we held back for him. He admitted that all the time in Shanghai he took no exercise and drank a lot of whisky, and Shanghai air is not good for the lungs.

"I am quitting and going back down," he said finally.

"Bad idea," I argued. "We are nine hours in, and only one hour from a place we can camp out of the wind and snow and make hot food."

"No, I go back."

I disputed some more, pointing out that we were at high altitude now, in a blizzard that made it hard to see more than a few metres, and only a couple of hours of light remained. "Besides," I told him, "you might get lost again. And where will you sleep? We only have one tent that is coming with us to the top of this ridge."

"Under a log, if I can get back to the treeline," he said.

I was not sure if he had ever before tried sleeping under logs in a blizzard, but I had settled for many such beds and couldn't recommend them. I turned to Simon, but he was being German.

"Each man must decide his own actions," he said.

Russian guides generally stay out of discussions like this, as they are not European guides; they are not responsible for you, nor should you want them to be. The idea is that they provide only the minimum help, so, in a sense, you explore as if they were not there. In many ways this is better, and you learn mountaineering skills faster, but this particular tradition was not helpful at that moment.

Eventually our Dane was convinced of the necessity to carry on, and it was the right choice. The guide showed us a place to camp in a high saddle of rock with a lake, out of the wind. Lovely days followed, with meadows softened by an abundance of wild flowers, the chirping of marmots, babbling brooks, and evergreen forests skirting peaks that towered over horse pastures far below.

Simon and I returned to Bishkek, the Kyrgyz capital, which is named for a milk-churn, as I needed to work some more on these interminable visas. It took me a day to discover that it wasn't any use to apply here, and that getting the Azerbaijani visa would be tough. I finally engaged a visa support company, Stantours, to help with Turkmenistan.

There's a drinking game in which you say, "I never did such-and-such," and those who *have* done such a deed must down a shot. Well, my hotel in Bishkek was not the finest, even though it was expensive—seven dollars a night for a dorm bed—and it was here that I broke my long streak of being able to say I'd never pissed into a hole in the wall of my hotel. An urgent bladder necessitated a visit to the communal toilet. The door was nailed shut with six-inch spikes, and a sign on the door said "Not Working" in Russian. Grumbling a bit, I returned to the dorm, put more clothes on, and tried the doors on the other two toilets, a floor up and a floor down. They were also nailed shut. Time to go talk to the administrator, but the woman wasn't there to bless me with her usual Soviet surliness. The locals didn't recommend going into the alleys at night in this neighbourhood, but there was no help for it. However, the only exits were chained and shut with padlocks. How's that for fire safety? I thought. Before noticing some holes in an interior wall ...

The next morning I asked Simon if he had detected a certain lack of hygiene in our hotel. He had, and we decided on a visit to the public baths. Here you stroll around with hundreds of men, all completely naked, between various pools and dry saunas and steam rooms. The employees are mostly Kyrgyz girls, who watch these men as they bathe or walk past, occasionally whispering to one another and giggling. Now I know the answer to this burning question: If staff consisting of teenage girls is working in a steamy bathhouse packed with naked men, should they wear hijabs? Answer: yes, otherwise a strange man might glimpse a girl's hair when he beckons her over to fetch soap or towels.

Feeling refreshed, Simon and I wandered down to the Ala-Too Square fountain in the city centre, where Kyrgyz youth hang out, and sometimes approach foreigners to practise their English or German. We stepped into the nearby national Gapar Aitiev fine art museum. After we had viewed some paintings, the administrator came over and said in Russian that we looked like strong men; could we help her move a statue to a new pedestal? She pointed to an unwieldy yet delicate life-sized bronze figure by a prominent Kyrgyz artist. It was darn heavy, but luckily we didn't drop it and cause an international incident. As a reward, the administrator showed us some extra art in a back room. She must have not had the funding to hire proper staff. Her colleague Mirfayz Usmonov, curator at the art museum in Tashkent, took more drastic measures than merely using volunteer labour: he raised money by selling off the most valuable paintings and hanging copies in their place, and had been getting away with it for fifteen years by the time he was caught in 2014.

DANA HAD SOME TIME OFF FOR A VISIT, SO I MOVED TO A NICER HOTEL for the weekend. When she arrived, she told me she had a problem: as part of her job, she was expected to go to Kabul in Afghanistan, but she was afraid of the Taliban and was planning to say no. Once, when she was in Tajikistan, she had looked out over the Wakhan Corridor, a relatively safe valley sandwiched between the Pamir and Karakorum mountain ranges, and that had been scary enough.

"Don't say no," I suggested. "Your colleagues will be angry. Say yes, and I'll go with you, and you won't be afraid." I sang her a verse: "Come, Mister Taliban, tally me banana; Daylight come, and I wan' go home."

This produced a smile, and she said she would go if I would. We agreed to meet in Dushanbe, Tajikistan, and cross together. This meant

I really had to get a move on and put in maximum effort on visa applications, so after Dana left I checked back into a cheap hotel, without water or electricity, filled out forms, and searched for clues online at an internet café.

Afghanistan did not have a working embassy in Bishkek—not for visas, anyhow. But in one of my pockets I had a scrap of paper, given to me by a local Afghan merchant, which had the number of an Afghan warlord in Uzbekistan, whose minions might be able to help. Perhaps fortunately, the number proved defunct. But I did manage to get an Afghan visa eventually, after a struggle with inept bureaucracy in Tashkent, Uzbekistan's capital, while I was staying near the largest twenty-four-hour melon market I've ever seen—perfect if you are hankering for a melon after a night out on the town.

Alone again, I hitched a series of rides with various locals, the last one an elderly Uzbek with a long white beard, who was proud of his reading skill, and kind enough to draw my attention to each of the cars we passed on the road, telling me how to pronounce crazy names like Ford, which was "Port." According to local and Russian rules, he was right.

The elderly Uzbek took me to Arslanbob, where Alexander the Great found a grove of walnuts. He brought some of those nuts back to Greece, where they were introduced to Europe as the Greek nut. The mountains here were sprinkled with walnut forests, and there was a home-stay well situated for day hikes that tended to escalate into mountain-climbing sessions. Each morning my grinning, black-bearded hotelier would send his daughter over with tea, fruit, and toast with quince preserves and honey, while I lounged on pillows and admired the view. Every time she put out that dollop of honey and departed, a swarm of honeybees descended and repatriated it, to the last drop. Reluctantly leaving this beautiful vale, I hitched along mountain roads to the ancient city of Osh, and then followed even more mountainous roads into Uzbekistan.

I was making better time than expected, my path carrying me to the more and less accessible Silk Road sites, in the company of a filmmaker, John from "Down Under," who would run his fork through every dish of *plov* (rice, raisins, and white or purple carrots, often with a cube of mutton or beef unwanted by John) because he would only allow the flesh of lizards and kangaroos to pass his lips, but was otherwise a strict vegetarian. Also we enjoyed the company of Lydia, a young American Peace Corps girl from the Dakotas, spirited, still gangly with youth, and somewhat idealistic considering her experiences abroad. She had many tales of drunkenness and games of "grab the goat" from her two-year stint with the Corps.

Uzbekistan and the former Soviet Stans are best to do as a quad: a group of four backpackers. It generally costs about ten dollars to get a day's ride by car, and the cars leave once they have four passengers. Often if you are missing one of four passengers to fill a seat, the wait is at least an hour or two, or five or six if you are unlucky. Our group of three—sadly one bum short of optimal—visited the monuments built by mighty warlords of the past, like Tamerlane and other masters of hordes of mounted archers that so terrified civilization until the invention of guns. There was Samarkand, Khiva—oasis of white slaving—and so many other turquoise and green-tiled ruins dotting the landscape. The whole area is prone to devastating earthquakes, so urbanization here alternately elaborates and gets wiped away like kid's castles in a sandbox.

These ruins, esteemed as centres for geomancy and as the haunts of powerful ghosts of ancient rulers, are an auspicious place for weddings. Troupes of angelic-looking musicians with long brass horns provide the fanfare, and children provide the shouting and wrestling in the dust. As ruins of conqueror's arches draw the nuptials of sweet youth, so ruined tombs attract the corpses: if a famous dervish or Islamic saint is buried there, he draws the freshly dead, for surely Allah will suck the holy one to heaven first on Judgement Day, and who is to say that bunches of nearby souls, even if not so saintly, might not be lifted up also in the hubbub, so benefiting by association? Shamans and dervishes knot Islamic prayer clothes to nearby trees and place enough relics to make any passing Saudi purist pull out his beard in righteous frustration. Islam is peace, it is said, but the people here want a wet, whirling, and fertile peace, not some dry and dreadful reading.

The three of us were making our way west to the Kyzylkum Desert, a vast expanse of red sand dunes between the rivers Amu Darya and Syr Darya. Lydia didn't have time for the deepest desert that now is the Aral Sea, but we exchanged contacts; she was planning to be in the Caucasus Mountains at the same time as me, and we might meet up. Also, she wanted to hear how Afghanistan went down, as did some other back-packers for whom I was serving as something of a guinea pig. With John I ventured far to the west, squeezing into speeding, clattering old sedans.

An atrocious singer kept popping up on the radio: a local explained that she was the daughter of Uzbekistan's president, who considered herself a pop star. She couldn't sing, but the stations had better play her, or else. The secret police were known to steam people's heads red as lobsters, then ditch the bodies of troublemakers, so what was a little mediocre warbling on the airwaves by comparison? Such tactics mean that Central Asian dictators are often surrounded by yes-men.

I noticed that balls of cotton fell off the trucks at highway speed and clung to bushes by the roadsides. A taxi driver told me that children are sent by regional bosses to scrounge them up, though he believed that "our children would profit more from school than from picking pennies' worth of cotton in the dust and heat." Anyhow, for the poorest children it may not have mattered; UN documents I'd read at Dana's flat said that child labour in the cotton fields was common, and we did see kids work-ing there, especially girls. John was tempted to do some filming, but local police and officials were suspicious of his camera, so he didn't dare take it out near the fields.

At last we got to Nukus. The area is not well known, being in the middle of nowhere, beyond the Kyzylkum Desert, near Dashoguz and Mang'it. Before Alexander the Great passed through on his armed tour of Asia, this whole Amu Darya delta was the heart of the land of Khwarezm; then conquering Mongols established the Chagatai Khanate in the thirteenth century, flourishing until Timur, also known as Tamerlane, a warlord who managed to kill 17 million people (one in twenty of the world's inhabitants at the time), invaded the capital of Old Urgench in 1388 and made a pyramid of the inhabitants' skulls.

Now, of course, the river is a trickle, and the inland sea is gone too, a victim of thirsty cotton fields and the hubris of Soviet hydraulic mega-engineering. We explored the hulks of rusting freighters and fishing boats, stranded forever in the dunes below the cliff that was once a shore.

This was as far as these roads could take me. Beyond was impassable Turkmenistan, land of an even more power-crazed dictator. I decided to try accessing the country from Afghanistan, entering through Herat and trusting my luck to manage the Turkmen visa from Tajikistan. Thus I had to get to Dushanbe, the capital of Tajikistan, as quickly as possible. I said goodbye to John and hitched a ride with a chubby trader from the ancient Silk Road city of Samarkand, who was carting east a couple of Uzbek prostitutes, their arms hennaed, braceleted, and bangled up, singing and otherwise festive from a profitable stop at an oasis of lonely men. I crossed the Tajik frontier in October 2008.

The roads were being resurfaced and mountain tunnels bored in this ancient and exceedingly mountainous land. The China Road and Bridge Corporation was doing the work using ten thousand Chinese labourers, and it seemed they had decided it was best not to brook delay and to do every road at once. The tunnels through the mountains were spectacular, and the rock still raw from blasting. After hours of waiting in whatever jalopy I'd managed to hitch a ride in, I would bump along for a half hour in the darkness, emerge into bright day, and then, around a corner, find yet more tunnel works. Our wheels scrambled for purchase on shards of rock, and we squeezed past pits of mud, cracked pipes spurting water, and little lakes shining in our headlights on what would be the highway when all was done. The valleys reverberated with blasts and the clatter of rocks loosened high above, and Chinese men with walkie-talkies and no knowledge of local language but admirable communication skills controlled traffic with joke words, gestures, and laughter.

Tajikistan holds many wonderful vistas and ancient towns, usually next to even more ancient ruins. Alexander the Great, fighting on to conquer all, and any moment expecting to come across the river "Ocean" that marked the end of the world, would have noticed beneath his sandalled feet the ruins of forgotten empires. He found no Ocean, but instead married the beautiful princess Roxanne. These ruins today echo with legendary deeds of the past: they are the haunts of young kissing couples, searching for their own ends of the earth, where love might conquer all.

My last ride before reaching the capital was with a Tajik man in an old Mercedes, who constantly played tapes of imams preaching. God only knows what he took away from these sermons, since he was so intent on finding ways he might cheat or turn a profit from me that he was reluctant to let me out in Dushanbe. It suited me to stay the first night at his house in a suburban slum, so I did, and in the morning I paid him and walked downtown, while he trailed behind, desperately suggesting other relatives for home-stay or restaurants owned by friends. I had to change money downtown, and had a laugh at the official name of the local currency: *somoni*, which sounds like "some money." With much effort I found a place to stay while waiting for Dana, down some alleys and across an enormous water pipe that bridged a gully, in a compound lush with persimmon trees.

Dana arrived in Dushanbe, and after some time lounging in the persimmon groves, eating bread dipped in honey, we were bound for Afghanistan, all smiles and excited to be able to enjoy so much of each other's company again, even if Dana had to accomplish a certain amount of work most days. Neither of us had any idea what to expect.

Dana was wheeling a big suitcase, and I assumed it must be filled with clothes she needed for work, absurdly heavy clothes. Anyhow, we would not have to lug it around, as we would be checking in to her room at the Intercontinental Hotel in Kabul. Security there was tight: mirrors on poles to look under approaching vehicles for bombs, an uphill zigzag through sandbagged machine-gun nests, metal detectors at the door, and a wide open space in front that armed guards could easily watch. As the hotel hosted wedding receptions, this space was occasionally taken over by rings of gleeful dancing Pashtun men, flipping their long, black, glossy tresses in unison.

We were handed Afghan cellphone SIMs so that we could be reached for security reasons, and were given cards with the number for Afghan

Logistics—really just a taxi company, but the drivers had been vetted and were almost certainly armed, and they didn't always stop for curbside prayers, as normal taxis did.

Dana laid her suitcase on the bed and popped it open, revealing a motherlode of vodka and Armenian cognac.

"Isn't alcohol illegal in Afghanistan?" I asked.

"Sort of, but foreigners are allowed to bring in a little for personal use. Besides, I'm UN, so they can't search my luggage."

"I'm happy they can't. That looks like more than personal use, even for a Kazakh."

She laughed and said, "The bottles are not only for me. It's going to be party in our room."

And so it was. This UN gig has some perks. There were a lot of interesting people in the hotel, many Afghan ministers and provincial governors, NGO types, Americans and Central Asians on business. Most enjoyed a drink or three.

The Intercontinental Hotel was like a little bubble of security from which we would venture out to explore, calling Afghan Logistics or climbing into one of a convoy of vehicles heading off to do something interesting: picnic in the garden surrounding the mausoleum of Emperor Babur; have a private tour of the bullet-pocked national museum, and hear from the director who hid the ancient golden treasures and many valuable statues from rampaging Taliban vandals; tour facilities that help women escaping gender-specific crimes against humanity. In the market we bought a blue burka for Dana; back at the hotel she put it on, and we roamed the corridors, Dana giggling like a little ghost on Halloween. We were considering going into Kabul like this for a joke, but a provincial governor warned us that the people might not share our sense of humour. Afghan women and girls have to wear a Halloween ghost costume every day, so it's not any fun at all.

I don't often spend so much time based out of a security bubble, what I think of as "the Palace of the Winds" after that enormous pink building in Rajasthan: a towering façade pierced with screened windows and studded with balconies for princesses to safely peek out at the wider world. The Intercontinental was one such façade in our "new world order." It had not yet been terror-attacked (that would happen three years later, in July 2011), but it was no surprise the Intercontinental was a target. Osama bin Laden was, and terrorists generally are, careful to always attack the Palace of the Winds for maximum effect wherever its tangle of gates and passages and corridors of global power touch base, such as here or at the Twin Towers or airports.

"YOU MIGHT BE BORED TODAY," DANA SAID TO ME ONE MORNING. "I have to go to a conference."

"Don't worry," I said. "I'll wander around Kabul."

"Or," she said, "you can come to work with me."

Why not? A search for clean clothes that might make me look like I worked for a living produced only a white raver T-shirt with crossbones and a black skull wearing headphones on the front, along with the words "Renegade Sound System." This would have to do.

When we arrived at the conference room, a man at the entrance said only, "Excuse me, sir, we seem to have forgotten to make your name tag."

"Yes, you have forgotten." They printed one out for me, and I pinned it on so I could look as business-casual as possible in that shirt.

We mingled and chatted at first, but then a commotion showed that the meeting had commenced, and we took seats at an enormous horseshoe-shaped table. I expected that Dana would sit beside me, but she had been talking with a colleague and sat near her instead.

"Tell a little about yourself and what you will contribute to this conference," a moderator said to the room.

Each of us had a stack of binders on the table in front of each of us, and rifling through them led me to believe we were to discuss electricity. Jonibek, energy advisor to the prime minister of Kyrgyzstan, was the first to introduce himself, and as I listened to others, it dawned on me that we were meant to be talking about hydroelectric development on the Amu Darya where it flows along the Afghan/Tajik frontier. Suddenly apprehensive, I wracked my brain for anything useful to say about hydroelectricity. Precious little came to mind until I remembered reading in a Central Asia guidebook that, some decades earlier, there had been a terrible earthquake at the headwaters of this very river, in the High Pamirs. Mud and rock had oozed down and plugged the river, and an enormous lake had built up behind this blockage. If there was ever another earthquake, which is likely as they happen very frequently in Central Asia, that mud and gravel would liquefy, and the whole lake would rush down at once, destroying every dam and village all the way out to western Uzbekistan. This little tidbit was my contribution. To my surprise, no one had heard of this before.

The more I listened, the less serious the project seemed. Hearing that the customer for the electricity would be Pakistan, I looked at the Tashkent businesswoman beside me, and we laughed. "The cheque is in the mail," I said. Jonibek maintained that all they needed was a stray billion dollars or so to get started running high-tension lines across Taliban-infested countryside to a feckless and habitually broke customer in Pakistan. And this is in Central Asia, where people are outraged if you ask them to pay for electricity, and even existing dams have trouble coming up with the funds for routine maintenance.

But the experience was worthwhile. There were opportunities to chat with some people, including Afghanistan's Minister for Preventing Corruption. He told a favourite joke: A senior minister invited a junior minister to dinner at his house. When the junior minister was getting in his car to leave, he said, "I have to ask, how you can afford this big house and three-car garage on a senior minister's salary?"

"See that bridge over there?" the senior minister said, pointing.

"Yes."

He rubbed fingers and thumb, saying, "10 percent."

A few months later, the junior minister invited the senior minister over to his new house, and now it was the senior minister's turn to be impressed. When getting in his car, he said, "Now it is me who has to ask, how can you afford this great mansion, and four-car garage, on your junior minister's salary?"

The junior minister said, pointing, "See that bridge over there?"

Look as he might, the senior minister couldn't see any bridge.

"100 percent," the junior minister said, rubbing his thumb against his fingers.

I made sure to get the minister's business card, as it would be useful at police roadblocks.

I also met the guy who owned Kam Air, a regional airline just for Afghanistan and, notably, the airline in which I've been frisked the most times before boarding a flight: eight times by my count, though it was occasionally hard to say when one frisk ended and the next began. He invited Dana and me to a party at his house that evening.

We dressed up (Dana was aiming for business-casual, given the country's conservative reputation, leaving me to rock my best "back-packer who has just laundered the collared shirt he wears for consulate visits" look), then cruised over to the address in an Afghan Logistics car and were ushered down some steps to the mansion's basement. The guy had a swimming pool down there, with mosaics of dolphins. And a bar, where who should I see but the Minister for Preventing Corruption. I said to him, "Here you are, Minister of Preventing Corruption, at an illegal bar." He laughed. The nozzle of a water pipe was handed to me and I heard "Kandahar hashish?" A glass of whisky was put in my hand, so I took a sip.

The minister was in conversation with an American businessman, who was saying, "I'll tell you what to do, to show them who's boss. Arrest the biggest baddest warlord you can find, and all the others will fall in line." I almost choked on my whisky and looked to the minister. He was admirably diplomatic, and thanked the American for the advice. This Minister for Preventing Corruption was a young man, energetic and smart, and probably on the way to a brilliant career as long as he didn't do anything stupid like arrest warlords. Afghanistan is a rough-and-tumble place, and people who arrest warlords find that after their family is kidnapped, tortured, and killed, they are shot through the back of the head.

It would be false to think that this minister was somehow corrupt because he was at a party where some people drank whisky or smoked hashish. In fact, he went to a lot of parties, as is only sensible for anyone who has this job. Businessmen have to bend the law to stay in business. The question is, who do you arrest? Because you have to start somewhere. If business is informal, then so must be the determination of who is and is not playing by the unwritten rules.

There was a young American NGO worker at the party, so young that I figured this must be his first experience out of university. He seemed stressed out, so jittery and yet so arrogant that if I'd met him in some other country, I would assume he was fresh from snorting lines of cocaine in the bathroom. He voiced his muddled thoughts on Afghanistan. I was without my notebook and pen, so his exact words are lost. But I got the gist, and, anyway, the same sentiment had already been expressed over a hundred years earlier by Rudyard Kipling:

> Take up the White Man's burden,
> The savage wars of peace—
> Fill full the mouth of Famine
> And bid the sickness cease;
> And when your goal is nearest
> (The end for others sought)
> Watch Sloth and heathen Folly
> Bring all your hopes to nought.

EXCEPT HIS VERSION WAS NOT SO PLAIN SPOKEN. SOMEONE SOMEwhere must have translated this into NGO jargon, because I've heard this stanza so many times worldwide. The new verses speak of developed country obligations and international effort to stabilize a conflict region, and end always bemoaning frustrations and challenges due to cultural differences exacerbated by poor regional education infrastructure. It is the lament of the NGO guy, who thinks he is here to do development and expects to see development. The original colonialist poem best captures the antiquated idea; these guys reciting the new jargon-filled version always seem so baffled by their own bafflegab.

DANA AND I CONTINUED TO GO FOR DAYTRIPS AROUND KABUL (THE city occupies a bowl-shaped valley that is also a pass into the Hindu Kush mountains), many arranged by Afghan members of the Central Eurasian Leadership Academy. We had some fun picnics in rose gardens and tried some of the best local food, though we continued to meet with NGOs. One agency was doing something so practical they could tell their own mothers, with a straight face, that they were doing development. This group had a building full of classrooms and was essentially teaching rural Afghans how to become government bureaucrats: how to answer the phone, run an office, deal with employees ethically, handle the payroll, and so on.

One day we went on a tour of one of the offices used by the Pajhwok (which means "echo") Afghan News agency. The owner, Mr. Karokhel, was a clever Afghan entrepreneur who was collecting all the news that was fit to sell internationally, Afghanistan being a veritable bonanza of newsworthiness at the moment. We very nearly became part of the news. We had just stepped inside, luckily, to see how the agency was run, when there were blasts out in the streets, and a pressure wave rolled through the room.

Nearly instantly, all our phones started to beep with explanatory texts and calls. The owner of Pajhwok was miffed that his was last to ring, but it was probably because our gathering included some VIPs.

We heard that a guy, or possibly three guys, had pulled out machine pistols and shot people on the street, then flung themselves into the Ministry of Information and Culture and detonated at least one suicide vest that killed three and injured twelve. Some of the people in our group were scared by this and didn't want to go to the restaurant that we'd planned to eat at. In my opinion, the chance of attack was the same if we ate at our hotel or at a restaurant, so we might as well go to the restaurant. But the "retreat to the hotel" advocates won the argument by showing more emotion, as so often happens. We returned to our Palace of the Winds for the rest of the day while some people settled their nerves. This was October 30; later I heard about an attack on the management of the DHL office a couple of days before we arrived in

Kabul. Two people were killed by rifle fire, and some Westerners trying to use the parcel service were injured. Kabul was otherwise relatively peaceful while we were there.

Soon Dana was preparing to go back to Almaty, leaving me to figure out how to get to Herat, a city of half a million in the Hari River valley, over 800 kilometres west of Kabul. The route from Kabul to Herat went through Taliban-infested parts of Afghanistan, so the planning was troublesome. Many people, including Afghan reporters and UN employees, who were very knowledgeable about the state of the roads told me it would cost a lot of money to get anywhere interesting. Lines labelled roads on the maps were in real life degraded four-wheel-drive-only tracks. And there were no buses going that way. I would have to rent a Toyota Land Cruiser and maybe hire some guards too, which would set me back thousands of dollars.

I figured talking to some of Dana's UN contacts was worth a try. I asked if they still had vehicles passing through the Central Mountains, and learned that they had deemed it too risky at that moment. Taliban fighters were plaguing the road: they stopped vehicles and asked everyone to speak in Pashto. If you couldn't, or even if you spoke it with an Uzbek or Tajik accent, they slit your throat. The odd plane might fly out there, but boarding was denied to anyone but members of a recognized NGO or the UN. I asked people at our hotel if they had any knowledge of rides I could hitch, but some of the other Western guests were visibly traumatized hearing of my intention to strike out cross-country, so I stopped asking. My attitude was calm and matter of fact. Day after day I was travelling to places that were more or less dangerous. This road would be in the more category.

I had one last hope: the founder of Pajhwok Afghan News, Mr. Karokhel, said he would get back to me with the number of someone who knew about the vans that ply the mountain roads. He also warned me that one road carried a 30-percent chance of death, and the other an 80-percent chance. Otherwise there was not much to tell the routes apart.

"In that case," I said, "tell him I'm mainly interested in hitching a ride on the road with only a 30-percent chance of death."

Dana had an Afghan friend, Irshad, who worked for a Danish NGO. He invited us for dinner at his house in Kabul. The food was superb, but his wife was always scurrying around in the background, afraid to sit with us. She was the daughter of a prominent Taliban family, and so very traditional. Dana especially was trying to convince her to sit and eat with us. The conversation was about the NGO work Irshad was doing—good works, of course, and not really development.

I asked him if he did any business, and he talked about his family farm. He had the usual problems: a medieval level of productivity, and no way to increase it. If he brought in tractors and fertilizer, what would he do with all the families living nearby, who had been hired every year to do the work on his land for as long as anyone could remember? I told him how the Europeans had dealt with the same problem: they enclosed and appropriated common land to themselves, kicking off the peasants, who were forced to scatter and find their own way or starve in the cities. Irshad explained that, in a way, he didn't so much own his land as hold it for the good of the community. He was the head and was obliged to look after those he and his family had traditionally looked after. But, as a result, productivity was low, so food was expensive. Some people lived on meagre rations even when he helped them, as he felt obliged to do.

I told him, "These were exactly the conditions prevailing in Europe at the time just prior to the enclosures that preceded modern farming: feudal."

"I can't do it," he said.

"I wouldn't be interested in doing it either," I admitted, "even as a last resort."

I figure that what will happen is someone will start the process—someone more strongly motivated than other landowners, often because bleak reality forces his hand. Then, to compete, everyone else will have to follow and generate as much income as possible to stay in farming as prices for food drop and other prices rise. The money will be needed for capital investment, and there will be nothing to compensate the serfs for the loss of their social contract. Nasty vicious stuff. That is real development. If you were helping people do that, you'd be doing development work, and you'd know it because the locals would want to kill you, and when you sat with your family after coming home from work, you'd hate yourself. Only locals can do that to themselves; there's no way foreigners can get away with it without bringing a tornado of hatred down on themselves, which is why they don't do it.

We talked about some of Irshad's friends who had managed to get help from foreigners to get out of the country. I'd been asked by more than a few Afghans if there was any way for me to help them move to Canada. This is not something that aid agencies like to admit, but when a country has a disaster, it is soon followed by what they call the second disaster: the swarming foreigners looking for food and accommodation as they scramble to set up shop. Least talked about is the third disaster, when well-meaning foreigners assist every other Afghan they befriend to skip the country and get refugee status in the West. These go-getters and high-net-worth Afghans are thus not forced by circumstances to bite the bullet and improve their homeland, which is functionally equivalent to a disaster from the point of view of the people left behind and economically struggling. Similarly, much of the profit that Afghan contractors made from supplying the Americans is safely out of the country, in Dubai bank accounts.

The NGO worker's wife did at last come into the room briefly to sit with us. She was very shy, and very young too, not embodying any of the fierce reputation of the Taliban, I thought.

The time came to return to the Intercontinental, and soon after was our last breakfast together before a taxi would carry Dana to the airport. I kissed her goodbye, checked out of the Intercontinental Hotel, and checked in to the Mustafa, an old backpacker place downtown, left over from when Kabul used to be on the Kabul–Kathmandu–Kuta hippie trail of the 1970s. From the Mustafa, I called the number I got from Mr. Karokhel, which connected me with a guy he knew who had family in Bamiyan, a former Silk Road caravan stop to the west in the Hindu Kush mountains. It was hard to hear or understand English spoken with an Afghan accent over the phone, but I gathered that maybe a van would be leaving near the terminal end of Chicken Street at one or two in the morning.

Bag packed, around midnight I checked out and wandered through Kabul's pitch-black alleys. As I hurried down one street, someone called out to me in an unfamiliar language. I looked back to see, in the glow of a lamp near a concrete barricade, a couple of soldiers in government uniforms with AKs ... just before stumbling into razor wire that hadn't been there the day before. They must have put it there in response to the suicide bombings, which had happened right around here. Bleeding and annoyed (flesh heals but trousers do not, and these, though costing only fifteen dollars, were supposed to last me a few more years), I moved around the wire and continued my search in the darkness for anything that might be a bus stop. Figures passed me in the dark on occasion, and donkeys with wagonloads of foliage headed in from the hills surrounding the city, making better time as everyone else was asleep. Down another street I joined a crowd standing in the moonlight as if they were waiting for something. Sure enough, after an hour or so, a white four-wheel-drive HiAce van pulled up, and we each paid some money and found a place to squat inside on low wooden seats.

A young Afghan man, perhaps a teenager, could speak a bit of English. He repeated the advice that there was a 30-percent chance I wouldn't survive. He said that they were all worried our van would be stopped and robbed by the Taliban, but they would cut off my head. He added, "I will try to protect you."

"What are you, then?" I asked. "Police, or military?"

"I carve wooden spoons," he said.

So a vanload of Afghans, some of them Hazara—mountain dwellers perhaps descending from a Mongolian bloodline—and I drove off, making good time out of Kabul. When daylight came, I could sometimes recognize where we were from daytrips Dana and I had taken with government and NGO people. By god, the villages are poor here: mud with holes stained with shit from open sewers, and the high street is where people shop for sticks to reinforce flat mud-caked roofs. Sticks and mud and shit and people in rags.

As we approached the snow-covered mountains and wound our way into the Shibar Pass, northwest of Kabul, the people were as poor or poorer, but it didn't seem so bad since they had fruit trees and usually a river, while the villages lent some charm. Passing orchards held smiling girls in colourful shawls, who climbed into persimmon trees to cut fresh leaves for their goats. Perched atop immense cliffs were ruins of mud forts from the time of the Mongol Empire, while yellow-leafed poplars, war-blasted Soviet tanks, and armoured personal carriers littered the roadside, and signs or paint markings indicated some of the minefields blighting the soil.

This road was marvellously rough. We were reduced to a crawl at times, and only a four-wheel-drive could have possibly lurched along it; even the huge trucks that shared the way with us, bringing out the red onion harvest, were only those off-road-capable Russian designs. There was not a lot of traffic, and I had this worry that around one corner the driver would call out "Taliban." I'd dressed in local clothes, but it was no use, unlike in Iraq. I'd tested the get-up on the streets of Kabul and near-by, and found that the Afghans knew me for a foreigner immediately. It would have been better to try to pass as Arab, but I hadn't grown a beard. Anyhow, the die was cast. Funny thing, if four different people had told me that my chance of death was 20 percent, 22 percent, 18 percent, and 25 percent, I would have tried harder to find some other way to get here. As it was, the chance of death had been assessed at a definite 30 percent four times over, making me willing to take the risk.

It was a long, beautiful, and tiring journey, and wooden-spoon man helped me the whole time, finding cooked food to eat and translating when locals wanted to know why I was here, "as a tourist," of course. Around one bend I saw through the window to my left a tire—our tire, actually—rolling furiously away up the nearest mountain. It had been ripped off by the rough terrain. Every passenger but me wondered why our van was grinding to a halt. The biggest problem would be deciding who would hike up through the ubiquitous minefields to get that wheel. But then, a minor miracle: the tire came to a stop, and rather than top-pling, it started rolling back down the mountainside, eventually flopping over right within grabbing range of where our van had skidded to a halt. Nearly everyone, including me, got out to stretch their legs and watch as our driver and a helper staunched the leaking fluids and crammed the wheel on in the most rudimentary way. At even more of a crawl, we carried on to Bamiyan.

It was dark and cold in the street, with no obvious hotels. Wooden-spoon man offered me a place to sleep in his uncle's house, and I said yes. His uncle lived up a rickety set of stairs, almost a ladder, terminating at a concrete platform that was roofed and served as a sort of restaurant or eatery. I was shown to a bare room, large enough for me to stretch out and sleep on the carpet, and was told that if I needed the toilet in the night, I should climb down the ladder to the alley and go there. Hot food was brought too, a camel knee on an aluminum platter. I requested soup and bread instead. Nothing against camel, but what was there to eat in those two cracked bones knit together with cartilage, with some boiled skin over all? Does one suck off the skin, or the marrow? I'll never know.

This was as good a place as any for an extended stay, as Bamiyan was beautiful, with cliffs holding ancient niches and the rubble of the largest standing Buddha statues in the world—and the graffiti-covered tank that had been shooting at the statues. It broke down from bad karma when it was trying to leave town. If I'd been in full business mode, as had been my practice until the end of 2007, I might have tried to buy the tank for scrap metal, carting it into Kabul on one of the passing trucks, and perhaps sending it on to Karachi eventually to try to get it on a container ship. But that would have been an effort of some weeks, involving tens of thousands of dollars, and there was no guarantee of a payoff.

Instead there was hiking to enjoy, trying to chat with locals, or picnicking on green patches among the rocks and dirt and ditches. Sitting beneath the yellow-leafed popular trees and watching the slow rhythm of life in the valley was my favourite pastime, and a clear signal from my subconscious that the journey on the 30-percent-chance-of-death road had left me in need of some relaxation amid nature to calm my nerves. It was getting cold, almost November. Ice was forming on puddles and persisting past noon the next day. High time for me to push on, as my visa for Turkmenistan stated that I was to be entering from Herat and specified the exact day. I packed and went to snoop around the street where the vans trolled for passengers. After climbing into one, wooden-spoon guy appeared and ran over to me.

"No, no, mister, that van will be taking an 80-percent-chance-of-death road."

I grabbed my bag and got out, loading it into the next van over.

"No, mister, that van is worse, much worse."

"What? The 100-percent-chance-of-death road?"

"I know that van from around town. It has no shocks."

Days later, after mucking about on even rougher mountain roads and not being able to get through, I gave up and buzzed over the Hindu Kush mountains in a small plane. The city of Herat had a different vibe; there was more commerce, and it felt friendlier on the streets, which were bustling, more like what you'd expect in India or Pakistan. There was a rather tasty chicken restaurant, an interesting old fort, and a collection of leaning brick minarets from century-old mosques. Locals didn't seem to mind me wandering around. Word on the street was that the regional warlord was fierce enough that the Taliban didn't often range into the city proper. One time a man snapped his fingers aggressively in front of my face as we passed one another, perhaps to show that he'd sussed me out as foreign, but most people were friendly, and I enjoyed being a tourist.

Herat used to be the centre of an old empire, and a woman who lived here was a renowned poet. She wrote about love, and it was love that ended her life: she was not allowed to marry the man of her dreams and committed suicide. Optimists might say she was born too soon, but that would be presumptuous, even though a thousand years have passed, women's lives have yet to take a turn for the better.

When I moved over to the Marco Polo Hotel, still in Herat but with a nicer bed, I found other Westerners at the breakfast table: American aid workers. Their conversation was easily overheard, and it was more iteration of the white man's burden. They had this notion that they were trying to do development but were being stymied by swarthy locals, half devil and half child. I ate my meal in peace, packed, and started hitch-hiking north. After two cars and 5 kilometres of trudging at the end, there was the bridge to Turkmenistan. An ex-Russian Army guy named Oleg was to meet me with a car on the other side, as we'd arranged by email. It took quite a while to get stamped through. When I made it, Oleg shook my hand, grinning.

"Sorry it took so long with customs," he said.

"No need to apologize," I replied. "If Canada shared a border with Afghanistan, it would take as long or longer to pass. Let's go."

He had a tape deck in his car, and I noticed a Boney M cassette. I plopped it in and heard "Ra ra Rasputin, lover of the Russian Queen" over the speakers as we accelerated to highway speed.

TURKMENISTAN WAS JUST GETTING OVER THE DAMAGE CAUSED BY the rule of the power-crazed dictator Saparmurat Niyazov. Soviet leader Mikhail Gorbachev had elevated him to high office, since he seemed like a grey apparatchik who kept his head down and obeyed orders. When the Soviet Empire broke up, he was suddenly absolutely powerful. If it's a rare person who can handle power, then this guy was especially common. He gave himself the title Türkmenbaşy (leader of the Turkmen) and wrote a rambling manifesto, supposedly laying out the mythical history of the Turkmen people, but actually about as coherent as something penned by the Unabomber.

Oleg explained that if you want a driver's licence here, the exam has little to do with the rules of the road; most questions are about the contents of this manifesto, *Ruhnama*, "The Book of the Soul." It is taught in a building shaped like a humungous open book. Printed copies of the dictator's feverish scribblings were blasted off into space, at great cost. We can only suppose space symbolized, for him, communication, strung as it is with satellites switching data at dizzying speed. His magnum opus will simply spin in a decaying orbit until burning up in the atmosphere, unread.

For the full measure of his megalomania, consider this: he built a giant "mosque" and demanded that each Turkmen visit at least once in their lives. This building is capped with a dome but has script from

Ruhnama instead of the Quran on the walls, so it wasn't clear to me that it could be called a mosque. What was pretty clear, Türkmenbaşy saw himself as another prophet of Islam. If you know anything about Islam, you will know that this sort of claim is bound to generate controversy. Luckily he was dead as of late 2006, not long before my visit. Oddly, but par for Turkmenistan, the new leader was the old leader's dentist.

The country is littered with Türkmenbaşy's pet projects; in fact, I slept in some of them: towering hotels such as you might see at tourist attractions in places popular with tourists. Usually I was the only guest, but one time there was another person staying in my cavernous hotel—not a Turkmen but a Western traveller: the author Mark Alpert, who was researching the sequel to his bestselling novel *Final Theory*. We went together to the national museum, which was worth a visit just to see their collection of *rhytons* (drinking horns). Most were carved ivory, set with precious metals, from the times of the Parthian Empire.

I also got to know Oleg as we spent a couple of weeks hanging out and camping well into chilly November. He had studied to be a philologist before joining the army, and he told me some old Russian sayings. One stuck with me: if you sleep with a Kazakh girl, you live two hundred years. He also told me a story about how he was duped into working for a company that had set out to defraud the dictator. A local businessman proposed to Türkmenbaşy that he would make a cotton-processing factory. He used the initial payment to buy an old Spanish factory that was being scrapped, shipping it to Turkmenistan so that it might pass for the latest technology. The businessman slowly put it together and hired some workers, including Oleg, to help with the project. This was all for show; he only wanted Türkmenbaşy to release the bulk of the funds. As soon as he had control of $10 million, he disappeared with his family to South America. The dictator was furious but the man and the money were never found. Oleg and some of the other employees were worried that they'd be blamed, but, luckily, no revenge was exacted on them—other than that they didn't get paid, of course.

The ruined city of Merv, though too ruined to be visually spectacular, is top-notch from a historical point of view, as it used to be one of the greatest cities of Islamic scholarship and Silk Road riches in Asia. That is, until the great khan, he of "What is best in Life? To destroy your enemies, see them driven before you, and hear the lamentation of their women" fame, demanded that the people turn over half their food and all their pretty women to him. When they refused, he levelled the site. If you visit after the rains, you can sometimes find beads and jewellery from a thousand years of history exposed on the surface. Oleg wore just such a millennial necklace strung with trinkets and beads collected over many occasions of wandering the ruins.

Ashgabat was an oddly lovely capital city from a certain point of view—the point of view of someone riding at the head of a convoy of limos: specifically, the ruler of the nation. Wide newly paved avenues were perfect for official inspections but a strange use of funds for a nation mostly lacking private vehicles, or many cars at all, really. All the buildings, by presidential decree, had to be faced in gleaming white Carrara marble from Italy, 4.5-million square metres' worth, to look splendid as his limo cruised past. One older building was clad in marble that was neither gleaming white nor Italian, so the walls were in the process of being stripped and redone in line with the dead leader's whim. Türkmenbaşy's statue poked up in the city centre: a gold doohickey to exalt a dumpy-looking bureaucrat in a golden superman cape, which revolves to face the sun. Other egotistical monuments littered the environment near and far, including a tribute to the guy's mother, after whom he had renamed a day of the week.

Ashgabat is old in a way, and new in another; the area is prone to some of the most devastating earthquakes on the planet, so a long succession of would-be kings of kings have built to the sky and been brought down to earth, contributing another layer to the interesting local archeology. The last major earthquake was in 1948 and killed a tenth of the republic's people.

People have been living in towns along the north slope of the Zagros Mountains for over ten thousand years. The plains where rivers used to flow are dotted with "tells"—mounds of accumulated debris of town life. One had been torn open in 1886 at the command of a Russian general,

Komarov, who was looking for gold. Its value to science was nil, but it was valuable to the visitor, as you could see the pottery shards from five thousand years ago under your feet, with fertility symbols, microliths, and clay spindles. Oleg told me there used to be a cult based on a yogurt drink called soma: it was like a bhang lassi, familiar to me from India, but as well as marijuana, it was laced with opium and a plant containing something like ephedra, a precursor to ecstasy. They had these wonderful white curvy bottles that they would drink the soma from, with a stylized black sketch of a pie-eyed girl on the side. I didn't manage to see one outside a museum, but I imagine it is a drink that would go down well nowadays at raves. Soma was the first known example of a drug concoction being frowned upon—the prophet Zoroaster preached against partaking thousands of years ago.

One valley in the southern Kopet Dag Mountains held Nokhur, a town of people who claim to be descendants of Alexander the Great, and to have only bred with each other since the days when chariots were hip. Maybe they were of a pure race: they sure had a similar look to them, like pod-people. And those who had the means put four spiralling horns of mountain sheep, projecting as if to the cardinal directions, atop their house's support studs and also atop their family grave markers. They resembled Ionic pillars, but made with wood and horn rather than stone.

Oleg and I went camping in the Yankala Canyon lands in the west, an eroded landscape of pink and white sandstone that dips toward the Caspian Sea, where I collected fossil shark teeth from the now-vanished Tethys Sea and lived off mutton cooked over the campfire. November days were cold and the nights colder, so much so that mutton fat would congeal in my throat after swallowing. It was probably just as well: normally the deserts hereabouts are crawling with aggressive fringed lizards. They like to flap open their fringes, hissing, and sprint over on two legs to chase interloping humans, only desisting when you are out of their territory. Of course, then you are in the next lizard's territory, and it is equally game to bite you. The cold had put them into torpor. We didn't see very many venomous snakes either, not even sunning on the black roads. A fair number of camels wandered about, however. They are an easy animal to keep, as they are loyal and recognize their owners. However far they might roam, they eventually come home. One day, Oleg told me, he had been sleeping out under the stars when a passing camel must have seen him there in the dark. This beast silently padded over on spongy toes. Perhaps it couldn't quite decide if Oleg was its human or just some random guy. So it loomed closer, closer, closer. Some sense caused Oleg to awaken suddenly, and by moon and starlight he saw this big goofy-looking camel face, lips nearly sucking his nose.

Later, on the shore of the Caspian Sea, I searched the beaches for the colourful shells of crustaceans scattered in white sand. I was staying in Türkmenbaşy, a town renamed after the leader, who proceeded to cram it with follies, including hotels meant to rival Dubai, I suppose. They were impressive from a distance until you realized they stood empty as tombs. It would have been fun to cross this great inland sea by boat, but the only way to get a visa to Azerbaijan was to arrive by air, so I returned to Ashgabat, had a last dinner to say goodbye to Oleg and meet his charming wife, then flew to Baku in Azerbaijan.

AZERBAIJAN MEANS "LAND OF THE FIRE GOD," A REFERENCE TO THE Persian religion from before the Arab conquest. There are still some remnants of fire temples around, including one built around a natural seepage of flame from the ground, where the priests used to deform, melt, and scar their limbs and flesh with fire as a sign of their closeness to celestial angels. Sacrifice of this sort is admired still in Central Asia, even if the religion has evolved: in Afghanistan, certain men had noticed potentially Quranic material burning in a rubbish dump near an American base and had rescued a few charred pages, at the cost of injuries much like those once admired in this temple. And the men put their scars to the same use, as they learned to show them off to their peers, gathering praise from this proof of piety.

Baku is an oil town, so energy from flames is still the bedrock of the Land of the Fire God, though now the energy is kinetic, for running our machines, rather than spiritual, for motivating believers. Apart from the oil, the city was reminiscent of some of those I had seen in southern South

America, emphasizing high-fashion shops; similar short, black-haired people; and the same Italian-style architecture. This civilized interlude was a chance for me to get on Facebook and link up with Lydia, who was making her way back to the United States through the Caucasus region, connecting the dots between groups of fellow Peace Corps volunteers.

We crossed into Georgia together. There, in keeping with my improved version of the "hundred-mile diet"—I sample all of the world's best food in season when I pass within a hundred miles or so of where it is finest and freshest—I made a most unexpected discovery. Although I assumed I had tasted all the world's famed cuisines by then, I was amazed by Georgia's tasty dishes centred on a tart wild-plum sauce. My vocabulary lacks the words to describe their unique cookery. Anyhow, writing about food is a bit like dancing about architecture, so it only makes sense to go and try it. Food tastes so much better when you are good and hungry from exploring the landscape that inspired it. Lydia and I would plan our days around restaurants, and we spent the time between meals working up an appetite, hiking in the wooded hills and seeing monasteries, castles, churches, and vineyards. (Georgian wine is still sometimes made the ancient traditional way, in great pottery urns filled with bunches of grapes, stems and all, and buried in the soil. It used to be customary for parents to prepare a few thousand litres in such fashion on the birth of a boy, and then open them up for his marriage when he reached his teenage years.)

We wanted to see Armenia on our way through, so after experiencing ballet in Tbilisi, and yet more excellent meals, we crossed over to Yerevan, in the shadow of Mount Ararat, mountain of Noah's Ark fame. In one of the villages we stopped so that Lydia could touch base with some of her Peace Corps contacts. As usual they were heavy drinkers, keen on the local hooch. This is common for Peace Corps members nearly everywhere. They are often young when they join, right out of university, so the idea of passing out drunk is new and fun. Then they get posted alone to tiny villages, where they soon discover that drinking moonshine is what the locals do to prevent boredom, and villages are very boring compared to university.

This was a jolly crew. One of the guys was a proud virgin in his twenties, which I suppose is not so unusual in modern American culture. Another couple of Peace Corps guys were telling a story about how they had been learning the language long enough that they felt reasonably fluent. It happened gradually and then all of a sudden. They remembered the day it really sank in. On a local bus they were discussing and joking about a particularly vulgar porno they had watched at one alcoholic session. One of them remarked, "Isn't it great that we have this secret language so that we can say what we want in this busload of old grannies and none of them have a clue what we are talking about, since it is all in English?" They laughed, but then the other guy noticed the baleful glances of the locals. "I just realized we're talking in Armenian."

That night I was hallucinating strange colours and had trouble sleeping. In the morning, when I mentioned this to the Peace Corps guys, they said, "Don't worry, the local moonshine always does that. We should have warned you perhaps."

It was lonely for the Peace Corps stationed here, and brain damaging too. Not only from the hooch. After a while they begin to speak in acronyms—a local becomes a third-country national, or TCN, for example—but they have acronyms for everything, which is a good habit to form only if you are comfortable being doomed to morph into a bureaucrat. The guys told me they also had to be careful not to chat too long with a village girl or else her parents and the whole village would assume intent to get married. It wasn't so different in the outports of Newfoundland in my grandparents' day, where if a boy walked a girl back to her house from school three times, it might be taken as a sign of an engagement. The Peace Corps guys couldn't chat readily with the village boys either, because of local resentment. Girls have been told by their families to have nothing to do with the local boys: they are expected to marry up, to a city boy. The local boys see an American who can have any girl in the village but spurns them all, and it eats their hearts out.

Lydia and I decided to tour a little wannabe country named Nagorno-Karabakh (Black Mountain Garden), and our visit ended in a fiasco. It's a breakaway region of Azerbaijan, spawned from a vicious little war between ethnic Armenians living in the hills and Azeri conscripts told to suppress rebellion. We needed a special visa to get in, but once inside the land didn't appear as militarized as expected. In the course of getting a feel for the place, we met a taxi driver who told us he'd show us everywhere of any interest for what seemed a fair price. We climbed into his car and started in on forests, monasteries, and one odd site: a ruined city that he described as Agdan. He told us in Russian that it used to be full of Azeris until the Armenians attacked and drove them out. They shot a bunch in the back, including women and children. He'd seen it with his own eyes. I believed him too, since he was ethnic Armenian himself and thought it was shameful.

Up in the hills, a convoy of black SUVs overtook us and boxed us in. Our driver seemed very nervous and told us that we were not supposed to visit the ruined city, and someone must have tipped off the secret police. He wanted us to promise that we would deny that we had ever seen the ruins, and Lydia frantically erased the pictures that she'd taken. I was glad that I hadn't kept the bullet a drunken Armenian soldier had given me that morning as a keepsake.

Lydia and I were separated, then driven to a military prison for interrogation. I had a very angry interior ministry policeman yelling at me in Russian that I would suffer worse than I'd ever suffered before. I doubted he would follow through on the threat, and decided to pretend that I could understand no Russian at all, not even "Da" and "Nyet." I simply stood there grinning. Eventually he had to call in a translator, who happened to be the only guy in the area who could speak English. Funny thing, but we were already acquainted; I had sought him out for advice on my first day in the territory, and we'd got on well over tea and cookies. The threat was repeated, and this time my main interrogator stood glowering and triumphant as he waited for the translator to convey to me the dreadful nature of my situation. The translation was merely "Relax, eventually this guy will run out of steam and let you go."

Now the advantage had shifted. I could use the translator's English-to-Armenian language skills to find opportunities to get everyone sidetracked into tales of misadventures trying to pick up women in bars in various countries, and eventually six of the eight interrogators assigned to me were laughing.

Obviously, Lydia, as young as she was, would break under interrogation, but I couldn't be 100 percent sure of this, so I had to maintain a line that would serve no matter what. My contention was that Agdan is a ruin, completely levelled, so who can say where the city proper once began and what were merely the outskirts, beyond city limits. Since I had not visited the distant ruin that was clearly once a mosque, in my opinion I hadn't been to the centre, and for all I knew, maybe I hadn't set foot in Agdan at all.

Many hours having passed, they brought me to the interrogation chamber were Lydia was being held. Clearly she had been crying a lot, distressed and slumped, as if she hadn't had any fun whatsoever, making me feel guilty about how much I'd been enjoying the game. It wasn't my first time in a situation such as this, and by my age I had learned how to handle these "bumps in the road" and disarm the secret police with humour. They kicked us out after searching our bags, but six of my interrogators came to the border to shake my hand and told me to come back and visit them one day. Lydia admitted that it was her first time being interrogated for real, and we laughed about it as we headed back into Armenia proper. It was a good and not too spicy sampling of interrogation for her, should she ever need to know the minimum to expect from secret police on whatever paths her life held in store.

We finished Armenia with some more church visits, sampling Armenian cognac and admiring local pink granite that figures in their architecture. The Debed Canyon held more monastery cave churches, and pagan Greek temples on a ridge we passed on the way. Armenia was perhaps the first nation to go Christian. I've noticed this about religions: they meld and evolve, and never appear as if out of the blue. For example, when the rulers of Armenia decided to push a new religion for their people and needed to choose one, what they picked out of the design space of possible theologies was not some outlandish thing, as different to what came before as Aztec is to Zen; rather, it made perfect political sense: with Jews to the south, angel-worshipping Persians to the east, and virgin-mother-goddess-admiring Greeks to the west, they split the differences.

We hadn't had our fill of Georgia or Georgian food, so it was north again, through the birthplace of Stalin, Gori, with the museum staff, including pouty Georgian girls in Soviet uniforms and tall black boots, selling kitschy memorabilia of the monstrous dictator. The Black Sea coast used to be malarial and swampy, so was never much inhabited, but just inland was the land called Colchis, Jason's land of the Golden Fleece, from the fleeces used to trap placer gold in the streams. By December we'd reached Batumi, on the seashore, and were wandering in forests and botanical gardens, picking mandarin oranges, and watching the butter-flies flit about in a grove inside an ancient Roman fortress. I wondered if some of the Romans of this legionnaire's camp had been the ones to fall victim to the infamous mad honey. Local honeybees have developed the ability to feed on rhododendrons, flowers normally relegated to bumble-bees. The resulting concentration of psychedelics made honey that ush-ers partakers into dizziness, paralysis and hallucinations. The forces of General Pompey were duped into eating honeycomb by King Mithridates of Pontus and were slain by sword thrusts in the ultimate "bad trip."

We crossed into Turkey and followed the southern shore of the Black Sea past Trabzon and its cherry orchards, ending up in Istanbul during an Islamic holiday. This was fine, as the city is plenty interesting even if the bazaar and buildings are closed. Riding around on the fer-ries and eating fish sandwiches from elaborately carved restaurant boats, their prows sculpted into dragons or mermaids and painted red and gold, made for a pleasant stay. Lydia took off back to the United States, while I stopped in England first, on my way to Canada for Christmas 2008.

Heathrow was more trouble than usual. They didn't like the stamps in my passport, especially the Afghan tourist visa. I spent nine hours in the glass box, a record even for me, with a guy guilty of flying while black, and a woman who just didn't have the right personality for getting through customs. She came across as spinny and happy-go-lucky, with no definite plans. My interrogation this time was a series of outlandish questions with a half hour wait between each. They confiscated some

Tic Tacs from my pocket so that I wouldn't do harm to myself or others, or so they told me. Eventually I got through. Western customs and security have dedicated hundreds of person-hours to interrogating me, and my backpack has got to be one of the most security-scrutinized bags in existence.

This border mania stems from unintended consequences that are the undoing of well-meaning regulation. For example, Europeans have made it very difficult to sack someone from their job; consequently, employers are reluctant to hire. There is no net benefit to society. Human rights campaigners have made a fetish of this line called the border, and all sorts of legal rights activate for the person who steps over it. The result is aggravation at the border, especially for people who end up lumped among those who make disproportionate use of these rights, such as those from poor countries or those not easy to categorize.

Any small social-justice triumph for those advocating that more extensive legal rights be granted to non-citizens is more than cancelled by the resulting hassles and denials of visas at the border. If a human rights group wins extra protection for refugees, the headline and story in the newspaper ought to read: "Do-Gooders Do Badly Yet Again. Travel and international business now more difficult for people whose lives don't fit into neat boxes and most especially for people of colour: several people in places such as Africa likely to be pauperized by the indirect effects of lost trade for each potential refugee helped by sexed-up legal protection."

On my return to Canada, I went to Vancouver for Christmas, where I was given a bag of dried mangos, and a present from beyond the grave: a bottle of homemade apple jam from Aunt Heather, who had died recently, when I had been in Bishkek. She must have put it in the mail before she went into hospital. I also renewed an otherwise perfectly valid passport so as to start fresh without the weird stamps.

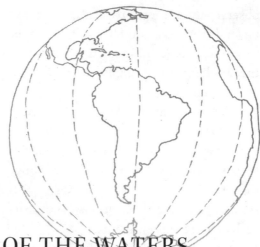

CHAPTER ELEVEN

THE MIXING OF THE WATERS

Brazil · Colombia

A SPIN OF A GLOBE IN VANCOUVER ONE NIGHT IN JANUARY 2009 showed me that another long South American trip, concentrating this time on the north of the continent, would put me among people and parts unknown. My practised eye took in the geography and estimated windows of opportunity for getting through mountain passes and over rivers and deserts, avoiding the sort of heat or rain that turned roads into ovens or mud pits. Peru was an excellent place to start, as my dad would be there with his wife, Maureen, who was working on an academic project dealing with rural development NGOs. What's more, cheap yellow fever vaccinations were available in Lima at a cost of $10, compared to $150 in Canada.

After meeting up with my dad and Maureen, we bussed into thin air, over 5,000 metres, to visit the valley of the condors, where we observed these impressive birds riding the thermals, often floating just beyond arm's reach of the road cut into the cliffs. With my dad I went to see Machu Picchu again, this time by train and bus rather than the Inca trail. I'd already explored this lost city the year before, but ... it's Machu Picchu.

North-central Peru had gone unvisited on my first trip to this country, but Dad and I managed to bus into the Cordillera Blanca in time for my fortieth birthday. I don't always mark my birthdays, as they aren't that special to me: it's not like there's anything more to look forward to; not like the Aztecs, who could legally drink alcohol starting on their sixtieth. But this one was special because it meant I'd had a birthday on each of the seven continents.

The Cordillera Blanca is the highest range of mountains outside the Himalayas, with deep valleys dotted with maize and potato farms, and rushing rivers. The high peaks are snow-capped year-round, and make a fine backdrop for green pampas meadows abounding with llamas, groves of eucalyptus trees, and titanka, a weird plant that looks like aloe vera and grows as much as 3 metres in diameter—after forty years of growing it sends up a 10-metre central stalk as big around as an alder tree, with flowers on top. Also catching my interest was talk of a ruined temple of the hallucinogenic-cactus-sniffing Chimú people, with underground passages and chambers, some of which are full of idols to jaguar gods and condor gods, as well as altars for human sacrifice.

Regional towns and cities in Peru proved a bit disappointing. They lack old buildings and are merely block after block of crumbly concrete with rebar sticking out of the roofs. Lakes are to blame: they build up behind landslides high on the mountainsides; then, after earthquakes, they pour into the valleys, destroying any urban areas in the valley bottoms and killing most of the people. This happens about as often as those flowering stalks on the titanka, which must be a huge disappointment to those trying to build a stable civilization.

One of the valleys, which can be reached only across a 4,500-metre pass, used to be prime habitat for pumas and the San Pedro cactus. And one of the Chimú civilization's temples, the oldest in the New World, is here to be explored, now a ruin. For 3,000 years, people have sought out this temple, through this valley that echoes with the calls of pumas, to worship by getting high on the hallucinogenic cactus. Instrumental for snorting the finely ground cactus powder is a bone tube carved with symbolic images of half-man half-animal gods and goddesses. The outer walls of the temple are decorated with a series of stone heads that show the process of hallucinatory transformation from man to puma. The first head is carved to appear entirely human; the second reveals he has sniffed some cactus powder, as streams of what is meant to be blood, carved in stone, come from his nose. The eyes of the following heads show dilated pupils and vacant stares as the features morph into an increasingly feline form, until the final head is that of a snarling puma. It had never occurred to me that a temple existed anywhere dedicated to sniffing hallucinogenic cactus, so you can imagine how happy I was to find one high in the Andes.

Lima is known to have the friendliest Brazilian embassy, and next-day visas are a shoo-in, so I bussed back there along the dunes and cold Pacific coastline, saw off my familial travelling companions, and got an excellent-value yellow fever top-up shot while waiting for my visa to be sorted before I struck out to float the length of the Amazon.

AT FIRST THE TRIBUTARIES OF THE WORLD'S GREATEST RIVER FAILED to impress me, as they were narrow channels with swampy banks, like those I had seen along the Bolivian Amazon the year before. The first major sign of civilization is Iquitos, deep in the jungle, the largest city in the world with no road access. A local guy standing on the riverbank tried to interest me in a necklace of beads that had a snake head hanging from it, a meaty pendant as big as a clenched fist: it would give me luck on the journey he said in Spanish. But I spurned this fetish in favour of a less arcane form of luck: a friendly Texan guy, well met in the hostel. We decided to travel together and help each other avoid thieves—we'd both heard that some local people steal from backpacks. He was muscular with a shaved head and a few tattoos. Rather than Tex, I'd call him Mex: his ancestors would have been besieging the Alamo, not dying in there with Davy

Crockett, and he looked it, apart from his eyes which seemed Asian. He told an anecdote about an old woman greeting him in Cantonese; when he said he couldn't understand, she scolded him for ignoring his heritage.

We shopped for hammocks to string on the deck of whatever boat we could find passage aboard. We wanted to be able to lounge and have somewhere to sleep during the trip, but ended up stashing the hammocks in our backpacks, as the best boat out of there, while fast, was too slender to hang them. We docked eventually at a small jungle town on the frontier of Peru. Many of the people there live in the swamp by the river on wooden houses perched up on stilts, and they get from house to house on wooden gangplank roads, also up on stilts. We asked around about another boat and were told to expect a wait of some days.

For something to do, Mex and I climbed into a canoe and crossed over to where Colombia owns the shore and rain forest. We were illegal aliens, I suppose, as we didn't get our passports stamped at Colombian customs, which we couldn't find. Our first jungle encounter was a pretty young gringo woman walking alone through the trees, with a tattoo of a yellow rose on the back of her neck. Upriver there had been a fat Texan who had a restaurant called the Yellow Rose of Texas. I'd gone in to try alligator nuggets with mustard and chips. Tasty, better than chicken nuggets—but what was up with all these Texans all of a sudden? None for months and now one a day for three days in a row.

"You must be from Texas," I said to the tattooed girl. "Did you go to that yellow rose place up the river in Peru?"

"I am from Texas, but the guy who works at my hotel told me about the Texan who owns that restaurant. The local people regularly hold demonstrations outside, because the owner gets drunk and yells 'Every woman in this town is a whore,' and he sticks any children who come near with a needle so that they don't bother his customers. I suppose he must have 'lost it' from being too long in the jungle. And the dude is married to a local woman, go figure."

"What are you doing way out here?" Mex asked.

"Do you want to come to the saloon out in the forest?" she said. "I'm on my way to it now." We joined her.

It was a proper saloon, complete with swinging doors and Amazonian girls dancing in feathered boas. We sat down at a small table near the dance floor, ordered ourselves a few beers, and started to drink. Then a guy, well dressed and confident, who might have been a bouncer or a waiter or even the owner for all we knew, came over.

"You can't sit there," he said in Spanish. "It's reserved for someone important. But I can put you at another table as long as you drink something more expensive than beer."

Mex's Spanish is perfect, so he understood all this. His reply was, "We can drink rum all night, sheep-fucker, show us this other table."

The guy was taken aback for a second, at a loss for words, and then recovered enough composure to say, "You must be from Mexico."

Afterward, we found that we were stuck in this small Colombian riverside town, at the tri-border area between Peru, Colombia, and Brazil, due to a lack of entry stamps. We tried to cross into Brazil, but they noticed our lack of a Peruvian exit stamp, or Colombian entry, for that matter; we'd have to work around that problem, but we were in no hurry, so we took a canoe back to the Peru shore. We'd only have been waiting for the next slow boat down the Amazon, which was slow in coming. All the more time for drinking beer, sweltering Amazon jungle heat, and gushing downpours of rain that made the metal roofs clang.

ANDERS, A NORWEGIAN DOCUMENTARY FILMMAKER WHOM I'D MET on the last boat, wanted to interview me; he was travelling around with all this mic and camera equipment, doing interviews for a documentary film on the strange people you can meet travelling in jungle wilderness. However, he was having trouble finding travellers to interview, and worried that perhaps he'd got into too remote a place. "I'm a strange person," I told him. He filmed me and recorded tales of my adventures. His body was shaking, and his skin beaded with sweat as he filmed, and later he messaged me to say it had been dengue fever, as feared.

We have since kept in touch through social media, and now he's married, but back then he was a single guy, out for fun. One night he had taken a canoe across from Peru to Colombia, much as Mex and I had, but encountered some scary turbulence and a hidden sandbank. He didn't capsize, luckily, and wound up at a party at a shack in the jungle. There was a lovely local girl who took a fancy to him and wanted to pull him into a backroom. He was very drunk by then, but still cognizant of his iffy status: "I can't spend the night here because I need to get across the river and come back when Colombian immigration is open. I'm here illegally," he said. She said, "I am the Colombia immigration officer," and whipped out a badge. Just as he was thinking, Oh no, I'm screwed, she said, "Come in here with me and I'll sort you out." She might even have given him multiple entry—lucky guy. As for Mex and me, an extra night to recover and a few bribes later, we got back into Peru and over to Brazil, and found spaces on the covered deck of a bigger boat to Manaus.

We passed some ports where fellow foreigners were getting off to go find shamans who would facilitate their taking ayahuasca, a mix of powerful hallucinogens from jungle vines. I had just assumed that Mex and I would end up doing the same, as the drugs are meant to expand the mind and provide useful insight into the human condition, so I was surprised to hear that he hadn't the slightest interest. That being the case, I gave it a pass too. There's always the possibility I'll come back one day to try some ayahuasca in the right circumstances.

We carried on down the Amazon. Our boat was stopping in Manaus, Brazil, a historic city at the merging of two great tributaries. Its glory years, during the rubber boom, were long behind it, happily, as this means the arrogant upper crust are gone, while the decaying but still lovely opera houses and mansions remain for more interesting people to enjoy. Not all the foreigners were off hallucinating in the jungle; we met an African American girl, tall seemingly no-nonsense Jocelyn, who, when we got to know her, turned out to be up for all sorts of nonsense, beer drinking, and chatting over Brazilian barbecue. She was going our way, to the mouth of the Amazon on the Atlantic coast.

While waiting out a tropical downpour, I popped into an internet café for the first time in three weeks. My stepdad Jim had sent news that the research vessel that had carried me to Antarctica the previous year had run aground in Marguerite Bay, near the Argentinean base. The expedition company had sent out a sister ship to rescue the stranded passengers. There was also an email from Brenda, who had done Central America with me when I'd first taken up my backpack, so long ago now. Her husband, Marty, had died, leaving her to raise the kids. I'd only really met him once, and could remember that he played piano. There was also some talk about him getting on the crew of a crab-fishing boat, and one of the questions the skipper had asked him was: "How many stories do you have? These are long hours at sea." I sent my condolences.

Mex, Jocelyn, and I were soon floating downstream from Manaus, through the mixing of the waters—one tributary coloured black, the other more like mocha. This last stretch of the 4,000-kilometre Amazon River would carry us all the way to Belém on the South Atlantic. The boat had a filthy smokestack in back, and the captain had flown the Brazilian flag just behind this stack; it was stained so badly it resembled, more than anything, a black pirate flag.

I slept in a hammock on a deck crowded with Amazonians. A cluster of women and girls had slung their hammocks under and over mine. They were fun and feisty, and though I couldn't speak their language, it was an occasion for much giggling when they discovered my lack of a wedding ring. One or more of them had a penchant for midnight bottom grabbing. Alas, along one lonely stretch of river, after goodbye kisses, they jumped into a canoe to paddle to their jungle shack in a muddy tributary.

It was a festive occasion when the boat surged past these isolated villages, and hordes of the residents would paddle out to wave at us as we passed. Mothers, too, would take their kids and babies out to watch us go by, and in one village all the kids flailed their arms and said, Wooo, wooo, like ghosts—perhaps imitating the forró music blasting non-stop from speakers in the stern.

Eventually the jungle banks of this mother of rivers widened so that no one saw land, even from the top deck of the boat. I could have fooled myself that we were at sea, if not for the kids in canoes surfing the wake until they could fling a grappling hook over our side rails and scamper aboard. Typical were a couple of brave boys, around ten years old or so, who positioned their canoe so they could surge into our bow wake, and got a hook onto the hull; then they pulled themselves in and roped on, all while their canoe was bucking like a bronco on the waves. They wanted to sell us passengers baskets of boiled prawns, and roasted palm nuts that tasted like buttered squash. They did a roaring trade; in a matter of five minutes they had sold out, unhooked the grapple, and got away through the wake without capsizing, somehow.

By late February, we'd reached Belém and had a little beer session to say goodbye to Jocelyn, who was going to Brasília and then turning north to visit Bahia. Mex and I were southward bound along the coast for Natal, city of dunes.

Our hostel there was made to be like a castle, with towers and a drawbridge; the dining hall had a big wooden table like what knights sit around in medieval movie sets, with lots of painted battle shields on the walls. The beaches weren't bad, with plentiful sand dunes, and dune buggies for rent, but first we had to get our visas extended. The border police can put restrictions on your visa when you cross over, and when Mex and I had approached immigration on that jungle frontier, the guy hadn't liked the look of us, and had given us only a month instead of the usual three. The situation was quickly repaired, and we hung around doing the usual beach and tourist stuff for a while, going to the bars to pick up girls, riding in dune buggies, swimming. My feet were very white from keeping them in boots since Central Asia the year before, and then covered all through the Amazon to guard against mosquitoes, and I burned one of them even hiding under a beach umbrella, just from light reflected off the ocean.

ONE QUIET NIGHT, SNUG IN MY CASTLE OF A HOSTEL, IT OCCURRED TO me it would be a good time to take a turn on the computer in the common room. I found an email from Dana with the subject line "Will you make baby with me?" Intrigued, I opened it and read that it was just so.

In Kazakh tradition, a daughter is not fully responsible for her first baby—they figure it is easiest for a dutiful daughter to get started on a family under the assumption that girls give their first baby to their mothers to raise. Dana had been such a baby, raised by her grandmother. Kazakhs have a rustic sense of humour, so she used to be teased that she had fallen off the watermelon cart. Anyhow, her mom was asking about that first baby. While Dana was already past the usual years for this sort of thing, she figured it was now or never.

I went down to the beach to deliberate, and decided, why not? My intuition raised no objections, and it is never useful to overthink big decisions. My intuition decides what is next in life, and overthinking only loads it down with excess baggage, taking the joy out of the inevitable journey. Dana had turned out splendidly from that same cultural childrearing practice, even if it seemed strange to Canadian sensibilities.

We agreed that I would meet her in four months, in the springtime, and multi-task. Conveniently, the north of Kazakhstan, where Dana's family lived, was new to me, especially the Altai Mountains, Outer Mongolia, and parts east. Dana would book time off work and we'd go north together. But for now, I was on the other side of the planet from Dana, bearing south.

SOUTHERN BRAZIL SUSTAINS TWO OF THE CONTINENT'S MEGACITIES; Mex and I headed south to take a look. He'd accompany me as far as Rio de Janeiro, where we would meet up with Jocelyn again.

Rio is a place of stark contrasts between rich and poor, with favelas encrusting the higher crevasses between sugarloaf mountains of granite, like colourful barnacles above the low-tide line of urbanization at Copacabana and the other bays and beaches. They say about real estate, location, location, location, but Rio demonstrates how this cannot be the final word. It has one of the best locations I've ever clapped eyes on in terms of natural beauty; even the bedrock is luscious and curvy, and the bays offer glimpses and teases of this smooth landscape, barely covered by its bikini of jungle. But most of the buildings are nothing special, as drab and ugly as the sweaty tourists and drunks leering at women's bodies at Copacabana. If you wanted to envision a dream city, imagine a colossal Christ the Redeemer looking down on the buildings of Buenos Aires, or better yet Barcelona, instead of what's there now.

Rio is also a violent city, which is disturbing if you are not born there or inured to it. One of the hostels down the street was invaded and robbed by an armed gang; the police caught them, as one of the robbers was recognized by the staff as a former employee. I was reasonably careful; Mex and I went together with a local guide when we visited the favelas, bringing nothing of value. And one night down on the beach, when it started to get dark, I returned to my hostel; everyone who stayed to see the sun set was robbed by a man with a machete. Here and in some of the other megacities of the south, the wealthy businessmen and their families have been driven up into the sky by threat of kidnapping; they shun the streets, keeping to penthouses that they flit between in helicopters.

My life choices had not rendered me a prime target for thieves, despite my personal treasure of experiences that would, given the extraordinary inflation of travel costs over the last few decades, cost another man millions of dollars to duplicate. All those experiences are a form of wealth like any other, but an intensely personal form that cannot be stolen or transferred, or taxed for that matter, despite paying rich dividends. And these dividends are all collected by me. In the way they appreciate and give pleasure and value over the years, travels of this sort are like antiques bought for pennies in a decade when few people appreciated their true worth; that they cannot be stolen or taxed more than compensates for the fact that they cannot be sold.

Millennials, who are counselling everyone to spend their money on experiences not things, have got the right idea, but it will create a headache for the taxman. A non-material multimillionaire such as me is just another guy in scruffy clothes, blending with the crowd, unfairly happy from living life as he wanted. Even if I could be detected and a wealth tax levied against me, my refrain would be, Can't pay, won't pay.

Mex, Jocelyn, and I did a farewell booze cruise in Rio's harbour; they were up for more drinking, while my path took me inland, alone, for another megacity. Most people's livers had already taken a beating from Carnival, which I'd skipped, leaving me healthy and good to go. São Paulo is a megacity of twenty million, with many successful businessmen but also crawling with homeless and landless peasants, and if a politician wants to get elected he has to pander to the masses without heeding their demands, since doing so would ruin the economy. And when they don't get what they want, or even when they do, they'll blame the politician, not themselves: Brazil regularly has massive street demonstrations that amount to chastising the government for giving demonstrators what they demanded the last time they took to the streets. It's a place where to be a politician is to be a cagey populist who thrives best by not believing his own bullshit.

A perfect example of this is a Brazilian back-to-the-land movement, a romantic notion of landless poor occupying cleared land that is now being used for soybean farming, and trying to grow food on it to live. This movement pulls on the heartstrings of foreigners, and appeals to Brazil's poorly educated slum dwellers and those intellectuals who make careers out of arrogating the right to speak for them. Politicians have to pay lip service to this ideal, but in their heart of hearts they know Brazilians are not satisfied by notions of subsistence farmers scratching a living in slashed-and-burned former forests, in what ought to be a powerful country making airplanes, computers, and robots, exactly like a first-world economy but with added bikini waxing. They don't want to fund or encourage further establishment of a peasant economy that will become a drag on the industrial and knowledge-economy transformation they imagine achieving in the near future. However, until they can fix their education system, they won't be able to leave peasants and slums behind, and Brazilians will keep telling the same joke: Brazil is the country of the future, and always will be.

Megacities are fascinating, but I was growing weary of them and it was time for nature and wildlife and the company of other backpackers. I set off for Campo Grande—called the swarthy city after the dusky soil, but the name could as easily describe the interesting ethnic mix of its people—to visit the famed marshland called Pantanal, afterward following the gringo trail north to Ecuador and the Galápagos, exploring the latter by sailboat. After all that fun came more of the same in Colombia, as a lively group of young backpackers coalesced into a crew that included me, as Uncle Mike, the freakishly well-travelled representative of the older generation. We trekked to the lost city of Tayrona, discovered only in 1972 by treasure hunters, deep in the jungles of the isolated mountains of Sierra Nevada de Santa Marta. Finally all that was left for me was to skip along the northern fringe of the continent, experiencing Venezuela, including Angel Falls, the world's tallest single drop, followed by the far north, including Guyana, where, in the middle of a raging river, I was faced with illegally entering one country or illegally returning to another. What saved me was the mess of shiny visa stamps and accompanying holograms that clogged my passport, serving as a lesson to bamboozled custom officials that "all that glitters is not gold."

The Venezuelan government had boasted that their nation's money was worth much more than the rate set by the black market. This preserves their sense of national pride, but they run the risk of vagabond backpackers taking them up on it. So, for merely a few hundred us dollars, I bought the flights I needed to carry me to Canada in late May 2009 and onward to see Dana in Almaty, Kazakhstan.

CHAPTER TWELVE

STEPPES TO THE FAR EAST

Kazakhstan · Mongolia · Japan

S PRING HAD SPRUNG IN ALMATY, AT THE BASE OF THE TIAN
Shan mountains; the trees were leafed-out and the air was
fresh. I'd flown in just as the World Cup qualifier game
between England and Kazakhstan was being played on June 6, 2009.
Forewarned of the contents of hundreds of England supporters' suit-
cases, spoilsport police warned that any fan inspired by the *Borat* movie
to show up in a mankini would be arrested.

On my way over to Dana's flat, I encountered the wallet scam. My
hopes had dimmed of ever seeing this much-talked-about, but ever-so-
rare scam myself. A man started walking with me and trying to chat. He
had to walk fast to keep up, but still did a good job of pretending that
the wallet he noticed in a gutter full of leaves was something we'd collectively discovered. I laughed at him and kept on walking when he held

his prize aloft. Of course, I was supposed to be interested, and we would both open the wallet and find money inside. Just as we divided it, the accomplice would arrive, frantically searching for his "lost" wallet. He would be relieved that we found it, but, oh no, where is the extra 300 dollars that was in it? After much arguing and threats to call police, the first accomplice would give in and "repay" 150 dollars to avoid trouble. The idea is that the foreigner would then feel pressured to do the same, for a profit of seventy-five dollars each to the scammers. This goes to show what types of foreigners frequent the city; usually only NGO workers or UN types would be naive enough to fall for this kind of thing.

Dana met me on her lunch hour and gave me keys to her apartment. It had only been a year and some South America since we'd been together in Afghanistan, so for me, for us both, it felt like we'd never been apart. We were soon back in our cheerful Almaty routines—wandering through the public rose gardens, watching the roller skaters circling the wooden tsar-era Zenkov Cathedral, and kissing behind the big oak trees. The next day we happened to meet one of Dana's sisters, who joined us for lunch. I answered her questions about my profession, while Dana nudged me under the table to make sure my answers were compatible with what she had told her sister on the phone earlier that day—her nudges were to let me know warmer from colder as I homed in on Dana's dissembling description of me. Her sister and I discovered that I was a United Nations official whom Dana was showing around the country.

Next came an invitation to go out for a meal with some of Dana's family who live near her in Almaty. I was this UN official who doesn't know Dana all that well, and we ate in an enormous yurt in a valley of the Tian Shan. Her elderly aunts made sure to keep me well supplied with powerful Kazakh cheese, which is a lot like parmesan but far stronger tasting and smelling, and so dry it bursts into powder in your mouth. Naturally they heaped my plate full of horse kidneys and raw onions, and we drank straight vodka by the glassful, chewing on green onion shoots as a chaser. I held up my end.

The same day, back at Dana's sister's flat, we continued to drink with Dana's sister and her husband; Dana was abstaining, for obvious reasons.

The neighbours came over when they heard a party going on, and these neighbours included a tall pretty Kazakh girl who worked in banking and was delighted to hear that I was a single guy who worked for the UN. She was finding excuses to give me kisses (for example, she made it clear she admired French culture, and then needed to leave the room, but now she was back, necessitating freshly demonstrated greetings), while Dana had to sit on her hands since she was pretending that she knew me only as a colleague from work. Later, in the car, we were laughing about it: so far so good.

Finally we had some time alone to get busy, but soon Dana had to get busy with work too. I tagged along with her for a flight to Astana, Kazakhstan's modern capital, since she had a stint of official meetings there—a conference or something—and this would be my first time in the capital. We took a taxi to Dana's elderly mother's home, where her teenage niece and brother live too, in an old Soviet-style flat in an area that was never supposed to be built on as it is right next to the sanatorium for treating tuberculosis. Dana's mother suggested that not many tourists visited this part of Astana, and I hastened to agree. Her mother looked like one of those nomad wise women you see in museum photos, and she obviously suspected that I was something other than a UN colleague of her daughter. She made a wickedly strong pot of tea.

That evening, Dana and I went back into Astana and bought train tickets to northern Kazakhstan for later use, then rented a huge flat in the government district for the night. It featured a giant television and a bathroom of white marble, with tiles decorated with hieroglyphics like you might see in an Egyptian tomb. Dana's other sister drove us around town, and we stopped to see the sights.

Astana is one of those super modern cities that I'm deeply skeptical of, where the architects make some snazzy model that they then bring to reality, but you never get over the feeling that you are walking around in the model. These cities are to architecture what the guitar solo is to rock music: a form of ostentation. You'll be walking in a colossal park next to golden-glassed towers, wondering why there is nowhere to sit that is out of the blazing sun, and nowhere safe from the wind. The answer is that this sector is designed in the shape of Kazakhstan's state bird, and is deeply symbolic—benches and windbreaker walls would be out of place. If only you could see it from the air, you'd realize it's perfect.

About half an hour after we'd finished complaining about how sterile Astana was, Dana and I were walking when a couple of well-heeled office women passed by. They were also complaining, speaking Russian, so we listened in. Dana is fluent in Russian, and she had taught me some. The last thing we heard was one woman saying to the other, "Do you know what I hate most about Astana? All the people walking around complaining about Astana."

We went to see the only oceanarium in Central Asia, and rode an elevator up in the tower that looks like a tree holding a golden egg. Inside the egg is a high platform where you can put your hand into a metallic cast of President Nazarbayev's hand. This is a sort of blessing, or so it would seem.

A few days later, back in Almaty, Dana and some other officials were going to give short speeches before a televised show of children dancing in one of the many excellent city parks, adorned with mature elms and oaks, among eminently livable streets. The office for preventing the worst forms of child labour, where Dana works, had been giving support and money to a neighbourhood program that gets kids involved in dance. Money for the program, and for Dana's wages, was being drawn out of a hundred-million-dollar fund set up by President Nazarbayev. In a case of bad luck involving an American merchant banker, James Giffen, and what should have been routine pay-for-play-business, the president had been caught with his blessed gold hands in the cookie jar along with a $78-million bribe for privileged access to oil for Exxon, BP, and ConocoPhillips. As atonement he said, Okay, here's a spare hundred million that will go to good causes.

We taxied out to the park and found the stage and a crowd of a thousand spectators. Dana introduced me to the other government representatives as a Canadian official, and I was game to play my part. After Dana and the others gave their speeches, everyone seemed to think that it would be splendid if I would stand up there and say some words on behalf of whoever it was I was supposed to work for. Dana said she'd translate for me.

A glance at the stage revealed that the youngest girls were starting into their routine: a score of girls between the ages of six and ten were tarted up as belly dancers, moving in a way that ought to be the preserve of women of an appropriate minimum age. After that, a dozen more girls, ranging from eight to twelve years, in burlesque costumes with long feather boas and feather bras, danced to songs that included such kid-friendly lyrics as "Do you wanna tap this ass?" and "Shake those titties." Few in the audience could understand English, of course, or there might have been some raised eyebrows and murmuring from the spectators. Meanwhile, the government reps handed me a shirt to wear in front of the cameras—a white T-shirt sporting the image of a little girl in a school uniform, holding a spiral-coloured lollipop. The Russian and Kazakh slogans below the logo could be translated as "Give little girls a try"—that is, the UN wants to give little girls their fair try at education and careers.

By then I'd decided against making a speech on that stage, thanks all the same. What would I have had Dana translate for me? Maybe "If anyone who knows me is watching, this is not what you think. Despite my shirt and presence on this stage, I am not advocating messing with any of these little girls." I was grateful when it came time for the older teens: fine Kazakh hip hop and breakdance troupes.

ONCE DANA'S VACATION BEGAN, WE RODE THE TRAIN NORTH ACROSS the Kazakh steppe to the Altai Mountains and the purported location of legendary Shambhala (the Buddhist Pure Land) at Belukha Mountain, now a ski resort. Ust-Kamenogorsk, Kazakhstan's leading city in heavy metals, immune system disorders, and former atomic weapons production, was a good first stop, with sunshine and skies billowing with poplar fluff. "But why is the city park full of hookers?" I asked Dana, after a group of them strode past us, one girl calling out "Sexy mother-fucker," and all of them in miniskirts so short that maybe if you sewed a crotch into them they might pass for panties. "Those aren't hookers," Dana explained. "This is a Russian wedding so they are the bridesmaids."

We retreated from the city into the Altai foothills; out in the villages, we stayed for nature hikes at an old Soviet Young Pioneer camp, now moribund but kept going by caretakers as a sort of back-to-nature bed and breakfast, *banya* (sauna) and birch branches included. An attempt to make our way deeper into the Altais to visit an isolated settlement of old believers, a persecuted sect that split from Orthodoxy in 1666 after dissenting to what it saw as that church's excessive modernization of rituals, ended in failure: the bridge had been washed out, and the settlement was completely cut off. We hopped on a prop-plane and buzzed over to Ölgii, a small town on the steppe, near the restricted military zone in the Mongolian far west; Dana had a police contact from whom we could get special permits to travel in the Altai Mountains within this zone.

The restricted area of Mongolia is a trackless wilderness, home to nomads and to archeologists, both foreign and domestic, with glacially carved valleys carpeted in larch, icy lakes where we could skip rocks ("licking the sour cream" in local parlance), and rushing rivers alive with grayling—tasty cooked over a fire with a dash of chili. We slept in a yurt provided by a nomadic family, under thick covers that kept us snug against the cold; it was worth my while to keep a supply of larch kindling gathered in the forest so I could get up a half hour before Dana to strike a fire and ensure that she woke to a warm yurt. We had our choice of horses, with names that translated literally as Brown, Brownie, and Brown Horse. Okay, not a lot of effort had gone into the naming. I renamed mine Stumbley, and not a lot of thought went into that name either, since he would stumble sometimes on rocky trails high in the mountains, or when trying to clamber up the boulder-strewn banks of rivers after he'd swum across with me on his back. We'd ride all day, often 70 kilometres or more, through wide glacier-scoured passes and along narrow mountain trails, looking at Scythian petroglyphs on high rocky outcrops (the Scythian women may have been Amazons, as described by the Greek historian Herodotus), finding waterfalls, and visiting nomads who lived alone in lonesome valleys.

For whatever reason, locals would come to me for medical advice; I tried my best. One complained of passing stones in his urine. I asked about his diet, and he said that he ate two kinds of cheese, curds, two kinds of milk, sour cream, butter, and little else. "Eat less dairy" was my advice to him. Another rode up with some companions and showed me where his leg had been split open lengthwise. The meat on either side of the slice was like two pink chicken breasts. I could finally use the medical kit I'd carried these many years. I asked if they had cleaned the wound. Dana translated my question, and they said they had poured a whole bottle of vodka over it. My kit contained a little bottle of more typical disinfectant, so we made sure everything was as clean as could be, then got one guy to hold it shut as I bandaged it. Really, lots and lots of stitches would have been in order, but that was beyond my competence so we had to hope it would just stick together and heal. When I offered some pills, Dana translated that my patient asked what they were, and on hearing that they were painkillers, he refused them with this explanation, "I am Mongolian."

When we'd first arrived, I'd gifted a sheep, bought at a stop in a dusty livestock market near Ölgii, to the elder in the neighbouring yurt. Late one night there was a knock on our door; it was the neighbours, inviting us over for dinner. We sat at a low table, in the middle of which was the cooked head of the sheep. The old man was there to assist and insist and, with a large knife, cut off delicacies that I was expected to eat, followed by cheers and a shot of vodka. First came an eyeball, which tasted just as you'd imagine, puckered full of slithering jellies, and a shot of vodka; then slices of lips and ears, shots of vodka; a chunk of brain and another shot of vodka. More brain was on offer, but I had Dana translate for me (since the locals can speak Kazakh) that there were so many hungry women licking their lips around the table, and, really, I shouldn't be greedy.

Another night there was a storm outside our yurt. We were fast asleep, but a noise awakened me: our door had opened and shut. There was a presence now, I could feel it, but I went back to sleep. In the morning the storm had passed, and it turned out there was a calf inside with us. It had stood all night just where it had been placed out of the wind, like a piece of furniture, except that it had reached its mouth down to nibble on our carpet of grass. The door opened again and hands reached in, removing our little visitor.

The locals were expert horsemen, and I was not, save in one regard. While riding out one afternoon, having done at least 40 kilometres, there was some talk, which Dana translated as a question: Is it time to rest? "No, I'm fine," I said. "But if they would like a rest, I'm happy to stop." She conveyed this information and we rode on. Another 5 kilometres and the question was asked again; my reply was the same. Finally, after one local fell off his horse, they admitted their backsides were sore and they needed a rest, but they didn't want to be the ones to stop first. My ass must have been tough as boot-leather from third-world bus rides, and thus inured to the saddle.

One local guy, who owned the horses we were riding, told us he was a big fan of Adolf Hitler, and said he would like to get a tattoo of a Nazi swastika when he was married the next year. I asked him what was so attractive about Hitler, who seemed to admire Aryan Germans and little else, and was told that he was great because he conquered and killed.

"Then you must be a fan of Chinggis Khaan too," I said.

"No, I hate Chinggis. Legend is that he killed people from my clan."

He was only a step away from the golden rule, so close and yet so far.

"There are no Jews in Mongolia. Who do you attack to show your support for Nazis?" I asked.

"We attack the Chinese," he said, "whenever my friends and I find them in Ölgii."

Meanwhile, I was pretty sure Hitler and his Nazis would see the Mongolian and Chinese races as a distinction without a difference.

Chinggis Khaan had been on the brink of ordering the genocide of all the Chinese when he first conquered them. He saw the way they lived, trapped as slaves to agriculture, and wanted them gone as a service to human freedom. Civilization was a way of life beneath the dignity of a free rider, or any human. Better if the land was denuded of all such slaves and reverted to pasture for horses. He relented, talked out of this strategy by a Han Chinese notable, and this doomed his empire to softening over time and eventual assimilation, as he must have foreseen.

Many of the Mongolians we met were proud of the time when they ruled the Eurasian sea of grass and the surrounding shoreline of civilizations, almost as if they imagined that empire might rise again if only another great leader appeared. But the days of the mounted archer were now in the past. They had taken advantage of the foot soldier's poor ability to cope with that paramount military problem: you cannot be strong everywhere. Nowadays the archer's advantage is thwarted by the rifle, just as the rifleman will soon be lorded over by the drone. What the Mongols achieved was not so far from the ordinary: history shows that each decisive military technology, once invented, is promptly wielded to conquer the known world. A notable exception to this rule is the Americans, who invented the A-bomb and, for the most part, declined the megalomaniacal prize.

Spying the white pennants of an encampment half a day's ride from a lake in a broad valley, we rode over and found French archeologists, who were excavating ancient Scythian burial mounds of Bronze Age warriors. When they saw us, they assumed we must be the National Geographic film crew they were expecting; who else would arrive on horseback across the trackless grasslands of Mongolia in a restricted area?

The principle investigator was a noted archeologist, Pierre-Henri Giscard—the man who claims to know the secret of where to find Chinggis Khaan's tomb—who looked as old as Gandalf, his teeth worn down nearly to stumps, but still camping here doing what he loved, in his seventeenth field year investigating Scythian burial practices. He was just about to open a mound, expecting to find a warrior with a bronze sword, but was awaiting the film crew. We talked about distant lands: he had been in the Pantanal as a young man, and had seen the herdsmen send the weakest zebu swimming first to test the hunger of the piranha in the rivers. He also had stories about the special birthmark on the bums of true Mongols, and told us there still exists a rump of this legacy in one region of France, suggesting Dark Age pillaging by Huns. Dana has such a mark, a sign, perhaps, of some Mongolian ancestors. In talking to the Frenchman, we were surprised by some news more current than the Dark Ages. This gossip invoked keen interest in locals when we passed it along in the days following: families in nearby yurts were not so remote that they had never heard of Michael Jackson, but they were too remote for the news of his death to have reached them.

We had been riding horses for so many days in a row that even Dana's ravishing Mongol bum was sore, so, in the morning, when we were asked if we wanted to go riding or perhaps fishing, she said, "Fishing, definitely fishing." A boy arrived and started saddling up the horses. Dana asked, "Why?" and he said, "You wanted to go fishing, so we ride to fishing river and back." Another long ride over rocky terrain.

IN EARLY JULY WE DECIDED TO GO EAST TO THE MONGOLIAN CAPITAL, Ulaanbaatar, so we returned to Ölgii and inquired about flights at the regional landing strip. They wanted $660 each for a flight. I complained to the vendor about the high price.

"Yes, we are charging you double since you are foreigners," he said.

"Is there any other way to get there?" I asked.

"There is always the bus."

Twenty-dollar tickets in hand, we awaited this bus one fine morning along with, by my count, forty-one Mongolians. It turned out to be a rather small bus. Sure enough, it was a shoulder-to-shoulder squeeze once we got settled. We were off, bumping across rocky terrain until we reached the road, or so it seemed. But instead we went up hills, down the other sides, splashed across rivers, and crossed plains of gravel and tracts of Gobi Desert.

"Don't you have any roads?" I asked a Mongolian.

"We are building some," he replied.

Sure enough, at some distant hour we encountered the signs of road construction across the steppe. While a progressive development, this was no use to us at the moment, as we bumped and bashed across terrain, splattered with the vomit of fellow passengers. We stopped only for pee breaks, and once for a chance to eat *manti* (dumplings). After an eighteen-hour drive, I asked that same Mongolian if we were nearly in Ulaanbaatar. He laughed.

"Don't you know?" he said. "This is fifty-hour bus. Two drivers, one sleeps, one drives, then change."

"Five zero, fifty?" I said. And he nodded, with a smile.

Dana and I looked each other. "Sorry," I said. "According to our map there is a dot with a name to it that we pass through. It must be a city or at least a town. We'll get out and find a hotel, and take another bus when we feel rested."

The next morning we reached that dot: it was a smattering of yurts on an endless horizon. The bus stopped so that we might crowd into one yurt (called *ghers* this far east), where a woman sat on a low stool. She listened for how many people called for soup, then pulled the leg and haunch of an animal out from under her and whacked off the appropriate chunks of meat with a hatchet.

"We can't stay here," I told Dana. "Living conditions were better on the bus," so after our soup we pressed in again for another twenty-five hours of discomfort that bordered on suffering. My main worry was that because I had purchased the bus tickets, the blame for everything that followed would naturally fall to me. Dana was suspiciously mild-mannered, making the best of the situation, but I supposed I'd find out what storm awaited me in Ulaanbaatar. Fifty hours of overland bussing accomplished, and many interesting sights later, we were in the capital and cheerfully getting settled in a hostel. Dana was remarkably resilient and easygoing, and voiced no complaints.

There was more horse riding, and more sights, in Mongolia, including a chance for international dining once we got to the capital. A Korean restaurant there presented a most incomprehensible menu: the Mongolian names were given for Korean dishes, written in Cyrillic. Our only recourse was to traipse into the kitchen to point at food. This gave us the idea to route through Seoul on our way to Tokyo to see some of Japan before Dana had to return for work, hopefully with baby on board.

We left sparsely peopled, wild, horizontal Mongolia for vertical, crowded, technological Tokyo, perhaps the world's greatest metropolis, a high-tech wonder, with three different interlaced subterranean train systems to get splendidly lost on. There is an excitement to the air, and a hum of vitality more pronounced than in other nation-defining megacities. The inhabitants are nearly all Japanese, which makes it, in a strange way, diverse, now that many technologically modern cities are becoming indistinguishable mixtures of ethnicities: Tokyo does not come to you; rather, you go to Tokyo, keeping it a favourite for travellers. Getting lost was as fun as finding things, or lounging in Yoyogi Park, eating extra-gooey octopus dumplings and drinking Kirin beer, watching rockabilly dancers and Harajuku girls.

Japan is compact, easily backpacked to experience honour, sushi, and karaoke, the three pillars of Japanese society. We rode the bullet train, sampled whisky in narrow back-alley bars, and walked Kyoto's philosopher's path through cherry trees, over arched bridges, and beside streams and pools that were home to watchful carp, connecting a string of Zen temples. These temples are deeply peaceful, beautiful, and ironic. For what is it to be inside a building, shelter and warmth aside, but to be everywhere reminded of human thoughts? Every wooden beam, every ornate flourish is a physical representation of thought, the most rigid concept there could possibly be. And yet the idea is that the Zen temple will help ease you out of the error of conceptualizing. They are koans written in architecture, inducing you to un-ask the question.

There can be metaphysics even more basic than the polished floor of these temples: to understand where you are going, where you are, and where you came from, hold these two thoughts in your mind at once: When you die you are reincarnated and There is no you. This is a little shiny beach pebble of a thought, two sided and flat enough to be a fine skipping stone. Sure, it's been smoothed by jostling with other concepts in the surf, so it's not a natural shape or size, and not identical to the vast bedrock from which it broke away, but it's still made of the elemental substance and, what's best, fits neatly in the palm of your mind.

DANA HAD TO RETURN TO WORK IN ALMATY, SO WE TOOK A TRAIN back to Tokyo and caught our flight. During our second stopover at the airport in Seoul, I saw a big advertisement for "traditional Mongolian jumbo-prawn soup." Having lately been living in the traditional style in

Mongolia, we were disappointed that we'd missed seeing a Mongolian jumbo-prawn round-up, with the Mongols driving herds of prawns across the Gobi Desert and into corrals, before wrangling them into the cauldrons for this soup.

In Kazakhstan I foraged for a Belarus visa, but otherwise spent my time hanging out, drinking birch tree juice, eating cabbage dumplings, and studying Russian most days, when I wasn't exploring canyons in the mountains. We discovered that Dana was not pregnant, despite our expedition to the valleys sacred to the ancient Scythians. I had thought that it would be sweetly romantic if she could conceive among these Bronze Age cairns of her Amazon ancestors, there in our lovely yurt by the edge of a forest, between lake and mountain, with an owl wing placed above our bed by a shaman as a fertility charm. Now my reason led me to say the fault was planning this overly complicated scenario—reminiscent of trying to finish off James Bond using sharks with fricking lasers strapped to their heads, instead of the tried and true. But Dana also admitted she was rubbish at maths, and we hadn't actually been together when it counted: she had twice left me alone for week-long conferences during my nearly three-month stay in Asia, exactly when she ought not to have gone.

In any case, I had to kiss her goodbye and fly to Belarus for September. And we decided that having a baby seemed like a rash choice in retrospect. I don't ruminate over decisions and instead just get on with things. My intuition tells me what is best, and if I doubt it, like everyone, I'll talk to a close friend. That friend's job is to listen and then tell me to trust my intuition, so often that step can be skipped. If a 30-percent-chance-of-death road is acceptable to me as an adventure, then so was a 5-percent chance of a baby bouncing along atop the watermelon cart on the road of life.

CHAPTER THIRTEEN

THE FOREST PRIMEVAL

Morocco · Rwanda · Congo · Gabon · Cameroon

MINSK, THE CAPITAL OF BELARUS, IS AS PLACID AS ITS oxbow lakes, consisting of broad, tree-lined avenues and giant forested parks that follow the rivers as they loop around the city. Perfect for long walks and catching some sun while lounging on the grass. Every neighbourhood looks like the kind of place where an embassy could be situated, and, in fact, I'd passed some of them, Ireland, Israel, Bulgaria, scattered at random. There are hardly any restaurants, and they are all places where you would feel out of place without a suit and tie. There was one McDonald's downtown. It was packed with customers, and bigger than it looked from the outside as an entire historic building had been hollowed out and colonized. My goal was to find an internet café somewhere, but I was barely able to find a café. Finally I asked a hip-looking young woman who was watching music videos; she'd never heard of an internet café. "A café with internet in it? Such a concept," she said, and told me there was no street life and only one bar nearby, and it shut at ten.

Adapting to circumstances, I spent much of my time in the museum, looking at art, and arranged to go driving around the country to the historical sites, finding ruined castles in the great Belarusian forests, where actors had been hired to imitate medieval peasants and knights.

After exploring Belarus, my travels took me back to Minsk to walk the riverside paths and contemplate the monument on the Isle of Tears that is dedicated to those who lost their lives in the USSR's war with Afghanistan.

I also went to the bar that shut at ten. The only other people there were the ladies who worked at my hotel. When they beckoned me over to their table, the waitress came past me to whisper in my ear "Dangerous." We began to drink full-glass toasts to Canada and international friendship, draining the glass each time, of course. When the bar closed at ten, I was spirited away, too drunk to object, to the manager's room, which was full of literally hundreds of statues of cats, in glass, wood, ceramic, whatever, arranged on shelves to stare at the central table. This display was like something out of ancient Egypt's temple of Bastet. In explanation, the manager lady said she likes cats. When all the booze made me sick, one of the ladies had a bag ready for just such an occasion, and we had to keep drinking. Then the ladies started competing with each other to get me to hook up with their daughters. They would say, "My daughter twenty-seven years old, very beautiful. I now call her on cell phone. Here, speak to her—speak." Then another would say, "My daughter twenty-six years and study law. Here, here, on this phone, you must speak with her." I blacked out, but somehow woke up in my room, lying atop the covers of my bed.

When the weather turned cold and the chestnuts littered the paths through Victory Park, I flew to Ottawa to start another round of visiting family and friends, and to renew my passport. I got an email from Dana telling me that there was certainly no baby. Also, a friend of hers had been shot twice, once through the head by a government sniper while protesting in Kyrgyzstan. She was especially worried since the guy's wife, also a dear friend, was pregnant with their second child. I wrote Dana to tell her to prepare herself for the very worst outcome.

My return to Canada in October 2009 was even more cross-continental than usual. I went from Change Islands in the Atlantic all the way to the shore of the Pacific, visiting both sets of parents, three aunts, four uncles, two brothers and wives, two nieces, two nephews, and quite a few friends. My dad wanted some company on a road trip: drive 1,600 kilometres from Ottawa to the Atlantic Ocean, then spend a day on the ocean (or more, as we had an extra seven hours at sea in a gale, waiting for the winds to die enough for us to dock in Port aux Basques), then drive another 600 kilometres to Change Islands, Newfoundland. We missed the ferry by ten minutes, so spent the first night at the Fogo ferry and arrived at Change Islands the next day to start charity construction work on his little museum of traditional knitting, the purpose of this excursion. Village ladies were knitting solid-colour socks for sale in craft shops, and Dad wanted to find out if they could knit stripy ones too, such as those worn by Pippi Longstocking and Newfoundland outport girls.

While we were there, Change Islands had a storm, the first of the year—powerful enough to shake my dad's renovated fisherman's house near Diamond Point. Most of the accompanying snow melted the day after. Out on a hike with my dad around part of Change Islands, we ended up in proper wilderness, skirting the shore, clambering over rocks covered with yellow seaweed—the locals call it "mermaid's aprons"—hopping between slippery boulders, and climbing cliffs into the dense stunted forests of larch and spruce, all of the trees weirdly sculpted by the wind. A solitary black fox allowed itself to be seen. After many hours the sun was going down, so we turned inland through deep cranberry bogs with pools of black water speckled with snow. We tried to keep to high ground and also out of the impassably thick forest, heading for an osprey nest in a high tree that my dad remembered was near the road. When we got back, cold and wet, it was time for a fish dinner at a local fisherman's house, where we drank wine and sang traditional songs when the fisherman brought out guitar and accordion: "Jack Was Every

Inch a Sailor" and "I's the B'y" as in "I's the b'y that catches the fish, and brings 'em home to Liza."

Farther west I stopped in to be Uncle Mike, and read 1960s sci-fi paperbacks while munching on colourful jellybeans, or took packs of dogs chasing balls in the forest. In Vancouver I met Chad for beers in the Cambie pub. He was just back from watching the world surfing championship in Tofino. Some of the best surfers in the world were there, but one local Canadian managed to stay in the contest and finally won the whole thing. The international surfing organization gave him the $20,000 prize and offered him a spot as a pro surfer, with jet-setting around the world and the potential for sponsorship deals. He told them he'd think it over and went for a walk on the beach with his girlfriend, after which he told them thanks but no, he was happiest where he was for the time being.

I admired the sentiment and felt somewhat the same way—except I was happiest where I wasn't. I unfolded a map of Africa and began to research this infamous Gordian knot of gratuitous visa and transport difficulties, not to mention the so-called impossible countries, which were written off rather than written about in the travel guides. There was no sense over-planning using notoriously outdated information; besides, my motto was "No travel plan survives contact with friendly forces." Africa was shaping up to be a wild ride, that much was assured.

DANA WAS IN FRANCE FOR A UN LABOUR CONFERENCE, BUT COME December 2009, we were going to kick off my Africa trip by hitch-hiking around Tunisia. We'd given up the baby idea, but still loved to travel together. Twenty-five hours of travel brought me to Tunisia's international airport at midnight, looking for a taxi into the city so I could start searching for a traveller hotel, cheap but not too cheap, as Dana would meet me there. The next morning I woke to explore Tunis, the city from whence was derived, according to a tourist brochure, the word "punish." It was a punishing series of flights to get here, for sure, but it was a lovely city, and the climate was fine and sunny: T-shirt weather for me, fur coat weather for the locals.

I cooled my heels until Dana arrived so we could look at museums full of ancient mosaics together, and bus to the isle of Djerba, the land of the lotus-eaters, where islanders had once drunk the intoxicating juice of the Barbary jujube. We watched a Berber beat his large octopus repeatedly against the cobblestone embankment. How they catch these octopuses is rather mean: they lower a lovely pottery house into the water, leave it there long enough for an octopus to move in, then yank it up and thrash the hell out of the occupant—a process strikingly similar to how the mortgage-and-housing crisis, then ongoing, must have felt to American workers.

We visited Tataouine, which is actually a village, not the planet Tatooine, Luke Skywalker's home. *Star Wars* was filmed nearby, and some of the locals do look a bit like Jawas—those little creatures who scavenged the dune sea for salvageable robots—as they wear the same thick hooded brown cowls, called jimbe. Hitchhiking was easy, and Dana could practise her French with smiling locals. Oranges were in season; peeling them was a fragrant pastime as we waited for lifts in valley air that was fresh, misty, and prone to rainbows. Or we could rent goofy-looking camels and lope around the oasis or salt flats near the Grand Erg Oriental in the Tunisian Sahara. Christmas passed more like Saturnalia in the green slopes of the Atlas Mountains, picnicking with Dana and exploring pagan temples and colourful mosaics of nude Venus with nymphs in an underground city, before hitchhiking back to the Casbah of El Ker.

Too soon, our romantic two-week vacation was at an end: Dana had to get back to the office, to strengthen worker's rights in Kazakhstan, while I had to carry on with my travelling to get in position for a rave on a beach in Morocco. From Tunis I flew to Casablanca, where I explored the third-largest mosque in the world and some of the old city before bussing south toward Essaouira, a coastal fortress where precious purple dye was once collected from the shells of murex sea snails. I stayed in a room with a view inside the crazy alleys of a seaside castle guarded by batteries of brass cannons. Here by chance was Mikko, a Finnish friend I hadn't seen since we'd met in a hostel on Easter Island off the Pacific coast of South America. Wooden ships were being built and repaired out near the crescent beach, and the shopkeepers sold pastries, cell phones, hanging carcasses of beasts, and women's underwear side by side in the kiosks: one-stop shopping taken to an extreme.

Moroccan cuisine is fixated on discovering which fruits, such as figs, prunes, or apricots, are best for stewing with beef, chicken, or lamb. And they have perfected the art of making tea, pouring it to maximize aeration. Just as Thais know how to cut pineapples in a spiral or Cajuns can shuck oysters, the Moroccans know how to pour tea at great height from spouts.

IN THE STANDARD CARTOGRAPHIC TRADITION OF THE MERCATOR projection, Africa always appears on maps to be smaller than it is. Travellers who fall for this illusion find their eyes are bigger than their stomachs when deciding what to see and do. Earth's oldest continent is also diverse, culturally and geographically.

My plan, after this swing across northern Africa in the winter low season, was to take in a rave on the beaches of Morocco, where my friend Molly would be DJ-ing, then head south to see if the West Africa overland route was open, as was rumoured among backpackers. From there I would carry on south as far as Dakar, where I'd fly to East Africa in time to catch the tail end of the great animal migrations, then cut inland to the Rift Valley lakes, try not to get killed in Congo, and eventually end up back in West Africa. This would involve striving to make headway going north against punishing red tape and border formalities while enduring increasingly intense tropical heat. When conditions proved unbearable, I'd retreat to England, attend my friend Ken's wedding, and rest up for another big trip. The map made it look feasible. Then again, there are many things that appear feasible in Africa.

Unavoidable Congo dangers were foremost on my mind. The Democratic Republic of Congo (DRC) was suffering from the Congolese civil wars, a pan-African war that had drawn in eight foreign armies and killed over five million people since 1996. Even the milder, smaller Republic of Congo, north of the DRC, was said to be corrupt and a poor base for travellers. The word in traveller circles was grim: if luck is on your side, soon after you cross into the jungle, corrupt police and militia will steal everything you own and you will have to retreat. Without luck, you could encounter genocidal rebels or bandits. The frontier roads were infested with both groups. While I was in Morocco, the cushy sort of place where a check of backpacker equipment was advisable, I had a chance to dig out the business card I had procured in Kazakhstan—the one with the UN logo and "Security Inspector" in English on one side and in Russian on the other. "Perfect," I thought. I'd had it laminated for durability, and even though my name did not match that of the inspector, I hoped it would be more than a match for the infamously corrupt and blessedly illiterate highwaymen of the DRC.

My Moroccan rave and the Atlas Mountains were fun but touristy, while the west-coast overland route proved feasible, allowing me to escape southward. Mauritania offered atypical adventures and sights: I met a sweaty South African on a bike with panniers, who was trying to camp and pedal all the way to the Cape of Good Hope. Local tribes were now sub-Saharan, without much mixing of swarthy Berber or Arab; many of them were fishermen or fishmongers, catching or selling fish of a species that has so much blood in them, it's revolting when you see one squished by a car tire in the market. While I waited for an iron-ore train that wends its way into the desert, sitting in stench with other people speckled in flies, one lad, who was interested in the contents of my backpack, kept trying to get me to go off into the desert behind an outcrop of stone 100 metres from everyone else so he could tell me a secret. I told him no, so now I will never know the secret. Was it something about a knife in my back, or maybe a rock to my head? I will go to my grave not knowing. Such are life's regrets.

Senegal and the Gambia were places of wild adventure, beaches striped like a zebra with black and white sand, strewn with purple jellyfish; a landscape dotted with bloated baobabs; and packs of Gambian bumsters and prostitutes who chase any white man, or woman, for that matter. Even the guards who stamped me past the borders, and the chief of police, seemed over-keen to procure something for me, with a consideration for themselves, of course.

Tanzania was staid in comparison—few pimps or hos, just regular people. I chilled on the beaches of Zanzibar, where Freddie Mercury was born, in Stone Town, to a family of Zoroastrian fire worshippers. That's how he turned out to be such a bastion of normality, I suppose. All is explained. There was a friendly South African couple to hang out with, and curried octopus to snack upon, and curious fruits on the trees lining the beach. Little kids kept trying to knock them down by hurling chunks of coral, which would sometimes ricochet and hit the hotel. The groundskeeper would chase these rascals on sight. One of the fruits was at hand for my investigation: tough, green, and shaped like the pit of a mango, with a thin, fibrous purple flesh. I couldn't fathom why it was worth the risk.

Viewing the migrations of the great herds, climbing Mount Kilimanjaro, visiting Kenyan cities and wilderness—including the amazing salty Lake Turkana in the volcanic Rift Valley, north near the rustler tribes—and the misty jungles of Uganda, kept the thrills coming faster than in my wildest dreams. In the world's newest, breakaway nation of South Sudan, occupying the ancient land of Kush, I hung out with a bush-war veteran named Bamboo. We met at a car wash/bar run by former child soldiers in one of Juba's back alleys. This capital city is built on savannah, with the odd forested mountain sticking up out of the plains. The Nile has been thrashing back and forth for eons, carving out a plain between the Dongatona mountains and the Imatong range, and leaving just a few stranded lonely mountains rising from the flats. Juba is like an absurdly overgrown village of round African huts, hugging both banks of the Nile, with concrete administration buildings starting to rise in its centre.

Transport in this part of Africa—rural Uganda and South Sudan—consisted of hitching rides on the back of charcoal trucks; my meals were whatever the villagers were eating, sometimes a tasty spinach and peanut butter dip. Often in South Sudan the roads were flanked by minefields, and burned-out battle tanks protruded from the dirt. People made a living as best they could, which might explain my encounters with men cutting wood that grew amid minefields to sell it as charcoal, a couple of young men setting out hunting with bow and arrows, and kids scrambling to dig up rusty metal, the scraps of which they traded for coins to a woman with a balance scale in a shed outside her hut.

At the end of February I was in Kampala, the Ugandan capital. In an internet café at the Red Chilli hostel, near where the Nile gushes out of Lake Victoria, I opened an email from Dana: she could make it to Kigali in Rwanda to meet me if it was possible for me to get there in time. I wrote back and told her to consider it a date. Then I took a boat to see Murchison Falls and all the hippos and crocodiles that gather there in north Uganda, rushed to skirt the eastern slopes of the Rwenzori Mountains (also known as the Mountains of the Moon), and carried on south to the cute little series of hills and lakes on the border with Rwanda, near the impenetrable forest. I didn't linger overlong in any one site, and crossed the border on a bus to Kigali with a day to spare.

Rwanda is a now a peaceful green land of mountains and valleys, its frontier guards cheerful and not obviously corrupt. The valleys are given over to a patchwork of small farms, and so are the mountains, which are often farmed all the way up to the peak. The locals are a mix of Hutu and Tutsi, with the Tutsi famous for being tied with the Dutch for the distinction of having the tallest people in the world. The Hutus are most famous for inflicting a terrifying genocide upon the Tutsi, killing 800,000 with axes, machetes, clubs, or their bare hands, but that happened a while ago now, in 1994, back when the colours on my backpack were still bright and all the zippers worked.

Dana was in Cairo, waiting on a flight; she would get her visa on arrival at Kigali the next morning, so I took a motorcycle taxi into town and found a nicer-than-usual hotel. After we got settled and caught up on news, we scampered over to the office that manages Volcanoes National Park in Rwanda, where the mountain gorillas live, and were pleased when we scored two permits.

A network of white vans connected the tiny nation handily, though it took longer than expected to get around on account of the winding roads and all the up and down. Plastic bags had been banned and replaced with paper to protect the environment. I had a few on me that

I used to waterproof my belongings, but I gradually lost my precious contraband bags. Rwandans tended to get motion sick very easily, and I would feel sorry for them and pass a plastic bag over to someone who needed more than a paper bag, for obvious reasons.

We hiked with a guide up the side of a volcano and spent some unforgettable time with a family of muscular apes. When the silverback beat his chest with his fists, his tough flesh resonated with a noise just like a xylophone. Some cute babies came over to play, but we tried to keep back so as not to transmit any germs: gorillas are such close relatives of humans that they might catch the common cold or flu. Afterward we drove through a park full of more wildlife—and biting tsetse flies; then on to lovely Lake Kivu, one of the African Great Lakes. Fishing is poor save for a few introduced sardines, since the lake is like a martini, with a suspended layer holding poison gas that wells up and kills everyone whether it's shaken or stirred. Only the bilharzia parasites are happy to dwell there, waiting for swimmers to latch onto. The Rwandan town of Gisenyi clung to the shoreline, in the shadow of a volcano that erupted not long ago and overran the nearby Congolese town of Goma with molten lava. Even poison gas and lava were not enough to discourage the locals, and once the flow hardened they moved back in, though their ground floors were now pumice.

Deeper in the mountains we did nature hikes in Nyungwe forest, one of the last montane forests. A flowering vine that is tasty food to elephants was growing like crazy and had overwhelmed and smothered half the trees. The elephants had all been poached, so there was no herbivore to control the vine. The bees were happy with the situation, and fern trees thrived in the ravines, the best groves of them I'd seen since Abel Tasman Park in New Zealand.

Back in Kigali we stopped in to visit and dine with the head of us Aid and his Kazakh wife. He was a young guy in a huge mansion with the usual tribal funky décor of the development set. He even had an ironic framed copy of the poem "The Development Set" among his eye-level photographs of dignitaries and villagers. And as he was somewhat too young, with too boyish a face to be taken seriously, he was growing a beard. This was an excellent idea. Someone heading up US Aid or even an NGO that wants to achieve anything resembling development needs to have local VIPs listen to him if he suggests that they modernize.

We talked a bit of Central Asian news and politics. Dana described the situation in Kazakhstan, which was more tense than usual because, in neighbouring Kyrgyzstan, Bakiyev, the president, didn't want to resign and was gathering his supporters; the country was dividing into two opposing parts, north versus south. Anything could happen, so the Kazakhs sent their army to the border just in case. Dana's friend who had taken the two bullets, one to his head and another to his arm, had undergone two operations thus far and was still having physical therapy. Doctors said he was lucky to live, but a long recovery period was needed, assuming nothing got infected.

When our hosts heard of my plan to cross the border into the DRC and try to hitchhike through the Rwenzori Mountains, their jaws dropped. The guy said that from what he'd heard and read, I'd never get out alive. The only way to do it was to go with armed guards and have a safe house and contacts in each community along the way. These diplomats and I go to the same places throughout the world: me with my backpack, them with their platoon of soldiers and armoured vehicles. That doesn't mean their way is always wrong, though; just that their warnings and advice don't necessarily apply to me. Backpacking is reckoned an esoteric skill, adolescent and a bit of a joke, like prowess with a yoyo. But just as someone who has practised yoyo for years can pull off some weird and wonderful tricks, so can someone who has lived out of his backpack his whole adult life. I assured them I would slip past any genocidal rebels, somehow hitchhike over the Rwenzori Mountains, and go deep into the Congo rain forest until I reached the river and finally the Atlantic.

After Dana had hopped on her flight out of Africa, bound for France, I hitched a ride to Burundi in a truck full of smoked fish, and spent some time on the lakeshores. On my way to Bujumbura in Burundi, a local guy commented to me that genocidal Hutu rebels were hiding out in the jungle near the Virunga volcanoes (on the west shore of Lake Kivu, the Congo side), killing any white man who tried to pass. Meanwhile,

instability had rendered my tourist information useless: even the top hotel listed in my guidebook was a mouldering ruin squatted by vagrants.
The hotel I eventually chanced upon was new and must have been
purpose-built for foreign NGO workers: the bed had its own mosquito
net already in place, like you see in tropical Asia. In any case, I didn't stay
long. It was now well into March, and I was worried that the hot season
would make the Atlantic coast of Africa unbearable for me if I didn't get
a move on and cut west across the continent.

I returned to Rwanda and gave the frontier south of Lake Kivu a try,
but the border guards wanted $300 to serve up a visa, and not even a
very good one for all that. My *matatu* (public transport) ride north was
nauseating: a great vat of sour milk burst inside the old Toyota van, and
Rwandans had a laugh as the contents sloshed around the feet of the
passengers, packed in like Lake Kivu sardines. My backpack, quickly
snatched up and held in my lap, had already been splashed. Some kind
local boys helped me to wipe it down, but it required a further soak in
a tub with detergent, and the hire of a woman to wash it again in a river.

I decided I would make my border crossing at disaster-prone Goma.
The lava-entombed rebar and concrete of the city were built up here
and there, heedless of any international frontier, and the people who
thronged therein, drawn to the fertile volcanic soil, took no special notice of the imaginary line. But in these regions, white skin is a beacon for
police harassment, so I needed the visa. A border guard on the DRC side
had good contacts, and when I slipped her a couple of hundred bucks,
she let me enter her country to wait in a rundown colonial-era hotel
until she could come back with my passport, formalities nicely skirted.

An old Belgian army vet was staying there too, and we'd sit together on a crumbling bench near the weed-choked fountain. He warned
me not to carry obvious valuables in Goma, and to wear a knife, since
gangs of local robber boys like to sneak up and stab people in the back,
especially around dusk. It so happened I'd already been roaming dark
streets the night before, but the only thing to be found on me was a knife.
I also learned that the roads around Goma drew bandits as numerous as
dung flies, most of them wearing uniforms of one sort or another. There

was an impressive UN military deployment, many of them Bangladeshi soldiers with blue helmets, in armoured personnel carriers and tanks under the UN flag. They were there to discourage genocides and the ongoing mass rapes of thousands of women, and so far they'd enjoyed some success: no crimes against humanity were happening within sight of these bases, anyhow. I'm not sure what more could be realistically asked of them: the UN has yet to be given a mandate to fight a guerrilla war, so it is more of a symbol than anything. As such, the UN logo was useful to me. Later that day I dug out my blue-and-white UN security officer card, switched to a neutral greenish tan shirt with collar and zipped pockets, and got a clipboard with various seemingly important documents on display as an accessory.

The next morning my visa was in hand, but I had a new problem: well-meaning but meddlesome local officials, including police and UN, had learned of my presence and were trying to save me, presumably, from myself. They wanted me to check in with them to ensure I was shunted to the airport and onto a flight to Kinshasa, effectively relegating me from traveller to stamp collector in the process. I had a message relayed back to them: my intention was probably just to hang around here and return to Rwanda, but I was grateful for their concern about my getting a flight, given my certain need of one if I decided to proceed.

At an internet café, in sweltering heat, with the roar of military transport helicopters overhead, and battling frequent power outages, I managed to log in to email and send a message for family: "I'm about to try to hitchhike through the Rwenzori Mountains, also known as the Mountains of the Moon, past the genocidal Hutu rebels, to head deep into the jungle to try to float the length of the Congo River." This took me an hour to send successfully, using every trick I knew. Though it was short, it would have to serve. Later I'd find it had been a mistake to communicate at all, because it was weeks until another internet connection became available, and by then everyone feared the worst.

Keeping out of sight and trekking through fields when possible, I got around the most problematic roadblock and started hiking. After an hour an old flatbed truck wheeled along, and I was able to hitch a ride with the friendly driver. He was taking a load of tires to a pineapple-cultivating town on the opposite slopes of this chain of mountains. The journey was a number of days, different every time, but he said sometimes there would be villages with huts for the night, or I could sleep in his piles of tires.

We wound our way up roads of dirt or mud into increasingly mountainous terrain. Sometimes the land was populated, and we passed men pushing two-wheeled carts of farm produce, something like wooden bicycles, or trying to sell hot potatoes: quite literally, they juggled them in the shrubbery as they wanted to show them off for sale, but they were too hot to hold. These cost only a few coins, as did a handful of minnows, grasped in some swamp, to round out the meal, or plump finger-length bananas. On three occasions swarms of armed men rushed out of the forest, and the driver bid them climb aboard the tire heaps—our truck was then fairly bristling with machine guns and rocket-propelled grenade launchers. At the other extreme, an afternoon or a morning might pass without seeing anything but lush green mountainsides.

There were no bandits out of uniform, or genocidal rebels for that matter, but the official bandits were intimidating to the max, pointing their guns and uttering threats. I'd pretend to take note of their behaviour on my clipboard, and play my UN card. If I thought there was any chance they were literate, I'd show the Cyrillic-lettered side, and always they would gaze at it and hand it back ... nobody ever asked me why the name on the card didn't match the name in my passport, so I never had to use any of my lines: "This is my boss; you don't know him? He passed along this road once. Probably he met with your commander." The logo worked its magic, and I always got through with little or usually no bribe. Inspecting road conditions before the big convoy that was about to come through was my stated purpose. Eventually I developed a better line, and perhaps it is true: "The UN is not allowed to pay bribes, and I have to have a receipt for whatever I spend."

This dry description fails to convey the level of threats, jeering, and intimidation, but if you ever find yourself on roads such as these, I can offer this advice: they are watching your eyes for signs of fear, and they ramp their threats up or down accordingly. In an all too real sense, driving in the DRC is like barging bears in the Canadian wilderness.

One night I slept on the floor of a circular mud hut, after the relative luxury of communal fish soup eaten by dipping it out by means of edible cups of cassava paste (*foufou*). The rest of the time I crammed myself into stacks of tires with whatever local peasants were also hitching a ride west. We were like human soup for the malarial mosquitoes to dip their wicks in. At the pineapple-growing town, I asked my driver what I might pay him for all those days and nights in his truck. He asked for twenty bucks. As I started digging for it, he beamed and clapped me on the back, and all his friends in the tire shack had a laugh, explaining that everyone knows the fair price is two dollars for such a trip.

"You drive a hard bargain," I joked, and paid him what he asked, but insisted that I also buy him and his friends some Primus beers from a shop.

A series of vans got me into the flats of the Congo basin, and on the way down I had my first views of that stunning spread of primordial rain forest. It is worth any risk to experience this sight of a lushly treed horizon clinching the mountain folds and then running flat and seemingly forever westward under sunbeams and cruising thunderstorms, a magical shade of green that tapped some primeval emotion, awesome and inspiring. The locals were long accustomed to the view, and their concerns were more practical. They'd offered to help me pay only the local price for an armful of pineapples, explaining that anyone could turn a fifty-cent profit just by carrying a heap of them in his lap for the six-hour ride into the lowlands. I surprised one and all by riding without spiky fruit bouncing atop my tender crotch. In the flatlands, more decrepit vans and buses carried me through identical settlements: grids of muddy red streets dividing a shantytown. I overnighted in one of these places, and by noon the next day had gone as far as local transport could take me. A lonely dirt track carried on, piercing the rain forest—a week's drive all the way to Kisangani on the Kiss-Kiss River, according to the locals. They told me a corporation owned by the Chinese state maintained the road, after huge bribes to DRC politicians—ensuring that no one was allowed to ask what minerals or how much of them they were digging and extracting, by way of this road, from giant mines encircled by armed men. There was a local bus, but it only ran every two weeks, if at all.

Roads such as these break up giant impervious chunks of rain forests into smaller plots that serve like kindling for pulsating civilization; the process had begun, with peasants settling in to slash and burn out a farm for themselves and their ever-growing families.

Testing my French skills, I chatted with various owners of motorbikes. My idea was that someone would carry me down this road as far as he felt comfortable travelling, then drop me next to another bike owner who'd agreed to do the same. One guy's bike looked a bit newer and still had some foam on the seat, but he was asking me to pay more. When I mentioned his higher price, the gist of what he told me was: That's because I don't intend to drive you out into the forest to rob or kill you, so what I ask has to cover my petrol and time. I'll drop you off only with someone of good reputation in whatever settlement we reach.

"A fair deal," I told him, and we strapped my pack onto the tail end of his bike.

Travelling like this is gruelling and painful ... You worry that your nerve damage is permanent (it isn't) and half expect to find your trousers dripping with blood when you stagger off for a few minutes' respite (sometimes they are.) My string of reputation-vetted motorcyclists carried me down this road, so unswerving, singular, and endless it felt more metaphorical than real, until I was brought back to reality by some painful bump, or a blizzard of exotic butterflies—as if I'd become a mad entomologist questing for another nameless species, using my face as a net. Increasingly, I noticed subsistence farmers with unusually short stature, chopping at the buttresses of titanic trees, until I felt that what I saw could only be pygmies peeking out from the tree line.

My last motorcyclist had to turn back, but felt sure I would find my own way from where he dropped me. A real hotel, of sorts, the Okapi Hotel, was within walking distance of the little town of Epulu. As soon as I staggered off the bike and wiped the red dust from my face, I noticed a big white man—a Slovak, I'd soon discover.

"How can you be here without armed guards?" he asked. "They told me any white man who dares this road will be instantly killed."

"That's what they told me too, warning of genocidal FDLR terrorists and M23 rebels," I said. "But here I am. You're the first foreigner I've seen since I left the shores of Lake Kivu, on the far side of the Mountains of the Moon."

The Okapi Hotel had three rooms, each a third share of a concrete slab with a corrugated iron roof. Beds were three inches of foam over plywood. An army of cockroaches climbed in and out of a stinking drop toilet in back of the usual sunbaked mud yard of chickens, papaya trees, and skittish lizards. I dropped my pack and had a chat with my fellow guest, who looked about a decade younger than me.

His name was Peter, and he was managing an entourage and a heap of film canisters, cameras, and photography equipment. Over a few beers I asked him how he got past all the armed robbery by police and army, and he showed me a document from the chief of this nation's secret police, instructing no one to hinder him as he gallivants about. It included the chief's personal number to call if Peter had any trouble, and cost $3,000. I showed him my repurposed UN card, which was working like a charm—but, of course, I didn't have any valuable cameras ... or any cameras. When Peter heard this fact, he asked if I wanted to join his expedition; I'd have to share half of the expense, which might run to a few hundred dollars.

"Sure," I told him, "but tell me what it's about?"

Because of security concerns, nobody had been in to photograph the Bambuti pygmies for many years, he told me. The Bambuti are indigenous to this rain forest, living either by poison-arrow hunting of monkeys or net hunting of antelope. It turned out Peter was a medical doctor and a photographer, a great skill set for making an immersive study of these iconic people, with a culture and even a name unchanged since the days of ancient Rome, when Herodotus described their hunting practices. Peter said he hadn't wanted to mention his plan until he was sure I was not a rival photographer, here after the same prize.

I assured him I collected only stories of personal adventure, not photos, and we talked for hours about the ethics and art of photography. In what was a stroke of luck for me, he'd been in this area several weeks already, following up contacts, trying to get an agreement to be allowed to venture deep into the forest to live with a Bambuti tribe and photograph them hunting antelope with spear and net. These weeks of effort had enabled him to assemble his entourage, including stout, easygoing Mustafa, an expert at contacting pygmies; Manuel, a professor qualified in pygmy-to-English translation (these people are as hard to find as you might imagine); and two Bantu tribesmen—Desire was a Nande from the Great Lakes, and Jacques a Budu from Wamba—who were forest rangers at the station here in Epulu, armed with AK-47s as protection from murderous gangs of elephant-ivory poachers. Peter had spent a month hiring them from far and wide; the first two were from the townships nearer the Rwenzori Mountains, but the rangers were from the nearby okapi breeding station; he had also found a dozen Bambuti porters, with backpacks they'd made of vines, roots, and bark, who could carry all the expedition's food and other supplies. He needed only a few more days to locate a better supply of dried fish, and something to leave as a parting gift for the tribe, and we'd be good to go.

It wasn't all planning and organizing. He'd already got a few photos of what he called road pygmies, the tribes that stick close to this road and trade fresh rather than smoked bush meat for imported rice, tinned sardines, salt, and biscuits. A poison-arrow-hunting tribe had allowed him to film them for a couple of days: they were eating a chimp when he first encountered them, and were down to the last arm. It looked entirely human as it cooked over the fire. These poison-arrow hunters are specialists in primates; they mostly eat monkeys, while the net and spear hunters feed mainly on antelope.

Over the next few days we went to visit the ranger station in Epulu and saw their successful breeding program for the okapi, those shorter-necked relatives of giraffe, whose chocolate-coloured bodies stand atop zebra-striped legs. Also, in what was a first for me, we got out hunting with the local road pygmies. This required finding the regional Bantu chief and paying him off. Pygmies are usually considered to be an inferior, subservient race by towering Bantu tribes, who feel a sense of ownership over them, like a lord would feel about his serfs. If you want to speak with Bambuti or visit them, you need the permission of their taller "owners."

While gathering supplies, we had some time to get to know the town. Epulu was founded in 1928, when an American anthropologist erected a mud hut to study pygmies and capture okapi for zoos, and stayed for twenty years before succumbing to dysentery. Over the decades, Bantu slash-and-burn farmers arrived and built a few more huts, and some Bambuti abandoned full-time forest living to cluster nearby.

A chatty road pygmy who called himself Botanique, the paragon of botanists, was always hanging around Epulu's local bar, a rudimentary lean-to of sticks and thatch. We'd buy him, and some of his friends, Primus beers, to a maximum of one per pygmy. They would hold the 720-millilitre bottles in both hands, as they were, relatively, sized more like a keg or cask. One was a walking pun, as he wore a filthy Britney Spears T-shirt, while holding some actual spears. Peter got the group dancing with a recording of the Red Hot Chili Peppers track "Californication," and I taught them how to open a beer bottle with a lighter, which they thrilled to, calling it magic. Road pygmies are city slickers compared to the more remote band we sought, but I figured they would still know their cultural proclivities. I asked Botanique what the pygmies liked best, and he said, *bangi*, which is just what it sounds like, marijuana, the word having arrived in the local language nearly unchanged from the Hindi source on another continent. Our parting gift to the tribe was sorted: I bought a huge sack of the pungent stuff to have on hand for later. Then we assembled our porters and set off deep into the forest primeval, looking for signs of a Bambuti hunting camp.

We had to dramatically scale back the quantity of food our expedition loaded itself down with, to the dismay of the porters and their rumbling bellies. Once, watching a pygmy tuck into a big pot of stew, Peter said, "I couldn't eat so much if there was a gun to my head." But they were amazingly tough and fast, and would zip away on bare feet, silently, through the trees. We'd find them lounging about the next good place to camp, with a fire ready to cook dinner. Desire and Jacques were deadly serious about their job and walked quietly with guns ready, as if they expected an ambush any minute. When we stopped, one would go find a place out of sight to wait, so that he had our position covered should it come to a firefight. This was one of the few times I've been accompanied by armed men who didn't seem to think that their presence alone was a guarantee of safety, and seeing these precautions reminded me that we were in the middle of the DRC.

So far we'd passed some signs of old encampments, and saw dried remains of those distinctive hemispherical leaf huts, but we had no certain knowledge where the band was now. The forests seemed to go on forever, and if I had been out there alone, I'm not certain I could have found my way back without a trail of bread crumbs, especially as we'd crossed small rivers bridged by fallen logs, and dark spidery understory, with nasty vines positively bristling with spines. We slept under a tarp while out on this quest, and bedded down on the forest floor. I pointed out a particularly vile and bulbous spider criss-crossing in the leaf loam, and Peter said, "I don't normally do this, but," and squished it. Each of the trees around our camps had to be a different species, despite indistinguishable bark, because they each bled a different colour of toxic latex where they'd been nicked by hatchet or nail for setting our tarp.

There were no mosquitoes whatsoever, which had certainly not been the case near the road. Was there something that preyed on them in the waters here, or was it strong tannins? It seemed a great mystery. In place of mosquitoes there were butterflies, lovely colourful butterflies, here landing on my hand—can you get a photo? One's on my nose now— hee hee—they are all over my pack, covering my arms, uugh. All up in my face, everywhere licking, licking, with those long coiled tongues, tickling the salt out of my pores ... Is there any such thing as butterfly repellent, do you suppose?

At long last we suspected we were very near, all the signs pointed to recent hunting in this area, and we burst into a clearing among gigantic trees, with sunbeams shimmering down through green canopies improbably far above. Little leaf huts were clustered here and there, and little people too, resting, spears leaning against hut and trunk. They left off mending nets and tending racks of smoking meat that gave off smelly wafts of burnt fur, and rushed over to greet our party. There were so many new faces to see, people who had never become accustomed to fading into anonymous faces in a city crowd; each was an individual, and everyone knew everyone else—in many cases, for all of their lives.

Peter and I arranged a hut to sleep in. The Bambuti sleep on a grill of green sticks, set above any nocturnal conflagration of centipedes and spiders. We draped the exterior with electronic camera gear and solar rechargers, so that it must have looked like a sorcerer's hut, from which, soon, music and strange lights escaped through the leaf-shingles at night.

When the chief, an old and renowned pygmy named Zaire of the Babeela, got back from hunting, he tossed his ceremonial animal skin (that of a jungle cat called a civet) over his shoulder and gave a speech of welcome, simultaneously translated for us by Manuel.

There was a vibrant routine to life at the camp, starting when we would eat breakfast of antelope in the morning, then go off hunting for several sets. The men would grab their spears and their nets made of woven bark fibre, carefully arranged and hung like floppy rings—imagine a hairnet for the biggest dreads in the world, but instead of dreads it is all net, draped from their foreheads down their backs. Most of the band would come to help with the hunt, following one another by leaving signs of bent saplings or broken twigs. Each man would suspend the length of his net on the many whip-supple saplings that grew up in the shade of the giant primary forest; adjacent hunters would string his nets together in a trap over a kilometre long. At a signal, shouting and singing women would drive the wildlife toward them, taking care to intercept escaping animals and get them fleeing toward the net. Dogs would reach the victims first and pin them down until the man arrived and slit the throat of whatever it was: common duikers, blue duikers, and other small antelope mostly, with some guinea fowl and the occasional rare or dangerous animal such as a leopard. They didn't always kill: we caught a chimp once, and they let it go, saying it is like grandfather. This is typical of the net-and-spear pygmies, such as the Bambuti we hunted with; pygmy bands that are poison-arrow hunters would have no such qualms about eating apes and monkeys.

On a few occasions Peter had me video the slaying of a screaming animal, while he took stills. He wasn't sure if the footage would be of any use, as Europeans were too soft to watch it, he said. Pygmies are one of the more carnivorous peoples I've ever met. Adults eat an all-red-meat diet, supplemented by red palm oil and sometimes rice and salt or whatever they can get by trading smoked bush meat with the Bantu groups settling along the road. The children worked from a young age, mainly carrying baskets with the quartered sections of the larger duikers, or a singular duiker of the smaller species with its hooves bound to make a leggy headband, so its body could hang like a meaty rucksack on some tiny kid's back. There could be a lot to carry: we'd sometimes harvest a dozen or more antelope a day. One little boy, maybe five or six years old, looked at my face as I watched the killing of a blue duiker: it screamed and then bled out. I could see that he found it distressing; perhaps he wondered if maybe an otherworldly White such as myself shared his concern. I smiled to let him know it was normal. After all, he'd have to be killing with his own hand soon enough, every day for the rest of his life.

Some children, who were not needed to carry freshly caught antelope, remained in the camp. A little girl and an even littler boy were having a contest to see who would flinch, each of them cocking an arm for a punch. They stared and stared but neither backed down. The girl clutched around her nipple, where one day she would have a breast, and wiggled it as a parting taunt for a boy who still suckled. Flowers rained down from the treetops, and other kids would try to drop-kick them before they touched the forest floor, calling out "ooh aye" if successful.

Peter believed the band lived in balance with nature; I was pretty sure they didn't. Despite many women saying they only ever wanted one or two kids, as they were too much trouble to feed, some of their sisters must be having more than their share: I saw far too many kids around camp. These kids are not a sign of good times and abundance, in this case, since the good times and the environment have been desynchronized. Population is not allowed to swing anymore, but only ratchets up. These extra children are cracks in the foundation of a culture that has scarcely changed for tens of thousands of years. If the antelope numbers sink, in consequence, to levels where you can't feed a family with net and spear, then their way of life will be destroyed, and you will only be able to comment on how weird it is that some Africans are so freaking short.

Supplemental food included opossums (caught with dogs and spear from tangles of brush), the occasional passion fruit, wild mushrooms, and copious pink kola nuts, of Coca-Cola fame. If we passed a tree of kola nuts, someone was sure to scamper up like a squirrel and bring some down, so that one and all could enjoy a chew, for the buzz. When Henry Morton Stanley, *New York Herald* journalist and trigger-happy colonialist explorer, battled his way across the continent in the 1880s, he remarked on the absence of provisions in these forests. If it weren't for pygmies bringing meat and kola nuts, his whole expedition would have starved. Mushrooms could be had if you kept your eye out for them, and the women would collect them in their baskets and bring them back to camp to add savour to the stew.

Wild honey was available for the brave, and Peter got some good photos of a pygmy smudging and chopping out a hive at some catastrophic height up a trunk. I filmed the process of him getting in place for these shots. The best honey was from a nest of stingless bees; one of the hunters caught the faint scent of the hive as we passed under it, and he shinnied up to plunder the honey, which tasted like a sweet balsamic vinegar. I felt lucky to have tried it once in my life. Imagine what you'd have to pay in a New York restaurant to dress your salad with the wild honey of stingless bees, harvested by a pygmy in the Congo rain forest?

The Bambuti know how to have fun. Even the families out hunting are smiling more than a Westerner on a bank-holiday weekend, and they dance and sing and tell stories and jokes. It's a common sight to see pygmies laughing so hard that they are holding their bellies, rolling around on the forest floor. Sure it was dangerous out here, with elephants, snakes, slips, and falls, but a pygmy who makes it to thirty absorbs more fun than an office worker who drags his living carcass around for three score and ten. Westerners want their lives to count, and some of us seem cock-sure that quantity beats quality of life, obsessed with how many years of age they've recorded, as if they were King Canute trying to hold back the tides of time. None of the pygmies in this band knew how many times they had whirled around the sun, or seemed particularly interested in even this most rudimentary life-logging.

The Bambuti can make a comfortable chair in ten minutes, with in-genious cuts and bends and bindings of materials within reach of where they intend to sit. I liked to sit thus at the campfire, swapping stories. They resented their status as an inferior race, so I guessed correctly that they would enjoy hearing about my travels among the Hmong of Cambodia, diminutive people who were fierce fighters, with rifles like the rangers, but even more deadly since they are so small, fast, and silent. The chief was widely travelled and had many interesting tales, including his comic first encounter with a zebu bull, and midnight raiding those ever-so-tasty banana patches of the tall folk. Pygmies are notorious ba-nana thieves; the stems of bunches may be too heavy for any one pygmy to hold, but three in a row can make off with it. Knowing how happy they were when puffing *bangi*, I tried to tell them how, if they would plant the seeds, they might have their own, and not be at the mercy of the stingy Bantu for their stash. While they understood the concept, Bambuti are rovers like me, and gardening of any sort calls for the gardener to put down roots. Mostly I told tales of hunting and camping in Canada, since they were so eager to hear these. Consequently, the chief announced a new name for me. I waited for Manuel's translation: "He calls you a big pygmy." The pygmies also listened to this translation, and one of them noticed that "big" and "pygmy" really ought to be one word. I was therefore a "Digmy." This was hilarious, of course, one of those rolling-on-the-ground-laughing moments of which these pygmies were so fond. That night, thunderstorms cruised above our rainforest canopy, sending lightning streaking across the open sky above our glade. Peter saw a flaming meteor.

If I've given the impression that life here was idyllic as a Disney film, with smiling happy families dancing and singing, I don't want to dispel this, since it was mostly true. But life in camp also had the usual frustrations and tensions, so it could go dark very fast, or very dark even faster, like a Quentin Tarantino film. It turned out that all it took was a dash of alcohol.

Tall strangers arrived at the edge of the glade, and the chief grabbed his civet skin and made a speech. I listened closely to Manuel's simultaneous translation.

"My fellow pygmies: big people have arrived to trade for our smoked antelope. They have red palm oil, salt, knives, rice, and more. Also, some of their women have come. Now, my pygmies, I do not need to remind you that if a woman sees an antelope on offer, or perhaps two antelope, she might forget that she has a boyfriend or husband back in her village. She will be behaving not good. Remember, one antelope, or at most two ... "

At this point in the translation I wondered if he was more concerned with morality or inflation.

He ended the speech, though, with an unambiguous admonition: "They have also brought alcohol to trade. Now remember, my fellow pygmies, what happened last time the traders brought alcohol." There were murmurs of assent from the band. "I do not need to retell, as each pygmy should have learned his lesson and we will be chastened and moderate pygmies this time."

For those hell-bent on moderation, there were alarmingly big jugs of moonshine changing hands. Peter seemed uncharacteristically worried. The Bantu women did a brisk trade, pairing off and disappearing into the forest for haunches of smoked meat; red palm oil was traded too, for whole antelopes—10 or as much as 15 litres for one. Apparently size mattered here.

At first everyone was merely getting jolly. Our rangers came back with a jug, and everyone had a swig. It was low-grade moonshine, part wood alcohol. I abstained after my next mouthful. As the sun went down, and the music of yelping dogs was replaced with singing and the giggling of children around the campfire, I thought, This is shaping up to be a fun night.

Then Peter tapped me on the shoulder and pointed to a muscular fellow, stumbling, his shoulders bunched and quaking. "He is going into alcohol withdrawal, see it?" he said.

"But he is still drinking," I said, noting the sloshing bin of moonshine in his hands.

"Some people are so bad at holding their liquor," he shot back, "that they show symptoms of withdrawal even while drinking."

Our forest rangers were drinking rather a lot too, but they seemed to have a higher level of tolerance and were getting only redneck drunk, if you will, rather than the hillbilly drunkenness setting in. "This will not end well," Peter said, and I had to agree. We wondered when it would kick off, and did not have long to wait.

The pygmies got obnoxious when drunk, and the quaking pygmy, whose name was Chi-chi-oo, and some of his confreres were especially boisterous. Now Chi repeatedly insulted the old chief. A hush fell over the encampment, as everyone looked to see how he would deal with this challenge to his authority, but he remained seated, his face showing concentration but otherwise inscrutable, and admonished them to cut out the drinking.

Then some of them began taunting the ranger Desire. He was older then Jacques but lower in rank, and he was often the one cooking and cleaning, as he did back at the ranger station. The taunts amounted to: you are not a soldier, you are a woman. We see you cooking and cleaning every morning.

That outrageously drunk Chi was also the instigator here, but it seemed that most like to stir up trouble when drunk, so it didn't take much to get them rowdy.

Desire had reached his flashpoint. He got up and walked to the far huts, where the women had assembled, and returned tugging a woman into the forest. She appeared to be about half willing. I'm not sure what she'd been offered in return.

"She is my wife," yelled Chi.

"I'm taking this pygmy anyway. She is mine for the night," Desire announced.

Chi flexed his extensive but pygmy-sized muscles and said something that, though Manuel declined to tackle it, I could well imagine. So Desire got out his AK-47 and waved it drunkenly around, yelling, "I'm going to kill the pygmies. I'll kill all the pygmies."

By this point, most of the women and all the children had scattered, or were hiding in the leaf huts. It was unusually quiet without any singing or dancing, and even the dogs were cowering in uncharacteristic silence. Everyone could thus hear the sliding of the metal bolt.

Mustafa, our level-headed expert in contacting tribes, was drunk and had gone off with a woman into the forest. Manuel was nervous, telling me repeatedly, "A bullet is now in the chamber."

"Drinking and assault rifles are a poor combo," I agreed, alert now.

I was paying close attention to the direction the barrel was pointed, seeing as Desire was so drunk he could hardly stand, with his finger on the trigger. I'd step behind a tree trunk when he waved it my way.

"Should we climb down that mud bank and go stand in the river?" Peter asked.

I looked to the chief, calmly sitting by the fire. His expression told me that there was more going on than first met the eye. While I tried to puzzle it out, I nodded at Peter's next suggestion: we should go to Desire's commanding officer and complain; we had hired them for a number of reasons, killing all the pygmies not figuring among them.

Jacques was drunk, slumped against a tree, but Peter managed to convince him that he ought to intervene. He stumbled over to Desire and stripped him of his AK-47, his bullets, and his knife, being firm but trying also to settle him down. Then Jacques was back in his cups.

Now Desire felt humiliated, so he threatened Chi with his fists. Chi sat down to show he was not afraid; also, perhaps, because he had trouble keeping his legs under him. Next, Desire took out the only weapon left to him, his leather belt, and began to thrash the man. And though Desire was smaller than Jacques or Peter or me, he was quite a bit larger than a pygmy. Chi didn't dare to stand, and Desire thrashed him till the blood streamed down his face, then declared, "Now you know your place." The guy's wife had stayed when the other women fled, and had been taking a keen interest in the goings-on; Desire clasped her arm and tugged her after him into the bushes.

Now Chi clearly felt humiliated and marched around the camp, yelling that he loved his wife (according to the translation), but kicking people's huts and making the children screech in fear. A series of fist fights ensued, as other hunters had reached their limit. One said, "You say you love your wife, but when I was out hunting, you slept with my wife." Bing, bang, they battered each other with fists. This seemed to have no end, as it was dark, and these fights raged in the black of night or against the last orange embers of firepits. Peter's and my boots had stirred up the thick layer of duff, leaves, and decayed wood, uncovering blobs of bioluminescent fungus, aglow now in the pervasive darkness.

"This muscular pygmy, the one making most of the trouble, is he one of the sons of the chief?" I asked Manuel.

"No, I think he married into the band. He is married to one of the chief's daughters."

Hmm. Interesting.

"We will get no sleep tonight, absolutely none," Peter said. "I experienced this before, when the traders brought alcohol to some poison-arrow pygmies. They got into a drunken machete fight. One guy had his collarbone cleaved in half, and another took a machete clean through the cheek that chipped out all the teeth on the other side of his jaw."

Peter was right; the camp was in turmoil. I had an idea: we should distribute the *bangi* early. Peter was not so sure. He was inclined to withhold it, annoyed with some of the Bambuti, especially the porters, who had been pilfering supplies. But in the end we decided we would give a handful of *bangi* for each leaf hut. I was fascinated how quickly the *bangi* worked its magic. As the spliffs lit up, the agro alcohol lost sway, and we settled in for a good night's sleep after all.

COME MORNING, THE CHIEF MADE A SPEECH AND CAPTURED THE mood of the camp. He said that one pygmy could not hold his drink, and as this was not his first offence, this pygmy was hereby banished forever. Camp life slowly returned to normal. Visitors to tribes see more than a normal amount of uproar like this, part of the reason some older tribespeople are suspicious of strangers arriving, as they seem to be bad luck. The wiser among them know this is not mere superstition; rather, tensions build among people living so intimately, and they need to be resolved and released. The arrival of strangers breaks the routine and provides cover for power plays and lesser social gambits; clusters of such events mushroom precisely when strangers can witness them.

This incident with the Bambuti taught me something about human nature, combining, as it did, violent social tension and banishment, both teeth on the key to the door of a mystery that had long bedevilled me. I've spent inordinate time alone in the wilderness, settling into a bush mode that entailed finding there was a flip side to what it means to be human. As I said earlier, this second half of human nature is just as powerful and fleshed-out as the first half, but so different as to mimic the alien mind of some other species, and always, when you return to "civilized" company, you are bush-crazy, a stranger in a strange land. This means you are exceedingly perceptive, so much so that everyone's face is an open book. You can practically read minds, and you do so with an energy bordering on paranoia. My unconscious mind has thus been trained to be that of someone who has banished himself from human company many times, and though I now dwell consciously as usual, my unconscious keeps to the old ways. It communicates to my "self" with in-tuition. That is why, when Peter asked, "Do you think we should go stand in the river?" I didn't try to work out bullet trajectories or otherwise apply myself rationally to the question; rather, I looked to the face of the chief in the light of the fire. He seemed alert, poised, smiling faintly with what could be satisfaction at a plan coming together.

If I had just been entering this camp after many months alone in the wilds, I would have been in that ultra-perceptive mode—a human trait, just like the mammalian diving reflex, or the instinct that has a person's limbs make a burrowing motion when their core temper-ature drops near lethal levels. Then, instead of mere hints from my subconscious, I would have seen in real time the machinations and tensions of this hunting band. I'd have known in moments what was what, instead of the slow seepage of understanding that gave me the answers to the incident of the calm chief, his wily daughter, and the brandished assault rifle.

The camp was now more tranquil than ever: skinny dogs back to whimpering, dreaming of stealing meat off the smoking racks; the women washing up in the river, with the suds of efefe fruit instead of detergent. A man clearing shrubs for a hut found a baby bird and gave it to the little kids to play games with, the final one being when they cooked it over a little fire and ate it.

I chanced upon a chameleon, no bigger than a fingernail, with only two toes on each foot. The Bambuti were dismayed and said this was bad luck for hunting. I told them through the translator that even if chameleons were bad luck, this minuscule chameleon couldn't amount to much of it. Sure enough, we caught eight antelope that day, and all were content that evening at the camp, save for one little kid who took to screaming and crying whenever Peter approached with a camera in front of his face. We were told that pygmies warn their children against being wimps, because if they are not strong and brave, a big white monster will come and eat them.

Sadly, the day came when we had to go. As we got everything packed away, Peter discreetly said to me, "Do you see the chief's eldest son there? He has AIDS. He probably caught it from one of these Bantu women who come in from the road."

"How do you know?"

"Notice his skin?"

"Looks like only a fungal infection to me."

"No. It's a fungal infection, true. It's ringworm. But it's not growing somewhere damp. It's on his chest and his forehead. Africans don't suffer fungal infections like that unless they have compromised immune systems, and what comes to mind when you think 'African with a compromised immune system'? It's AIDS, but he'll have a tough immune response. It might take years to kill him."

I felt worried, especially knowing that the pygmies sleep around as much as they do. "Are you going to tell him?"

"No," Peter said, getting out his medical bag. "I'm going to give him cream for the fungus, and he'll enjoy a better quality of life for a few more months. There are limits to what I can accomplish, and telling someone they have AIDS is just making trouble if they don't and can't understand it, and will only cause a momentary terror—for nothing, as then the disease will progress and spread the same as before. AIDS is untreatable without a healthcare infrastructure and an economy to support it."

Peter gave the man a tube of cream and instructions as a final parting gift. He also helped any others medically as best he could, and we slipped a whole pack of cigarettes to an old woman, Tee-ti-moh, who stifled a cry of surprise when she felt the pack touch her hand, hiding it before the others could see. She was too old to get more than a few cigarettes a year, if that, out of what was swapped with the faraway road, and now she'd have this whole pack to savour and trade.

The band all assembled for our departure, and the chief made another oration, thanking us travellers from such distant lands, and saying any time we returned we would be welcome.

A squishy half of a yellow-and-black lizard found itself somehow under my boot on the long trek to the dirt road. It was the front half of the critter, and hollow, like a meat puppet. Usually you will encounter a lizard or you won't; it's rare to see nature split the difference. A tick crawled on my skin and was brushed off, a strange caterpillar stung my neck with what may have been hairs or bristles, and a barbed vine cut my bottom lip. But the only worry that mattered was crossing high above streams on logs, and there my footing was firm.

AS SOON AS WE GOT TO THE SLASHED LANDS NEARER THE ROAD, Peter, weary of a diet consisting overwhelmingly of meat, traded with a slash-and-burn farmer for a whole sack of passion fruit and ate them on the spot, to the laughter of our porters, who consider passion fruit only fit for children. We got another sack of the fruit for later, and stashed it back at the hotel.

A white man, a kid really, had come to see us. He probably had heard that there were a couple of white people at this hotel. He looked to be a bundle of nerves and just needed to hear some English and see familiar faces after being out here too long trying to run a development project. He was an American, and his name was Joel, Joel the geographer, and he haltingly explained that he was teaching the squatters who had invaded along this road through the park how to farm more efficiently.

I was about to say, I am also trying to teach more efficient farming: I was trying to instruct the pygmies how to grow marijuana.

But Peter beat me to it, saying, "How do you morally justify what you are doing? Are you going to come back next year and hand out AKs to thin out the resulting overpopulation?"

Now I was forestalled and couldn't poke any fun at him, so I asked him if he was headquartered locally. After all, even if he did think he was doing development, wasn't that more the fault of all the adults who kept putting such ideas in the heads of impressionable youngsters? And who can say? In some distant era, after the info-tech solution of the economic question, when the great national parkland forests of the Congo basin thrum to commerce amid green fields of GMO maize tended by robots, fun-employed locals, rather than tapping their toes to old-timey Nashville tunes about John Deere, may well sing of Joel the geographer, the stuff of legend, like rainforest trees, okapi, elephants, and other fanciful things.

But the kid was now reduced to mumbling to himself, pacing in a tight circle. "You broke Joel," I told Peter, who roared with laughter. I would like to have told him how brave I thought he was to be so young and out here in a place like this doing good works, which should be cherished for their own sake. But we weren't likely to get much more out of Joel.

We left our intrepid geographer where he was and caught up on something we'd missed: beer drinking. Peter launched into a tirade against Médecins Sans Frontières. I've heard it three times since, whenever I drop in on him in London, where he settled to practise surgery, but he never starts this story until at least pint number six, so I've no idea what he's on about: something about institutional corruption of one sort or another.

Peter was also keen for advice only a guy like me could give him: where was the most dangerous place? Because he still had time to rush over somewhere and get pictures of dangerous derring-do, the hope being any competition would be frightened away.

"South Sudan," I told him. "I was just there, and if you're looking for trouble, you'll find it. Even if you're not looking for trouble, it'll find you."

"Then I'm going there next, after I find a way to airmail these boxes of undeveloped film," he said.

We decided to try to hitch a ride together to Kisangani. He'd finish up with this pygmy expedition, attempt to get photos of some jungle mining by profiteering warlords, and carry on to South Sudan. I was hoping to catch a barge down the Congo River; the Kiss-Kiss is a tributary, and Henry Morton Stanley had managed the journey from Kisangani (which used to be called Stanleyville after its founder).

Jacques and Desire, who had both recovered nicely from the moonshine, pointed out a transport truck that would carry us westward, and we bid them goodbye after a last look at the okapi they were husbanding for later release. Just before we left, a convoy of latter-day journo-jeeps pulled into the station. Rather than a mustachioed Stanley, the VIP passenger was a blonde woman, perhaps French. We didn't have time to speak with her, but it is always a good sign for the stability of a region if you see Western women, so I decided this place might be a little island of peace in an otherwise appalling neighbourhood. Mind you, she was guarded by four dudes with automatic rifles. Later, this illusion of stability was shattered: I read online that a gang of elephant poachers attacked this very ranger station, massacring locals, including some of the rangers and all their precious okapi.

A semi-trailer trundled along the road toward us and we flagged it down ... it was the Primus beer truck. After stowing our packs and a burlap sack of passion fruit, we were on our way. Our truck was carrying empty bottles only, but we met the outgoing beer truck not long afterward, and had the driver pass some full ones over out his window.

The DRC police were as rapacious as ever, but with two of us, and Peter's genuine document to provide cover for my bluff, we sailed through without too much trouble. The trucker seemed to have his customary whorehouses in settlements strung along this road, and if we saw him changing to his one nice pair of jeans and shirt, we'd head for whatever passed for a tavern while he took his time. The food on offer included a lot of bush meat, so we continued a diet of smoked antelope, almost certainly caught by pygmies. There were often pangolins for sale, and usually a guy would come through with a wheelbarrow full of smoked monkey corpses ... these reminded me of photos I'd seen at Auschwitz. I always declined, but locals sitting at the bar would munch them like pub food with their beers.

One morning I kept trying to buy bananas, but our driver was telling me in French, "No, wait, not here, better up ahead." It was afternoon before he stopped to shop for some bunches, and I wish I remembered the name of that village. They were by far the finest bananas I've ever tasted, then or since. They put all the others to shame.

Some days later we got to Kisangani in the pouring rain. Rather than looking for a hotel, we spent our first hour in a restaurant seeing off a police chief who arrived literally rubbing his palms in glee for what he felt certain was payday. I ordered him a soda as we waited for him to get around to the shakedown. He did not disappoint and soon produced a list of bogus charges he'd gone to the trouble of typing up: licence to own a camera: 300 dollars; video camera: 700 dollars; ten dollars for each roll of film; licence to photograph in the environs of this city: some other tremendous charge. I would have paid someone 700 dollars just to have the video of us inviting him to sit with us while we listened to his demands, and to see his grin fade as Peter showed official permission for all such things, signed by the chief of the secret police, and disappear completely as I said I was UN and neither owned a camera nor intended to film anything. Glumly he ended by asking if we'd pay for his soda, since he'd used so much petrol coming out here from the station.

We had to check nine hotels to find one with a room because of all the NGOs and UN in town. The price of a ten-dollar room was a hundred dollars. The locals know their customers have no idea what a hotel usually costs—and simply pass the expense on to the UN anyway—so the hotels charge as much as the daily accommodation expense account covers. Our hundred-dollar room was the bay of a warehouse, with dirty rags for dividers.

Now Peter wanted to show me something. We'd been talking about why I didn't own or carry a camera, and I'd said it was partly because I felt it would fragment my experiences, obligating me to capture and preserve them instead of living in the moment. Peter wanted to show me that the freestyle travel I favoured might not even be feasible for a photographer. He hung a big camera around his neck and suggested we try to walk down to the river. The fifteen-minute walk took an hour, most of it spent in the stations of four different branches of suspicious police as they made threats and tried to extort money from what they assumed must be a pair of journalists, a choice prey of police in corrupt nations everywhere.

One of the bars near the river was a favourite of ours and of UN big-wigs, some of whom had mercenary bodyguards. One of these guards understood his real job all too well. He was looking daggers at everyone else in the room, hand hovering above the hilt of his machine pistol; the white-haired gentleman being "guarded" seemed well chuffed. Peter and I had a laugh about this, since clearly there are two kinds of threats to guard against: random violence, like a drunk or belligerent local; and organized violence, such as a hit squad in town told to kill some UN functionary as a reprisal. This mercenary would be doing his job best if he practised concealed carry and tried to blend in to give himself more options should he be needed, rather than annoying locals by trying to intimidate everyone and, thus, serving as a beacon to any assassins while indicating that the man he was with would make a superb target. But this mercenary must have understood that those are secondary concerns next to his real job: to make his employer feel powerful and important. His role was similar to that of a sexpot model hired as a gentleman's escort for a posh party, here with the UN picking up the tab.

The local girls were just as creative in defining their roles; one had busy hands rubbing my leg under the tablecloth while carrying on a conversation with her boyfriend. When I mentioned it to Peter, he laughed and said, "She was trying the same with my leg too."

MY FAMILY FINALLY GOT A TRAVEL UPDATE, AFTER I'D LOCATED AN internet café with semi-reliable connection and an archaic computer that had all the letters on the keyboard rubbed off and used a system that wasn't qwerty. My efforts to arrange a boat or barge down the Congo River failed. There had been some difficulties involving a zany Spaniard, Dr. Manresa, who had given it a try; word had just reached the relevant authorities that he had been captured by an Enyele rebel group that had been attacking the city of Mbandaka on the river. Their superstitious leader, Mr. Mangbama, had shaved off every strand of the Spaniard's body hair to fashion a pungent amulet, whose "white" magic would make him immune to bullets. Those same rebels still held choke points on any river route, ready to ritually shave any white man they captured until he resembled a baby's bottom. And all indications were that extra-ordinarily low water levels meant it might take months to float down, longer than my visa would allow. The local secret police chief insisted that if I wanted to go, it would be in the company of one of his officers, who would be travelling at my expense, so the venture was looking more like a plan to hang out with a policeman, and nothing like the freestyle adventure I'd been hoping for.

While I thought it over, Peter and I went to look at traditional fishing at Boyoma Falls, where locals fish from weirs, lowering huge baskets that look like cornucopias into the current. I used this time to make up my mind: floating the Congo, my dream since reading Stanley's *Through the Dark Continent* in high school, just wasn't doable or likely to be any fun under the circumstances; the plan was nixed. Instead, there was an old beater of a cargo plane, the aviation equivalent of a propeller-driven dinosaur, whose pilot could fly me to an airport close to Kinshasa. I said goodbye to Peter (who'd sent his film to Europe and was heading east to South Sudan), then climbed into the hold of the plane, among a pile of crates, and got a good look from on high at the spreading rivers and jungle around Kisangani—formerly a slave raiders' lair, then

Stanleyville and the den of mercenaries, before settling on its present name and becoming a haven for UN types.

Next day, after napping against the wall of the N'djili Airport, I was approaching the megacity of Kinshasa, astounded by the horizontal forest of titanic logs afloat in the rivers and streaming into town on the roads. I worked my way toward the central cluster of skyscrapers, figuring that was where the action and the embassies were; besides, the outskirts included a whole lot of what looked like filthy slums. My experience as a backpacker told me that now would be a good time to splurge on posh accommodation.

Sub-Saharan Africa generally is poor value for money, so fifty dollars a night got me a room on the seventh floor of a ratty-looking hotel high-rise, no elevator, aircon, or running water. If I needed to wash, the staff would lend me a bucket and I could find a burst pipe somewhere in the street, fill the bucket, and stagger up seven flights of stairs in the tropical heat. There was a restaurant on the ground floor, but it had degraded into a bar, and not a popular one. A lonely hooker sat nursing a Fanta, trying to pass as a hotel guest. Soon I befriended a Cameroonian who lived out on the street. He'd been trying to get to South Africa, but his passport was stolen right about here; he decided to spend a few years on the curbside selling goat-meat skewers while he considered his options, as might we all if we were in his shoes.

Kinshasa's banking was modern enough for me to get a cash advance and start work on visas for Congo Brazzaville (that's the Republic of Congo, as opposed to the much larger Democratic Republic of Congo) and Gabon. While exploring the downtown area, I passed a pub that lured me in with a promise of air conditioning. It was gloriously cool, and it seemed I was not the only customer reeled in out of the heat. Two foreigners were downing pints and invited me to join them. They were Carl, a Quebecois mixed-martial-arts practitioner, and Spencer. "I'm also from Canada," I told them, "and something of a Spencer too, but Spencer is my middle name." This Spencer was a Swazilander, riding a Yamaha Ténéré motorbike all around the periphery of the African continent, filming his experience to raise money for Save the Children, and posting it online as Africabikeadventure. This was later to become a show on the Travel Channel (as of this writing he's filming another show, in South America). They were both interesting to talk to, unsurprisingly: off-the-beaten-track places like the DRC are excellent for filtering out boring people. No scrubs here: everyone I met could hold up a conversation better than the top one in a hundred vacationers you might meet at a resort or popular tourist site. Even Joel the geographer would have been interesting, I'm sure, if we'd given him a chance, although he was just starting out as an adventurer.

We called for food, but the only thing on offer was a bowl of peanuts. There was another restaurant downtown, so we ventured into the tropical heat once more.

The restaurant, L'Orangeraie, was a fancy French joint said to be favoured by expats, and there was an expat to prove it. As soon as we walked through the door, he invited us to dine with him. Food on its way, beers in hand, we swapped stories with this jolly Belgian, whose name sounded like Yves. Carl told of getting into martial arts battles with Africans: he broke the leg of an aggressive drunk twice his size; another was initially eager to come at him with a machete, but then his courage failed him and he turned tail and skittered away, waggling the machete behind his ass. Spencer told of having his bike nearly shot out from under him by Samburu bandits on the highway south from Ethiopia. His back brakes were destroyed, but the Yamaha ran another kilometre or two before he had to ditch it and hide in the shrubbery. The Samburu fellows showed up, looking to find him, rob him, and perhaps kill him. He had a special device given to him by his sponsors, a button he could press to summon a crew of armed mercenaries who would set out by helicopter to home in on the signal. As the Samburu searched for him, Spencer was tempted to push the button, but he reckoned it was useless. Night was falling, and these tribesmen would either find him or not before any helicopter could arrive. Also, his sponsors would be charged $20,000 for any push of that button. The Samburu searched a while, but gave up.

I told some of my own travel tales, and Yves had stories galore. He was in charge of Reuters news for the entire Congo basin, so he'd had lots of run-ins with insurgents and minefields.

When I'd checked email back in Kisangani before my flight, I'd seen a message from Anders the Norwegian documentarian who had filmed an interview with me back in South America while we floated down the Amazon. He wanted to know if I could ask about the guilt or innocence of two Norwegian guys who were in prison in Kinshasa for murder. The allegation was that they had killed their driver, and a film found by police that showed them posing with the body as a trophy seemed to belie their protests of innocence. Yves here was the guy to ask, since journos have to maintain shady contacts to do their jobs. He told me they were guilty as hell ... everyone knew everyone in this little expat crowd, and these guys had left jobs at the Norwegian embassy and took to dealing in cocaine. Their driver noted what they were up to and tried to blackmail them, so they killed him. They would have got away with it, too, if they hadn't vanity-filmed themselves with the corpse.

Carl, Spencer, and I were surprised to hear about this cocaine in Congo. Yves told us, "Congo has the best cocaine in the world." We were not convinced, and each of us suggested another country that should, by reputation, have better: Colombia, Venezuela, anywhere but here. Who ever heard of Congo being praised for its cocaine?

"You don't understand, it comes across the Atlantic pure, it's like what a dentist would use ... absolutely pure, in order to be smuggled north toward Europe overland. Here, I'll prove it to you guys. If you don't believe a European, you can hear it from a local." *Beep beep beep*, he made a call, and a few minutes later a Congo dude showed up on a motorbike and sat with us.

The horrifying scars on the motorcyclist didn't escape my notice, but I felt it wouldn't be polite to pry. Carl had no such qualms. Before we could ask about DRC cocaine smuggling, he said, "I have to ask you, what is this, and this?" pointing out the man's scars.

"Motorcycle accident," he mumbled, then promptly got up and left the restaurant.

"I should have warned you," Yves said. "You touched on a sore point there. It was no bike accident. He and his pregnant girlfriend were stopped by the police at a checkstop. The cops must have wanted to steal his bike, since they hacked him up bad with a machete, then cut his unborn baby out of his girlfriend before his eyes, strangled it, and killed the mom. He was left for dead in the ditch. By some miracle he survived, but his respect for police did not, and he lives as an outlaw now."

On hearing this, I felt the DRC was not ready for mass tourism yet. There is a term for when stuff like that happens: T.I.A. (This Is Africa).

THE NEXT DAY I HAD ALL MY VISAS. SPENCER WAS RIDING NORTH TOO, but he had to wait on some replacement parts for his bike to arrive by express mail. We agreed to keep in touch by email and try to meet in Cameroon after I'd made my way through Gabon to see the surfing hippos of Loango National Park. I said goodbye to Carl and Spencer, and we wished each other luck and happy trails.

The public ferry carried me across the river to Brazzaville, capital of the Republic of Congo, on the north bank of the river. People in wheelchairs swarmed aboard alongside me, trying to manipulate heavy packages without the use of their legs; they got a discount on ticket prices, so, according to the law of unintended consequences, traders who were disabled had a comparative advantage over the able-bodied and drove them out of business.

Brazzaville was less crazy than Kinshasa, more laid-back, and the buildings had somewhat more character, but otherwise it was a similar capital: vital for its region but internationally little known. A train carried me south, and from then on it was a matter of hitching in the back of trucks from town to town. The land was somewhat hilly, denuded of trees but lush with weeds or crops, and the roads dominated by flatbed trucks taking bundles of rainforest hardwoods to be sawed into boards. Battered old trucks handled dry goods and necessities between the farm towns, and the people crammed themselves in among the supplies.

It proved wise to pre-empt any problems with police by sitting with the first one I met and buying him a beer. Problems were sometimes unavoidable. Once rival factions of police were beating each other bloody outside headquarters in a free-for-all over who would have the right to try to extort money from me, and my misleading UN card was frequently in play. Outside the same headquarters a bleeding police-man smiled and said, "There is another white man in town, perhaps you know him?" I strolled over and, as a matter of fact, I did. This seemed completely normal to the policeman, but the South African bicyclist and I were surprised: he was the guy I'd met in Mauritania months earlier, still pedalling his way south. You can tell that a place doesn't get many travellers when you meet only one other and happen to know him.

Carrying on north, surviving off the occasional tin of sardines and biscuits, I neared the frontier of Gabon, a country named for a now-unfashionable style of coat. The shakedown from corrupt cops became more extreme the nearer the border I was, and by now the people riding in the trucks with me were all making for this same border into Gabon. A lanky African dude also had a foreign passport, and I could see that he was avoiding me and my presumed miasma of bad luck attracting police corruption. I needed to up my game and adopted a fierce attitude with any policeman, pretending to be enraged by the mere thought of corruption. Miraculously, by the tenth shakedown that day, the lanky dude was manoeuvring to be called into the private offices right after me, and finally was standing by my side if he could, so I must have been doing something right.

Blustering my way past an angry demand for ten euros to get my stamp at the border, I hopped in a pickup truck heading for the coast. When I reached a stretch of lovely white beach, I decided to stay a while in a little town, Mayumba, population a few thousand, but spread out, with a hotel and even a motel, a bar, and a restaurant. The sand felt won-derful on my toes, and when the sun was too high in the sky, I could hide under the spreading limbs of trees just like the ones I'd seen in Zanzibar, on the opposite coast. They were exactly the same species, I thought, noticing those weird green fruits. A nearby stone looked like it had been used as an anvil, and a hand-sized stone as a hammer. Testing, I plucked one of these fruits from a branch and hammered it till it split lengthwise to reveal a tasty white almond-like seed inside. The mystery had been solved: they were enjoyed as nuts, not fruit.

I might have stayed longer in Mayumba, but an incident weighed on my soul and forced me to push on to Gabon's capital, Libreville. It happened around ten one evening, when I was already in bed. I heard a knocking at my door in the Mayeye Foutou hotel, got dressed, and found my torch. It was two little girls, one maybe ten or eleven, the other at least two years younger. They asked me in French if they could come into my room. I asked them where their parents were and told them to return to their village, assuming they were from the fishing village I'd come upon once, a couple of kilometres to the south. Just as I was getting back into bed, there was a louder knocking ... it was the older of the two little girls, asking to come in again, having left the younger (her baby sister?) out in the bushes. Again I told her to go home, and then I had difficulty getting back to sleep. I found it disturbing that they would have this routine worked out where they come at night to knock on hotel rooms with strange men in them. It was not for their health that they were walking so far from their village so late at night. And how did they know I was out here in the darkness anyway, as all the rooms were empty but mine, and there was no manager or receptionist at night? That was the last I saw of them.

Riding in the back of a pickup truck, I went far enough inland to get around impassable marshes and lagoons, then headed farther north and cut in toward the coast again. My goal was to get to a town called Gamba, from which I might boat into Gabon's Loango National Park, which contains the only protected lagoon ecosystem on the West African coast. The people here now are recent immigrants, as in many areas of Africa: they came south just before the time of the American Revolution and ethnically cleansed the indigenous pygmies into oblivion.

Everyone got around in these pickup trucks, riding in the back, wedged between stems of green plantains and bananas. It was a strenuous workout to stay in the truck; you'd find a piece of metal or another man's proffered limb to cling to as you were bashed and jolted and twisted side to side. On three occasions, on three different trucks, men were flung out of the moving vehicle onto pavement or into swamp. We'd shout, and someone would bang on the cab to tell the driver to stop and go retrieve him. I held my place in the truck's bed by strength of arm as civilization dwindled and my surroundings looked more and more like some set from a Tarzan movie. At one point, someone had to swim across a river and come back with a primitive raft. The truck drove onto it, and we pulled it to the opposite bank. The roads became braided tracks and finally muddy ruts, and the landscape a mix of primary forest and swamp. Sometimes the only way to the next passable set of ruts was by boat, and whoever was going that way would try to find transportation onward from whatever godforsaken village we'd ended up in.

At last I found the town of Gamba, peopled mostly by members of the Fang tribe, where I'd been told I could arrange a visit to the park. The town was surrounded by golden grasses and was hot and flat, with not much for the locals to do but eat chickens (tough as vulcanized rubber from a diet of lizards and beetles, and always served with lots of mayonnaise and cups of instant coffee that were half sweet condensed milk) and attend noisy Baptist revival meetings, from which they'd stream home in the wee hours like ravers, eyes gleaming in anticipation of eternal life in heaven.

A friendly guide with a motorboat was willing to take me deep into the park. He had a dangerous job on account of all the buffalo and hippos, and especially the forest elephants. I didn't get to see the hippos in the lagoon cross over the bar of white sand to do any "surfing"—they only waddle out of the lagoon to roll around in the surf when they have parasites they want to scrub off in the grit. The woods themselves, while chirping, buzzing, and rustling with life, had been stripped of all the valuable ebony timber long ago, leaving mainly towering bloated cheese trees (named for their pulpy wood) and other non-commercial species, but there were plenty of animals to see, especially as we were spending our nights camping among them. One type of tree might have come in handy, as it had a cage of roots like staves skirting the base of its trunk. If a buffalo or an elephant was trying to kill me, I was told to squeeze in there and take cover, moving around the trunk inside the cage to keep the tusks from poking through to spear me.

My guide took us on a route that passed near a tree house a BBC filmmaker had been living in the previous year to make a special, *Living with Monkeys*, about rare red-capped mangabey monkeys. It was an amazing three-level tree house with ladders and a homemade rope walkway leading over to a second house that was way up in a tree and had no access from the ground. The walkway consisted of a rope that you balanced your feet on, and a rope for stability on either side at about armpit level. It looked to be still in good condition so I tried it out, making my way to the otherwise inaccessible tree house by inching along far above the forest floor, which was alive with hordes of little crabs searching for organic detritus to nibble.

Another day's hike took me deeper into the park, where a forest elephant with long pointy tusks, like skewers, and angry red eyes charged me ... but then let his attack trail off. I'd backed up near a cliff above a beach, and he may have decided that it wasn't worth the risk so close to the drop-off. This elephant's family had been accidently surprised by our presence; he had crept out of the forest with a female and a little baby, and got aggressive when he smelled us. After that encounter, we beachcombed our way back to the motorboat, a day's trek, with lovely islands, forest, lagoons, and deserted beaches—deserted except for frisky mudskippers, one buffalo, and five more forest elephants. Somehow it was more fun hiking when you had to sneak quietly past huge grey beasts that want to kill you on sight, something grand, like being transported back to the Stone Age, when I imagine such experiences would have been commonplace.

Leaving the park and pressing on through yet more jungle, I ended up at a crossroads, enjoying beers with three Gabonese men. We were talking about how many children we each had: eighteen, fourteen, twenty, and none yet. I pointed out to them that if their kids behaved like they did, everyone in Gabon would be standing shoulder to shoulder just to fit in the country. It's a good thing that as cultures modernize, they invent other ways to gain prestige, including cars, vacations, motorboats, and big houses, because there are few deeds more permanently damaging to the environment than everybody having loads of kids.

The Catholic mission in Libreville had some rooms to accommodate visiting priests at a reasonable price, and there was a fun group of travellers, including a German and a Kiwi, attracted by the same deal. We were all working on visas: I was going north; they were going south on the London-to-Cape Town motorcycle safari. The visa fairies favoured me: as compensation for being turned back by Equatorial Guinea, I got a visa for Cameroon, the only country named for an edible crustacean, as well as a São Tomé visa that allowed me to swiftly fly over to the island for some beach time and relaxation in an old sugar-plantation mansion that served five-course meals by candlelight for a price that wouldn't get you a flophouse in much of Europe.

The other guys were not so lucky. They really had a tough go of it, and our beer-and-fish sessions at the market became glum and, quite frankly, horrifying. First off, a German guy crashed; his friends feared he might have lost an eye, and he had other serious problems besides, so he wanted to be flown out to Cape Town for further medical care. Another guy was sliced up and bleeding from the same accident. He had been helping similarly bleeding truck drivers and was worried, justifiably, that he had exposed himself to HIV. When I got back from São Tomé, another one was gone, the youngest—I think he was only twenty-eight, and named Mike, like me. He'd taken a corner too fast riding up in the hills and had clipped a metal bar used to secure logs on a semi-trailer. The other two guys found him on the road with his helmet split open. They'd tried to help him but it was no use ... one guy said he tried to push his brain back inside. He was upset about it, of course. They told me his brain was only a little out, and they had put it back as fast as they could, but he did not revive. I told them that my understanding was that once the brain comes out, the person has died instantly without suffering; it's extraordinarily delicate, not like some other organs, such as intestines, that can withstand rough treatment. There is no three-second rule for dropped brains.

These two guys did their utmost to get their friend's body embalmed and all the paperwork done so they could send his coffin home to his family in New Zealand. To my relief, a message arrived later without mention of any further disasters as the last two friends completed the trip. Motorcycle travel in Africa is often the most dangerous kind of transportation for both visitors and locals, and everybody has some stories of close shaves. Often survival is not a matter of skill but of merely being lucky.

Eventually I got into Cameroon, enjoying the beach at Kribi, a town at the mouth of the Kienké River. I chatted with an elderly guy who sold beads to visitors. He had done this since the 1960s, had never changed and adapted, and was now being pushed out by energetic youngsters copying this idea, which was a problem as he had staggering heaps of children to raise. He shook his fist at the oil rig offshore, flaring gas in the darkness, saying he would destroy it if he could. Honestly, he was as much a beggar as a bead seller at this stage in life.

My wanderings ceased for an interlude at the Ideal Hotel in Yaoundé, the capital, foraging for yet more visas, and unsuccessfully going after Equatorial Guinea for the fourth time in my life. Spencer, the Swazilander from Kinshasa, met me while working on his own visas, and we toured around in Cameroon for a week or two on his motorbike, taking on the 370-kilometre mountainous ring road, home to the Fon kingdoms. He was doing a lot of local media, so kids and villagers would recognize him in the street, cheering and waving as we rode by; the only way I could get into a building with him and the British High Commissioner once was by pretending to be his cameraman.

Spencer wanted me to film him paddling rafts around soda lakes— volcanic lakes with deep layers of fizzing carbon dioxide that, when disturbed, off-gassed and killed every living thing for miles around—and doing crazy stunts in the vibrantly green hills near Bamenda, as I hung off the back of his Yamaha Ténéré with the video camera. We didn't crash or come off the bike but it was a near thing a few times, and it took a month for the nerves in one of my hands to regrow. They were numbed from gripping a metal bar so tightly to stay on the bike while my other hand held the camera.

Bamenda, a city that is largely English speaking, was great, especially the streets near the market, where we'd spend afternoons drinking beers and snacking on grilled mackerel with chili. One night, though, as I was putting up my mosquito net, I heard gunshots, *bang bang bang*. I thought: I should stand away from the window. Then came another loud bang. It was dark, so slipping into bed won out over any notion to open my door and investigate. Spencer was staying in the room next to me, and when I knocked on his door in the morning, I found he had already been out to ask around about what had gone down last night in front of the hotel. As far as the locals knew, a twenty-two-year-old man had been murdered from four bullets in his back. Lovely people in Bamenda by and large; this incident was sheer bad luck and could have happened anywhere.

Spencer was carrying on north, so I wished him a safe journey and booked myself a flight to England. The heat was getting to be too much: at night, drops of sweat would tickle my skin as they rolled down to the sheets, and I'd shower with my T-shirt on so it could cool me as it dried on my body. It was no use flying south to relieve the heat, as the 2010 World Cup had inflated hotel prices in South Africa. Besides, it didn't make any sense to try to squeeze in another country before Ken and Sally's wedding in the UK in August.

CHAPTER FOURTEEN

HORN TO THE BIGHT

*Greenland · Sudan · Somalia · Puntland ·
Malawi · Madagascar · Namibia · Angola*

B Y JUNE 2010 I WAS IN ENGLAND, WITHOUT MY BACKPACK. It had skipped a connection in Paris, but the good news was that it had since made it as far as Heathrow, though it was not yet delivered. My mom and stepdad were in the country, having just finished a vacation to Scotland and the Cotswolds. We had a couple of days in London, visiting the Docklands museum, where we learned about British involvement in the slave trade (the 400,000 taken to North America were only 4 percent of the total Atlantic trade, I was surprised to learn; trade with the Caribbean and South America constituted the bulk of the crime). We also looked at the house where the fictional detective Hercule Poirot is imagined to have lived.

Then Bruce, my friend from Calgary, flew into town and wanted me to meet him at the Saatchi Gallery. I was standing out in the square a few minutes before I noticed there was a private function going on, with people in suits and fancy dresses. Because of my missing backpack, I was in shabby clothes and borrowed trousers; my hair hadn't been cut in seven months. Hmm. A possibility occurred to me. I approached the door, and the security for the party thought I could only be an artist and let me through, even though men in suits were denied entrance beside me. It turned out that Bruce was at the party to meet Charles Saatchi, as they were then in business together. So I got a private viewing of the gallery, and free champagne all night served by girls circulating through the crowd with trays of drinks and snacks.

We carried on for sushi and drinks in central London, and Bruce invited his friends. As far as I could determine, at least three of them had interesting jobs: a woman who directs PR for Getty Images; Nick, who runs an internet site that allows you to remix music tracks online (he is a young man but also the Earl of Shaftesbury by an odd twist of fate); and a guy I recognized from music videos as the singer from the Fine Young Cannibals. Telling bear stories was my principal contribution to the evening. Having just come in from sweltering mud huts in African villages, I found the whole week random and absurd.

As best man for Ken and Sally's wedding ceremony, I needed to work on a speech and figure out the difficult question of a stag. Ken had given up drinking, so I didn't see the point of, for example, setting up some vast piss-up where he had to endure a bunch of drunks boring him all night, and possibly ending with him off the wagon for his wedding night. I asked him what he'd prefer, and he mostly talked about how he missed exercise and fresh air and seeing remarkable sights. I decided to take him to Iceland, as I'd seen it before and could guarantee it held all he was after. It was the perfect choice, with a healthy 15 or more kilometres of hiking a day, and remarkable sights to boot.

Ken returned to England for wedding planning, while I had time enough to see Greenland before his big day. I caught a small prop-plane, full of Inuit throat singers, to Nuuk, at the mouth of a long fjord system on Greenland's western coast, where the icecap calves icebergs. There were also whales and Viking ruins. These former arctic dairy farmers had been starved out and either left or died off. Some people said it was a great mystery why they didn't just eat fish to tide them over when the climate cooled and made dairy less viable. The answer seemed pretty obvious to me: I'd heard someone in Reykjavík say that Iceland has a rate of seafood allergy that is higher than the rate among the founding population in Scandinavia. It makes sense to me that if you have population pressure and lack farmland, and someone says, "Follow me on a dangerous voyage into frozen oceans in return for a promise of land to farm," it stands to reason that a disproportionate number of people who take you up on this offer will be especially eager for land—many of whom will have no choice as they can't eat fish. Then, when land becomes scarce in Iceland, if another captain says, "Follow me for free land in an even more godforsaken and icy land," the only ones to take up the offer will be those with seafood allergy. The others will say, "Never mind, I'll eat more fish, less milk and grain."

There were two Swiss journalism students in the only hostel in Nuuk, and an internet connection to use while we waited out cold, rain, and ear-piercing wind. When I tried to add Greenland to the places I'd been on a travel map, the computer wouldn't allow the update, saying I was trying to access obscene material. I joked with the Swiss that while I'd travelled extensively enough that many people might find it annoying, I hadn't considered that I might be obscenely well travelled.

Ken's and Sally's wedding proved splendidly fun and was a rollicking start to their married lives. It took place in a marquee in a field by the seaside in Climping, near Bognor Regis, with a theme of the 1920s and 1930s. Everyone was camping in the field, and many of the girls had prepared by learning how to dance the Charleston. A swing band was hired, along with an Argentinean barbecue. My duty as best man included giving a speech, dressed in the Dirty Thirties suit I found at a charity shop, that noted the cognitive dissonance in Ken's coming to England to study technologies and formalities associated with architecture, when his family's Sons of Freedom sect rejected property rights, building permits, and property taxes, and had a penchant for destroying buildings. On the occasion of his father's funeral, Ken had been asked by his aunts to break with tradition and forgo burning down his house while singing in the nude in a ritualistic rejection of materialism.

IT WAS ALREADY LATE SUMMER, AND I NEEDED TO PLAN AND VISA-UP for another go at Africa. One trip I'd not yet had a chance to make was to follow the Nile River to one of its sources in the Ethiopian highlands. Returning to Canada on another of those astonishingly inexpensive flights, I got my teeth checked in Alberta to make sure no toothache would strike in the next year (I don't worry about much, but dentistry in the Sudan would be one of those things), and after a side trip to LA I was good to go, hopping on a flight to Cairo in October.

Egypt was the same as always, with social and economic systems locked up like a population pressure cooker. Getting a visa to Sudan was a Kafkaesque experience, both good for a laugh and instructive, illustrating the pernicious bureaucratic mess that keeps the third world just so.

After a train ride south to Aswan, a city on the Nile's first cataract, ticket in hand, I jumped on the boat across Lake Nasser, a reservoir created by the Aswan High Dam. A young German blogger, Johannes Klaus of *The Travel Episodes*, was sheltering from the baking sun under the same on-deck lifeboat as me, and we travelled up the Nile together, past the pyramids of the ancient Nubians. On the Sudan side of Lake Nasser we carried on south, hitchhiking along the green patch where the Nile valley cuts across the Nubian Desert. An elderly Irish guy joined us and got himself chased through the streets of Khartoum, as the locals thought he was most certainly a spy. The angry mob had evidence: they saw him take a photo of a teapot at a market. But before they could lynch him in front of our hotel, a policeman arrived and sent them away, yelling that they were a bunch of imbeciles.

The three of us took a left at the Blue Nile—one of the two Niles that join to become the main Nile in Khartoum—and headed up into the Ethiopian highlands past the fortress city of Gondar. The Irishman stopped in Gondar, but Johannes continued on with me to explore most of Ethiopia before our paths diverged—his to a bubbling lake of molten lava in the furnace-hot Danakil Depression; mine returning to the cool air of the Ethiopian capital.

A string of local buses brought me to sprawling, fascinating Addis Ababa, with hilltop shrines and churches, and modern office towers. Ethiopians have a unique urban culture and sophisticated ancient civilization, with their own church, their own cuisine, and their own coffee and style of café to serve it in. Never colonized, they could have, would have, and should have adopted modern economic best practices and been rich and powerful. Sadly, they made that ever so common mistake: when deciding how to develop, a place with such reverence for King Solomon is likely to make the "wise" choice and try to plan their economy. Following the bulk of Africa, hoping to steal a march on the despised capitalists in their metaphorical top hats, Ethiopians laboured under a planned economy as pinko as a baboon's ass. Only recently have they switched over to Chinese-style capitalist development, with spectacular results for the city's skyline.

There was an impossible country I wanted to visit from here: Somalia. It had split into at least three pieces: backpacker-friendly Somaliland and the "here be dragons" regions of Puntland and Somalia. As Addis Ababa was the place to apply for a Somaliland visa, I decided it would also be the best place to tackle the formalities of accessing the other two fragments.

First I tried online searching at one of the many business-quality internet centres, logging about twenty hours of research before deciding I had as good an idea of the risk profile as I was likely to obtain. There was no up-to-date or official information. It changed by the week and even by the hour; most of the testimonials were outdated and from military or NGO people who hadn't handled their own paperwork anyway. Most importantly, as I researched more, I got more points on a graph rather than homing in on any single truth. People who ought to know and do know, speaking from experience, advise that to go to Mogadishu (the capital of Somalia) or Puntland is instant death, or likely to result in your kidnapping. Or they assert that these places are okay to visit but somewhat dangerous, or easy-peasy requiring no preparation at all. The more you research, the more dots you can plot. They make it easier to visualize the risk profile, like a bell curve, but in this case it was a wonky one, heavily skewed toward saying the trip was impossible. There is a point of diminishing returns for further online research; past that point you are just plotting more dots that support the same curve. If you want to know for sure, you have to go in and try it. Also, it turned out that the biggest factor in determining how dangerous Somalia would be was not nationality, but race and, especially, ethnicity.

The Somalia embassy employees thought it was hilarious that someone wanted a tourist visa, and for fifty bucks the ambassador agreed to glue one into my passport. He was curious to know if it was possible for a non-Somali and a tourist, especially a white man, to go there and come back alive. I promised him I'd stop in on my way back and tell him how it went, but I asked, "Shouldn't you already know? After all, you are the ambassador, so you must fly over to Mogadishu from time to time."

"Sure, I'm the Somali ambassador, but that doesn't mean I'm crazy enough to go there. I haven't been to Mogadishu since the fall of the central government so many years ago. It's a war zone, practically all the government controls is the airport and the presidential palace and the road connecting them, and all around they are besieged by Al-Shabaab terrorists."

Out on the street, as I returned happily with my visa to book a flight for the next day, one of the beggars tried the common line "Can you help me out? I'm from Somalia."

"I'm going there tomorrow," I said, smiling. "I finally have my Somalia visa."

There was a French businessman staying at my hotel, and we started chatting in the courtyard while waiting for dinner. He seemed fascinated by all the risky countries I had visited, but announced, "Aha, there is one you will never dare to visit, Somalia." When I told him I had just booked a flight to Mogadishu, he said, "You are not even human."

The usual route to Mogadishu was through Djibouti, so I delayed long enough to see that country before carrying on to Somalia. Djibouti is little known, a land surrounded by harsh desert, bays of whale sharks, and deep blue seas. The capital, also Djibouti, has a heavy French and American military presence manning this strategic chokepoint at Bab-el-Mandeb on the Red Sea shipping routes. This military presence encourages the proliferation of local scammers, who try to prey on the naivety of the foreign soldiers. One lake, Assal in the Afar Triangle, has the second-lowest elevation of a salt lake after the Dead Sea, but is much saltier, so you bob around like a balloon on the surface, flippering your feet and hands to save your skin from being punctured by the sharp salt crystals that make up the pure white pillars and salty pseudopods on the jagged glistening shorelines—kind of like the oozing crystals and stalagmites normally discovered only deep inside caves.

I toured around in a jeep with a couple of local guys who taught me how to properly chew khat—a narcotic shrub with an effect much like the rave drug meow meow. We stopped to camp on a geothermal brine marsh with clouds of flies, and visited attractions for local tourists, such as a place where we could shoot things with an AK-47, which is considered family fun.

We saw some furtive men out in the desert, and more along the road. They were Omo tribesmen on the trail of dreams, I was told. Basically, Omo tribesmen in southern Ethiopia try to live by milk and blood from cattle herding (much like the ancient Irish). Their families already tend as many cattle as the land can support, perhaps more, so expanding the herds is not an option when their sons need a way to make a living. If a family has seven sons, they will keep one and tell six to be on their way to the Arabian Peninsula to work as illegal immigrants. The food and survival that this work might provide are the dream at the end of the trail. Mostly the police ignore them as long as they retreat to the deserts when a squad car approaches. They are just passing through anyhow, on what is a long overland slog, and no policeman wants to be out in that dreadful heat chasing them.

Back in the capital, I made my way to the airport and found that it was filled with what seemed to be Somalis returning from Mecca, since they were toting plenty of Zamzam water. When they heard I was a tourist going to Mogadishu, there was a hush, followed by whispering—then many crowded around, especially old men with orange beards, happy to shake my hand and congratulate me. Most were old enough to remember when Somalia was relatively rich and beautiful, and perhaps they thought the first tourist returning boded well, like thunder at the end of the dry season.

The flight was normal enough, other than the plane approaching the runway in a way that would minimize the chances of attack from the ground, and at the airport I found the expectation was that I would purchase a visa on arrival, with the same fifty-dollar fee I'd already paid. Customs didn't recognize the validity of visas obtained elsewhere, though I needed the documentation anyway, since there's no way they would have let me on the flight without the visa in my passport to confidently show I was welcome.

The Ugandan commander of the African Union (AU) troops in charge of the airport saw me lined up with all the visiting Somalis at immigration. When he heard that I was a tourist, he said, "Don't you realize this is a war zone?" and tried to have me thrown back on the plane without my backpack, which was unloaded but not yet retrieved by me from the baggage room past customs. I managed to convince him that I was just the sort of person who could be what I claimed to be, an actual tourist, but I also let him know that I would follow his rules. It was a fine line to tread. If a man named Bashiir had not been there, the owner of the aspirationally named Peace Hotel, I would have had to sleep in the airport, as the commander was not willing to let me step out on my own. My experience as a tourist was much enhanced by the laughing of the AU soldiers and the incredulity of the officials.

The airport was the most fortified I'd ever been in, with gun emplacements and dug-in tanks, and thousands of AU troops, many from Uganda. There was not even a proper gate: when enough people wanted to pass through the fortifications, a soldier in a forklift would spring into action and remove immense concrete slabs, people would squeeze in and out, and the slabs would be set back in place. Already I heard the crackling of rifles and the occasional boom of tank fire. Bashiir explained that I would have to ride in a car with blacked-out windows in a convoy of soldiers so that no one could see my white skin.

"What about that journalist who visited a year or two ago?" I asked. "He hired some guards and went walking around the city. I was hoping I could do the same."

"No longer possible," he said. "That was a unique few-months-long window of relative calm, when it looked like the Islamic Courts might be able to set up a stable government, before they started attacking all their neighbours. It's much worse now. Nearly all the city has been conquered by Al-Shabaab, and the front line with trench warfare is never far away."

There was another hotel that took foreigners, but it had recently been raided, and two French secret service men captured to be held for ransom. The Peace Hotel was guarded by thirty-five soldiers, with armaments including belt-fed machine guns. There were a few other guests to chat with, all friendly guys: two white Americans, experts in fortifications, and a black Zimbabwean on the same project. I said to the Zimbabwean: "You are black, so does this mean that you can go down to the market and shops?"

"No," he told me. "At first the people won't realize who I am, but as soon as they see I am not Somali, someone will lift a machete and chop my head off."

Xenophobia was rife in Mogadishu, apparently. He told me to be careful even sitting out in the courtyard, as someone he knew had been sniped. Bashiir also told me to stay out of view and not go to the roof unless it was dark enough that no one could see I was white; if they scoped a white man on the rooftop, Al-Shabaab might think it worth their while to expend a bullet, even for a long-range shot.

A friendly Somali guy, Mustafa, was also staying at the Peace Hotel. An Agence France-Presse journalist, he was reviewing some of his war photos with other Somali journalist friends. I took a look: many of them were far too gruesome to be released, and it took a practised eye to choose the ones that were just gritty enough for people to think they told the truth, without showing more than they could handle. Mustafa was enthusiastic when he heard that I was a tourist and seemed to think

I would make an excellent international story. I couldn't see why, as it seemed to me it would be more a local interest piece, but he was the expert in the global news market, so I went along with it when he asked for an interview and photos.

We went up to the roof, where there was an open shed full of weapons, including rocket-propelled grenade launchers. The youngest Somali "guest" at our hotel had no trouble getting one out of its box and set up with a grenade, and Mustafa had me pose with it, and with some tripod-mounted machine guns. It was dusk anyhow, so the chance of being sniped on the roof was low, he said, and I could enjoy the sunset with this trove of weapons. I supposed us guests were meant to use them to help with the defence of the hotel if it came under attack. I'd be okay with an assault rifle, having owned one before, but I didn't know much about RPGs and had never fired one. All I'd ever heard was that you should open your mouth when you fire it so that the pressure wave doesn't shatter your teeth.

Luckily it didn't come to that, and I had fun hanging out with my fellow guests, Somali visitors, journalists, and the Americans, who were probably military. I didn't think it polite to ask, especially if they were not supposed to tell, as is the case with many military advisors I've met in out-of-the-way places over the years.

Mustafa was clearly going for the comic crazy-tourist angle for his story, as he had me pose for more machine-gun pictures with AU soldiers and took some notes as he questioned me on extreme travel. He also tried to set up a meeting between the Minister of Tourism and me, with an armed convoy taking me to the presidential compound, only to find that the Minister of Tourism had recently been dismissed because the president said there were no tourists in Somalia. If only I had managed to arrive a bit earlier, I might have saved him from the sack, unfortunate fellow.

I listened and learned, as it was like taking a crash course in Somali politics. For example, originally I'd thought that the United States probably messed up by not allowing the Islamic Courts to try to form a stable government, but the Somali journalists said, no, the international community was as patient as it should have been. The problem was that the Islamic Courts were not behaving like a normal government; instead, they immediately tried to expand as if they sought a Greater Somalia, to the consternation of neighbouring countries. There were no easy answers in this big bloody mess.

Later I met some of the Somalis who were going back and forth through the front lines to visit friends and family on the Al-Shabaab side of the trenches. One guy told me it was nerve-wracking, as he had a US passport. Oddly, he found the US dollar was a more accepted currency in Al-Shabaab–controlled Somalia than anywhere else, including the United States. You were liable to be killed if you did not accept these notes at face value in Somalia. This was because the terrorists had plenty of cash from piracy and other international business, on top of their usual charcoal dealing, and they became irked when they had trouble spending some of the older bills—a result of that persistent third-world failure to see a bank note as a legal document and not a market vegetable that goes down in value with declining freshness and condition.

I left Mogadishu with an impression of Somalis as bright, interesting people, natural entrepreneurs. The enemy occupied 90 percent of the city, so I didn't see much of it, despite another excursion in the convoy to view ruined Italian colonial-style buildings, shabby and bullet pocked. I slept well despite the shelling and small-arms fire, which I always find kind of soothing for some reason, like when you hear thunder while out camping.

The AU troops were supposed to search me thoroughly before my return flight, and they had tables set up for it, but everyone was rushing over to get my autograph, joke around, and take pictures with their first tourist, so my bag never got searched, even though I came from a hotel crammed with weapons, where the guests have access to grenades. When the jet landed, they said, "Run, run, get on your flight."

"Run out onto the tarmac?" I asked.

They said, "Yes, run." So I grabbed my backpack and ran out to where the 737 had let down a stairway, waved goodbye, and ducked inside. I was looking down an aisle full of Kenyan businessmen in suits, finding my seat, and stuffing my pack into an overhead compartment. It had a knife in it, but nothing more—I'm not one to pinch monogrammed towels from my hotel rooms, so I'd felt no great urge to tuck an RPG in there as a souvenir.

I knew from an earlier email that Johannes Klaus expected to be arriving in relatively safe, backpacker-friendly Hargeisa in Somaliland, staying at the retro-chic fifteen-dollar-a-night Oriental Hotel. I already had the visa so I dropped in for a visit. He showed up, travelling with a Swedish friend, Hans, who was helping him on his quest to play the ukulele in countries that do not officially exist. They'd done Kurdistan and Nagorno-Karabakh earlier that year and were composing and practising a song to perform here on the roof of this hotel in Somaliland, a suitably informal place, not recognized by the UN as the powers that be are still holding out for a unified Somalia one day. It was great to see Johannes again, and he suggested that I check the computer, as I was in the news.

When I got to a computer, I discovered something was wrong with my Facebook account. I use it to communicate with family and friends, so this was annoying. It seemed to be broken: three fields were blinking at the top of the page and showing numbers in the thousands for friend requests, messages, and notifications. For whatever reason, the boxes were now red, and the fields seemed to be roiling under the strain of incoming data.

It turned out that Mustafa's silly human interest story about me had gone viral and been picked up by thousands of newspapers and magazines. I was now "The first tourist in Mogadishu," a title that perhaps had struck some chord with popular fancy or satisfied a deep-seated desire for light-hearted news out of this grim part of the world for once.

This was the first time anything about me had gone viral. Normally I just keep to myself, so I wasn't prepared for it and had to stop travelling for a couple of weeks to try to get a handle on things. It took that long to peruse thousands of friend requests and messages on relatively slow computers. I was looking to sieve out media requests or messages from friends and family but more kept piling in, such that my Facebook page was crippled as if by a denial-of-service attack. Someone told me a special warning came up on the screen of anyone who tried to add me as a friend, telling them to desist unless they knew me personally. I decided to accept friend requests of people who had bothered to explain why they wanted to be my friend, but I mass-deleted most of them—kind of like sweeping a mess under the carpet. What else could I do with thousands of friend requests from people I didn't know and who gave no reason for wanting to know me? If the profile photo of a decaying skull with the name "Destroyer" was really the alias for a newspaper editor trying to contact me, I'd have to apologize later.

A few requests for interviews were among the messages (my brother Steve told me the phone had been ringing at his house, as loads of journalists trying to contact me were asking for information from him), and I accepted the ones I could, doing a Radio France interview over the phone in my hotel room (fortunately no blaring call to prayer from the mosque outside coincided with the recording), and a BBC one from a dusty shack with a slightly better phone connection as donkeys shuffled around in the heat outside. Reporters were fairly clueless about what sort of questions to put to me. Much of what they asked I would have expected to hear if I'd been a diplomat or security expert: about the progress of the war and the machinations of regional politics. If I hadn't just been hanging out with exactly those sorts of people, I wouldn't have been able to answer them coherently.

Most people travelling so extensively would have had a blog and commercial sponsors and a web page already set up; I was meeting more and more of this sort of traveller, who had clued in that there is money to be made and travels easily funded if you can provide a vicarious travel experience for people doing the nine-to-five thing. But I was glad I hadn't taken that path. I suspected it would have had insidious effects on my travel style and world view. It entails selling yourself and packaging your experience so it can be better received online; in subliminal ways, the market for vicarious experience would have manufactured my consent to change the nature of my wanderings. I wanted to see the world for its own sake but would have ended up seeing the world for my own sake, not at all what I set out to do. My backpack holds plenty, so no need to stuff a persona of "me" in there too.

What happened next tested my philosophy more explicitly. A few days before Christmas, the owner of the hotel knocked on my door and said, "I can hardly believe it. Mr. Ferrah called my hotel, asking to speak to one of my guests. He wants you to take his call from Saudi Arabia."

This Mr. Ferrah had read about my exploits in the international news, perhaps one of the newspaper interviews I did that went into greater depth than the little comedy wire-service piece, and he had his assistants track me down to the Oriental Hotel in Somaliland. He was extraordinarily kind and asked that I provide him with a Western Union number so he could send me as much money as I wanted.

The strangest things are always happening to me. If I were keeping a list, I could now check the box for "Receive call from rich sheik in Saudi Arabia offering to shower me with money." I imagined one of those Aladdin stereotypes: guys sitting on cushions in a perfumed pavilion, surrounded by turbaned guards in parachute pants with scimitars, though of course he is more probably a famous ethnic Somali industrialist or oilman with a kind heart. I thanked him for his amazing generosity, but I declined to receive any money, even though I could have done with some as I gave lots to charity and my travel fund was running low (I'm kind of "opposite man" when it comes to charity. Some people say nice things about charity but seldom give, while I am reasonably critical of charity but give for the sake of giving). After all, I had enough to eat and to stay in a fifteen-dollar-a-night hotel, which is more than most people on earth.

Some of my backpacking friends heard me politely turn down money and were dismayed, saying, "You could have said yes and passed it to me." But I couldn't. That would have been dishonest to an honest man deserving of respect. If I'd accepted money, I would have been obliged to spend it on my travel, since that is what it had been given for. It's hard to explain, but easy to see how I would have trouble fitting in among the modern cohort of professional travellers. My views are a throwback even among many people of my own generation, or the hippie generation, who would have said "Groovy, man," and accepted the money. If anything, I'm more of a beatnik. My money supply is never more than what is needed to get by. I remain unconvinced that someone with a heap of money can travel at all; it seems to me they end up only going places.

At the other end of the spectrum from Mr. Ferrah, I had my first experience with internet trolls. I knew little about what was a new phenomenon at the time, and, my, do they go wild when you call them trolls. Some people have no sense of humour and take the news so seriously. It didn't help that Mustafa had compressed my answer to one of his questions so that he had me saying, "Mogadishu, checked off the list," in what amounts to taking-the-piss-out-of-dangerous-country backpacking. Or that he'd taken my overly long, very polite-Canadian statement about trying my best to avoid being immediately deported and translated it to shorter sentences filled with action, expressing what a Somali might mean, such that he had me shouting at the AU guards. Naturally I didn't shout at any of the 8,000 AU troops in the vicinity of their airport fortress, or anyone else for that matter—instead, I spoke in a respectful manner as would be normal and expected, and posed for their souvenir photos with the soldiers, all of whom got the joke. No one was angry, and before I left I tried to ensure someone would relay my thanks to the commander for putting up with me. Alas, for those who like to dispute over the internet, short wire-service articles lose much in the translation and in the compression needed to keep them snappy, and are not exactly literature suited for textual analysis. The article about me was amusing, so, close enough. What more could anyone ask from a zany traveller comic piece?

The worst of the trolls were attacking my unrelated attempts on traveller forums to give advice for getting visas to tricky countries. Some disputed my very existence. There is only so much pleasure one can get from chuckling at notes that argue: "No one could possibly have lived the life you claim to have lived; therefore, you do not exist." It seemed kind of sad to me that people could have such limited horizons; I go out and travel and have adventures, sure—but so do most of my friends, in their own ways. And the ones who are living quiet lives are doing it by choice, not because they don't know what's out there. I could only conclude that these people were like fish in very small ponds, and not big fish either, but minnows. I wasn't even trying to get involved with all the discussion and tweeting, which was taken by some as evidence that a grand conspiracy was afoot, and all was not as it seemed. It's funny to read commentary saying I was CIA or part of a plan for a NATO invasion of Somalia or some other preposterous claim. The fact that I might actually be a backpacker whose only connection to the world was Facebook and email, malfunctioning under the strain of too much traffic, didn't suit them. Neither did they guess that there were better uses of my time than disputing the fact of my own existence on the internet when there was travelling to look forward to.

A development that I'm rather chuffed about is that people started to contact me online about how to go about visiting Mogadishu safely, and I was able to provide exact names, numbers, and contacts to get in and see things smoothly, allowing me to play a small part in putting Somali tourism back on the map. Also, journalist and author Robert Young Pelton, of *The World's Most Dangerous Places* fame, congratulated me.

Puntland was next but while doing research there was time to get a feel for Somaliland. At the time, you had to hire a soldier to sit with you in the taxi if you wanted to use the main highway to the coast. The beaches were fun, as was sitting with camel traders in the afternoons to chew khat. Boats, some of them wooden, did a lively business picking up tasty little black camels and shipping them across the Gulf of Aden or into Arabia through the Red Sea. Out in the desert, within jeep range, there were some ancient cave paintings, 7,000 years old, that travellers could view as long as the armed guard was tagging along. Some of them were said to be lewd—unintentionally, I'm sure, since the Stone Age was clothing optional.

Hargeisa is a placid town by Somali standards, with a few quirks. The Somali shilling must have suffered hyperinflation, since it took a brick-sized wad of them to buy anything worth having. The money needed to purchase something often outweighed the product you toted away;

the money-changers shifted shillings around by the wheelbarrow's worth. There was an interesting open-air camel market. And compared to Mogadishu, they enjoyed relatively quiet nights, sometimes 20-millimetre cannon fire popping out in the suburbs, or assault rifle fire close by the hotel, once followed by a woman's screams.

Try as I might, Puntland wasn't accessible from Somaliland, so I returned to Ethiopia to work on the problem. My persistence eventually got me a meeting with the Puntland liaison officer and, through him, a flight on Puntair to the capital, Garowe. The liaison officer's business card ended up being very useful to me in the days that followed. After a short stop to chat, as promised, with the Somali ambassador and give him up-to-date information for anyone else who asked about the procedures for travelling to Mogadishu, I taxied out to the airport and to a distant gate, where I climbed into a little prop-plane with a Russian crew. Both had seen better days. All passengers were Somalis except for me.

The guy in the seat next to me was Mr. Dude, pronounced Doo-day, but he was fine with Dude. He'd just set up a business buying fish and flying them back to Addis Ababa to sell to the kitchens at luxury hotels. He told me how, as a boy, he had looted his first assault rifles from the armoury when the government had collapsed, making Somalia a failed state. He traded them for a camel, but now he'd boarded the camel so long with his uncle that it would feel weird to ask for it back.

Our plane was buzzing along, and out the window was the desert, coloured all sorts of orange with strange shapes from fossil flows of water, like the plains of Mars. I told Mr. Dude that Puntland was the object of the first recorded national joke: in the temple of Queen Hatshepsut on the Nile, I'd seen an engraved graphic novel showing a trading expedition to the land of the Punts around the year 1480 BCE. One frame depicts the meeting of the Egyptian captain and the king of Puntland. The king's enormously fat wife is shown astride a donkey. In hieroglyphics a caption reads, "I feel sorry for the donkey."

We landed on a desert airstrip and were told not to leave the plane. I wondered what the holdup was. The aircrew left, pushing a wheelbarrow through the sand to a crashed plane similar to our own. They stripped parts of it, wheeled them back over, and stowed them, while the captain walked atop our plane, inspecting and tapping on the hull metal and giving the engines the once-over. Then we were off again, better safe than sorry.

I told Mr. Dude about the Omo guys I'd seen on the trail of dreams, and he was reminded of an odious business meeting he'd had on his last trip to Bosaso. An acquaintance prevailed on him to visit a man who had a business proposition. They sat and chewed some khat before getting down to details. This guy had a clinic on the shores of the sea, and he would bring in Omo tribesmen. They wanted to get on the wooden boats so they could be smuggled to Arabia, but they didn't have the $100 for the passage; in fact they had no money at all. This guy would tell them, "I'll buy you your ticket, but only if you give me one kidney." (A person can still function pretty normally for up to twenty-four years with only one of the usual two kidneys.) The clinic would then sell the kidney on to China, but it needed investors to expand. Mr. Dude threw money on the carpet to cover the cost of the guy's khat he had chewed and stormed out. All the while the other guy was cajoling, "You are missing out on big profit."

THE AIRPORT FOR PUNTLAND'S CAPITAL LOOKED LIKE A STRETCH OF desert that a bulldozer had rendered unnaturally level. We climbed out of the plane and approached immigration, which consisted of two empty oil drums with a plank of wood laid on top as a sort of rudimentary desk. Men with assault rifles and Uzis were there to greet us, and there was a lot of excitement, waving of weapons, and talking in Somali when it came to my turn at the plank. Mr. Dude translated and helped to explain that my intent was visiting Garowe. After much confusion it was decided that I would be put in detention, guarded by two guys with automatic rifles.

The best place to keep me was a walled compound with ample guards that encased Mr. Maxmud's Maka al-Mukarama hotel. The compound containing the hotel was built with slabs of reinforced concrete. Access was by a metal gate, and colourful pictograms nearby showed various modern and tribal weapons, including a club, all X-ed off to show their inadmissibility on hotel premises. Everyone was armed regardless, and there to greet me was the owner himself, an energetic man with a black beard that curved at an angle exactly matching the curve of the banana magazine in his Kalashnikov. Mr. Dude had ridden in the car that took me to the compound, kindly using an hour of his time before seeing to his own business to make sure I got this rather cushy and better-than-expected result.

The terms of my detention seemed mild: I was confined to this fortified hotel. I tossed my backpack in a corner and went to the only other room available, a sort of foyer with some seats and a television showing football. There was a young American man there; when he saw me, he explained that he was also detained and had been for a number of weeks. He advised me to show my captors that I couldn't be pushed around, as this was the only way to deal with these sorts of people.

"Is this your first time being held like this?" I asked.

"Yes, but I know how to behave from dealing with Indians."

"I find it better to be my normal friendly self in these situations," I said, thinking that this predicament was not the same as when a rickshaw driver doesn't give the correct change.

The American was happy to have some company at first—it turned out he was a student of Arabic language—but as we were talking, he realized who I was.

"Oh no, you are that traveller guy who goes to dangerous countries. You are notorious. It is because of reading about you that I got the insane idea to come here."

This was funny to hear, so I explained that I do all the countries, not just dangerous ones, though I admitted I'd done a few countries where the average backpacker who went there by mistake would come back with post-traumatic stress disorder.

"Please don't talk to me. I can't be seen with you," he said. "I've spent weeks waiting while my father tries to get help through the US embassy. He thinks he may be able to convince them to deport me. If I'm seen with you, I might never get out of his place."

Every man for himself, then. I returned to my room so as not to get the guy any more worked up. This was certainly not my first experience of being detained as a suspected terrorist; it happens to me disturbingly often, and I had no intention of spending much time in this room. The American guy's kung fu was weak, I suspected, obviously, given that he'd wrong-footed himself straight away by being unco-operative and working the us embassy angle. That adversarial approach of insisting on rights is narrowly suited to domestic detention in America.

I looked out my window and saw my guards near the gate, chumming around with some of the perimeter security guys; later that evening a group of Somalis, including some elderly gentlemen in embroidered vests, sat on plastic chairs out in the courtyard. I was served a platter of goat liver and onions, standard fare for Somalis. Soon afterward a convoy of cars arrived, and the metal gates opened to admit a VIP and many bodyguards. Then came a knock at my door, and I opened it to find the corridor filled with Somalis, most of them armed, and a man who had questions for me: the Minister of the Interior.

He was shouty, prompting me to ask if there was something wrong with my documents and visa. He said, "The documents are in order. Our government's concern is that nobody in his right mind comes to Puntland State of Somalia. The few that do are infiltrators trying to join with the terrorists, and are packed off to prison." He kept shouting. "You had better be a journalist, or things will go very badly for you."

I showed him extra supporting documents, including the card and note with telephone number of the Puntland liaison officer, and explained that while not technically a journalist, I sometimes had journalists write stories about me. Fortunately, I had something more in my backpack: a folded Somali-language newspaper with a long article and interview about me, saved in anticipation of just this kind of situation. My memory was vague as to what questions the reporter had asked, and there was no way I could read what he had said about me—all good I hoped—and what was written of my enjoyable stay in Mogadishu, and how friendly everyone was.

The Minister of the Interior repeated that I had better be a journalist or things would go very badly for me, so I said, "In that case, I'm a journalist." Oddly enough, I have done some journalistic writing since then, a bit for *Esquire* and a few other magazines, but I suppose I have an amusingly precise answer if I'm ever asked when the idea that I might become a journalist first crossed my mind.

The minister left in his convoy. My next thoughts were about how to get out of this hotel or, should that prove impossible, how to make the best of the situation. I had questions for my guards, and someone who could speak English was kind enough to translate: "Can I go across the street to where I see a mango tree, and pick some fruit?" No, came the response. "Can I go into town and look for an internet café?" No, no, no. "Then can I sit out under the moon and the stars in this courtyard with these men I see who are gathered near the gate?" They conferred and said, "Yes, that would be okay."

I went out to introduce myself, and someone brought an extra white-plastic chair. These guys were drinking camel milk, taking each other's blood pressure, and discussing whether the numbers boded ill or well for their health. Many of them could speak English, and my hunch was confirmed: they were interesting people and more distinguished gentlemen than they might at first appear, which only stands to reason, as who else might gather so near a posh twenty-dollar-a-night hotel?

We sat around telling stories and laughing. One man, Mr. Kasim, who was in the process of starting a local bank, told some spectacular tales, including how catching a giant shark led to the birth of his first child. He'd been looking for some way to make money back in the '90s, and an Australian had said, "Catch some fish and sell them to me." So Mr. Kasim bought a wooden boat and hired a captain and crew, as he was neither a sailor nor a fisherman and had never been to sea. They were doing well and catching some hefty fish, as the war had scared away many of the international trawlers. Next they hooked a giant shark and got it hove in close to the hull. Being Somalis, they pulled out a wide array of guns and riddled it with bullets. But then what? So they landed on a sand island that bulged up from the waves and proceeded to cut into the shark.

As they mucked about, an old man approached and remarked, "You don't know what you are doing, would you admit?"

"Okay," Kasim said, "I admit this."

"Look here," the old man said, "this is the liver. You can take that for the oil. And these are the fins. They can be sold and end up in China."

They thanked him, and Kasim was invited to sit at the old man's beachside shack for tea.

He noticed that the young woman who brought the tea was alluring, enough so that he announced, "I will marry that girl."

The old man said, "That is my daughter. She is seventeen, and she will not marry unless I allow."

So Kasim snuck off to where the girl was fetching more water and said, "I will marry you."

She replied, "Not without my father's permission."

When he returned to shore to sell his catch, he was saddened to hear that, while he'd been at sea, Al-Shabaab had severed the Australian's head, and it took some work for Kasim to flog his load of fish. But he couldn't complain. He spent two weeks getting to know the old man and his family, and the permission was granted, so that he was married and has had many babies, and it would not have happened just so if not for this giant shark.

There were all kinds of stories: hunting for blue ostriches, peculiar to this part of the Horn of Africa; the tactics of Al-Shabaab in trying to embarrass the government; the real reason for the rise of piracy on this coast. My own travel tales were readily told when called for. Finally, after the second night, the gentleman beside me was making a phone call. Kasim said to me, "Mr. Abdullahi Ali is asking His Excellency the President, Why is my Canadian friend in detention? He should instead be a guest of the government."

It turned out that these men I'd been sitting with were all VIPs: former federal ministers of Somalia, important businessmen, and one was the former mayor of the town of Eyl, popularly held to be the lair of the pirates.

From then on, instead of detention, my days were spent enjoying the hospitality of the Puntland government, driving around in technicals (pickup trucks with belt-fed machine guns in the back) with the

Minister of Education and the Minister of Good Governance. I had a memorable time with some other officials, including the Minister of Counter Piracy; he was responsible for other ministries as well as preventing piracy, and did not like to be described only as the Minister of Counter Piracy. Some of that reluctance stemmed from what had happened to the last guy to accept the job: he was kidnapped by the pirates, who were keener on milking the irony than on any ransom.

The minister was having a special military unit trained to go after the pirates in their hidden coves. He told me that Israeli security guards were being hired to defend against the pirates, as they had the advantage (from the employer's point of view) that they could not surrender and would have to resist any pirate attack to the death. He explained how the piracy originated with fishing boats from other nations that were plundering Somali waters—in essence, they were pirating fish—and when one boat got stuck on a sandbank, the locals were surprised how much money the foreign owners were willing to pay them to help free it. This got locals thinking: why not catch these pirate fishing ships and hold them for ransom? Those ransoms proved so lucrative that events had spiralled out of control; the Somalis had become pirates in their own right, preying on ships far from shore in international waters. The minister was angry that South Korea had recently dropped millions of dollars from a helicopter to pay the ransom for a ship and crew. How could he fight against swarms of pirates, he asked, when outside nations complained but also dropped millions of dollars from the sky, enabling the pirates to buy the latest arms and thus encouraging them to proliferate? There were some rumours that the West would get more serious about helping once Lloyd's of London had finished profiting from the jacked up insurance rates, but he felt that that criticism was perhaps overly cynical.

The Minister of Education was kind enough to show me what he was doing with the schools, and the humanitarian Dr. Abdi Artan showed off the new public hospital being built, which would have modern medical equipment, including a CT scanner, Somalia's first. A funny thing: I was reading *New Scientist* magazine some time later, and a researcher was describing her new approach for detecting pirates' lairs remotely. A satellite had scanned Somalia, and she duly noticed frenetic activity in one place in the desert: this town of Garowe in Puntland. Ahoy, this X must mark the spot where the pirates are stashing their loot. I chuckled while reading, as it goes to show the difficulty of delving into geopolitics from the vantage of outer space. According to the dates on her research paper, the satellite she was using had been orbiting above us when I was there, looking down on the same buildings that I was given tours of—except she saw evidence of pirate booty, while my eyes noted schools and hospitals, which is what they were.

On the terrace of a popular restaurant I was introduced to a tall, ninety-six-year-old man who had a bone-crushing grip and had just been married, again. He had fought in Mussolini's army in the 1930s and worked in the 1950s on the oil rigs in Texas, and was now back in Puntland as a sort of living national treasure.

He joined us, and while we sat waiting for our food, I mentioned that the outside world thinks Puntland is overrun with pirates, describing how the first three times I tried to fly to Puntland, someone from an airline stopped me and said, "No, too much danger, pirates," and when I tried to get advice from the biggest Somali-owned tour company in Somaliland, they said Puntland was full of pirates. I replied that I would ask the Puntland Minister of Tourism for some advice on what places were okay, but the guy at the tour company said, "The Minister of Tourism must be the Chief Pirate. As soon as you step off the plane he will hold you for ransom." The Puntland ministers scoffed at this. Dr. Artan and Kasim asked me if I would be willing to take a bit of a risk to show that it is in fact the Puntland government, not the pirates, that has the upper hand. I could go to Eyl, Pirate Bay, with the protection of an armed convoy and do something for the news to show it was safe.

"Sure, I'd be willing," I said. "You know what would really get the pirates' panties in a knot? Take me across the desert to Pirate Bay and I'll go for a refreshing dip, maybe wearing a pirate hat and an eye patch, and waving a scimitar. We could call it 'Tourist takes swim in so-called Pirate Bay,' and have a photographer take some photos for the wire news."

The ministers agreed and organized a couple of truckloads of soldiers to drive me across a very rough desert road out to Eyl for the Pirate Bay swim. However, later that evening we found that I would need another day in Puntland to get there and back, or else I'd miss the Puntland festival I'd been invited to, where I was to hear Somali poets and meet His Excellency the President. And my flight was on Monday, without another until the next Monday. We decided it was not feasible, sadly.

A multitude of technicals spun into town for the Puntland festival, leaving clouds of bright dust in the air, and a couple of them came to fetch me. My seat was beside the Minister of Good Governance, Mr. Muxamad, who had agreed to translate for me, as there would be speeches and many fine poets and minstrels. My notebook was out and ready, as a journalist's would be. Mr. Muxamad was the first to take any sort of notice that it was a bright blue child's scribbler, with a drawing of a boy playing with a football on the front.

"You should get a more professional-looking journal," he said.

"Yes, of course. My old one was black leather with gold embossing, but it was stolen in Ethiopia," I explained.

"Those Ethiopians," he said wryly. He translated while I jotted down thirty pages of detailed notes, some of which were consulted for writing this chapter, making me, as anticipated, a sort of journalist, and I'm grateful for his help.

He enjoyed the stories I told him between speeches about his counterpart, the Minister for Preventing Corruption, in Afghanistan. Mr. Muxamad was surprised and amused that, unlike him, the Afghan minister attended parties, but he understood my reasoning when I explained the wisdom of arresting the unpopular corrupt people preferentially, especially when one is surrounded by warlords—a different situation than in Puntland, where the pirates are no-shows at parties.

Poets and politicians spoke, and cameramen recorded the festival, and all the while armed men wearing sunglasses sat around the stage, facing the audience and alert for sudden movements. Near the end I went to meet His Excellency the President.

It was hard to move on, but I wanted to visit Central Africa again, and the security chief was perpetually alarmed at having a foreigner about, worried in case something happened to me. This has been common for at least the last few centuries in Somali culture, as someone always takes serious responsibility for the welfare of a visitor and ensures that he is in good hands when he passes to the territory of the next clan. I thought to myself that this was the greatest change of circumstances in the shortest time that I'd ever encountered while travelling: from being detained as a suspected terrorist to becoming a guest of the state, and being brought to a festival to sit with the ministers and shake hands with the president. Later I learned that my cause had been helped by expat Somalis in Canada, many of whom had called the government to say they had been welcomed so kindly in Canada after the war, it was not right to detain a visiting Canadian. So I benefited to some extent from the accumulated goodwill of Canada's refugee and immigration policy.

Before leaving, Mr. Abdullahi Ali, one of the VIPs I'd met in the compound, wanted my opinion as to whether the American in their custody was a terrorist. Though I'd been held many times as a suspected terrorist, and a terrorist had mistaken me for a fellow terrorist, this was another first: the first time I'd been asked to help determine for a government if another guy was a terrorist. The American stirred my pity. As he'd languished in his room, or killed hours watching football on the television, he'd seen me being picked up every morning by a convoy of technicals, cheerfully greeting locals and ministers, and then sitting safely wedged between soldiers for various tours. The American had wanted me to promise not to mention him or have anything to do with him, but I figured if he'd known the circumstances, he would have made an exception. Before he knew who I was, he had told me that he crossed the border in order to see the first all-Somali football tournament. He hadn't known that it was going to include some Al-Shabaab players. I told Mr. Abdullahi Ali that in my opinion the American was not a terrorist but just a guy who found himself in over his head, and I imagined that his father would be very relieved if he could simply be deported.

Some soldiers and I piled into a waiting technical and sped off toward the weekly arrival of Puntair's little old prop-plane. This would be the end of bright blue skies with billowing white dust, goat liver and onions, and herdsmen with an equal affinity for mobile phones and guns. I'd miss Somalia. The chief of security didn't speak English, but he had some fun teasing me with my passport, which he knew I wanted back and preferred to hold; eventually, just before I boarded the flight, he handed it over and I waved goodbye to Puntland, and to Somalia—said to be impossible to visit, but proving instead to be interesting and home to friendly people and some of the best fun on my journeys to date. The Puntland State of Somalia ministers had been extremely kind and generous, and even (jokingly?) offered me citizenship in their exciting state. I was invited to return any time, and I may take them up on that offer, with so many friendly Somalis to talk with, and so much more to see there.

A bad case of African flying disease meant that I had to buzz back on a prop-plane to Addis Ababa, even though it was Harar I wanted to visit next, and the routing was through Hargeisa in Somaliland, which is not so far from Harar. African flying disease is what I call the frustrating tendency of African nations to force you onto planes flitting between national capitals. If you don't strive to remedy the situation, your African trip can turn into jet setting. For example, if you arrived in Somaliland from Ethiopia by air, then you cannot return overland; you have to fly into Ethiopia. In this case I needed a visa on arrival, so I had to go all the way to the capital. This is why it's important to go overland as much as possible, since once you are airborne, it's hard to get your feet back on the ground.

AFTER A FLIGHT TO THE CITY OF HARAR AND A RETURN OVERLAND to see the places I'd been forced to fly over when arriving the day before from Hargeisa, a helpful consulate official in Addis Ababa allowed me to obtain a multiple-entry visa for Cameroon. Then I flew west, to the other side of Africa, to use Cameroon as a perfect, and perfectly charming, base of operations for visa foraging and overland visits to the surrounding nations. Between excursions there was no better place for me than holed up in the Ideal Hotel in Yaoundé, Cameroon, which was ideal for my purposes: close to the embassies and not too much of a brothel, by African standards. I visited the Republic of Chad and the supposedly undoable Central African Republic by hitchhiking everywhere with an Italian medical doctor and nun, Dr. Ione, who warned me against taking a dirt road plagued by Lord's Resistance Army terrorists, whom the locals accuse of black magic and cannibalism, and who had just killed the niece of one of the doctor's colleagues the day before. Hitching north carried me into Chad, with its fascinating Lake Chad, where I was the only tourist. On my return through Kousséri, across the Chari River in northern Cameroon, a swarm of bees descended from the heavens, stinging me hundreds of times. On the bright side, it proved that I am not allergic to bee venom.

Back in Yaoundé, there was no choice but to launch a harrowing three-week effort to obtain a visa to the elusive and odious dictatorship known as Equatorial Guinea. After enduring a bout of malaria in the Ideal Hotel and working for weeks manufacturing fake documents, I finally hit upon a ruse that got me the visa. The woman in the embassy guard house gave me a high-five: she had never seen someone persevere and actually walk away with the visa before. The country itself was most notable for corruption and flocks of smelly bats.

Nigeria proved more amenable, and I swept into the Cross River delta in a fibreglass boat hauling sacks of edible foliage. The Nigerian police eventually found out, telling me that the delta there was as dangerous as the Niger River delta. Concerned for my safety from hostage takers, they insisted I sleep in the police station on an island in the delta. A jolly policeman let me have his spot of concrete floor to stretch out on, and we shared my last tin of sardines for supper. In the morning he fetched some bread and a few mangos from the nearest tree. I roamed around Nigeria for two weeks and got a good feel for the exceptionally vibrant and friendly people. Nigerian hospitality is such that after an evening spent talking and telling stories in an eatery, I often got up to pay and leave, only to have the waitress tell me that someone had already paid for my meal. To understand Africa it is necessary to get a good feel for Nigeria, a microcosm of the risks and promise of Sub-Saharan Africa.

But now the heat was rising and my forty-eight-page passport was full to bursting. I needed to return to Canada to get a fresh one. The rest of West Africa would have to wait, but not for long. My flight took me from Lagos back to Canada at the end of March 2011, stopping in Ottawa for a fresh passport and then in the Rocky Mountain town of Canmore to endure a terrible blizzard that dumped 10 centimetres of snow and brought brutal cold for transplanted Africans like me. After the blizzard I carried on with family visits: five cities in three weeks before starting my fifth major Africa trip.

BEFORE I HAD BOUGHT ANY FLIGHTS TO AFRICA, WHILE I WAS STILL in Alberta, Dana emailed me to suggest I visit her in France, where she was improving her French by living in the Alps for a summer. Just a year had passed since we'd last been together, and Dana was my most stable relationship in a lifestyle that seemed to be turning my every "hi" and "goodbye" into "long-time no see" and, far too often, "sayonara." We hiked through valleys of Savoy, visiting old monasteries and shimmering mountain lakes, eating picnics of bread, cheese, and wine. After a month I was on a flight to South Africa, an excellent place to start any African trip due to its easy visa-free and hassle-free borders. I arrived on June 9, 2011, for six arduous, punishing adventure-filled months.

The Drakensberg Mountains, on the rim of the Great Escarpment of southern Africa, and the mountainous nation of Lesotho were charming, with African horsemen wrapped in colourful blankets against the chilly mountain air and snow, and petroglyphs of the San Bushmen who used to hang out in this mountain vastness. I had entered through Monantsa Pass without an entry stamp, but managed to talk my way out through Van Rooyen's Gate after circling Lesotho.

Turning east, I passed through green Swaziland and carried on to Mozambique, enjoying long beaches, sugarloaf mountains, and all the mouse-kebabs I could shake a spear at. I visited old Portuguese forts and sleepy towns by river deltas, connected by abysmal bumpy roads that were tackled in ramshackle old vans. The locals knew the merits and deficiencies of every seat and would jostle outside like penguins until some foreigner entered and was stuck with a perch that was little more than a rusty blade-edged steel bar, that he would bounce atop for twelve-hour stints as the van smashed over rocks and ploughed through billowing dust. My northward progress was good, past the Limpopo River, which flows from the distant edge of the Kalahari Desert, and the Zambezi River, with its source in the jungles of northern Zambia, on bridges rusted or collapsing or never having existed in the first place— the vans crossed on rafts if need be.

The Island of Mozambique, where Admiral Vasco de Gama landed and built a fort 500 years ago, is connected to the mainland by a 3.5-kilometre-long causeway. I relaxed inside the old slave market, a former dungeon turned restaurant, looking out toward the beaches and the passing wooden dhows with their lateen sails, while drinking baobab fruit soup and reading a book of Zen koans. The island is a World Heritage Site, so it had more travellers than was the norm for Mozambique. It also had internet connection. I accessed my email for the first time in a couple of weeks and immediately saw a slew of emails from my stepdad, Jim. It is the traveller's worst nightmare to see a note from home labelled "Cancer Update," with two other unread emails: "First Chemo" and "Second Chemo." My mom had been diagnosed with stage 4 cancer.

Mom had written to assure me that there was no need to break off my travels, saying that if the cancer killed her, it would not be during chemo but after I'd returned to Vancouver. But I didn't want to be away from the internet or stuck in a place too isolated to have an airport should her health take a turn for the worse. The best plan was for me to make my way out into the Indian Ocean and swirl around the islands of Comoros, Mayotte, Seychelles, or Madagascar while waiting to hear the results of the last courses of chemo. The islands had better international flight connections, so I would be able to rush to British Columbia if need be. However, flights to Comoros were no longer available from the Swahili coast of Mozambique, and there was no way to cross the country's trackless, bridgeless northern wasteland. I made my way west to Malawi, which was in a rowdy mood when I arrived. I fell asleep to the sounds of gunshots and rioting around my hostel, and it was hard to get around the cities during the day, as I kept running into gangs of drunken men carrying bricks. Lake Malawi was lovely, however, with bulbous lakeshore baobabs and red sunsets. After a swing around Zambia to see some wildlife, I headed out to the Indian Ocean islands.

Madagascar has its lemurs, spectacular baobab species, weird tsingy (tippy-toe) rock formations, and, if you know where to look, eggshells from the elephant bird, most massive of the flightless birds, weighing up to half a ton (the last one eaten only a few hundred years ago). And the restful pink beaches of the Seychelles restored my will to press on despite the terrible news from Canada.

Back in South Africa, hitchhiking proved best; I got nearly every-where this way, chatting with friendly locals. In the town of Kimberley I saw the pit from which almost three tons of diamonds had been re-moved, to be sold by Cecil Rhodes, a laughing con man who had much in common with Nigerian internet scammers. After experiencing the blooming Karoo, a semi-desert region awash in colours, Namibia beckoned, with its red dunes, oysters, and oryx, and I hitchhiked north with a semi-trailer rig hauling between Cape Town and Windhoek. The driver let me out on the side of the highway 70 kilometres from the Fish River Canyon as the bird flies, and made a gift of a bottle of cola: he was concerned that I'd dry out trying to cross 80 kilometres of desert on foot. This was where I had one of my worst nights of ac-commodation, lying on my back in the freezing desert (with a large black hairy wide-bodied scorpion making a guest appearance), and then the next night one of the best, a gratuitous luxury hotel cabana in a field of immense boulders.

When I was assured my mom was doing as well as could be ex-pected, and since there was nothing I could do to help, I started into the rougher leg of my journey: north up the Atlantic coast. A friendly woman, Georine, in Windhoek, Namibia's capital, told me the secret for getting an Angolan visa, something I'd been unable to obtain so far. She described a little town in northern Namibia with a Kentucky

Fried Chicken, a youth hostel, an Angolan consulate, and not much besides. If I stayed in the youth hostel, ate KFC, and waited a few days, presto, the impossible Angolan visa would be in my hand. Visa obtained, I drove into Angola with a Portuguese guy from the Canary Islands, past artillery-scarred roads, destroyed battle tanks, and primitive mud villages, where people ran around naked carrying spears. My driver, as an expat, had a lot to say about the very real risks from police of DWW ("driving while white") in Africa, the correct way to manage a lifestyle that includes hookers (fascinating information but not for me), and the pink-champagne antics of the Angolan oil lords.

We parted company after passing through Lubango in the dry hills; he carried on north while my path took me down the canyon into Namibe, which was also enjoyable. I speculated about the identity of weird deep-sea fishes washed ashore, and circled a shore fort armed with anti-aircraft cannons. One complaint, however: I was attacked by a gang of Namibe's plentiful muggers who punched me in the face on a shipwreck-lined misty coast. This was unusual for me, but these things happen. That coast was too dangerous to explore alone, and a different gang of muggers had fought with me the night before, but—and this is one of the advantages of not carrying cash—when they ripped open my beach bag and ran away with half the currency that spilled out on the sands, it was not much of a loss. It's hard to evaluate what-ifs, because if I'd been carrying more than what I needed for a few days of travel, I would never have wandered out alone on the skeleton coast in this place the bushmen call The Land God Made in Anger.

I spent some time in what was then the most expensive city on earth, Luanda, in a fifty-five-dollar-a-night skid row room. From Angola, I flew west to Cape Verde, hoping it would be a good place to get a visa to Guinea-Bissau and places on the Bight of Benin, the wide bay that hollows a 640-kilometre chunk out of West Africa ("Beware and take care of the Bight of Benin, for one that comes out there's forty goes in" as the old sea shanty goes, warning of the ferocious local malaria). On a lonely jungle frontier, a menacing and corrupt Guinea policeman stole what was actually my expired medicines bag and gobbled all the pills, as if he was eager to test meds like a certain Peruvian rodent. I was all the way south in Liberia before meeting another Westerner, an American man, thin and rashy from raging malaria, who turned out to be a diamond dealer, or, as the terminology goes nowadays, a blood diamond dealer. I came down with malaria again myself while going to see soldiers feed live chickens to the crocodiles in the presidential moat of Yamoussoukro, Ivory Coast, and self-medicated with Coartem pills before carrying on south across the bay, getting the hang of this string of tiny former slaver kingdoms that line the coast of the Bight of Benin. ·

Bussing inland through Benin and Burkina Faso, I was soon back in the dusty Sahel (where Sahara meets savannah), crossing and recrossing the Niger River as it wound through Mali. I was just in time for some trouble with Tuaregs, a Saharan Berber pastoralist tribe noted for camel herding and favouring the colour indigo. Terrorists from AQIM (Al-Qaeda in the Islamic Maghreb) or Ansar Dine, a Tuareg terror group, shot a German tourist in Timbuktu, and kidnapped some others, so the police were thick on the ground, and travellers were even more scarce than expected.

This didn't stop me from exploring the Dogon escarpment, home to the pagan Dogon tribes who make their tombs by burrowing into rock high on the cliffs. There I met the Ogon (shaman) of the Dogon and tried my luck at a medical intervention, discreetly nudging a guy to seek help at a nearby NGO clinic; he was too tough for his own good, so had not complained as a fungus stemming from an undiagnosed AIDS infection ate away his lips. Over the week I made my way to Gao, a former capital of the sixteenth-century Songhai Empire made largely of mud, before being stopped by the Nigerien police. They tried to force me into a compound in Gao where they could guard me against attack by AQIM, but I managed to talk them into letting me stay at a place called Euro Camping, a former watering hole of the Peace Corps before those volunteers fled the country the year before. It was still open, now full of Nigerian (as opposed to Nigerien) prostitutes from the Christian south (luckily they assumed I was an Arab and unable to speak anything other than Arabic, so they were no bother). On Christmas morning 2011 they gathered in the hall, and I woke to their enthusiastic singing, "But for the love of Jesus, I'd be a sinner."

There was an Algerian consulate in town, but Al-Qaeda killed the consul just after I'd asked him about getting a visa. By donning an Islamic cap, I explored deep into Niger, all the way to the foot of a massif of dark rock called the Aïr Mountains, and reached the town of Agadez before the police realized I was a foreigner and confiscated my passport. A week earlier I could have obtained an Algerian visa there in Agadez, but now all visas were off. My best efforts to find an unconventional way forward always led me to people smugglers working the Libyan and Algerian frontiers, who promised that if I paid them a few hundred dollars they could have me picking cucumbers in Spain before the end of the month. This was not what I had in mind, but my French wasn't good enough to fully explain my intent.

Aha, a Tuareg rebel commander active during an earlier rebellion that ended in 1995, was happy to chat over beers, and through him I met an Italian NGO group. We hired some government soldiers, ethnic Hausas, with belt-fed machine guns and ventured into the Aïr Mountains—armoured tourism at its best. Bandits were robbing the buses and killing people, so our precautions were necessary. The only bandits we saw quickly ducked down in alarm. The mountains held oases with orange trees and lush gardens, and outcroppings with blue marble veins in black rocks; we also met a camel-mounted nomad who was injured from a recent sword fight over a woman. Meeting someone like him was the sort of experience that would normally require a time machine, so this excursion had been worth the effort.

While simulated time travel is fascinating, there was no way forward from here either. My path to the north led through Arab-occupied country, and Arab bureaucracy is the most difficult to work around; the channels of informal influence are not as blatant as in other places, but are based on close relationships. There was only one choice left: backtrack south, alone, to Niger's hot and dusty capital, Niamey, where the main entertainment was watching hyenas and crocodiles devour stillborn camel fetuses in the zoo, and where the only hotel was a filthy brothel with a mean bouncer who started as many fist fights as he stopped. I bought plastic bags full of soup from street vendors. Since there was no table, dishes, or cutlery of any sort with which to drink the soup, I had to find a cockroach-free spot of floor, put the bag down, and use my hand like a ladle. The only other food was chunks of chewy goat, wrapped in paper from Portland cement bags.

After a week of waiting, I learned that if I waited three more weeks I might hear yes or no about getting into Algeria. I was worn out, and Niamey was not the place for cooling my heels. I flew to Tunisia, known to be difficult for visas, and sure enough encountered only "No." Trying for Libya was little better. The embassy was controlled by the anti-Gaddafi rebels, and the only way to get service was to stand in a huge crowd milling about in the street, surrounded by barbed wire, soldiers, and armoured cars, and shout at a tiny window high on a granite wall of the embassy. After four days of this, a guy threw a scrap of paper at me with the phone number of a corrupt official who could get me the visa for a bribe of $750 and three weeks' wait. I was freezing on the rainy Punic shore and exhausted from my prolonged trip in Africa. It was time to fly, at last, to Vancouver, to see how my mom was getting on with her cancer treatment.

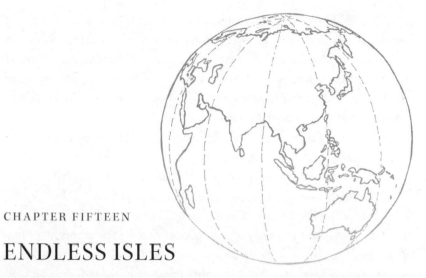

CHAPTER FIFTEEN

ENDLESS ISLES

Caribbean · Bangladesh · Bhutan · Korea · South Pacific

MY MOM WAS MINUS HER HAIR AND RESPONDING AS well as could be expected to chemo, given that it was a stage 4 cancer whose tumours had broken her bones. She was more worried about my brothers and me than herself and was carefully trying to prepare us for the possibility that she might not be around much longer.

Once in Kanata, Ontario, when I was five years old, my two brothers and I had been playing with one of our cousins. He was a little kid like us but bald, with scars on his head from brain cancer surgeries. After some hours playing in and around a cardboard box that once held a canoe, we asked our mom if we could run off into the forest. She told us to play some more with our cousin because this might be the last time we saw him. My brother Steve, a couple of years older than me, said something like "But he told us the doctors fixed him. He won't be sick anymore."

"That's just what he's been told so that he will not be scared," our mom explained, adding that we should be sure to let him believe the doctors had fixed him, and then telling us to play with him now because we would probably never see him again.

So we did, and we had fun, an experience that we all would have missed if our mom had not been honest with us about life and death.

I couldn't have asked for a better mom, and my stepdad, Jim, was a pillar of support. My family is loving and thoughtful, but lacks any penchant for drama, which is deemed sappiness by all of us. We chatted about my travel plans and my mom's genealogy hobby, and there were hugs all round before I left for Alberta to visit my brothers and their kids.

By February 2012 I had returned to Ottawa, family visiting all accounted for. A month had passed since my flight out of Africa, and February in Ottawa, with its bitter cold, ice, and deep snow, is enough to drive even the locals out in search of sun and sea. I wasn't as tolerant of cold as a former North American should be; for ages now, if it was too cold I'd adjust my location on the planet, north or south, elevation, whatever. But now my money was running short. Operating off credit and bank cards instead of a massive "float" of cash had drained my ability to instantly exploit opportunities and to make money from time to time during my trips. The Caribbean was close to Canada, compact, and I'd only ever dabbled in the area, so there was a pleasant arc of tiny nations I'd never visited. Also, as a fun fact to boost morale as my funds ran out, if I swung through there I would have visited the entire Western Hemisphere.

Island hopping in the Caribbean is not as easy as island hopping in a similar archipelago in a less-developed country, such as Indonesia's Nusa Tenggara. The transportation is much worse. By which I mean, instead of convenient and inexpensive wooden ferry boats linking one island to another, all that can be had are expensive modern ferries or planes, and they are set up to bring visitors in or return them home to distant places. Each island is a realm unto itself, idylls for the package tourist. I elected to see this as a challenge, so I tried to be patient and waited for mail boats or studied flight paths with an eye to minimizing them. Even so, I had to pop out to Miami and back a few times just to get to the next island nation.

Upon arrival in the Bahamas, the airline told me they'd lost my backpack and offered a couple of hundred dollars' compensation. I'd lived out of this backpack my entire adult life, though I wasn't sentimental about it. The pack was like my now-lost Colt lighter: it was fun to see how long it could last, but if it was ever gone for good, it would be replaced, as would its contents, without fuss, even if they were all my possessions. Well, not everything, I thought, taking stock. What was left to me was a metal cup, a white shirt from a pirate museum with a skull and crossed sabres on it, and a bottle of rum. Was the universe trying to tell me something? Should I embrace the moment, don the shirt, pour some rum into my cup, and say, "Arr?" Tempting, but instead I spent several hours tracking down my backpack, which had jetted off to explore North America without its owner, and retrieved it in the end.

Haiti stood out from the other Caribbean islands, still trying to get back to normal and clear the rubble from the earthquake that had killed a quarter million people. The presidential palace was a collapsed ruin. The domes slumped like a white wedding cake, fallen and crumpled in some kitchen misadventure. It rained inside my first hotel in Port-au-Prince, but not as hard as it rained outside, so this was some comfort. Besides the bad roof, rooms were rented by the hour, and girls kept knocking on my door all night, which was annoying enough to prompt me to change to a fancy hotel near the market. This place had a security guard who walked around twirling a sawed-off shotgun. Often he held it by sticking his trigger finger in the barrel, a bad habit if ever there was one.

The Grenadines had a laid-back feel to them, with colourful breezy cottages and rum punch on the porch, but most of the Caribbean is not for me, especially for a two-month trip such as I did. Mass tourism is not so much travel as the outsourcing of heavy drinking and noise. The region lacks a flow between places, the sense of learning something and getting somewhere, though there are some picturesque locations. For me, travel is best when you can trace natural features and get a feel for the lay of the land, the mix of ancient cultures and changes of ecology unfolding at a human pace.

There was another trip with substantial flow, one I'd been saving as a treat. I could see it in my mind's eye: I wanted to arrive in Bangladesh, float down the Irrawaddy River by paddlewheeler, continue on to the Sundarban swamp to view tigers if I could, then head inland to see if it was possible to cross over and climb to Sikkim, lofty Gangtok, and green-terraced Darjeeling. Next I'd roam the forts and cliffside monasteries of the Thunder Dragon kingdom of Bhutan, skirt the Himalayas across the Gangetic plains of India, bus up into the Vale of Kashmir and see the house boats of Srinagar, then back to circumambulate the Golden Temple of Amritsar. The sweltering Indus flood plain of Pakistan would welcome me in prime mango season, and then I'd veer north to hike among the apricot orchards and glaciated valleys of the Karakorum range, finally crossing into the high Pamirs, where I'd follow the Silk Road through the Tarim Basin and past Uyghur oases and Buddhist caves, east to China's ancient capital of Xi'an. This would be my third trip to China, but my first to its far west. I would also take time to visit the megacities lining the east coast and try the high-speed trains, with side trips to the totalitarian fiefdom of North Korea and the islands of Japan, Hainan, and Taiwan. Finally, I'd get a better feel for South Korea, where the difference between the feudal north and capitalist south is most stark.

The trip played out just so over the summer of 2012—I was able to do all that was planned and more on a fun and, overall, relaxing journey with nothing too stressful or dangerous. In Lahore, Pakistan, I met a young American blogger, Steve McDonald of "backpackology," and carried on with him to China. What struck me most was the warmth and friendliness of the Pakistani people, contrary to all ethnic stereotypes fomented by network media.

North Korea had to be done as part of a tour. There is plenty for travellers to see in North Korea, but since it all has to be done by efficiently planned tour, it doesn't take long. The kinds of things that make me want to linger in some countries—hanging out with locals, wandering aimlessly around—are forbidden. What you get instead is an orderly whirlwind of sightseeing. My little group was assigned to charming but sharp-eyed Miss Yu, whose brother was an army physicist in the nation's nuclear program. Often we got around by bus, and at one point another tourist started a game: we each had to think of the one thing we would grab if our houses were on fire. This required careful thought from some of our group, but it was easy for me and Miss Yu. I would grab my backpack, and thus lose nothing. Miss Yu would grab her framed photograph of the Dear Leader, so that it would not suffer the indignity of flame.

We ticked all the boxes: the propaganda shops, the astoundingly deep subway that serves double duty as an atomic bomb shelter, the gigantic humanoid monuments in Pyongyang. I came to appreciate the aesthetics of dictator statues. Many reused techniques invented by the ancient Greeks for representing divinities and heroes. One marble chamber had a statue of the paramount leader plumped down in a comfy chair, but it is carved as if it is emerging from the living rock, as the thrones of the gods on Olympus were imagined. Behind was the sacred mountain of his birth, according to propaganda, which also insisted that flying horses and rainbows danced in the air.

We stood on the balcony from which the Dear Leader makes his speeches and watched people practise spelling out words en masse in the square below by holding up different-coloured placards and rearranging themselves according to little cues printed on the ground. On Victory Day they would be spelling out entire slogans at night, by the light of torches raised in their fists.

Not all was pomp and glory in this most old-fashioned of countries. Nobody was allowed to take any pictures of villages, where I saw some peasants not worthy of loyalty badges (those little pictures of the family of the great leader that they wear pinned on their chests). The maize crop was dismal, damaged once again by torrential rain or perhaps a typhoon. Not since El Salvador in the early '90s had I seen a situation where peasants were desperate enough to slog up a hill, mostly bare rock because of erosion, to plant a few dozen kernels in cracks where some residue of soil had lodged.

Sometimes a land is a throwback that provides a window onto vanished cultures. In the case of North Korea, historians interested in the pre-conquest Inca would do well to study the prevailing ideology and mentality in Pyongyang. North Korea has a deified royal family, feudal economic system, and militaristic outlook like that of the Inca in the Andes, and the analogy extends as far as keeping mummies that never relinquish their royal titles. The founder of the dynasty remains the leader for all time, and his mummy is maintained in its own palace/tomb, revered as an eternal ruler. The people, especially ruling bureaucrats, are also addicted to stimulant drugs—not cocaine, in this case, but the crystal meth they manufacture for sale abroad. And it's no wonder Dear Leader and his family love classic Disney fairy tales, as they so mindlessly espouse a cheerful and unquestioned divine right of kings by virtue of bloodline: grandfather, father, and son are the spitting image of ancient Inca lords, with their mummy palaces, sacred mountains, and bogus divine lineage.

The highlight of North Korea was crossing a bridge that was in danger of being washed out. Companies of soldiers had waded into the river, stripped to the waist, to pass sandbags hand to hand, bolstering the foundations. Several remained on the riverbank playing accordions, and they all worked cheerfully, singing revolutionary songs. Of course, photography was forbidden.

After dodging typhoons along the East Asian coast as the summer ended, I knew it was time to return to Canada for a couple of weeks and plan the most disjointed trip imaginable: skipping among the South Pacific islands sprinkled across the watery world of history's greatest dead-reckoning navigators. It was September 2012, and the end of my travels was in sight.

OUR EARTH IS THE BLUE PLANET, AND THE BLUEST OF THE BLUE IS the Pacific Ocean. While it is nearly all water, there are spots of land, millions of them really, but only thousands with any size to impress. I had to decide which ones to visit, and it made sense to visit all those claiming to be bona fide nations, plus those that had something intriguing in their history, geology, or culture. This came to a large number, and I was worried I might not have the cash to do a proper survey and still have enough for my final trip, "mopping up" the world. Fortune favours the brave, so I set out, travelling solo as was my new normal, and hoped for the best.

I had travelled through Polynesian islands only twice before, so the area was practically terra incognita. I certainly had a lot to learn. The locals were usually friendly, and the islands, such as Tuvalu, Niue, Vanuatu, and Tonga were far less touristy than I'd imagined. Some of them scarcely see visitors, and those who do visit come mostly for business or governance purposes. The Pacific was never more strategically important than during World War II and many of the atolls are littered with gigantic rusting guns, shipwrecks, and other evidence of humanity's bloodthirsty nature. It is easy to view these roadside relics, as many Pacific nations are banana-shaped strands, not much wider than the trans-national road itself. The only battle still raging today is human against bedbug and the news is not good. Fiji, in particular, has the world's worst infestation, with no armistice in sight. Young backpackers spread the problem, as most wouldn't know a bedbug if it bit them in the ass.

All in all, flights and boats landed me on a hundred Pacific islands, many of them little known yet fascinating. Just a sample: Tarawa is the capital of Kiribati (pronounced "Kiribas"), a country named for Georgian-era British explorer Thomas Gilbert. Kiribati is how "Gilbert" is pronounced in the local language, known as Gilbertese. Etymologically speaking, his mother ought to have been proud of her son's perpetual fame. Like many inhabited coral atolls, one road arcs around a crescent-shaped island, with ample smoke-spewing cars and vans blaring Korean pop and Rihanna songs. The beaches on either side of the road are home to pigs and piglets that use giant clamshells as slop buckets. My rental shack was daubed with blue paint and perched up on stilts, with a ladder to reach my front door; each morning presented me with the choice of taking a van left or right to explore.

My first day I went to the Betio side, where the port of Betio is found, and the entrance to the lagoon. Eight huge tuna-fishing mother ships were anchored just inside. This was the site of a bloody American victory in World War II, when they invaded at Red Beach. Busted Japanese bunkers and eight-inch guns remained near the causeway. One of these enormous guns took a hit from American bombs or shells. The barrel is shorn off a metre out, and the residual metre of steel is slumped and cracked from the force, like a snapped tube of lipstick. Shrapnel penetrated the crew compartment, which sustained a spray of hundreds of pieces that cut an inch deep into the steel like hot knives through butter.

If our species ever needs to escape the clutches of gravity to colonize another planet, the search for astronauts with the right stuff need go no farther than these little Pacific nations. Residents here grew up on homelands sometimes no wider than a ship's deck, and a day's jog from end to end: maintaining social order with strict taboos in tight quarters with a minimum of fuss is their cultural forte.

NAURU, WHOSE NEAREST NEIGHBOUR IS THE SMALL ISLAND OF Banaba, 300 kilometres to the east, has a peculiar backstory: it is the island of fertilizer that sold itself by the boatload and now has to reinvent itself as a concentration camp. From there I went to the Solomon Islands, crossing Iron Bottom Sound to Savo Island. I observed the hot sand in which megapode birds lay their tasty eggs, near where hundreds of dolphins constantly play in the cerulean waters. Hiking brought me to nearby volcanic fumaroles through vegetation that looked like the setting of a King Kong movie. Even the local girls fit the part—they had long perfectly blonde hair and often light-coloured eyes, but otherwise typically Melanesian characteristics. Some of them had lovely designs scratched onto their cheeks with the sharpened wing bone of a fruit bat when the girls were babies; these designs showed now as fine silver scar-lines against their dark skin. Other girls, all Asian, could be found in cage-like shops spaced around Tonga, keeping them safe while they sold peanut butter and canned fish. Many of these isles had five thousand citizens working abroad for every thousand stay-at-homes, which was just as well: there was no room for them. In a way, these islands were rookeries for people more than birds.

Before reaching Papua New Guinea, while sleeping for a few days on a bench in the Brisbane airport, I got an email from Molly saying she wanted to travel with me again. I told her Papua was not a good place for women travelling on a budget, but she insisted she didn't mind. I flew in a day early to Port Moresby, the newly crowned most expensive city on earth, and one of the most violently criminal. The absolute cheapest hotel on the market was $170 per night. It had sewage leaking out of the bathroom and staining the carpet, and I heard the distinctive *tap, tap, tap* of M16 assault weapons in the dark outside my window. Molly flew in the next day and, thankfully, there was only pistol fire to "soothe" us into sleep that night.

The staff was friendly but security was tight. If you wanted to get to the hotel bar, there was no use to try the metal door from the restaurant. This was kept locked to force everyone to go outside into the car park, where you'd ask a guy standing at a heavy gate like a blast door to let you into a caged corridor tracing the outside of the reception building. This terminated in something like a zoo-cage or aviary for humans, with chain-link mesh all the way over the ceiling to prevent attack by missiles such as rocks. Here, should you hanker for a beverage, you might slip cash to a woman between some bars set in the wall. These bars were spaced just widely enough that she could push a beer bottle back through them to you.

There is not much to do in Port Moresby, so we flew in a little prop-plane to Mount Hagen, from where we could access the highlands. We developed a routine of staying in Seventh-Day Adventist guesthouses when possible, and saving money by travelling in public buses (PMVs). As many people, babies, produce, and live animals were squeezed in as could possibly be accommodated, entertained by loud Christian radio; the locals were surprised to see white people riding with them and not in armoured 4x4s.

Violence against women is rife in Papua, but as is often the case with anti-social behaviour, a minority perpetrate nearly all the crimes, and we enjoyed the kindness and care of many locals. Often our PMV would drive us directly to where we were planning on staying instead of dropping us off at the station, and men would get off with us to ensure we made it in the door of whatever house or mission hostel was expecting us. Their concern was heartwarming.

The day after we passed through Mount Hagen, a mob stripped naked and bound a young woman, Kepari Leniata, and burned her at the stake for the crime of witchcraft, filming her agonizing death on their mobile phones. In another instance, a woman carrying a baby ran out of our bus, chased by a bunch of men. They stripped the baby out of her arms, and thrashed her within inches of her life. The nearest villagers rushed over to watch the scene and intervened ... not to save her, but to strike powerful blows to her prone and soon unconscious body. This commotion all happened as the crowded PMV we were wedged inside accelerated to highway speed.

Occasionally, if I'm advising someone about to travel to PNG and bring up that story to illustrate some of the extra precautions women ought to take, I'm asked why I didn't step up to help the victim. My answer demonstrates the sorts of travel skills needed to visit places like Papua. Let's break it down. What if I had intervened? This would have entailed jumping out of the bus, where I was already travelling in the company of a Western woman carrying valuable cameras, obliging her to watch all our bags while I waded out into a mass of angry and often armed tribesmen swinging their fists. What motivated this violence? Was it revenge for a murder she committed? Did they think she was a witch? How should I know? I could not speak a word of their language. What would their reaction be, when their blood was up, to a foreigner babbling away at them and daring to chastise them? Travellers and Westerners in general had best keep their wits about them.

The most I could sensibly do in a situation like that was try to get information from communicative locals. As we slowly discovered, after the bus had proceeded out of the village, the beating was a domestic attack, and the woman's husband was the principal abuser. He was the father of the baby, and the beating was set off by the wife insisting too publicly that if her husband was continuing on down the road, he had to leave enough money behind for his family to eat. He exploded into violence at being publicly disrespected.

Let's say I had been foolish enough to intervene, and let's even assume, by some miracle, I was able to stop the beating without becoming a victim myself. Then what? The Papuan woman was still there, about to be beaten as soon as I left—probably a particularly horrible beating, as the interference of a foreigner would have caused the husband to lose face to a degree that would have dwarfed what he lost from his wife talking back to him in public. Realistically, and this is one of the most profoundly painful truths of travel, I was a backpacker visiting for a few weeks who had no surplus resources (my bank card was barely working in PNG, and we could only withdraw enough money each day to pay for our bus fare and scarcely enough to eat). We could do no more good for that poor woman than I could for those little girls in Gabon a couple of years earlier.

Unless I were a government administrator who had a relationship with the regional boss and a long-term commitment to peace in the district, any intervention would simply have stroked my own ego by letting me pretend I'd done a good deed, and paved the road to hell for that abused woman. Serious social problems of 50,000 years' gestation are not resolved by casual visitors, no matter how good their intentions. Better to set the bar lower and try not to make things worse. Sometimes a traveller comes across opportunities to help people, and I've saved my fair share of people from terrible situations, even saving lives, but the circumstances have to be right; this was not such a time, sadly, and the cultural divide was too wide to bridge.

I WAS EXPERIENCING AGAIN A RARE AND CHERISHED FEELING: THESE highlands of PNG held cultures and landscapes the likes of which I'd never seen before: naked tribeswomen who smeared their bodies in ash; hillside yam gardens; Huli wigmen with their eponymous fetishes, adorned with boar's tusks and bird-of-paradise feathers, and kept dry in special ceremonial houses. Despite the abundance of brilliant feathers, they were not above coveting certain of Molly's blonde dreads to add to their wigs, and she ended up parting with a few snippets. The men played a particularly aggressive sort of darts, with the boards up high and far away, and otherwise schemed of tribal war amid a grid of walls and trenches, as their women toiled rain and shine. One woman taught Molly how to break open white pandanus nuts with her teeth.

Highland rascals who noticed us pass by made three attempts at theft, all unsuccessful. One time the PMV we were riding in lurched to a halt, and the passengers took to a bit of petty thievery themselves. Three boys carrying seed-bearing red pandanus stalks had tried to cross the road in front of us. The men in our bus rushed out, shouting with glee, stole the stalks from the kids, and laughed as we drove away. The driver had positioned fern decorations on the cab, like the antennas of a ground-creeping bug. And creep we did, past cavernous potholes and rickety bridges. Despite the country being so expensive, the infrastructure was primitive: mineral exploration, not civilization, had driven the exchange value of the local money so high, and the roads billowed with white dust from passing trucks. In the highlands near Tari, a grass hut in a former eco-camp was eighty dollars a night; any cat-food-grade tuna to heat up over a campfire was extra.

Especially interesting to me were new friends who had one foot in the modern world and one in the past, like the young woman who was studying to be a legal secretary but lavished much of her potential study time taking care of a menagerie of prize pigs and cassowaries that would enhance her family's tribal status. In Papua, animal husbandry is often done by the women, while the men preen and dress up in costumes. Some aspects of traditional culture, particularly *wantok*, the intense obligation felt between those who speak the same dialect, can be wonderfully adaptive but not to modern living. The process of development is, necessarily, a process of weakening tradition.

We met two young pilots from the Seventh-Day Adventist airline, one of them a betel-nut bootlegger, who were skilled at landing on ridiculously steep grassy runways cut from forested mountainsides. One of the pilots took us on a road trip to see some Asaro mudmen, who skulk around in heavy clay monster masks, befanged with pig's teeth. We had a look at one of their prize pigs—the biggest can sell for $3,000, priced not for the meat but for the bling factor. There we enjoyed an afternoon buzzed on betel nut, our mouths dripping crimson juices.

Shortly after, Molly jetted off to visit some friends in Indonesia, and I connected through Cairns to Guam. We'd travelled through one of the most dangerous countries for women, and men, on account of certain "rascals," as they are called, but had met mostly the charming and generous people who are the majority of Papuans.

CIRCLING BACK TOWARD NORTH AMERICA AFTER FOUR MONTHS IN the Pacific, I spent some time in US-associated islands, such as Micronesia, the Marshall Islands, and Palau, where I spent a week at year's end. New Year's Eve was pretty low key, as usual for me. Most of the day was spent on an airplane, then hiking along a highway into the main city. A drunk guy who worked at Immigration picked me up and drove me to town just before a squall would have soaked everything, and this enabled me to get a hotel room before midnight. It was well out of downtown and far from any parties or bars, so I just went to sleep.

Palau was ideal for swimming and snorkelling, easy and carefree. I took boat trips to snorkel around an island in the Rock Islands group, and to explore the top of an undersea wall, seeing a shark and a turtle and thousands of fish. Later we passed the cave where the Japanese used to hide kerosene barrels for float planes, and Clam City, where tourists snorkel around a shoal of giant blue clams. Most intriguing is Jellyfish Lake—a briny lake in the centre of an island, where millions of pulsing stingless golden jellies migrate up and down with the sun.

Pohnpei was another gem of Micronesia, especially exploring the ancient lost city of Nan Madol, built out on the reef. Hexagonal columns of black basalt were stacked like logs to form palisades and temple enclosures, spread over ninety-two artificial islands. Imagine if the ancient Irish had used the rocks from the Giant's Causeway to build a city in the sea, and you'll have a picture of it—as long as you envision Venetian-style canals among the temples, and decidedly un-Venetian flooded pits for keeping eels and turtles. The remainder of Pohnpei offered interesting hikes; on the ridges on the other side of the island were many abandoned Japanese guns, some of them looked to be 12 centimetres or more, so massive they required engines to spin them in their bunkers.

As I made my way east again, because of fuel problems at Majuro Atoll I was dropped at the Ronald Reagan Ballistic Missile Defense Test Site on Kwaj Atoll, part of the US Army Space and Missile Defense Command. This place is off limits, so those without clearance are not allowed to stay at the base itself—an army ferry took me to a little island crowded with shacks, where the locals who work at the test site keep their families. The base is an atoll ringed with high-frequency radar domes for tracking the telemetry of missiles and spacecraft, like an enormous catcher's mitt for ballistic missiles. Residents are not allowed to climb to a height above 15 feet in some places on the atoll without a permit, as a body can begin to cook as if it were in a microwave oven.

There were no ATMs, and no businesses took Visa, so by the time I left I had only one dollar and seventy cents to my name. But I had a flight to Vancouver, and my mom and stepdad were going to meet me at the airport.

CHAPTER SIXTEEN

AN ARAB SPRING

Eritrea · Yemen · Kuwait · Spain · Italy · Cyprus · Greece

I WAS BACK IN CANADA IN LATE JANUARY 2013, AND MY MOM HAD tested clear of cancer. This was the test that showed if she was in complete remission, so further monitoring was needed only once a year. Beach walks are cold this time of year, but they felt warm to me, full of the hope of spring. My mom was already planning what new flowers might do well in various parts of her garden.

I had a short visit with her and my stepdad, then rushed off to Ottawa to stay at my dad's. Now that other worries had been dispelled, I was planning my final trip, through the nations rocked by the Arab Spring of 2010–2012, but only if I could get the frustratingly elusive visas quickly enough. Otherwise, the rising desert heat would turn the area around the Red Sea into an oven, and I'd have to delay my trip. I put in a six-week stint working every day to get the visas, calling every contact and trying every trick gleaned from a lifetime of travel. In the end, enough progress was made: I had a couple of visas in hand and a line on a couple of others. The missing visas would haunt me on this last trip, a tour of the ancient lands of the Mediterranean and Red Seas.

Hard to believe, but I had nearly run out of planet to explore. What was left was concentrated in an area that would have been familiar to Ptolemy or Severus thousands of years earlier. This was no accident. My travels had become increasingly methodical over the last few years, and I had made sure to leave myself with a regional trip instead of erratic dilly-dallying. On my final list were Eritrea, Yemen, Kuwait, Libya, Algeria, and some of the Mediterranean islands. I also needed to see Saudi Arabia, the most difficult country to get into, and then Israel. Saved for last was one of the easiest countries, and the best for raising a celebratory pint: Ireland.

A jumbo jet carried me across the Atlantic, through London, and onward to a nation known as the North Korea of Africa. Eritrea is a former province of Ethiopia, whose president was a friend of the Ethiopian president when they went to school together. But Eritrea broke away in a civil war, in apparent violation of the words of the Prophet Muhammad, who was heard to say: "Listen and obey your chief, even if he is an Ethiopian with a head like a raisin."

Eritrea is little known, the only country named for toxic algae. Its map decorated the palace wall in Sacha Baron Cohen's movie *The Dictator*. In Asmara, the capital city, I marvelled at fascist art-deco architecture from Mussolini's empire, such as the Cinema Impero from 1937, and the Fiat Tagliero building that looks like a petrol station for flying saucers; visited the fertility tree near Keren; saw the forest on the escarpment and the coastal city of Massawa; tried my hand at black-market currency exchange (without which the cost of everything is triple); and drank Asmara beer with the ebullient and long-suffering locals. Come the end of April, Eritrea was done for me. Even with a canny tour operator, who was willing to help convince the authorities to let me see as much as possible, they only agreed to four places. I'd seen these four, and since nothing more was on offer, I flew to Yemen to stay in Sana'a, the amazing ancient city of high-rise mud-brick apartments.

Yemen was a medieval holdover: every man a swordsman, every woman compelled to dress in what is colloquially referred to as "full ninja." Sana'a was also not shy about putting more modern weapons on display, with tanks strewn about at strategic intersections and at the remains of street barricades left over from the protests and revolution that flared up with Yemen's Arab Spring in 2011.

Day one was spent having a good wander through the Old City, and the street markets of Souk Al-Milh the day after, ending with a sit-down to talk with a lad who was running a roadside knife shop. Yemenis love their crooked knives, which they tuck under their belts. The teenager also traded in repacked AK-47 bullets, which he would assay carefully before buying, as he didn't want any dented or duds. His friends were chewing khat, but not him. He asked me if I had ever chewed it, and I told him once, in Djibouti, and that it was very strong.

He said, "Yemeni khat is the strongest of all." He indicated the sorry state of his friend's teeth, and added, by way of example, "After chewing, even this guy dreams he will one day have a wife."

"Yes, a wondrous drug," I agreed.

Two-thirds of Yemen's precious desert water, and 40 percent of the arable land is used to cultivate khat, akin to the entactogenic drug methylone, which even the children get buzzed on, chewing away until their teeth are as yellow and worn as those of their livestock. But if Yemenis had chosen to maximize crops instead, would there be twice as much population, with all the resulting stress, and, worse, no druggy shrub to chew and relax with?

A shady antiques dealer haunted the hotel gardens. Antiques dealers are typically laconic and suspicious, but I find it worthwhile to make an effort with them, while appearing casual. Eventually this man was willing to swap tales of eye-popping profit from an Ottoman swagger stick with Islamic inscriptions, sold to a filthy-rich sheik, and a deftly smuggled casket of yellow silken handkerchiefs.

A single-minded young East Asian woman was usually about the premises, or else at the tourist police, a force dedicated to the control of foreign visitors, begging them to give her permission to visit the town of Tarim in the Hadhramout Valley, home of the bin Laden family. To her mind, everyone she met exuded an aura of a colour that determined their temperament, and she'd become upset if someone acted at cross-purposes to what she'd expect given their aura. Her maniacal persistence paid off after some weeks, and she obtained permission after agreeing to cover herself with an abaya, the Arabian concealing dress, so no one would see she was foreign, and to ride the long series of buses in the company of an armed policewoman, similarly cloaked. The security situation seemed fine in the city; no muggers accosted me while I was walking round Sana'a at night with my backpack. But I did see a slender and elegant young woman in a black abaya and full-ninja black veil; she had a dainty black sequined purse slung under one arm, and a black MAC-10 with a high-capacity magazine slung under the other, ready for whatever the morning might bring, be it shopping or assassinations.

In my travel bag was a printed authorization from London's Libyan embassy to pick up a Libyan visa here in Yemen, but I wasn't going to pick it up until just before leaving; as soon as it was issued, the month-long period to activate it began counting down. Instead, for now, I got authorization from the tourist police to visit the Jabal Haraz mountain region, where I could see the forts of the Yemeni tribesmen, mad, bad, and dangerous to know. For afterward, I'd booked a flight to Socotra, an island off the Somali coast that was famous for its dragon's blood trees. I'd stay there a week, then fly to Aden and overland it back to Sana'a. Not much more was possible. There was a Japanese guy asking for everything and getting turned down, as there was rampant kidnapping in the north by ethnic Houthi insurgents, and in the east by an infestation of Al-Qaeda in the ruins of Ma'rib, the Queen of Sheba's ancient city. We ended up getting permission for the same places. There were not many tourists in Yemen: just me, the Japanese guy, a tour group of young Russians with a guide, and one other. This was more than the previous year, according to the locals.

First up was a stop to see Wadi Dhar, a beautiful castle perched on a spire of stone, on the edge of the cooler and misty Jabal Haraz. Some local characters were about, strutting around with their dagger belts. One guy had his white thobe (robe) rolled up so that his legs were bare; he tucked the fabric of his kilt-like clothing over the pommel of his dagger, which jutted up from his belt at a 45-degree angle like a ship's bowsprit. No doubt he could enjoy more breeze this way, but it was "not a good look," if you care to picture it.

As I enjoyed stunning mountain scenery and charming villages of traditional stone high-rise apartments, it struck me how easy it would be to turn a traditional Yemeni village into a castle. They are all built on the highest, most defensible outcrop of rock anyway, and a Yemeni house is often a six- to eight-story high-rise of quarried stone, with little windows high on the walls, like murder holes and gun ports on a block house. These stone towers, looking like the keep of a European castle, are crammed together side by each; all you need to do is whack up a few walls between the outermost keeps, and there you have it, a proper castle.

Kawkaban was one such fortress atop a mesa, with a neatly engineered cistern of fresh slimy water. I walked down the *jabal* (mountain) along a path that traced a gorge to the fort-like town of Shibam far below. A local boy accompanied me, using his limited English at intervals to teach me this and that. First he explained that his father had shot himself through the head, leaving him an orphan. After a decent interval, he further explained that he had no television or football, but then, straying somewhat off topic, the next thing he said was "Yemen safe, never any shooting," and mimicked firing an assault rifle. His assertion was somewhat undermined by the inopportune burst of automatic gunfire from Shibam a few seconds later—locals celebrating, I imagine. Halfway down the *jabal* he added that his mother was both crazy and completely blind. At this juncture I paid him a small "guide fee" to save us both the embarrassment of his having to concoct further tales of woe.

Hababah was another fort with a huge cistern, subject of much civic pride, and green slime and tadpoles too. A friendly old man "salaamed" me. He had thrust a bouquet of sundry flowering weeds into his turban, to debonair effect.

Another man walked with me through town to practise his English. Mostly he talked about women. He had met a Dutch woman once. She was old, but very pretty: huge breasts, he explained, making the traditional cupping-of-the-hand signals. His wife also had "huge breasts, very pretty," hands dextrously indicating their breadth. Changing the subject, I asked him what he did for a living. He claimed to make handicrafts and showed me an array of Egyptian, Indonesian, and Indian boxes, necklaces, and charms. "This one is ruby," he said, fingering a string of marble beads, clumsily dabbed with green paint. He found it difficult to sell me on his wares, so instead he offered to find me a wife, suggesting marriage to an eighteen-year-old Yemeni girl, whom he would provide.

Leaving him to contemplate my profound indifference to his salesmanship, I searched out and found a tall white tower of a hotel in Shibam, taking a room on the highest floor. Lit through stained-glass-window alcoves, with pink and blue plasterwork, it was a perfect place for me to contemplate my own profundity, as the only reading material remaining to me was a vexing article on quantum gravity in a crumpled science magazine.

The next day, yet more amazing mountain views culminated in the most stunning of them all: Ar-Riady. Imagine a seascape, but petrified. The valleys seemed to be a groundswell peaking in the perfect cliff I stood atop, with a dozen neighbouring peaks like white-capped waves jostling on the swell. Where there would be a crest of white froth, a rock pinnacle was capped with a forlorn ancient castle, and rather than concentric oceanic ripples, I saw concentric green terraces of khat and crops. Compact groves of forest bobbed in the vista like flotsam on a big sea. And all was shot through with steep-walled canyons, like the troughs betwixt waves, as the groundswell relaxed from this uttermost dizzying height toward distant haze in the far foothills of the Red Sea's coastal plain.

In a fort on this landscape I met Omar, who told me he counted himself among the blessed. He gestured to indicate this stone tower, his to dwell in, and, beneath our feet, his balcony for chewing khat, until his hand swept up with a flourish to draw my eyes to our splendid view overlooking the town and the huge khat field that was his family's birthright.

He would chew until he had a buzz and enjoy the dreamy view, centred on the field that made his fortune. He asked me twice what Canadians thought of Yemen, but I had to tell him the truth: it is a rare Canadian who has ever heard of Yemen, on the other side of the planet.

Not all of Haraz was these lofty mountains. One section of the road dropped low into lush wadis (seasonal river gorges), where the air was hot and humid, and the damper soil at the bottoms of the gorge was planted with mango and banana. Here the Yemeni tower homes were dwarfed by gigantic boulders that had rolled down from the cliffs above and become wedged in the narrow wadis. For a few kilometres the road itself was a wadi, following the course of a rushing stream. During any steady rainfall it would have been impassable.

In Manakhah, a market town high again on the peaks, it was my pleasure to attend a Yemeni wedding. The only thing you might recognize from a Western wedding was perhaps the wedding singer; everything else that transpired was indistinguishable from a battle scene. Wild screeching and shouting, powerful concussion firecrackers (thunder claps) that exploded with deafening force, stunning the village dogs into silence and setting off all the car alarms in town. Into this barrage, automatic gunfire erupted: picture men armed with AK-47s, M16s, Uzis, and the occasional sad sack with a lowly bolt-action, each and every one of them emptying magazines into the air in every direction. (Yemeni people are the second-best-armed, per capita, in the world—after the Americans, of course.) It is a status symbol to blast through a clip, as it costs 7,000 rials for thirteen bullets (if I heard correctly). In the midst of this, the guests made a circle and danced the traditional Yemeni dance, brandishing daggers and feigning thrusts and jabs, the groom borne aloft on the shoulders of the best men, one of whom held a large scimitar and scabbard crossed behind his back.

I couldn't help but think, Please, President Obama, don't drone-strike us here. If you are poised in the White House, considering the infrared intel from your circling drones, remember: if you see bombs exploding, machine guns blazing, and knives and scimitars wielded to terrifying effect, it is only a wedding. Or maybe an Al-Qaeda attack.

Anyone's guess, I suppose, because, honestly, from an intel perspective, there would be precious little to tell them apart.

And now I know if I ever see a man so calm he could thread a needle while the ground around him is being peppered with bullets and vibrating with explosions, he's not James Bond or a Navy Seal, but a Yemeni wedding singer—all in a day's work for these brave souls.

MY LAST DAY IN THE LOVELY JABAL HARAZ WAS SPENT IN THE company of a trekking guide who in North America would be called a hillbilly. In this case, he must have been a "Jabalbilly." He guided me over peak and dale, but women were on his mind.

"My wife, she is good woman," he began, "but I don't like that she is daughter of my uncle."

"Your first cousin," I said. "But if you don't like her, why did you marry her? Why not marry a woman from the next village?"

"Are you crazy? How do I know she is not ugly?" (True enough. In my time in Yemen I had not seen any women, as they were hidden behind black abayas.) He continued, "Her parents will lie and say she is pretty, but after wedding you look the face, and ugly."

"Lots of cultures marry first cousins," I told him. "In Europe this used to be the practice."

He said, "Okay she is cousin. Problem is when we make relations, she lay still like donkey. Even donkey make more action."

I thought, How would he know? And probably she is thinking: I'm doing my first cousin, ewwh.

My Jabalbilly friend was on a roll. "What I want now is this: What you call when you go to Africa and take persons for to sell?"

"That would be a slave raid," I helpfully suggested.

"Yes, slaves; I want slave girls, small the age, virgin."

"Hmm," I said. "I know for a fact that there is still slaving going on in northeastern Niger. But most Africans are now skeptical of ye olde slave trade, having formed this notion that slave taking was not an altogether good thing." I tried to imagine the possible paperwork problems that might arise if you tried to revive the cursed trade. First, when filling out your landing card on the flight to Africa, which box would you check for the "What is the purpose of your journey?" question—conference, family visit, vacation? I supposed you'd want to check "Other" and hope the border official didn't ask for specifics.

Sadly, conversations like this were too common to be considered merely a joke in villages where old attitudes endured. The history of slaving was thousands of years old hereabouts, and not so easily extinguished by Yemen's 1962 law ending the practice. In the countryside, existing slaves and their children were still passed down as property. One town I'd passed through, Hajjah, held 300 enslaved Africans according to a count done in 2010.

I had to take leave of this man of deeply conservative ambitions and loop back to Sana'a, stopping only to buy a whole bag of mangos and put in a day's work doing a test run for my Libyan visa attempt so I would be ready when I got back from Socotra.

A couple of short hauls on dilapidated aircraft brought me out over the Gulf of Aden to the legendary island of Socotra off the Somali coast. I'd arrived with neither plan nor reservation, intending to do the place freestyle, as was my preference. But there was no getting around a need for a four-wheel-drive truck and camping gear, so in order to save on costs I hooked up with Tammy, the only other tourist, who I met in the airport.

Camping on Socotra is greasy and hot, with salt in the breeze. Ironically, the only time your skin doesn't feel like a sardine is when you are swimming. Luckily there are natural horizon pools in the highlands with views to distant seas, and fantastic beaches with spinner dolphins, caves like dragon lairs, and abundant seafood. Here and there, yellow-headed vultures boldly scavenge for scraps, hissing and glaring out of beady black eyes.

The peculiar local trees didn't amount to much of a forest. They were only about eye-height, sized as if for tiny fairies, which would not be out of place given that the trees are shaped like vases of a silver or bronze colour. Instead of leaves, each sports a sprig of pink blossoms. Less of a draw for fairies were the lines of rusting T-34 battle tanks, left over from the last civil war. Farther inland, vanishingly rare dragon's blood trees resist extinction, looking like alien mushrooms with silver cords for gills, and a tightly knit saucer of spiky leaves perched like a green UFO on top. Apparently they drink the morning mist.

By day we swam or adventured in our Toyota, and before nightfall and stargazing our guide would have cooked us some giant grouper fish or lobsters, purchased from fishermen in passing sailboats, and set up a tent.

It is all normal, which is to say marvellous, I thought as I tossed the vultures some fish bones. I'll never tire of exploring our wondrous planet.

From Socotra I returned to Aden and had a week of fun hitchhiking through rural Yemen, checking out the surprisingly atmospheric ancient mountain city of Ta'izz. I enjoyed five times good fortune soon after returning to the capital. For starters, the Libyan ambassador was in his office, and after only a couple of days of asking, he gave me my visa. They'd claimed to have the visa ready for me in the embassy, but my mind was only at ease after I held it in my hand, worried that entry requirements might change as a result of the terrorist bombings in Tripoli, especially the car-bombing of the French embassy just before I'd arrived in Yemen. With the visa in hand, I could get into Libya no matter what happened with the security situation. The ambassador also agreed to return to me the lab report stating my disease-free status in case it was needed for my last visa application, Saudi Arabia.

The next task was to change my flight so I could get to Kuwait early and reroute to Libya. When the woman at the travel-desk found the flight on May 22 was full, she spent an hour getting me on regardless, without charging me the typical $192. My subsequent search for flights to Libya from Kuwait scored me an onward flight to Tripoli. All was set for me to finish Africa over the next month. What's more, the pie-eyed taxi driver who took me back to the central square following my day of logistics work gave me khat to chew while we were stuck in traffic.

Kuwait could be a set for a sci-fi film. The place is built for cars, and the only people seen at street level are the South Asian and Southeast Asian servant class, who do the logistics and street cleaning, like in

Planet of the Apes before the ape insurrection. The Arab ruling caste lives up in the air-conditioned glass monuments to high technology. It's interesting, especially for architects who get to design these skyscrapers, but I'm not convinced it's socially sustainable. At some point the Kuwaitis will have to either give all these people citizenship or send them home, and it could be messy either way.

I found a Kerali Indian-run hotel for twenty dinars a night (the elevator shook and groaned like a submarine going deep to escape depth charges) and had fun walking around in the 40-degree heat, sampling Pakistani curry, soft dates, and iced fruit juice. The museums were free, and with heat like this, Kuwait could market itself with the slogan "Every day is a museum day in Kuwait due to the stifling heat" if they ever valued truth in advertising. It was by cool night that the markets came alive with shoppers, and the mosques were lit by an eerie green glow.

Following Kuwait I flew to war-scarred Libya. My first walk around Tripoli showed bomb damage near the airport and on the road in, and one of the military compounds was entirely destroyed, but the city retained some charm. The Libyans were friendly, but many shops, and everything touristic—castles and museums and whatnot—were closed because of the war. They don't want to reopen the tourist places until the tourists come back, but the tourists are not likely to come back until the tourist places reopen. This presupposes that the shooting stops, of course. I talked my way into the main museum in Tripoli, having nothing better to do. It was inside a Spanish fortress (the Spanish have left fortresses everywhere, like cigarette butts). There wasn't much to see, and it wouldn't surprise me to hear it had been looted.

Just as in Tunisia, the economy seems to be based on street vendors selling one another sunglasses and dresses, coffee, fruit juice, and shawarma—and the old town proved to be a satisfying place to hang about for a few days. After getting my hair cut one fine day in a market stall, the barber handed me a note where he'd written how much he felt he was owed: seventy dollars. Maybe he reasoned that anyone who didn't speak Arabic must speak stupid. I put down my best guess of what his service was worth and walked out. He had given me the look of an extra hired as a villain's henchman in an action movie, my hair slicked back with lots of product.

As far as I could tell, I was one of only a smattering of people poking around Libya's abandoned archeological sites of ancient pillars and sacred fountains. Visitors had been scared off by this war, which had begun only a couple of years before my visit, in 2011, when I had been travelling around Madagascar. Several militants told me that Libya was unsafe, but I found it rather peaceful. They all warned of trouble if I went to Derna or some of the towns deep in the desert, but I hadn't intended to go there anyhow. Having looked at all the ancient ruined cities, most of which it was possible to visit by sneaking through holes in fences, I thought the most impressive forum was the one built by Severus, in Leptis Magna, but the best overall ancient city was Cyrene, with a spring-fed pool in the temple of Apollo, home of the now extinct wonder-spice silphium (it is said Nero ate the last sprig). The location is spectacular, on a hill with mature trees, overlooking the Mediterranean Sea in the distance. A visiting scholar was shown inside the building that houses the statues from the façade of a major temple, so I got a peek too.

The food situation was dire. With the old package-tour-only model under Gaddafi, the hotels chose locations out in the light-industrial areas of cities, where land was cheap; the idea was that they would monopolize all services for the captive hotel guests, so it didn't matter that they were far from the restaurants. But now the hotels couldn't be bothered to serve food, and if you went out looking, you'd end up walking for an hour or more in the dark through dusty alleys with broken sewer pipes, past sheet-metal fabricators and bins of Chinese clothing for sale, hoping to find a shawarma. Often the meals I'd end up with were something like a bottle of water, handful of dates, bag of potato crisps.

The roads east of Misrata showed more signs of artillery duels and bomb-blasted armour, the asphalt pockmarked with shell bursts, mostly tank or artillery fire, and the occasional bomb crater. Destroyed armour was tanks for the most part, but some armoured personnel carriers and truck-borne rocket launchers. I've seen so much destroyed Soviet armour around the world that if someone said, "Quick, picture a tank in your imagination," a burned-out Soviet tank with the turret blown off would spring to mind.

There weren't as many destroyed tanks on the highways west of Misrata, the military presence was a little lighter, and the roads didn't show nearly the level of shell burst. Instead, houses and businesses were ventilated in places by 20-millimetre cannon fire, and buildings were blasted out by rocket-propelled grenades, which were not nearly so much in evidence out east.

All things considered, the Libyans trying to help me greatly outnumbered the people trying to rip me off. The best fun was just hitchhiking around to look at this and that, and talking to whomever I met along the way. Even the sandstorms were fun, provided I could get to shelter in time.

To return from the coast east of Benghazi to Tripoli was a chore. The road trip just from Al Bayda, east of Benghazi, to Tripoli exacted a twenty-four-hour effort of no-sleep, non-stop driving through a raging sandstorm that reduced visibility around the Gulf of Sirte. It should have been only a ten-hour drive, but we filled up on bad benzene from one of the gas stations. The engine kept cutting out, and the fuel filter was gummed up; once we had slowly burned through that tank-full and refilled, all was well. There were oodles of police, army, and militant checkpoints on the coastal road. One of them was very intrusive: a bunch of rifle-toting militants stopped our car and commanded that any foreign-seeming passengers had to give blood on the spot for an AIDS test.

This had happened to me in Iraq a decade earlier, but the Iraqis weren't serious about it; they just wanted each person to pay one dinar as a bribe. The Libyans were actually taking blood, and everyone had this ominous wait as they tested it. I wondered what the scientist who developed the fast test would have thought about his invention being used this way. Luckily for me, I didn't have to submit to the dirty needles. The Libyans were amazed when I produced a legal document, written in Arabic, stamped, signed, with photograph attached, proving that I was free of this and other diseases. If Libya wants to be welcoming to more tourists eventually, they'll have to drop this custom of random blood tests at gunpoint.

The Tripoli-to-Tunis run took another twenty-four hours, which is typical, mostly due to the long wait for enough people who want to go, and a longer wait at the border. The police search and ask questions six times, but I'm not sure they are getting security "value for money," as it were, since they ask the same questions and look in the same tops of the same bags, six times over. I made my way to my usual hotel in Tunis, Salammbo, and slept away my exhaustion.

Continuing west, Algeria was a colonial-era time capsule: urban cafés and fields of red poppies little changed from descriptions in the novels of Camus, generations earlier. The south was forbidden, as it had been since at least my last attempt in December 2011, due to kidnappings and terrorist attacks, but I managed to get there anyway, using misleading but objectively true documents. I really wanted to see the Crying Cow rock carving and the famous sinuous sand dunes.

By now it was mid-June, the border west of the city of Oran was shut, as it had been for twenty years, and there were no flights available to hop over to Morocco's Tangier. I decided to fly to Barcelona. Tendrils of a dozen strategies for obtaining a Saudi visa might still be viable, and each needed cultivation to have any chance of bearing bureaucratic fruit, something best accomplished by going into a holding pattern over the Mediterranean Sea. As long as I stayed in places with sufficient access to working internet cafés, I could travel aimlessly. From Barcelona, my next stop was the Balearic Isles and Palma de Mallorca, on to ancient Cádiz, then the fortress of Gibraltar, legendary site of the Pillars of Heracles.

Spanish attempts to conquer this strategic rock from overland faced devastating British fire from the cliffs. The Rock of Gibraltar is riddled with tunnels and cannon galleries, including the formidable King George Battery. Longer tunnels were made during World War II, but only the nineteenth-century tunnel works are safe for visitors. The modern wartime works, excavated quickly with dynamite, are prone to collapse, while the nineteenth-century works, done with blasting powder, remain sturdy and passable.

After a flight to Sardinia, I took a boat to Corsica, and another to Italy, wending my way south to Sicily. Europeans suffer no shortage of travel options. On the same day it is possible to take boats, planes, trains, and buses. My favourite was ARST Bus Company in Sardinia, as in "I can't be arst to rent a car, so this bus will have to do." I crossed the channel with the legendary clashing rocks of Scylla and Charybdis on both a train and a boat at the same time; the train is split in half, stuffed on the boat, we cross, and then it is reconnected.

Arriving very late in Syracuse, the only thing available for food was the special Sicilian pizza—a pizza rolled up in another pizza. The ancient ruins of this former Greek colony, home of Archimedes, were excellent for wandering and daydreams. I saw Mount Etna, the volcano without which you can't complete a *New York Times* crossword, and the following day snuck out into some overgrown ruins near Naxos, a city destroyed by the tyrant of Syracuse over 2,000 years ago; wild fruit grew there, four black figs that were ready to eat, one lemon, and mulberries. When it was time to go, I bought a ticket for a boat to Greece so I could make my way to Athens, with a mind to reach Cyprus and get back to the Middle East.

Boarding the ferry to Greece, the guy checking my ticket said, "Let's see where you are bunked ... deck?!" Yes, I was sleeping on the deck, with the Bulgarian babushkas and the scruffy types. There were only about a dozen deck passengers, and most of us ended up sleeping in the landings of stairwells, as it was cold and windy outside. Even the touring American high-school kids had bunks, and when they came into our "steerage-class" stairwell by mistake, you could hear them giggle and say, "We made a wrong turn."

In Athens I walked to the top of the Hill of Muses for my favourite view of the Acropolis. After only an hour and a half trudging around with my pack, I found a hostel that offered a free shot of ouzo for checking in. My intent was to make a beeline for the archeological museum at first light. It had been closed for upgrades to make it ready for the 2004 Olympics the last time my wandering had brought me to Athens, so this would be my first opportunity to marvel at the collection of marble statuary.

In the morning light, I was astonished at the amount of destruction and graffiti marring the centre of Athens, with countless shops closed or struggling. The youth had been revolting in the streets, and the elders ought to be hanging their heads in shame. Everybody is always looking for a free ride off the labour of others. In this case, it amounted to an obscure form of slave trading, since unborn future generations were being saddled with the requirement to work literally decades of what will be essentially unpaid labour in order to cover the lifestyle loans taken out by their ancestors. In ancient Greece, some fathers without honour might sell their children into slavery and go to orgies on the proceeds. If a portal opened between ancient times and today, and a Greek baby boomer found himself sitting as a critic beside such a disreputable Ancient, how long would it be before the Modern Greek was found out? An equal amount of shame ought to be felt by the Western Europeans, for having lent them this money in the first place.

Museum visited, I made my way to the Greek Republic of Cyprus, positioning myself to do Saudi if a visa should ever materialize. This southern portion of Cyprus was new to me; I'd seen the north a long time ago, but had been unable to get into the south. I was just checking in at my hotel when the lobby was suddenly swamped by buff, shirtless guys with spiky black arm tattoos, vying to see who could best say "waaah" while sticking their tongues out, all of them stinking drunk at eleven o'clock in the morning. It was going to be one of those places. Oh, well. If I meant to see all the different cultures, this had to include modern European culture.

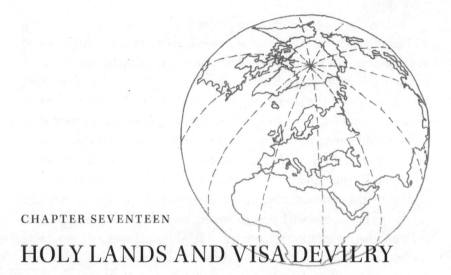

CHAPTER SEVENTEEN

HOLY LANDS AND VISA DEVILRY

Jordan · Saudi Arabia · Israel

Q
UICKLY MAXED OUT FROM THUMPING AND BEEPING
Europop-techno, I plotted my escape from package-
tourist purgatory on a Friday. The ferries didn't run
anymore, so my best option was a flight out of the city of Larnaca
to Amman, Jordan, for the next Monday. Flying on the weekend was
pointless because the embassies might be closed, so I decided to accept my fate and chill on the palm-lined seafront in Larnaca, birthplace of the Stoic philosopher Zeno, for a couple of days. I arrived
in Amman on Monday as planned, but it was the start of Ramadan,
so embassies might be closed anyway. People are very grumpy at the
start of Ramadan, so if the embassy was open, I could maximize my
chances by showing up as early as possible, before the embassy staff's
blood sugar levels fell. (Ramadan was no problem for me otherwise,

as I usually ate in the morning, then travelled or hiked all day before eating again at nightfall.)

Nothing I'd tried to this point had brought me any closer to a Saudi visa, so my plan for Amman was to go to the Saudi consulate on Rainbow Street and ask to be let in. I thought it might be worthwhile to try to talk to an actual human Saudi; perhaps they were less formal in person.

By chance or by trace of ghostly memories, I took a bus to one of the oldest neighbourhoods of Amman, within walking distance of the Citadel, and checked in to the Cliff Hostel before realizing that this was the very same place from which I'd set off and survived my Iraqi wartime hitchhiking adventure a decade earlier. This time the images of war on the common-room television showed Sunni and Shi'ite fighters in Syria rather than Iraq; my fellow backpackers were mostly Chinese rather than Western. Israelis were altogether absent. But for me it was a familiar feeling and a familiar challenge, although the insanity I was facing was visa bureaucracy rather than bullets and bombs.

My health was not good, and I suspected the insidious influence of a single-celled parasite called *Giardia*. In someone who is highly resistant, it manifests as mild depression and energy drain. Intuition told me I'd acquired it in Papua New Guinea, but my immune system had forced it into dormancy: I'd been suspicious enough of its presence to take a course of Flagyl months ago while visa foraging in Ottawa. If you don't exterminate *Giardia* right away, ideally within the first three days, it can be hard to completely clear, and in hindsight, I thought maybe it had re-emerged in Algiers, causing me such trouble with situational awareness that I'd lost some money to street thieves.

Visas and *Giardia*, while both traveller's banes, are not equally vile. Visas are much the worse of the two. In my psyche they were closely linked, since half the times I'd come down with *Giardia* were while I was waiting in the fetid slums of a capital city for a visa to be issued.

The very first time I'd encountered *Giardia* was in 1992. It hammered me as I ended my eighty-six days alone in the Valhalla Wilderness. I'd been reduced to lying in a steep meadow, soaking up the warm rays of sun, watching yellow swallowtail butterflies cavort above the wild flowers, and reading Hunter S. Thompson's *Fear and Loathing: On the Campaign Trail '72*. I'd lost ten kilos from my already lean "living off the land" weight, and my trousers were kept up with a rope after the last of three buttons proved too loose. My emergency food was long gone, rendering me barely strong enough to fish or pick berries most days, while marauding bears had destroyed my tent and had been circling just beyond the light of my flickering campfire come nightfall. I laid a twelve-gauge shotgun loaded with rifled slugs across my chest, and in this position I'd watched the sun come up, the sun go down, the moon come up, the moon go down, for three days and nights, conserving my energy by not moving except to keep the gun levelled at bears that were getting impatient.

Soon after returning to civilization, I had encountered my first visa annoyance. And now, with my last visa attempt, my old enemy *Giardia* was back again, making me feel sluggish and miserable.

Granted the power to swap my current ordeal seeking this Saudi visa in Amman for a repeat of that first *Giardia* experience in the Valhallas, I would have taken the trade and counted my lucky stars. As it was, well over two decades of relentless travel later, here I was in my mid-forties, propped on a cot in a hostel in Jordan with nearly no money and no possessions that I couldn't lift with one finger after fitting them in my trusty backpack. I wore my visa-application shirt, my only collared shirt, a hand-me-down from my stepdad. Piled around me was all that I owned: boots, old clothes, a mosquito net, some camping stuff, in that same backpack from the Canadian mountainside, now faded, mended with copper wire and electrical tape, and missing many zippers and clasps. The possessions were uncannily similar to those I'd had as a lad, except the backpack alone was over two decades older, like a backpack of Dorian Gray that waxes shabbier over the years, while my other possessions, replenished, seem ageless.

What had changed? To the untrained eye, not much. But to my own satisfaction, I'd seen the world.

As a side effect of seeing the world, I'd been to nearly every country and non-country on earth. It was Saudi Arabia next, now or never.

While awaiting the results of my first concerted visa effort in Amman, I bussed a few hundred kilometres to the south to Petra, the city the Nabateans excavated into sheer gorges of rosy pink sandstone millennia ago. It was Ramadan anyway, so there was no beer drinking on offer. I'd bought Flagyl pills and resolved to do a full course of them to clear my mood along with the dark circles that had formed under my eyes.

On the day I arrived in Petra, Alicia Keys gave an impromptu concert at the Treasury, just where the Siq opens up for the world-famous view. This sure beat my experience of ten years earlier, when the VIP was Tony Blair, who did not sing (for which I was profoundly grateful). Even though I was feeling exhausted from the Flagyl and the *Giardia* and the hike to the site, Petra was as spectacular as I'd remembered.

With so much time on my hands, I made my way to nearby Little Petra, which is just as it sounds: a smaller version of Petra. One sandstone chamber had seen so little vandalism that the plaster and painting remained on parts of the wall; the whole room was decorated with a colourful, intricate, and well-balanced painting of looping vines with bunches of purple grapes in homage to Dionysus. Naked cherubs frolicked among the vines, playing instruments and whatnot. The room gave me a whole new perspective on the original appearance of those now austere chambers in Petra. The ancient Greek historian Strabo said that the Nabateans loved to drink and party and would do so in groups of thirteen, with two additional dancing and singing girls for each group (not a bad idea even in modern times, actually); they would line up eleven cups, of gold for the king, normal cups for other people. So democratic was the rite that often the king would take his turn to fill other people's cups. After the eleven cups were drained, the wine was done for that session, to prevent excessive drunkenness.

The Nabateans who'd built this city, so marvellously tucked into crevasses in rose-coloured sandstone, were one of the most advanced of the Arab cultures, and more comfortable with nudity and alcohol than most of the Muslim Arabs who followed them. Nineteenth-century Bedouins used up many a cartridge shooting off the faces and breasts of ancient decorative statuary.

I was a big hit with the many Chinese backpackers at the Valentine Inn in Wadi Musa, the town nearest to Petra. They christened me "god of travel," took dozens of photos with me, and made me offerings of apples, nectarines, and pears, so I had plenty of snacks. There was an older guy on staff at the hostel, infamous for rudely and comically messing with all the other travellers, but he called me "sir." And the Bangladeshi indentured servant women from the kitchen brought me hot water on request to make noodles or coffee. The perks of being the god of travel, I supposed.

When I stepped into the hostel's common room, I was in for a surprise. A 2,000-year-old pattern had been extinguished in the decade since my previous visit in late 2003. The wine drinking, chatting, camaraderie, and playing of musical instruments that mirrored the reverence for revelry seen in the ancient wall frescoes were gone, and the scene in the common room was unrecognizable from any era of human history. By age-old tradition, our families took surnames from what they did: smith, forester, fisher, tanner. Following that example, there is only one surname fit for us now: scryer. Every one of us gazes as if to scry into a crystal ball, peering into glass all day to gain or send information. And so it was in the hostel, as it was in most places, now that I thought about it: everyone scrutinizing Gorilla Glass, big-eyed, their faces illuminated by glowing screens, ominously tapping.

One of the age-old characteristics of travel will be negated by the smartphone and other technology. What does it mean to say you return home to see it for the first time if you can never disconnect from home? Are we all now homebodies, or e-turtles, hauling around the home-shell of unbreakable communication, plodding out to cover territory, and sending back telemetry? Or else hermits if we deliberately disconnect, snubbing those left behind with our WiFi silence?

The change came slowly and then suddenly. Compare the modern backpacker, feeling poorly connected to home when his Skype signal will support voice but not video, to the loneliness of the ancient traveller, making his way through a strange and dangerous world. Before transatlantic cables, before telegraph, before even the pony express, there was the ultimate old-skool traveller, in comparison to whom my quest to find a rotary phone in the no man's land of Burma pales. Consider this traveller's message from the days before email and Facebook, slower even than snail mail; he only half delivered this message on foot before he died, so he had it chiselled as the epitaph on his gravestone, perchance to be delivered by the next brave soul to pass.

I am the grave of Biton, traveller:
If from Torone to Amphipolis you go
Give Nicagoras this message: his one son
Died in a storm, in early winter, before sunrise.
—Nikainetos, Third Century BC

Now, instead of lively conversation, the hostel was hushed but for the occasional noise or word, like the grunts and groans of an athlete's concentration on a task. Perhaps modern travellers see themselves more like crews of siege-style rock climbers, exploring a rock face that represents the unknown to them. One leads and puts in safeties, what Tyrolean adventurer Reinhold Messner called "the murder of the impossible," while the others follow in person later, or vicariously through up-to-date file sharing. Smartphones are the ropes that link them together. In this new zeitgeist, the traveller not only travels for himself, but travels "lead" for his crew, drilling safety bolts into the face of adventure.

Such an ethos, while odd to traditionalists, must represent the new paradigm for travel. Perhaps there are profoundly interesting experiences possible from such a hive-brain effort, or perhaps techno-gypsies can achieve feats beyond the dreams of individual travellers, such as me.

The world moves on. The modern travellers are qualitatively distinct from the travellers that came before, and something is lost when something is gained.

BACK FROM PETRA, I SHOWED UP AT THE NEW BUILDING WHERE THE Saudi consulate staff in Amman had directed me to pick up my passport with the coveted visa. Not so fast. The relevant official said that the passport had not been entered correctly into his embassy system, I had not OFFICIALLY been waiting at all, and my passport, which already contained the visa, would remain gathering dust until ten days had passed.

I'd done all I could, so I hopped on a bus to the Dana Nature Reserve, a place of hauntingly beautiful valleys and hills, where, a Spanish cyclist had assured me, there was a hotel with three highly skilled Filipina cooks, and full room and board cost just fifteen Jordanian dinars. I would have time for another look in on the Saudi visa process come mid-August.

Most afternoons I'd trek an hour or two in the hills fringing the Qadisiyah Plateau, along winding trails scratched in the gravel by hooves, and crouch in the shadows of pale cliffs or eroded pinnacles and caverns striped with layers of purplish stone. The landscape was ancient, silent save for the occasional "salaam" of passing shepherd boys bounding after jingle-belled flocks. There was much time to sit and to think, and I revelled in it.

At first I puzzled over an emotion lately conspicuous by its absence. When I'd started as a young backpacker, with mindsets schooled into me, I used to get caught in moods of cognitive dissonance. Travel does that, and then makes you adapt to be suppler in thought. For me, the first adjustment had been to reconsider an assumption rising from formal education itself: that there was no harm in appearing smart. Unwise, as it turns out; I learned the importance of not being earnest the hard way. Not everyone has your best interests at heart, and if you know what's going on, often the best strategy is not to let on. Draw out any machinations so you can observe and counter them, and thus dodge traps and cons as if by dumb luck. This is a habit foundational to street smarts, which so frustrates teachers with a class from the 'hood.

The ultimate cognitive dissonance to trouble me concerned religion. I'd never understood what people got out of it; superstitions and ceremony, anniversaries like holidays and even birthdays, were important for others, not me. Now, in just these last few years, I'd found myself fully as comfortable saying an Islamic prayer before slitting an animal's throat as I was perched on a mountainside reflecting on Zen koans. A formerly alcoholic Christian could babble about being born again without my feeling the temptation to draw his attention to glaring inconsistencies of doctrine; rather, I'd appreciate his unspoken hope that his religious habit would save him from his drinking. Likewise, if a tribesman wanted me to assist in a magic ceremony involving mud and leaves and some creature's tongue, I'd stand with him, my toes in the dust. None of these felt foreign to me anymore; there was no cognitive dissonance between touching lifeways shaped before Western science, all the while dwelling comfortably in my own excessive worldliness.

IN EARLY AUGUST I RETURNED FROM THE DANA NATURE RESERVE and the village of Dana, which looks out on Wadi Dana. It had helped me while away the days of visa purgatory but left me feeling lonely. Perhaps I was thinking how much Dana would have enjoyed this place; she was still in France, attending conferences. My solution was to return to Amman.

A couple of guys from the Cliff Hostel—Adam and Felipe—left with me on a road trip to see the ruins of ancient cities, as well as castles built by crusaders, including one made by command of Saladin. Adam nearly fell to his death when a sudden wind gust struck us on the crumbling castle walls. Our conversation turned to matters of life and death and chance, and Adam shared his superhero origin story from the UK with Felipe and me. His mother found out she was pregnant and had terminal cancer on the same day. She didn't tell the father, who had been a one-night stand, and she refused all drugs for the cancer. She died and her son was born, like a Hail Mary pass in American football, throwing a precious life into the future. Adam bounced around between various relatives of the deceased mother and grew into a kind and introspective young man. Felipe was South American, of Lebanese ancestry, thoroughly modern, socially conscious of the plight of Palestinians (he helped out at refugee camps), with a body covered in colourful tattoos, including one of Buddha. Each was excellent company. On the road home we bought a huge (15 kilogram) watermelon and lugged it into the hostel common room. Everyone was daunted by it, but I managed to weaken it with stabs of my camping knife so we could pry it open enough to crack it into four pieces. This made it manageable, and by three in the morning it was eaten.

The next morning I took a taxi to see how my visa application—more a supplication—was going. My hopes had been dashed so many times that I approached the counter without emotion. This gong show had been going on for exactly forty days and forty nights, including two long periods of special penalty, which I suspected were to punish me for being Canadian, as there was a diplomatic spat going on at the time. Now, after an effort that rivalled Noah's floating at sea in his own Arkful of wild beasts: success. The Saudi embassy up Rainbow Street had finally issued me the worst and most restrictive visa I'd ever received for any country or quasi-country on earth.

It took me a couple of hours to find a bus that would agree to take me into the Kingdom. Before taxiing out to get on the bus, I showed my final visa to the other travellers in the hostel common room. My new friend with the tattoos, who was here to study Arabic, informed me that I had a religion listed prominently on my visa: Islam. Though I'd made a declaration of United Church, since a relative was the United Church moderator, and everyone had to have a religion to get into Saudi, I knew as much about Islam as any other religion, maybe more. My hope was that no one at the border would put it to the test by asking me to recite passages from the Quran in Arabic. As it turned out, this was but the first of a series of assertions concerning my person I would have to contend with that day.

Three hours bussing on the highway landed me at the Al-Omari border crossing. The driver had assigned one of our busload of chain-smoking Palestinians to shepherd me through the process. He asked me if I was Muslim. My answer was "yes" as he would be asked to translate questions for me about the visa, which clearly stated I was, though I told him that my knowledge was not as deep as many who follow a religion—giving an excuse in advance in case I should be questioned on memorized doctrine and forget some things. He took this to mean he should serenade me with Arabic Islamic sutras for the hour we stood in line. Then, after being singled out for fingerprinting and a photo, I had to sort myself into one of three lines: Jordanians, Diplomats, or Arabs.

I figured I would have to wait in the Arabs line, as I was more demonstrably *not* a Diplomat or a Jordanian.

Customs singled me out again, and the man told me that there was a gun in my pack, he had seen one on the X-ray. Here I had to put my foot down: I was okay with them making me a Muslim Arab, but then to add that this made me a gunrunner? Racial profiling, that's what that was. We Muslim Arabs had to stand up for our rights!

"No guns in my bag, or metal objects. Only clothes and a mosquito net and books," I insisted.

After checking everything in my backpack, they had to agree that a gun was not to be found. I was inside the Kingdom, on the home stretch of a lifetime devoted to travel.

MY THREE-DAY TRIP ACROSS SAUDI ARABIA WAS DWARFED BY THE many weeks of work, over an elapsed time of many months, even years, to obtain the visa. Naturally I made the best of the situation, and squatted on my haunches with the men in their white thobes to chat while munching on soft dates and mutton with fragrant rice. But thematically, the real story Saudi had to offer was one of baffling and obstinate bureaucracy. One great irony I noticed during my travels was that there was often an inverse relationship between how much time I spent obtaining a visa for a country and the likelihood that it was a country I truly wanted to visit. All countries and cultures are interesting in their own way, naturally, but the government structure in certain places really detracts from the possible enjoyment of the culture and people who live there.

The Kingdom of Saud is the latest in a storied lineage of feudal economies going back to the days of the Queen of Sheba. An odour of religiosity lingers over this land that once operated as a racket for temple aromatherapy, selling frankincense so that, as in Babylon, "hungry gods smell the fragrance, and gather like flies over the offering." Machines have replaced temples in the West, but they are no less hungry for burnt offerings, of oil. With no shortage of this commodity, the Saudi rulers see no need to collect a few additional dinars accommodating curious travellers such as me.

And yet, I had more fun in the Kingdom than I would have expected. Riyadh rose like a beacon of skyscraping technology obtained by rubbing the oil lamp of foreign ingenuity, so that the Arabs could remain men according to the Quran, as it were. This nation was only now beginning to realize that this was not the only moral choice; both man and jinn can serve Allah. Guards let me visit the national museum on a day normally reserved for families, and I experienced some local colour, particularly after sunset. The air was insufferably hot and dry, 46 degrees Celsius, so families picnicked in the parks at night under sodium lamplight—the women swishing past, black wraiths against brash green lawn, their children giddy with pent-up energy. Outside of Western rave culture, it's rare to see people so pumped and pie-eyed in the pitch dark. Gangs of friendly boys showed me around the streets, cheerful, their lone complaint that the weed they get to smoke in Saudi is weak and they only get properly high on holidays. I found hotels in the guest-worker ghettos when possible, and otherwise stared out the dusty windows of buses at stretches of barren and surprisingly unlovely desert, marred by trenches and obscure earthworks, rusty metal objects, construction rubble, and dumps of trash.

Some travellers have since asked me, "Why didn't you make it more exciting and go to Mecca? You were listed as a Muslim on your visa, so the police would not have stopped you."

Ought I to have gone crowding in with the devout to circle the Ka'aba, that great black box of fabric that conceals a stone, perhaps fallen from the uttermost void of outer space? No, Mecca is a place of ritual, while circumambulations and other rituals are a barrier to spirituality for me. They are not my sacred wilderness. Yet Mecca is what it is, so even after dropping in, and though I might tick off a box, only my ego would have visited the place.

Just before my visa expired, I crossed into Qatar and bussed to a Filipino-staffed hotel just outside Doha city centre. That evening I concocted a plan for the morning. I knew where all the air-conditioned places were from three prior visits, and I could roam in comfort along the corniche by the waters of the Gulf by connecting these dots of precious compressor-driven chill. A walk through the oppressive heat brought me to depot number one, the Museum of Islamic Art. But it was closed with hazard tape because of cracked and shoddy construction. Pathetically, I hid under a shade tree, sweating profusely, to the point that each of my fingers was individually dripping like a leaky faucet, then retreated to my hotel. And that was it for my day until my night flight to Jordan, where I crossed over with exuberant crowds of Palestinians into the West Bank.

ONLY WITH SAUDI UNDER MY BELT COULD I TRAVEL OVERLAND TO Israel free of consequences. Many Islamic countries don't permit visitors whose passports betray evidence of travel to this much-fought-over jot of scrubland.

First stop, after an hour's drive, was Jerusalem, a house famously divided against itself. The Old City in Jerusalem was a bit of a tourist trap, granted; but visitors have been coming here expecting to be awed—now mostly settling for wowed—for so long that the hospitality industry itself is ancient. Jerusalem is one of the few cities that need to be touristy to be authentic.

Long interested in history, stories, and myth, I enjoyed finding myself amid people whose passions exceeded my own, even if their fervour was sometimes parochial, kindled by the notion that Abraham's god comes in only one flavour. Other passersby, taking a lesson from the Good Samaritan, saw a naked need for assistance, and were eager to offer their help. The Citadel Youth Hostel, which was my base, in a convoluted medieval building set in the labyrinthine Old City, a maze within a maze, was full of such well-meaning youngsters, opining from where we reclined on comfy red cushions, "If only the Jews, Christians, and Muslims could get along, no matter what direction they pray in, and find common ground."

But Israel already has Samaritans, and they are not passersby, having made their homes in the Holy Land since before Solomon built his Temple. They once dominated the West Bank and have their own house of god (Mount Gerizim) to pray toward, viewing the upstart Jews little differently than some Jews view the Muslims. History has reduced them so that they number not millions but hundreds, attacked from all sides. My lesson from the Samaritans is a warning for passersby: while kindness is welcome, it's best not to meddle in domestic political disputes. Instead, soaking up rooftop views, walking the narrow alleys at night, marvelling at the Orthodox Jews praying at the Wailing Wall with their old-school ghetto-style clothes and even older-school worship, puzzling over the golden pedestals and graven images in the Church of the Holy Sepulchre, pacing the ramparts of the nearby Citadel that Herod built, and chatting about history while sucking ruby pomegranate seeds would more than do for me.

By late August I'd gone to the Palestinian city of Nablus in the West Bank to see the ancient and new ruins, and various castles and towns along the seaside. Masada holds its own among the planet's mesa-top forts. There are remains of the Roman military camps from the siege of Masada, and the ruins of Herod's palaces on the mountaintop, evidence of a Jewish defeat here that became symbolically important 2,000 years later. Looking down, the sense of what it would be like to be surrounded by the Roman legion was palpable.

After testing the waters, I ranked the Dead Sea, glistening below Masada, as a worthy float, only bested by the saltier salt lake in Djibouti, where you bob higher in the water. An urge to dip in a sweeter sea brought me to the Mediterranean at a swimming beach along the promenade from Tel Aviv to the old city of Jaffa (named after one of Noah's sons—Japheth). Afterward, a stroll to drip-dry evolved into a hunt for the rocks of Andromeda. I finally found them, I think, just offshore, and they looked like the perfect place to chain a lovely princess if you were going to sacrifice her, and also the perfect place to rescue a princess from a sea monster if you were a hero cruising the skies astride his Pegasus. However, I was not totally convinced I'd found the right rocks, because there is no information plaque or statue or anything but a smelly dock area. Yet the tourist information said that this was the place.

Might Israel have so many tourist sites and historic rocks that it is not worth making a fuss about this rock of Andromeda? Or perhaps it is not the real rock. I decided to test, saying, "Release the Kraken." Nothing. Granted, there was no Greek princess. However, several Jewish girls were sunbathing in bikinis on the nearby beach. Mightn't they have served in a pinch? One would have thought the monster might at least poke up an eye-stalk to scope out the "writhing scantily-clad sacrifice situation."

FOLLOWING AN EXCURSION OF A FEW DAYS TO SEE THE NORTHERN crusader castle and Roman-era ruins at the port of Acre, I bussed back to Tel Aviv to meet with a selection of Israelis for drinks. These were people who knew me from their travels and had kept in touch through Facebook. One guy had funny green hair when we'd first met in Addis Ababa, both of us tramping around the city searching for a place with hummus on the menu. The dye had worn off or grown out in two and a half years, and he was back to brown.

I got some laughs from him and others with a joke that was long in preparation. After saying my travels had taken me everywhere on earth except for one place, they began to guess: Was it Somalia that daunted me, the Congo, South Sudan?

I replied, "Ireland, and I'm going there next."

Ireland is the opposite of Arabia: wet, green, Guinness-loving, and easy to visit. A desultory glance at my passport, it was as simple as that. I'd travelled in forty-two European nations already, so you might think I'd have known what to expect. But I experienced a cascade of good luck, such that I'll always have a special place in my heart for the Emerald Isle.

CHAPTER EIGHTEEN

EMERALD ISLE: MAKE NEW FRIENDS AND KEEP THE OLD

Ireland

A FEW DAYS BEFORE EMBARKING FOR IRELAND IN September 2013, I arrived in Luton, UK, from Tel Aviv, bought a bottle of wine as a gift, and made my way by public transport to a house in South Chessington, where I thought I might find some friends, including Tim. Nobody was home. A trellis in their garden held bunches of ripe grapes, so I munched on some of these. Finally the housemates came home to find me passed out on their doorstep, clutching an empty bottle. I shifted over to sleep in the back of the white van Tim uses for his heating and plumbing business.

While waiting for Anders—the filmmaker who had interviewed me nearly five years before in the Amazon—to get funding from the Norwegian government to film me, there was a rave called Mischief to spare me from the temptations of idle hands. My friend Molly couldn't go; she was working on an article about the free-party scene in Lebanon for *Dazed and Confused* magazine. Anders arrived from Norway just in time to join another party, buy some more video memory cards, and jump on the train with me to Holyhead and the ferry across the Irish Sea.

As we neared the port, Anders phoned a television news crew in Dublin and told them that a man was about to complete his twenty-three-year journey to see the world with his last country, Ireland, stepping off the ferry that night. The news crew caught up with me on the promenade. After a chat, the interviewer said, "You are a natural for interviews. My friend works for the Ray D'Arcy talk show. Would you like to be on it?"

He made a call and managed to get me on the show the very next morning. Anders found a hotel and I found a hostel and had to set my alarm, as a taxi was being sent from the talk show to fetch me in the morning.

Catching a good sleep in a dorm room requires great peace of mind. Twenty-three years' experience allowed me to absorb the usual noise and weird goings-on, or both, without being disturbed. At first there was a couple whispering, so a man lunged out of bed and chastised them. Soon after, another guy began to snore, not too loudly, but the same man lunged out of bed, woke him, and told him to be quiet. Twice more, another snorer started up, but the man jumped up to menace the reprobates. He must have been a menacing man indeed, because his technique was to perch on the snorer's bed, saying, "We should chat. I can't sleep because of your snoring, so I've decided to keep you awake too. How was your day?" If the snorer let the least bit of annoyance creep into his responses, he would be asked, "Are you getting smart with me?" and would be cowed into promising never to snore again. The oddest thing was that this approach worked, and eventually every last snorer mended his noisy ways.

Thus it would have been a quiet night if the couple had not decided to giggle and fool around, and if a drunk had not burst into the room, turned on the lights, and fumbled into his bed, all the while carrying on a loud phone call in which he gave a live-action play-by-play describing exactly how he was trying to get into his bed while drunk. Then he called out, "Does anybody want to buy any drugs?" I half expected that he'd get a talking-to from the man who thwarted the snorers, but this did not happen. Perhaps our paladin of noise control was himself sound asleep.

RAY D'ARCY'S TALK SHOW HAD A "GREEN ROOM," A PLACE WHERE guests waited before going on air. It occurred to me, even though I was experiencing a green room for the first time, that the place was not fit for its purpose if the idea was to let people relax. This was on account of its glass floor, under which sat the engineers and techies in their tech-support cubicles. Anyone who was scared of heights would be uncomfortable, and a woman in a short skirt would have to keep her knees constantly closed as a precaution. How could she trust the techies below were perfect gentlemen? I noticed the numerous pretty young ladies who worked in the building stepped gingerly around the edge of the room when passing through.

As it happens, I'm not a pretty young woman, nor scared of heights, and I'd been swapping travel tales in thousands of hostel common rooms the world over for practically all my adult life, so I had no worries. Storytelling was second nature to me, as was inadvertently generating a lot of commotion and attention. It was normal for me to arrive in a village and have the local chief or shaman invite me to speak by the campfire. That the chief and the shaman were now called the interviewer and the sound guy, and the campfire was a microphone, made little difference. Call-ins to the show produced hundreds of offers for free accommodation, offers to guide me through Ireland's mountains, lakes, and historic towns, and invitations to drop by for beer. Ray said I was the most interesting guy he'd ever met, and he's a talk show host—however, perhaps handiness with flattery was a bonus in his profession.

Afterward, I resolved that I would say "yes" to every possible offer from newspaper, magazine, school principal, international media, or what have you for the next few months. It thus became a simple matter of connecting the dots of kindly offers from some of Ireland's friendliest people. Word of mouth is powerful in the tight-knit communities of this smallish country, and soon strangers recognized me in the street and came over to shake my hand, waitresses brought managers out to meet me, and I couldn't dream of paying for a drink. The Irish gave me a warmer welcome for the end of my wanderings than I ever could have hoped for. Pretty hotel receptionists slipped notes under my door, saying such things as "You fascinate me, please call," with their number beneath, even though I might only have chatted with them for a few minutes. I didn't let things like this go to my head; instead, I put it down to the media attention, while also apprehending why celebrities find it hard to stay married. Oddest for me was staying in posh hotel suites, all expenses paid, or eating in fancy restaurants and having oysters on the half shell with pomegranate drupes delivered by a waiter saying, "compliments of the chef," while I tried to figure out which spoon was for what.

All the while, every conceivable media request flooded in, from being filmed for charity documentaries while kissing the Blarney Stone or being interviewed atop one of Cork's belfries, to newspapers, internet blog Q+As, and speeches to the assembled kids in various schools. My intuition to say yes to everything worked some magic. Soon the media storm was going viral, similar to what had happened after I visited Somalia. I experienced the same online difficulties—having to respond to thousands of new friend requests on Facebook, which spiked again whenever some new media mention came out, like being listed as newsmaker of the week in Canada's *Maclean's* magazine. My email and Facebook handled the traffic without freezing up this time, probably because I had access to technology more advanced than that found in a shack near a sand dune with donkeys parked outside, and the internet sites themselves must have become more resilient. A fun superpower that I've noticed both times I've been viral on the net is the ability to crash people's servers with traffic by mentioning their blog or site.

THROUGHOUT THIS MEDIA STORM, IT DIDN'T SLIP MY MIND THAT MY travels would have taken in every country not on account of stepping off the ferry, but, rather, only after exploring Ireland. Luckily, my resolve to say yes to everything included saying yes to offers from kindly strangers. Only through their help was travel still possible given such overwhelming demands on my time and attention.

An example of Irish hospitality was Travis and his family in Westport, County Mayo, who taught me how to gather and cook black mussels the Irish way. Travis, who runs a bike-rental business on the west coast, also invited me to hear a woman named Gemma Hayes singing and playing guitar. At the same time, he asked if I would give a lecture for assembled kids at the local school. In keeping with my resolution, I said yes to both. After the concert, we drank until morning, and I stumbled back to my suite at Westport's Wyatt Hotel. I slept in my clothes atop the bed, and somehow I must have remembered my promise to speak at the school. I awoke in an hour, without an alarm, and just made it in time to talk to the kids, who had gathered in the gym. I was probably still tipsy, and I definitely hadn't showered, but the kids loved to hear tales of foreign adventure, bandits, lost cities, landscapes of salt, streams of lava, and superstitious tribesmen of the tropics. That day I climbed Croagh Patrick, a site of pagan and now Christian pilgrimage since 3000 BC, and enjoyed views of the sea from the sacred mountaintop during breaks in the fog. In the 1980s, quartz veins holding half a billion dollars' worth of gold were discovered, but violating the mountain to mine the quartz is taboo.

A ferryman taking me to the picturesque Aran Islands, near the Cliffs of Moher on the Atlantic coast, recognized me and said, "I get travellers who are in the news through here from time to time. I'll wait for you a few minutes at the dock. I suppose you want to touch your boot to the sand and get back on the boat?"

"I'm not that sort of traveller," I said, and explained my intention to hike around the island, find anyone who fancied a chat, and gain some impression of the place.

He seemed pleased to hear this, and by his tone of voice afterward, I felt I'd come up in his books. I resolved to use some of my media opportunities to educate the public about the difference between travellers and country-counting passengers.

In Europe, most travellers laugh and roll their eyes when they meet certain tourists with rail passes, who say they are doing every country in Europe—and they are now adding France, for example, because their train is passing through Paris. Usually these people are young and naive, and the assumption is that they will eventually learn how silly this is, and will stop to speak to the people, enjoy the food, hike in the mountains, or otherwise actually experience the different cultures and nations. But what if one of these kids carries on like that and does a hundred countries, or even all the countries? It is a tragic waste of what could have been exciting journeys, and a terrible shame. I, for one, will do what I can to shift country-counters off the use of the word "travel" in their blogs and websites for what is clearly just transportation, and dispensable transportation at that.

While country-counters are ridiculous with their transportation gimmickry, it's also fair to say I respect practically all other forms of travel. If someone tells me they tour in a band or sell food from the back of a truck following the summer festivals or sail the ocean wide or even go on jaunts as an astronaut in space, all power to them: these are examples of the many interesting forms of travel. Pretty much the only forms I cannot respect are the abomination of sex tourists prowling for children, and the mild silliness of country-counters. Yet these two disparate forms seem to fascinate the media, who rightly seek to eliminate the first, but wrongly encourage the second.

SOMETIMES, AS I TRAVELLED AROUND IRELAND, I'D TRY TO STAY incognito, if only to give my liver a rest. It worked in a way while I was at the Parkview B and B in Cork, but only because I snuck up the stairs. Some ladies nearby had figured out who I was and were waiting to ambush me with a bottle of wine when I came in.

When I was in Cork, an offer came in to sign with the William Morris Agency in Beverly Hills. I found a post office to send off the completed contract, only to realize I needed a postal code. A second later I realized it had to be 90210, from the teen television show once popular in North America.

The next morning I responded to an earlier offer. A friendly gentleman said he wanted to set up a film crew on top of the bell tower of the largest church in Cork to do something for a UN-affiliated charity. My answer was yes, expecting he'd want to talk to me about some international subject for the cameras. With any luck the questions would be the sort I could answer, especially with a working film crew I'd be sorry to disappoint.

The next afternoon I wandered in the direction of the highest steeple in Cork. There are four clocks up there, all of them slightly off the correct time, so the locals call it "the four liars." Did the sponsor think through the implications? People on the street were offering me drinks and pulling me into pubs as I went, and I finally had to ask one publican to save my drink for after the filming or risk arriving more than half-cut.

I met the crew, and we shook hands all round; then they said they wanted to film me climbing up and down the tower steps, and greeting the custodians of the church before we climbed the tower. I still hadn't sussed-out what we were meant to talk about.

The weather was gusty, but the crew found a place in the lee of the steeple, and it went very well. Turned out the subject was technological change and how it is transforming the world. I was supposedly an expert although I don't even own a television, and I'm the last guy you'd ever ask for help navigating menus in devices. My contact had presumed that, like all the other famous travellers, I was travelling the world using technology and blogging to support my effort. A fair guess, but dead wrong. However, technological change was something I'd seen first-hand everywhere, including the least-developed countries, with satellite dishes in Rajasthani slums and solar-charged mobile phones in the camps of tribal cattle rustlers east of the Omo Valley. We did the interview in one take.

DINGLE WAS WITHIN EASY BUSSING RANGE OF CORK AND PROVED TO be a lovely peninsula. My plan was to go kayaking. This didn't happen, as the kayaks were all booked in advance by a college class. Instead I walked along the sands and hung out with Johnnie, a guitar-playing Irishman who was allergic to hops, so he had to make the best of it and drink Dingle-brand gin. I enjoyed fish and chips on the house when I happened to pass the shop, and a local hippie came out into the street to kindly offer me tea and cake, and get a photo with me.

The day before that I was at the West Cork Hotel in Skibbereen, a little boat harbour in the south, and a local man took me to see the sites: the caves, the castle owned (and painted pink) by Jeremy Irons, and Mizen Head, a zone of rock and swirling waves with an antique lighthouse, the most southwesterly point in Ireland. Even the seals were finding the sea too rough, and were hiding in the coves below the towering sea cliffs.

By the end of October I had so many media requests that I had to take three days off from exploring Ireland for a media blitz. There was an *Esquire* interview to be done, then major newspaper interviews and a Yahoo news interview, a long phone call to an online writer, UK radio and Canadian television to set up, lots of web articles, and more radio. Whenever I did a newspaper interview, they sent out a photographer who would pose me in various places and take whirs of shots with a large camera. I began to get used to it. Sadly, none said, "Work with me, baby. Yeah baby, yeah."

I headed back to Cork and did a couple more talks for schools. One assembly was little kids in their Halloween costumes, which prompted me to tell tales of spiders and snakes and lizards from around the world. The other group was somewhat older kids, who were excited to hear about unusual places and people. They had oodles of questions. Following a call-in talk show, I was off to Blarney Castle, in amazing park-like grounds with black oaks and meandering streams, flanked by druid sites of dolmens and sacrificial altars.

In what was becoming the new normal, I was being filmed, with a soundman and a cameraman and all. When the guide heard that I was the most travelled man, he agreed to take me on a special tour. Afterward, he told me that he really appreciated how I listened to him and had a chat; the other travel bloggers he had through were constantly uploading photos and tweeting as they went, and hardly paid any attention to where they were. A huge group of them had come through the day before, he said, and they had their faces in their phones the whole time. He asked me what I thought about the powers of the Blarney Stone I'd journeyed here to kiss, said to magically confer the gift of the gab.

"It's all a matter of taking the long way around to the Blarney Stone, stopping in every country," I said. "Then you are so used to chatting in hostel common rooms that the stone works and you feel eloquent and can say it's practical magic."

After that day-long shoot, I made my way north and east to Waterford in the company of Keith Daniels, the manager of the Barley Field hotel. The weather was blustery and chilly, but this was okay as Waterford is the oldest city in Ireland and had plenty of good museums and pubs. It used to be a Viking settlement until it was conquered by Normans (a different sort of Viking, with more military prowess if such a thing is possible). Living was rudimentary back then: people used to hang their clothes in the drop-pit toilets at night—the ammonia fumes discouraged lice— and all the staircases were narrow and spiral so that any attacker would have to fight someone above him while using his left arm.

After Waterford I rushed to the far north and looked at some of the places around Belfast. There is a famous rope bridge out to an island, Carrick-a-Rede, that was used for salmon fishing back in the day. I'd heard the bridge talked about as if it was rather dangerous, and I was half expecting to see something like the rope bridges in Nepal, before the Gurkhas upgraded them to steel construction. In truth it was a rather small bridge, only 100 feet high and nothing treacherous about it, but it was fun to see the kids getting happily scared on it. A local legend says that a man-eating sea serpent lives nearby and can only be slain by a man named McCurdy wearing clothing made of calf skin, wielding a club with three nails in it that have never been used to shoe a horse.

The Giant's Causeway in Northern Ireland was worth a look. I've seen a few of these black basalt formations around the world, including by the roadsides in Ethiopia and at Nan Madol, the city out on the reef that I'd explored in Micronesia. But the Giant's Causeway has got to be the most famous, and it looked to be a strand where mermaids would frolic. There was a blustery wind when I was there; it whipped up a deep froth of foam and drove it into the coves and shoreline, a metre deep in places.

The weather had turned to rain and driving sleet, and I had pressing demands for studio time in London, so I rode the train to Dublin to catch the ferry back to Holyhead. After a final appearance on Ray D'Arcy's show, I collected some swag from the host, including a hoodie, and hiked over to the port just in time for the afternoon sailing. The Irish Sea was rough, and some people were getting ill. The décor in the lounge didn't help: copies of Andy Warhol's photos of Marilyn Monroe, with her face coloured various shades. In the one opposite the bar she was completely green, and some of the passengers' cheeks went a similar hue after looking at it.

On reflection, another week or two would have been perfect for Ireland, but it was the end of October and I had work to do: interviews at studios in the BBC's Broadcasting House near Regent Street in London, tall and traced with blue glow, with curious Dalek robots from *Doctor Who* on the ground floor; interviews with NPR to go out over the whole United States; and other radio and internet news interviews for about six weeks solid. A lot of media requests arrived over the next six months, and they still have not completely abated, even after several years. It was a fine feather in my cap for the end to a life's journey.

My hair was greying on the sides and I was now in my mid-forties, with nothing in the way of possessions: no car, no house, no suits, and no stuff, just a wealth of experiences, my family, and friends on six continents. Thinking of what I had gained and what I had sacrificed following life's less-travelled path—which is to say, the path of most travel—I asked myself, was it all worthwhile? The answer was yes.

Canada beckoned for more scheduled media events. I said goodbye to friends and headed for Heathrow at four o'clock in the morning, flew to Paris, changed planes, and flew to Montreal before heading on to Ottawa for national news interviews. Montreal was a fun city to visit, especially as I hadn't been there in a few years. The first snow of the year came while I was visiting a friend—ice crystals in the air that did not accumulate, but sparkled in a way that was especially lovely viewed from the top of the Oratoire Saint-Joseph du Mont-Royal shrine.

In mid-November 2013 I had an article on the front page of the *National Post* and was working on pieces for various international publications, including ones in China and Pakistan. My plan was to sweep west across Canada, doing interviews and radio call-ins as I went, ending up on the Pacific coast. I needed to record a *Canada AM* interview for CTV before leaving Ottawa, but I kept being bumped by coverage of Rob Ford, the crack-smoking mayor of Toronto. He had me waiting in Ottawa a week as the media focussed on his extraordinary antics. If he'd known I was waiting in freezing Ottawa, I'm sure he would have been a gentleman about it and apologized. Apologies seemed to be his go-to tactic.

In the meantime, there were many international and smaller interviews to do, in keeping with my continuing resolve to say yes to everything. Sometimes it was impossible, such as when a frantic reporter from a Bangladeshi newspaper called me to say he had only an hour to write an article about me—could I quickly send him dozens of photos of me in Bangladesh? But the wait for Rob Ford gave me time to fit in interviews and shoots that I wouldn't have been able to do from western Canada. For example, in late November I got up early and trudged out into the snow to do some filming by the Rideau Canal, the longest skating rink on earth, with Arda Ocal of the Weather Network and his very cold-resistant cameraman. We chatted about extreme or unusual weather around the globe, and about travelling. I did a couple of live segments and told some typhoon and hurricane stories, among other things, but wrapped up just in time to scurry back into a warm house before my face froze stiff.

My *Canada AM* television slot was finally confirmed early one morning. Reaching the studio entailed waking up dreadfully early and trudging through the nearly deserted streets of Ottawa. It was starting to feel like winter, getting close to minus twenty overnight, with wind chill to consider. The green room was full of experts dressed in suits and tweed jackets, and me in my shirt with a collar. One guest was a former ambassador to Iran, there to comment on the recent progress in international nuclear talks, and two others were experts on vaccinations. They asked me what my expertise was. I answered, "Travel." The former ambassador asked about my experience of Iran, and we chatted about the underground party scene and the Bam earthquake.

The process for the interview involved the guest sitting alone in a room with a light and a camera, answering questions that came from Toronto, fed to the guest through an earpiece. Now I know why people on television news sometimes seem like talking heads: I sat alone in a cell painted battleship grey, staring at the hulking camera that was the only thing in the room besides myself and my chair, and listened to voices in my ear. Each expert went into the room, did the interview, then came back out to watch it "live" on the television in the green room. We provided good-natured critiques of each other's performances.

By December I'd done enough of this media stuff. While fun, it pays nothing beyond the occasional free beer or coffee. And it was costing me plenty of money to hang around places with access to these studios or where I was within driving range of reporters. On December 2 I flew west and ended up in Okotoks, Alberta, home of my younger brother, where I stretched my legs on a stroll in the forests of the Sheep River Valley. I was glad to have had the sunlight and peaceful air, since the next day the weather turned and I was staring out the window into a fierce blizzard. A bald eagle was being tumbled and blown down the valley, flapping like crazy to fly where it wanted to fly—but there was no chance against those winds.

Soon after, I returned to my love of travelling the world, and now, with my experiences compiled here, the publication of this book is my latest scheme to replenish my business float and keep on travelling. If enough copies sell, royalties might amount to sufficient money to fix my teeth, chipped as they are by pebbles in the rice I ate at rural villages over the decades. If it does really well, I'll be able to backpack for some time more.

Despite answering reporters' questions for months, I'd had to think long and hard on one that was both frequent and difficult to do justice to in the few sentences allotted for my answer. This was the big question of why. I'd never given it serious thought before, my lifestyle being just what I did and who I was.

There are myriad reasons to recommend travel. One of the more splendid things is its efficacy as a filter. If you are on the beach in Cancún and strike up a conversation with a passerby, you'll pass some time; perhaps the experience will be interesting or stimulating, though more likely it will be shallow, or dull. But if you are, say, chopping your way with a machete up an overgrown jungle stream in search of the lost Temple of the Jaguar God, and you meet another soul who has the same motivation, you can guarantee an interesting conversation around the campfire. Travel sifts away the dross and connects you with people who realize they are alive on our wondrous earth and are game to seize each day. This filter serves you well on every splendid adventure, but clogs when you stick to the well-worn tourist paths.

That's why set plans often do a traveller a disservice, as no travel plan survives contact with friendly forces. I've said on more than one occasion that good people greatly outnumber nasty people worldwide. There is a network that existed long before social media: the network of persons of good will, who will introduce and pass you to other persons of good will, such that you can take a friendly look around a town, a nation, or the world, as you like. There is no similar network among nasty people. They are on their own, and if you know what is good for you, you will leave them alone.

MY MOM FEELS HEALTHIER THAN SHE HAS IN A DECADE, AND HAS returned to her habit of long walks in the fens that line the shores of Boundary Bay, thick with bulrushes and the calls of red-winged blackbirds. My nieces and nephews are getting to be teenagers now, and will soon be travellers in their own right. One of my nieces just went on her first trip, flying solo to Maui from Alberta for some beach time, age twelve. My old friends are enjoying themselves in whichever home fate has settled them. Ken is living in Calgary with Sally, and they find plenty of time for fun in the Rockies. Chad has found balance between a meaningful career as a negotiator and his desire for weeks of surfing and backcountry skiing. Molly is in Bristol by the sea, taking photos and giving lectures on ethics in photography. Last year many of my European friends, organized by Tim, took a road-trip vacation through Transylvania, which gave me time to catch up and also to see the occasional place that I'd missed when first visiting the Carpathian Mountains in the summer of 2004. Brenda in Victoria and Joanna in Bali helped me remember details of 1990s trips. Bruce lives in Victoria now too, enjoying the salmon fishing from his new boat. Barbara is back in Winterthur, and Dana in Almaty—keeping in contact with friends is easy now in this era where WiFi has replaced black rotary phones in no man's land.

Lately I've been spending more time in Russia, Turkey, and Ukraine, making new friends and staying in touch with the old friends, travelling at a slower pace to allow more time for writing and thinking. Mostly, going somewhere new has been replaced, necessarily, by return visits, and that brings its own rewards, to see what has changed and what remains. Life is endlessly fascinating.

The traveller who loves travel for its own sake is found, at the end of the journey, in possession of a treasure that cannot be picked apart or taxed, or fought over after death. A person who put as much energy into building a mansion would find the taxman assessing it, and having to pay property tax accordingly. There woud be jealous neighbours to endure, and it would have to be sold eventually to pay the owner's death taxes. If that mansion, even built by owner's own hands, was assessed by the government at millions of dollars, then people would curse that person as part of a "1-percent elite," hoarding the resources that ought to be distributed among the needy. And yet, a traveller like me has accumulated experiences worth millions of dollars; actually, many of my experiences are, or will soon become, priceless. They will be impossible to duplicate as nature and our surviving relics of antiquity disintegrate or are sequestered for the lucky few. And no taxman can come away with so much as a smidgeon of my rich experiences, any more than it is possible to get blood from a stone. This alone makes experiences garnered through travel a superlative store of value in a time of strident talk of income inequality.

But my wealth can be shared—not with the taxman, but with anyone who asks for a story. And its value does not diminish in the telling. In a sense, the traveller can have it all *and* give it all back to the community, as long as the travels were adventures and fun or interesting for the listener, and not mere box-ticking or country-counting in the service of tedious one-upmanship.

Roald Amundsen, the early-twentieth-century Norwegian polar explorer, once quipped, "What is the point of going somewhere someone else has already been?" He invented the concept of independent adventure travel in its modern form. Indeed, he was ahead of his time in many ways, and more like a modern adventurer than I am, a blogger and crowdfunder who concocted the idea of working the media to raise funds, and attracting an admiring audience of vicarious armchair travellers. But we are in a post-Amundsen world now. Humans have become numerous, and it is in our species' nature to spawn adventurers, so it's a tall order to find feats of derring-do yet undone, and many of those remaining seem contrived. Consider the man who set out to walk the Amazon, a first. It took him years of squelching through mosquito-infested muck instead of a swift and sensible float of a couple weeks. What will he do for an encore? Canoe the Sahara?

Some people say it's a small world now. And certain adventurers have a visceral need to feel caught up in events on a scale far bigger than themselves, a need that cannot be satisfied in such a small world, or with good works done for their own sake. So what is the point of travelling to places where someone else has already been? I hope that I've helped to answer that question. Because otherwise we are left with good works that do not scale, and the threat behind the anonymous quote "In a society that has destroyed all adventure, the only adventure left is to destroy that society."

Villagers and tribal people often have a tremendous sense of fun and can get a laugh at the absurd, including the unfathomable ways of nomadic backpackers. They were happy to tell me why they make a home where they do and behave as they did, what they do for a living, how they raise children, what they expect from life. Their answers have given me much to reflect on. Importantly, comfort is not all it's cracked up to be, and can be dispensed with. Naturally, I was at times lonely, bored, and frustrated. But most of the time, I'm happy to say, I accepted, with as good grace as I could muster, any obstacles and ill-luck.

My understanding of the world comes not only from common sense, but from gleaning the un-common sense that comes from chatting with a rogue's gallery of bandits, tour guides, tribesmen, subsistence farmers, students, terrorists, ministers, businessmen, police, and exhausted NGO workers at their local watering holes. These moments can be had in the most out-of-the-way and unlikely places. The single greatest revelation from my two decades of more-or-less constant travel is something that probably should have been obvious before I started: the world is not small. The people who share our planet are diverse, and there is no simple answer to the meaning of life.

Yet hidden behind some very peculiar customs and cultural differences, people are basically good and are worth knowing whatever the race or culture they hail from, and in this way we are all remarkably similar. If you are accepting of their circumstances, rather than being judgmental and rigid, you will have no problems getting along with people anywhere on the planet. To avoid the trap of the soft racism of low expectations, I am always mindful when making comparisons between different races and cultures to compare hillbillies in Malaysia to hillbillies in the Appalachians, rednecks to rednecks, scholars to scholars. When I do this, the commonality of our human experience jumps out at me. However, anyone who insists on comparing a Mongolian redneck to a Melbourne white-collar worker, and is bullheaded with their opinions, arrogant and condescending, will have to get used to suffering a narrow mind and wearing an appalling frown. The world is not a simple place of firm identities suitable for constructing some ideology. We all have opinions, of course, and most people can be diplomatic if they try hard enough, but I think that effort is better directed, instead, at understanding where people are coming from.

As compensation for my outlandish roving, I've amassed a body of knowledge and a collection of adventure stories of a breadth to satisfy my own curiosity. Because I had put my whole adult life into it, reporters called me the world's most travelled man, and I suppose, according to the backpacking, freestyle travel so dear to my heart, I am—having followed my dreams to explore our planet free from gimmickry, not to prove a point, but to let the adventure teach me what it means to be alive in what is a chaotic, alluring, and tremendously large world.

The author's trusty backpack, photographed in Kiev, 2017.

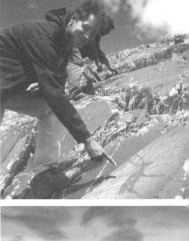